PENGUIN BOOKS

MY LIFE IN POLITICS

Born in 1913 to working-class parents, Willy Brandt was involved in Socialist politics from an early age. By 1933 he was an active anti-Nazi and at nineteen had to flee Germany for Denmark and Norway. He remained outside Germany for the next eighteen years, actively involved in the Resistance and as a radical journalist, and was stripped of his German nationality in 1938; it was returned to him only in 1948.

However, within a year of his return to Germany he was a deputy for Berlin in the first German Bundestag. From then on his rise was rapid, and by 1957 he had been made Mayor of West Berlin – a pivotal position in Germany – and in 1964 was elected Chairman of the SPD. Passionately committed to internationalism, Brandt was on the front line when the Berlin Wall was erected in 1961 and welcomed Kennedy to the city when he made his famous 'Ich bin ein Berliner' speech. In 1966 he was made Foreign Minister and three years later Chancellor. He was awarded the Nobel Peace Prize in 1971, and countless other doctorates, awards and prizes followed.

In 1974 all this came crashing down over the DDR spy affair. Nevertheless, he was re-elected to the Bundestag, became President of the Socialist International and was a tireless internationalist, his work culminating in the 'North–South Commission' of 1980. To the end of his life he retained an unflagging commitment to a single Europe and a unified Germany.

Willy Brandt died in October 1992.

WILLY BRANDT

———————

MY LIFE IN POLITICS

PENGUIN BOOKS

PENGUIN BOOKS

Published by the Penguin Group
Penguin Books Ltd, 27 Wrights Lane, London W8 5TZ, England
Penguin Books USA Inc., 375 Hudson Street, New York, New York 10014, USA
Penguin Books Australia Ltd, Ringwood, Victoria, Australia
Penguin Books Canada Ltd, 10 Alcorn Avenue, Toronto, Ontario, Canada M4V 3B2
Penguin Books (NZ) Ltd, 182–190 Wairau Road, Auckland 10, New Zealand

Penguin Books Ltd, Registered Offices: Harmondsworth, Middlesex, England

First published in Germany under the title *Erinnerungen* by Propyläen 1989
Translated, abridged and with a new Preface, *My Life in Politics*
first published by Hamish Hamilton Ltd 1992
Published in Penguin Books 1993
1 3 5 7 9 10 8 6 4 2

Picture Acknowledgements
Archiv des Autors 1 (J. H. Darchinger, Bonn), 2, 3, 4, 5, 6, 7, 9, 13, 18,
22, 23, 25, 26, 27; Wolfgang Bera, Berlin, 16; Bildarchiv Preussischer
Kulturbesitz, Berlin 8; dpa, Frankfurt/Main 28, 31; Landesbildstelle, Berlin 17;
Studio X, Gamma, Paris 32; Ullstein Bilderdienst, Berlin 10, 11, 12, 14,
15, 16, 19, 20, 21, 24, 26, 27, 30, 33 (ADN-Zentralbild), 34 (Gunter Peters);
Dave Valdez, Washington, D.C., 29

Printed in England by Clays Ltd, St Ives plc

Contents

Select List of Leading SPD Politicians

Internationally known figures such as Helmut Schmidt and Karl Schiller have not been included; nor have lesser figures whose status or role is made clear at every mention.

BAHR, Egon (b. 1922) Willy Brandt's chief press officer when he was Mayor of West Berlin. Instrumental in drawing up the Moscow Treaty, and led various West German delegations in negotiations with East Germany. Became director of the Hamburg Institute for Peace and Security Policy in 1984.

EPPLER, Erhard (b. 1926) Federal Minister for Economic Co-operation, 1968–74; subsequently Chairman and Parliamentary Party Chairman of the Baden-Württemberg SPD.

ERLER, Fritz (1913–67) SPD Party spokesman on defence in the late 1950s, and subsequently Chairman of the Parliamentary SPD.

LEBER, Julius (1891–1945) Pre-war trade union leader and socialist politician; active in the July 1944 plot against Hitler, and marked out by the conspirators as a leading member of a post-Hitler government. Betrayed and arrested several weeks before Stauffenberg's assassination attempt, and subsequently executed.

NEUMANN, Franz (1904–74) Prominent SPD leader in Berlin; outstanding for his firm resistance to Soviet threats at the time of the Berlin blockade. SPD Party Chairman in Berlin.

OLLENHAUER, Erich (1901–63) Succeeded Kurt Schumacher (q.v.) as leader of the SPD. Had spent the war years in London.

REUTER, Ernst (1889–1953) Became a Communist after being a prisoner of the Russians in the First World War, subsequently rejected Communism and joined the SPD; member of the pre-1933 Reichstag. Arrested in 1933 but released, and spent the Second World War in Turkey, returning to Berlin in 1947. Was Mayor of Berlin during the airlift period (although his appointment had been vetoed by the Soviets, he continued in the post with his deputy Frau Schröder officiating).

SCHMID, Professor Carlo (b. 1896) SPD politician and chairman of the steering committee that drew up the Basic Law of the Federal German Constitution. Minister for Bundesrat Affairs (liaising with the *Länder*) in the Grand Coalition.

SCHUMACHER, Kurt (1895–1952) Post-war leader of the SPD in the Federal Republic. Arrested when the Nazis came to power and spent eight years in concentration camps. Fervently anti-Communist; urged the creation of a new Germany under SPD leadership. Politically very active after the war despite ill health.

WALCHER, Jacob (1887–1970) Colleague of Willy Brandt in the breakaway SAP. Remained on friendly terms with him although Brandt returned to the SPD while Walcher embraced Communism and favoured the merging of the SPD and KPD in the Soviet zone to create the SED.

WEHNER, Herbert (b. 1906) Former Communist, post-war SPD politician and Bundestag member. Organizational manager of the SPD at the end of the 1950s. Minister for All-German Affairs in the Grand Coalition. Chairman of the Parliamentary SPD.

Abbreviations of German Political Parties

CDU Christlich-Demokratische Union (Christian Democratic Union)

CSU Christlich-Soziale Union (Christian Social Union; Bavarian counterpart of CDU)

DKP Deutsche Kommunistische Partei (German Communist Party, founded 1968)

FDP Freie Demokratische Partei (Free Democratic Party *or* Liberals)

KPD Kommunistische Partei Deutschlands (Communist Party of Germany, banned in the Federal Republic from 1956)

NPD Nationalsozialistische Partei (National Democratic Party)

SAP Sozialistische Arbeiterpartei (Socialist Workers' Party; SPD splinter group, 1932–45)

SED Sozialistische Einheitspartei Deutschlands (Socialist Unity Party of Germany; governing Party of the German Democratic Republic, founded in 1946 by a merger of the KPD and SPD within the Soviet zone of occupation)

SPD Sozialdemokratische Partei Deutschlands (Social Democratic Party of Germany)

Preface

When I was completing my memoirs in the late 1980s, it could be sensed that Europe was on the brink of far-reaching changes. The decomposition of the Communist social and state system was far advanced. Even after the fall of the Berlin Wall, however, the headlong speed at which fundamental change would occur on German soil, and far beyond it, could not be foreseen. The East–West conflict was nearing its end, but it was not clear what would take its place. The division of Europe seemed to have been overcome, but long-suppressed disputes were breaking out. The collapse of Communism was followed initially by confusion rather than a new order. It was probably inevitable.

I was one of those who had hardly ever doubted that the divisions arising from the Second World War would not last for ever. Yet I had not thought it very likely that it would be granted to me to see new unity grow from new freedom in my own country. It was a unique experience, extending far beyond my own sphere of activity, but in that sphere, as elsewhere, there was some talk of a precipitate hastening of the historical process.

In the late autumn of 1989 Federal Chancellor Kohl outlined the possibility of a 'confederate' association between the two German states – instead, nine months later they had united, and in early December 1990 the Germans in East and West were voting in the same election for their representatives in the same Bundestag. A few weeks earlier, at a special summit meeting of heads of state and government in Paris, a declaration announcing a state of peace for the whole of Europe had been made; the Warsaw Pact had outlived its usefulness and the proceedings of the Helsinki Conference were validated. New opportunities for fruitful co-operation were the order of the day, but quite a number of the imbalances and strains resulting from different rates of development still remained. Reconciling the principles of democratic order, national self-determination and European responsibility turned out to be unexpectedly difficult in parts of what had previously been Communist-ruled Europe. The clamps holding Yugoslavia together as a state broke.

A man with a life such as mine behind him should not be surprised to see democracy in Europe faced with new challenges. Nor indeed should he complain of the fact that, to a considerable extent, it was the impatience of the very peoples of the countries concerned that determined political change. It is something else again to say that the series of great leaps taken by history was liable to cause great concern. We certainly learned that stocks of poisonously destructive nationalism were far from exhausted. But from where I stand the great and noble nature of the events through which we lived as the century moved into the nineties cannot be denied: Europe was given the historic chance of overcoming its divisions in a substantially non-violent manner. Success depended to some extent on whether the Germans did their part to fashion European unity in freedom.

So far as the progressive achievement of German unity is concerned – unity of content as well as form – I am confident that it will have natural repercussions on the process of the unification of Europe. Whether the Federal Republic of Germany, now rather larger than it was, will be equal to the international responsibility expected of it will be shown first and foremost in its commitment to Europe. There is a direct link here with the European Community, which must both enlarge and consolidate itself.

By now everyone can see that getting German unity off the ground proved more difficult than most people assumed; it will be more expensive than expected and indeed than necessary, and there are considerable social and cultural tensions. However, I have come to the conclusion – leaving party political disputes aside – that on the whole there was no reasonable alternative to the decisions the Federal Government thought it right to make. That applies not least to bringing what was then still the GDR into the Western Deutschmark currency area on 1 July 1990. Where the procedures themselves were concerned, the Bonn Government could have done with better and more forceful advice, but in answering the fundamental question it was guided by the simple logic expressed by our East German compatriots in the words, 'If you don't let the D-mark come to us then we will go to it.' The rapid tempo at which state unification took place – by the amalgamation of the revived 'East German' *Länder* with the Federal Republic in accordance with an appropriate clause in the Basic Law – may also have been determined by less relevant considerations, but here again the deciding factor was the weight of expectation exerted by people demanding their rights. Let it be emphasized that the resultant collapse of previously existing markets could have been cushioned better, and less could have been expected of the Deutschmark in the medium term.

But however acute economic and political foresight had been, it could hardly have been imagined that the Eastern bloc would disintegrate so fast. The sensationaly uncomplicated manner in which the Soviet state leadership thought it expedient to give up its German pawn were astonishing, too. Any German head of government would have laid himself open to accusations of neglecting his duty had he not acted when the chance of an early and agreed withdrawal by the great Eastern power arose – particularly as no one could know whether there would be an opportunity later on to take up the offer Mikhail Gorbachev had declared himself ready to make in the summer of 1990 in the Caucasus. The key role still accorded here to Germany's relations with Russia (and what was still the Soviet Union) in no way detracts from the importance of those changes in Central Europe instigated by our immediate neighbours: Poland, with its remarkable tenacity in asserting itself over the years; Hungary, extraordinarily helpful in perforating the Iron Curtain, which was partly the work of some of the old leadership; Czechoslovakia with its so-called 'velvet' revolution.

It was only right and proper for Germany to adopt a policy of going to meet Gorbachev and smoothing the path which brought the Soviet Union, still in its old form, to the international economic summit meeting in London in the summer of 1991 (whether it always pursued that policy compellingly enough may be left an open question). Nor was there anything surprising about the fact that the Bonn Government formally agreed to back the application of our immediate Eastern neighbours, mentioned above, to join the European Community as soon as the requisite conditions existed. No new geopolitical special account was being set up, nor was any special claim being laid to new markets. The point at issue, rather, was to stand by those declarations of the Cold War years that the border of Europe is not situated on either the Elbe or the Oder – that Warsaw and Prague and Budapest are indubitably European cities.

The German agreements with Moscow were to go through in the context of the Western Alliance, since their relevance to global interests meant that Washington could be relied on for great goodwill from the start. Western European objections and reservations about the form and tempo of the changes affecting Germany scarcely did anything to slow the pace. Moreover, even confirmed sceptics were not always immune to the fascination exercised by this unexpected prospect for European and international co-operation and security. Yet it is still a remarkable achievement of Germany diplomacy to have changed the formula of 'four plus two' (four victorious powers and two German governments) into a formula of 'two plus four' as early as the beginning of 1990, banking on the likelihood that any further talk of two Germanies would be only cursory and for form's sake.

On the other hand there was a failure, which is hard to

explain, to mobilize all available expertise for so unprecedented a task as the ushering-in of German unity, and to bring as many well-disposed forces as possible to bear. The size of the task was underestimated, and the governing group tended to over-estimate itself. Greater co-operation could at least have helped to promote social adjustment, keep profiteers from the uni-fication process under restraint, and prevent flooding of the labour market. It is true that international statistics had given a thoroughly inaccurate picture of the GDR economy which now had to be integrated with West Germany's. With some exceptions, the machinery of production was much more back-ward and inefficient than had been generally supposed in the West. Furthermore, the extent of ecological damage was alarm-ing. The Eastern markets of the old GDR economy collapsed. Disputed titles to ownership blocked the revival of a market economy. Meanwhile, West German producers and commercial firms were exploiting the opportunities offered by a labour market unexpectedly opening up, and did not show much fore-sight about it.

I found it easy enough to form a picture of all this and point out that parts of the East, after an admittedly difficult transitional period, would become highly modern economic regions. Meanwhile, however, there was an alarming amount of discouragement to be dealt with, as well as unemployment problems. The social security systems established in the former Federal Republic were transferred to the East and swiftly adapted in line with material requirements. The same thing happened in those publicly answerable areas of the infra-structure which had long been neglected and are of such import-ance for economic development. All this will mean a large transfer of public funds from the 'old' Federal area to the 'new' Federal *Länder* for some years to come. The rash claim made in the summer and autumn of 1990 that this could be done without raising taxes could not be maintained for very long. Moreover, there were considerable calls on the capital market to supply increased borrowing for public budgets. No wonder that in Europe (and beyond) people began asking what would become of the Germans, once regarded as such shining examples of stability and growth. It was legitimate to question the effects of German interest rates and monetary policies on other countries. However, I did not and do not think there is any justification for doubting my compatriots' ability to deal with these problems in the course of the nineties.

No one should have been surprised to discover that more was involved than a comprehensive process, however important, of economic adjustment and the adaptation of financial and social policies. Another factor was the widely divergent development of the ordinary lives of the two separated parts of the German people. The spontaneous delight shown when the Brandenburg Gate was opened and the barriers were removed between Lübeck and Hof (and from Mecklenburg to the Vogtland at the same time) did not yet quite match the new reality. There certainly was and is a feeling of great relief in many reunited families. Bridges of solidarity and goodwill were built between many municipalities, associations, political and non-political groups, unprompted by central authorities. The fact that great efforts had been made to enable people in a divided Germany to visit each other, at least from West to East, now paid off. Of course it had also meant a good deal that West German television as well as radio could be received almost everywhere in the GDR – and in recent years even without obstruction from the 'organs of state'. Yet there were obviously problems of communication between the two parts of a nation no longer forcibly divided. A certain mutual sense of strangeness experienced by both those parts is one of the new features of life in Germany, though it will surely continue only for a transitional period.

Risky as generalizations about social psychology are, it may be said that the Germans of the former GDR did not feel inferior; instead, they felt that they had drawn the short straw when Germany was occupied in 1945 and divided into zones. Compared to their Western compatriots, they had to bear the greater part of the burden that had to be borne after Hitler. Now they wanted compensation. By no means everyone thought that all the institutions and arrangements of the old regime – in the field of child care, for instance – should be abolished wholesale. Even more important, as was shown by the change to democratic self-determination and the transition to a market economy with its social side-effects, was the fact that in the 'other' part of Germany more than two generations (counting from 1933, not just 1945!) had grown up without ever learning to develop freely, something that was bound to have had an effect. Moreover, the secret police had cast its net over society as a whole, and such unpleasant memories could not immediately be blotted out.

When I opened the newly elected Bundestag in the old Reichstag building in Berlin on 20 December 1990, as Chairman by virtue of seniority, I referred to the subject in these words:

'Fears about the harshness of structural change are circulating, and the humiliations of the decades of dictatorship have their repercussions, even if they amount to no more than a sense of having brought less with them than others on coming into our common home. Walls in people's heads are sometimes more durable than walls made of concrete blocks.

'I entreat our compatriots: do not let the feeling that history has given you a rough deal express itself in discouragement or perhaps even aggressiveness. Let it be offset by a feeling that it is never too late to make the most of life when the opportunity comes. We must go ahead rapidly and deal with the aftermath of the old system of rule, legally and in as fair a manner as possible. In my view, and speaking from experience, I would say that means distinguishing as clearly as we possibly can between those who behaved and enriched themselves in such a way that they deserve to be called to account for it, and many others who were politically misguided, or just cheated in a small way to get by. Democracy will not forbid them the chance to join our society and prove themselves.

'I would like to add this: the criteria of the democratic

constitutional state simply cannot be applied to life in a dictatorial unconstitutional state, nor to a system that lived at least as much off small-scale as off large-scale corruption. That is what makes passing moral and legal verdicts on conduct and misconduct, swindling and double-dealing so extremely difficult. One thing is certain: not many could be born to be heroes in the state ruled by the SED. And there is something else: who feels competent to judge his brother?

'We in the old Federal Republic have not requested our compatriots in the East to leave their homeland; indeed, we have asked them to stay if they can. The task of building bridges between our societies, with their contrasting developments and very different ways of life, is a challenge that will face us for some time to come.'

Disappointments in the East were met by a feeling, on the part of a good many West Germans, that they were not responsible for other people's misfortunes. And where would a willingness to make an appreciable national sacrifice have come from when leading sections of the community neither urged any such thing nor gave forward-looking reasons for it? Some singular hypotheses could be heard, to the effect that the burden of German history properly lies in the East ('Protestant, Prussian and Nazi'). In the argument over Berlin – should it resume the duties of a capital in more than name? – it became clear that rule by force and foreign rule can bring terrible confusion in their train.

Superficially, it might seem that the enlargement of the Federal Republic strengthened the coalition of Christian and Free Democrats which had held power in Bonn since 1982. In fact the first elections in the former GDR had to be seen as a vote in favour of the Western economic and legal system. The Christian Democrat and Liberal parties, in addition, had the advantage of having an organizational framework available in the East, although one that, until the 1989 revolution, had served as an auxiliary to the ruling Communists. The party offering itself as successor to the latter (under the name of the 'Party of Democratic Socialism') did not win the voters' confidence. Intellectuals who had foreseen the revolution and voiced their protests with increasing clarity – usually under the sheltering roof of the Evangelical Church – found hardly anyone to go along with ideas of a special way for East Germany. The notion of a 'renaissance' of Social Democracy in those regions where it had grown up in the last century proved illusory. However, there are now many indications that a relative balance between the two big national parties will be found, in the new part of the Federal Republic as well as the old. At the same time, and far beyond Germany itself, we can see ideas of social democracy (though under various different names) gaining ground in a new way in what was once Communist-ruled Europe.

Not surprisingly, questions are being asked about the role of a unified Germany in world politics – in international and especially in European discussion. It soon becomes obvious that the essential significance of the subject relates to Europe. No one of influence in the Federal Republic wants to diverge from the European course. The general opinion is that the Community may be able to forge stronger links between its parts, and yet enlarge itself. Meanwhile the Federal Republic, at the very centre of Europe, is doing all it can to avail itself of all-European co-operation and the opportunities that have opened up since the East–West conflict ended.

The perspicacity of the Moscow leadership – which, as it was to turn out, was no longer firmly seated in the saddle – meant that Germany was spared having to consider a new position in military policy. The country's membership of NATO was not called into question; acceptance of a certain limitation of the German armed forces was a result of the negotiations on arms reductions in Europe which had been in progress for some time. Special provisions came into force for the former territory of the GDR: the arrangements applying to NATO as already integrated were not automatically transferred to it. A time-scheme was agreed for the withdrawal of Soviet troops, and financial aid provided. As a result of world-wide changes in the field of security policy, it was natural that the number of American and other Western troops on German soil should also be reduced, without jeopardizing Germany's firm alliance with the West.

In my Berlin speech of 20 December 1990, I said:

'But for those claims of freedom asserted by the German West and Berlin, every hope entertained by our compatriots between the Elbe and the Oder would inevitably have been extinguished. And we know that we could not have preserved our freedom if it had not been protected by the Atlantic Alliance and, to an increasing extent, by the prosperity and solidarity of the European Community. In that context the founding fathers of the united Germany include – and we should not forget it – the originators of the Marshall Plan and such men as Jean Monnet, who helped to show our peoples the way into Europe even before Hitler had met his end. A little later Thomas Mann coined a phrase which could well be applied to our present constitution: "We must aim not for a German Europe, but for a European Germany."

'Building Europe is certainly not Germany's task alone, but we are jointly responsible for ensuring that the European East, hungry for prosperity and thirsty for freedom, is not left stranded. The European Community will reach one of its more crucial stages during the present legislative period of the Bundestag: comprehensive economic union in 1993, the subsequent important step to monetary union and then, we hope, to becoming a social and ecological community, a political union, and a union in the field of security.

'The Community of Twelve must first be truly democratic, and second must not put up barriers around itself. When the EEC, the European Economic Community, came into being, it was stipulated that democratic states from all parts of the continent should be able to join it. That is still a reasonable stipulation, for in the long run there ought not to be any second-class Europe. At the same time, sober experience tells us that if we want to help our neighbours in Central and Eastern Europe, we must not expose the house of the Community as it now stands to any danger of collapse. Perfectionism will achieve nothing and threaten everything, but creative policies have always called for the courage to take risks, and that is still the case. People who are well disposed to me sometimes suggest that the day on which the Germans united in freedom must have represented the fulfilment of my political life. That view falls too short and is too narrow. What I would like to see is the day when all Europe is united.'

It has been asked, mockingly, how much more sovereign a state Germany might yet become (Germany within its new borders, and not contesting that the border with Poland is at the Oder–Neisse Line) if it were not wisely determined to hold to its anchorage in Western Europe and its alliance with the United States. Without a hint of mockery it may be said that Germany – historically, geopolitically and as a part of Europe – does have more responsibility than it could bear on its own. Incidentally, Bismarck in old age advised his compatriots not to try to be everywhere at once; he said it would be 'against the real interests of Germany'. In today's context, that means not aspiring to outdated Great-Power status, but letting our own interests – well-founded interests in whatever field – become a part of the development of European objectives.

Germany will work to enlarge the European Community, within an appropriate framework of time, for its own real and not merely economic interests. Enlarging the Community does not mean simply including those partners of the old free-trade area, EFTA, who are willing to join, but our Central and Eastern European neighbours as well. Appropriate forms of association or co-operation, however they are described, will have to be found for the Baltic republics and the Balkan states, as well as the European East itself (including Russia and whatever other territories may join it to establish a new Union). Overt influence will play a part in the new markets, but no one should have to fear monopolies or other untoward consequences. The geographical situation, however, does mean that problems affecting Europe as a whole – perhaps problems of environmental damage, or of increasing emigration – will be felt more keenly in the German capital than in peripheral areas.

The European Community has made a successful start to its development and to promoting the common good of its member nations. It was set up, not least, to achieve joint security (and security between those member nations). The actual closeness of its joint structure was left open, although there was much to indicate that the individual weight of its national components would be reduced but not eliminated. Its foundation in principles of human rights, the democratic separations of powers, and parliamentary control, remains a crucial factor.

Germany has good reason to be grateful for the protection and support of the United States. It will be in our interests for the European Atlantic partnership to continue in existence and go on developing to the best of its ability. I believe that this partnership will thrive better based on the idea of support by twin columns (as held by President Kennedy in his time) than if it were guided by vague ideas of a larger area stretching eastwards from San Francisco to Vladivostok. The opportunities for useful co-operation with those entities that succeed the former Soviet Union will depend on circumstances which cannot yet be clearly discerned as I write. But Germany, of all states, and on the basis of a wealth of experience, will hardly wish to lose sight of the fact that Russia is still a great power.

In the early and middle months of 1991, and faster than anyone could like, first the Gulf War, then the tragedy of Yugoslavia and the confusion accompanying the collapse of the Soviet system, showed how far removed the European Community still is from playing a relevant part in security policies. Indeed, the same is true of Europe as a whole: it is not short of good intentions, but it does lack effective institutions to back them up.

The question remains of how far Europe in lieu of its constituent parts (or over and beyond those parts), working within and together with a stronger United Nations, will be ready and able to help settle conflicts in the developing world and to solve global problems of survival. I hope I am not wrong when I say that such a readiness will be found in Germany.

Willy Brandt

Unkel, September 1991

1

Return to Freedom

At the Limits of the Possible

13 August 1961: it was between four and five in the morning and the election special train from Nuremberg had just reached Hanover when I was woken. A railway official handed me an urgent message from Berlin. It was from Heinrich Albertz, head of the Senate Chancellery. It said the East was closing the sector boundary. As Mayor, I was asked to return to Berlin at once.

Albertz and Police Chief Stumm met me at Tempelhof airport. We drove to the Potsdamer Platz and the Brandenburg Gate, and saw the same scene everywhere: construction workers, roadblocks, concrete posts, barbed wire, GDR soldiers. At the city hall, the Schöneberg Rathaus, I heard reports that Soviet troops were stationed in readiness around the city, and that GDR Party leader Walter Ulbricht had already sent congratulations to the wall-building units.

At Allied Command headquarters in Dahlem – it was my first and last visit there – I was surprised to see a photograph of General Kotikov, the former Soviet Commandant of the city; his Western colleagues evidently thought it proper to pay tribute, in this respect at least, to Berlin's Four-Power status. However, the Soviet side had trodden the city's status underfoot that day in transferring power in their sector to the GDR authorities who were bent on division.

How would the Western powers react? How would they take

being dictated to over sector crossing-points? After a few days they had just one left, Checkpoint Charlie in the Friedrich-strasse, and nothing had happened. Or almost nothing. Nothing, at any rate, that was likely to do the many separated German families any good.

Had I been feeling cooler during those morning hours of Sunday, 13 August, I would have realized that our esteemed friends the commandants were bewildered and at a loss, and had been given no instructions. The American Commandant hinted, looking doubtful, at what Washington had told him: on no account must there be any hasty reactions, any 'trouble'. After all, West Berlin was not in immediate danger.

The President of the United States was on his yacht. I learned later that he had been told the news promptly. What interested him was whether Allied rights had been infringed in West Berlin, not whether the rights of Berlin as a whole were being thrown into the dustbin of history. In fact, as the memoirs of his colleagues indicate, President Kennedy was concerned about the possibility of war. At the very beginning of the crisis he had commented that he could involve the Alliance if Khrushchev took any action against West Berlin, but not if he tried anything on with East Berlin. On 13 August the White House assumed that the flood of refugees passing through Berlin would slacken but not dry up entirely.

This was a serious error of judgement, but it was more than came from official circles in Bonn. On the day the Wall was built I had a telephone call from the Foreign Minister, Heinrich von Brentano, saying that we had to work closely together now. That was all. Konrad Adenauer, the Federal Chancellor, wrapped himself in silence. An American observer commented later that fears in Bonn had been twofold: that the Americans might prove weak – or that they might stand firm!

I myself could think of no effective counter-measures to propose and, without concealing my emotion, I appealed to the commandants: 'At least protest, not only to Moscow, protest to the other Warsaw Pact capitals as well!' The Central Committee of the SED had just announced that East Berlin had been sealed off in accordance with a decision taken by the governments of the Warsaw Pact. I added: 'You could at least send patrols straight to the sector boundary to counter the sense of uncertainty and show the West Berliners they are not in danger!'

Twenty hours passed before the first military patrols were seen on the city's internal boundary. Forty hours passed before any formal protest was sent to the Soviet Commandant. Seventy-two hours passed before the protest reached Moscow: it had the ring of mere formality.

Meanwhile, many tears had been shed. In my own electoral district of Wedding people jumped from buildings on the sector boundary into blankets held by firemen, and not all of them landed safely.

On 16 August I wrote to President Kennedy, mentioning the gravity of the situation and the existence of a severe crisis of confidence. If the drift towards making Berlin a 'free city' continued, I said, an exodus of refugees from West Berlin was to be feared. I suggested that the American garrison should be strengthened, the responsibility felt by the Three Powers for West Berlin should be emphasized, the 'German question' should not be regarded as settled, and the problem of Berlin should be laid before the United Nations. It was with some bitterness, I said, that I remembered how negotiations with the Soviet Union had been rejected on the grounds that one ought not to negotiate 'under pressure'. However, I continued, we were now in 'a situation of outright blackmail, and I am already being told that we shall have to negotiate. In such circumstances, it is all the more important at least to show political initiative, however slight the chance of showing any in action. After accepting a Soviet move which is and has been described as illegal, and in view of the many tragedies now being played out in East Berlin and the Soviet zone of Germany, we shall none of us be spared the risk of showing the utmost resolution.'

Kennedy had an additional combat group stationed in the city and sent me his answer by a special messenger, Vice-President Lyndon B. Johnson, who arrived in Berlin on 19 August and endeavoured, with Texan nonchalance, to play down the gravity of the situation. In his letter Kennedy frankly admitted that military conflict could not be contemplated, and that most of the measures proposed bore no comparison to the enormity of what had happened. Was it this letter that raised the curtain to reveal an empty stage?

A few days after the first anniversary of the building of the Wall, on 17 August 1962, Peter Fechter, an eighteen-year-old construction worker, was shot and bled to death on the Eastern side of Checkpoint Charlie. We were unable – forbidden – to help him. His death had far-reaching consequences; indignation ran high. There were demonstrations of grief and anger. Young people spoke of blasting holes in the Wall; others dug tunnels and worked to help their fellow citizens – until some irresponsible people began making money out of the operation. A popular newspaper accused me of treachery because police had been sent to guard the Wall. One evening I was called to the Rathaus: a procession of demonstrators, most of them students, was on its way. I used a police-car loudspeaker to tell them that the Wall was harder than the heads they were trying to run against it, and it would not be removed by bombs.

Immediately after the building of the Wall there had been terrible scenes: scenes of helpless rage that had to be voiced, and yet had to be controlled. There could hardly be a more difficult task for a public speaker. After the August 1962 crisis I went visiting businesses and administrative departments, trying to explain to the people of Berlin what was possible and what was not.

What *was* possible, and what was not? That question was my constant companion over the next few years. After the building of the Wall, people went on uttering much the same platitudes for some time, but it was clear that nothing was the same as it had been before. A search began for possible ways of alleviating the hardships of the division. If we had to live with the Wall for any length of time, how could it be made less impenetrable? How could we find a *modus vivendi*, a settled relationship between the two parts of Germany? What precautions could be taken to make the centre of Europe a securely peaceful zone?

I had become Governing Mayor of Berlin in the autumn of 1957. I had shared responsibility for the people of that hard-pressed city for a decade. As a member of the German Bundestag since 1949, I had also been pushed into the front line of German politics. As a young man I had resisted the Nazi rule of tyranny and war. In Berlin, I ranged myself beside those who opposed the Communist imposition of conformity and the Stalinist strangle-hold.

This was pure self-defence: an obligation towards people who had suffered greatly and wanted to make a new start. At the same time, there was anxiety over the fragility of peace. Later it became clear that we had been right not to give in over the Berlin blockade in 1948, the ultimatum from Khrushchev in 1958 or the building of the Wall in 1961. The right to self-determination was at stake, and it was important not to surrender it and thus help to set off a chain reaction which might have led to renewed armed conflict.

My Berlin experience also taught me that there is no sense in running your head against a wall – unless the wall is only made of paper – but it makes good sense not to accept arbitrary barriers. Working hard for understanding and communication will not bring every individual an immediate profit, but many lives depend on it. Human rights do not fall from heaven, nor do civil liberties.

In Berlin we were right to take account of new developments in the world around us and look out for that 'wind of change' of which John F. Kennedy spoke to the Berlin students a year and a half after the building of the Wall, only a few months before he was assassinated. It was important not to hang back as if expecting some natural event to happen of its own accord.

There was no point in wasting too much time crying woe and demanding our rights; instead, we had to concentrate on making such improvements to the situation as could be made.

I do not overestimate my own achievements, working first from Berlin and then from Bonn. But I do know I could have done nothing of any value if I had taken what seemed the easier way in my youth; if I had not frequently accepted the risk of being misunderstood and hurt, even of physical danger; if I had not first guessed and then learnt that I must not be deterred by stupidity, and had to be able to endure unpleasantness if I was to do any good to the community, both nationally and beyond. politician who learnt his trade in Berlin had not only to face reats from outside, but to stand up to those in his own camp – Germany and the West – for whom the flight from reality had become a substitute for politics. That became my resolve, and I exerted myself to use the key that lay in German hands to open the door to more than surface, minimal détente, so that arbitrary division could be overcome, however small the steps along that way and however tortuous at times the path itself.

Circumstances, my office, and also, I am sure, the experiences of my youth, gave me a chance – first as Mayor of Berlin, then as Foreign Minister and as Federal Chancellor – to reconcile the idea of Germany with the idea of peace in the minds of large parts of the world. After all that had happened, that was no small matter, particularly since history has caused hatred to build up, but at the same time has shown that the Germans as much as anyone have a part to play in European peace. And not just the West Germans. Indeed, that ersatz nation did not exist at all when I first saw the light of day on Hanseatic soil, on the eve of the First World War.

I was convinced that the unnaturally tense situation in a divided Germany had to be eased, for the sake of peace and the human beings affected. Europe could not be constructed around or in opposition to Germany. Obviously I had to abandon the rose-tinted spectacles through which I saw the future in my very early youth. But I was confirmed, time and again, in my belief that the future cannot be built without a certain amount of hope. However, even a man convinced he has made the right decision cannot be sure of avoiding errors and mistakes. I have sometimes said things I regret. But I can say with a clear conscience: I have always been aware that a freeze demands a thaw and must be overcome as far as possible.

Berlin itself was credited, unduly, with much of what should really have been laid at the door of Nazi rule (and the Kaiser's Germany before it). Obviously a city from which Hitler had governed could not stand very high in the eyes of the world, but it was forgotten that on average the citizens of Berlin had been not more but less pro-Nazi than their countrymen. In the immediate post-war period, however, many people found it convenient to put up vigorous opposition to any idea of the old imperial capital's becoming the seat of German government again. In the west of the country they called Berlin a 'heathen city', and in the south it was said that the new capital should stand among vineyards, not potato fields. I may claim some of the credit for helping to restore the image of Berlin.

I will admit frankly to thinking and acting with self-assur-ance – although I am well aware that self-assurance is no safeguard against errors and inconsistencies. In retrospect, there are certainly things one wishes one had not done, or had done differently. Or that one would like to do better another time, should the opportunity arise. There are things one would rather forget than boast about, others from which it would have been better to refrain in good time, or into which one should never have let oneself be drawn. For the rest, a man like me who has seen so much confusion and destruction over the years, but moments of quiet contemplation and much renewal too, feels that comments on the tempo and diversity of change in the lives of people in our time are commonplace understatement.

I aimed for co-operation wherever confrontation could be avoided. I hoped fervently for renewal after every disaster. I was writing about collective security even before the Second World War ended. I did not set too much store by discussion of the Allies' peacetime aims, but I did think that a document such as that signed by Prime Minister Churchill and President Roosevelt in August 1941, on board ship in the Atlantic before the USA even entered the war, was more than just a piece of propaganda. If the Allies could have gone on working together instead of being divided by the Cold War, it would have helped the process of reconstruction and the understanding of European responsibilities in the world. Even as a refugee twice over, exiled in Sweden, I feared that the East–West controversy, relentlessly inflamed, would not only divide Germany but cause the whole continent to drift apart. From the positive viewpoint, I saw that co-operation between the victorious powers would have provided a better chance of dealing effectively with the tasks of the post-war period.

The Cold War and the disintegration of the wartime alliance led, among many other things, to the long Berlin crisis and the existence of two states on German soil. The breach between East and West cast the west of the country in the part of both victim and profiteer. This made it increasingly difficult to restore state unity, but the problem was pushed aside: there were more urgent matters on hand. I too have had to bow to the demands of immediately pressing concerns, thus laying myself open, at a later date, to critical questions: why did I not speak up more clearly in discussion of such international problems as the future of the post-colonial peoples?

My answer was simple: in foreign policy, you cannot start changing direction on several lines at once, or I for one could not, in the circumstances of post-war Germany.

In the transition from major war to modest peace, I had been occupied with ideas which were distinctly over-optimistic, especially where they concerned the prospects for international co-operation. Only too often the wish was father to the thought. But why would a German exiled in Scandinavia know better than the assembled heads of government of the democratic powers, or others with a wide experience and a good vantage-point?

Years followed in which I had to defend my own German and European identity and that of others. Years when there was great disarray in the West, while what might have been feared came to pass in the East. But I never entirely abandoned the hope that even the tensest situations can be eased and opposing interests reconciled.

I have had critics who assumed, simplistically, that only practical experience of the Wall in Berlin led me to adopt the *Ostpolitik* and peace policy that I carried through, in the face of much opposition, in the early seventies, but here they were wrong. The conclusions that lay at the root of my Berlin 'small steps' policy and of my endeavours in office in Bonn were actually very close to the ideas of what would be needed that I entertained during the war.

I have not always been able to feel part of a majority on this subject, but I never felt isolated. Moreover, true as it is that reliable guidance seldom comes from the crowd, and however much experience shows that even with a democratic mandate one cannot expect agreement from all of the people all of the time, it must not be forgotten that if policies of peace and reconciliation are to prevail, they must be firmly established in the minds of large sections of the people.

Berlin – a Testing-Ground

'Our Currency – Berlin Free, Never Communist!' The meeting was as huge as the headline announcing it. That day, 24 June 1948, I was there at Ernst Reuter's side in the Hertha Stadium at the Gesundbrunnen when he addressed the crowd: 'People of Berlin! In these hours of difficult decision, we call upon you: let no one and nothing delude you. Go forward unchallenged. Only if we are resolved to take every risk can we have the one kind of life worth living: a decent, honest life and, poor as it may be, a life lived in freedom.'

Reuter, the elected Mayor of Berlin, repeated what he had said at the first of the great freedom demonstrations, on 18 March of that fateful year: that after Prague, Finland was to have been next in line. Finland had not been next because the Finnish people stood up for their freedom. 'Nor will Berlin be next in line if it stands firm at this time of crisis. In this crisis we do not merely ask you to trust us. We want you to trust yourselves. That is the only way to find the path to freedom; and freedom, we know, is the breath of life. We must and will fight for it.' The danger to be averted was that Berlin would fall victim to the Eastern zone if it was kept outside the Western Deutschmark currency.

How important are the personalities of those who bear responsibility at great historical turning-points? It was a stroke of great good fortune that Ernst Reuter was there to steer Berlin through the post-war years and carry the Berliners along with him. His previous career and his temperament enabled him to make the best of the difficult but challenging situation.

Reuter was a man who had emerged from that chaos of which Julius Leber had said that it alone produced great leaders. He had fled from a sheltered middle-class childhood into Social Democracy; he served his apprenticeship travelling the country as a public speaker. He was wounded on the Eastern Front in the First World War, was captured by the Russians, and was a spokesman for those prisoners of war who supported the October Revolution. He even became a commissar, with a mission from Lenin to the Volga Germans to set up an autonomous republic. Once back in Berlin, he joined the KPD, which expelled him in 1921 – he was unwilling to accept the deranged directives of the Comintern – and he returned to the fold of the SPD. He became editor of *Vorwärts*, Berlin City Councillor for Transport and Mayor of Magdeburg. After being arrested twice, he emigrated to Turkey and entered the service of the Ankara Government. That accounted for his nickname in Berlin, not always kindly meant, of 'the Turk'.

In 1946, when Reuter returned to his old post as Councillor for Transport, he had abandoned many but not all of his hopes for the unity of the state and the city; in any case it did not seem to him a matter of the very first importance. Six months later Reuter was chosen to head the Magistrat [the Berlin city administration] by the members of the City Assembly, but the Soviet Commandant vetoed the appointment. Louise Schröder, a former Reichstag deputy who inspired great confidence, became acting Mayor on his behalf. He was concerned with those very simple tasks which still partook more of the nature of clearing-up than of reconstruction. At the same time he warned us against illusions. We were also saved from those by the rough methods with which the Cold War was being waged on our doorstep, as it were. They included the abduction of some of our own acquaintances.

Reuter did not believe in 1947, and still less in 1948, what all parties were saying: that the Soviet Union was merely satisfying its own need for security and must not be provoked. The Soviets had left the Allied Control Council in March and the Military Command in June. The transport of supplies to Berlin was impeded from the beginning of the year, and there were repeated statements to the effect that the Western powers had forfeited their right to a presence in the city. A realist could therefore be under no illusions. Had it been otherwise, would Reuter have urged the Western powers so incessantly in the early summer of 1948 to include Berlin in the currency reform (which had not been part of the original plan), or at least not to give up control over the city's currency? Would he have given such a free hand to his militant colleague, the head of Berlin's Economics Department, the never-to-be-forgotten Gustav Klingelhöfer of Metz, who had once stood on the barricades of the Munich republic and spent several years in Bavarian prisons? Would he have read the riot act to the opposition within the party at its *Land* conference in July 1948? Everything that was going on, he said, had been ruthlessly planned in advance by the persons responsible on the Soviet side. Western policy should not, therefore, take its cue from Soviet sensitivity.

Reuter also took the leadership of his own party to task, although not for any such reasons as taking offence at the rather disparaging description of him by Kurt Schumacher as 'the Prefect of Berlin', or Erich Ollenhauer's criticism of the emphatically pro-American policy of the Reuter wing. Ollenhauer, then deputy leader of the SPD, inquired at this same Party conference whether 'we really had to be more American than the Americans', thereby showing that he was insufficiently aware of the possibilities and necessities of life in Berlin in the year 1948. Reuter wanted positive steps to consolidate the west of Germany: this was at the heart of his policies and consequently of his criticism of the party leaders. It would not do, he said, 'to go on standing between two bundles of hay, like Balaam's ass', and coming to no decision. If the West was to thrive and Berlin survive, something must be done to put an end to the confusion of zonal administration (and maladministration). I had drawn up the appeal which the *Land* SPD committee dismissed in almost the same terms, or indeed rather more strongly, as befitted our division of labour: the Soviet policy of the last three years, I said, was responsible for the failure to find an all-German solution to the currency issue. I described the economic and political rise of, in the first instance, the Western zones as the only way to restore German unity and freedom.

Politically and personally, Reuter and I were close, almost entirely of one mind. I was regarded as 'Reuter's young man', and I was proud of his liking for me and of being able to give him support. What drew us together? On my return from wartime exile in Scandinavia, I felt attracted by his humane and sociable manner, his warmth, his wit, his courage in standing up for his convictions, his readiness to shoulder responsibility, his optimistic nature and his assured but not arrogant way of expressing himself, even to the Allies. We had both been in exile, but so had others. What counted was how you had coped with your experience of emigration, of party history, of the Weimar Republic, of the path you had taken or from which you had strayed, and whether your sense of reality had been sharpened. 'The Federal Republic has made enormous progress in the past few years,' Reuter reminded his own party in 1953, adding, 'our frequently propounded thesis of a collapse tomorrow, or at the latest the day after tomorrow, is completely out of touch with reality.' As a reformer who strove for agreement, Reuter was thinking not only of electoral defeat for the Social Democrats, but of his long difficulties in his own local party in Berlin; in 1952, weary of controversy, he encouraged me to stand for the chairmanship of the West Berlin branch of the party. The voting went against me: Franz Neumann, a brave but rather narrow traditionalist, was elected by 196 votes to 135.

On 24 June 1948, as I stood beside Reuter at the Gesundbrunnen, we guessed that decisions of the utmost importance lay ahead. We did not know what they would be or where they would lead: even, perhaps, to a turning-point in world affairs. The previous evening the Deutschmark had been introduced, with some restrictions, in the American, English and French sectors, and the East's answer came next morning with the Berlin blockade. We knew that the currency issue was merely a pretext for the battle for Berlin, and that the Western powers were only just beginning to understand how set their Eastern wartime ally was on seizing the city, and perhaps more. On 11 April 1945 the Americans had stopped at the Elbe; if they had marched on they would have saved themselves a good deal of trouble and given the world a different face. But they left the triumph of marching into Hitler's capital to the Russians. One reason was that General Eisenhower, the Supreme Allied Commander, no longer considered Berlin an especially important objective. He failed to understand the symbolic value of the place, regarding the German capital as merely a point on the map. At the end of the 1950s, when I broached the subject with Eisenhower, then President of the United States, he freely admitted that he had not foreseen the consequences of his order not to advance on Berlin. The Americans and the British had therefore entered the city only later, the French later still, and they had omitted to make any clear agreements about access. None the less, common sense showed up more clearly in the orders issued by the victorious powers than on the subsequent bureaucratic battlefields of the occupying administrators.

Road and rail access from the Western zones was blocked. The electricity cable from the Eastern zone was cut. All deliveries of supplies from the East to the 'rebel' Western sectors stopped. No bread, coal, milk or electric current was to reach the defenceless population until they had forced their elected representatives to capitulate and made the Western powers withdraw. Ernst Reuter said privately: 'Even if we can only hold out for a fortnight or a month, the fact that we resisted at all will influence historical development.' From the first moment of the blockade Reuter had known and said that our own determination to stand firm was the only chance of mobilizing Western aid. In 1940, when almost all seemed lost, Churchill had said the British would fight on 'if necessary alone'. Outside all considerations of party thinking, Reuter had admired Churchill, and so had I. We were aware that enthusiasm for Berlin was lukewarm in the west of Germany and anti-Prussian resentment was in fashion, but just then we did not think it particularly important. However, the Finance Minister of Hesse was not alone in believing, as he said, that it was inadvisable for the Germans to expose themselves by 'financing a political action by the Americans against the Russians'.

Late that June I accompanied Reuter to the Harnack building in Dahlem. American administrators told us that it would be possible to supply the city by air. Reuter, sceptical rather than surprised, said, 'We shall go our way. Do what you can. We shall do what we feel to be our duty.' He had previously been assured by General Clay that the Allies would give what help they could – provided, it was intimated, that the Berliners endured all trials and stood by the Western powers. Reuter had replied: 'General, there can be no question of where the Berliners stand. They will stand up for their freedom and be glad to accept any help they are offered.' A little later I heard a comment from Washington to the effect that suddenly they were coming across people who did not hold back but let it be known they had made up their minds. The description of Berlin as the cradle of German–American friendship had its origin here.

When Lucius D. Clay, the American Military Governor, organized the airlift and got the consent of his President (Truman, who said, 'We are in Berlin and we are going to stay – period'), he was thinking of an arrangement to last a month and a half, not 322 days. At the height of the operation an unarmed bomber was landing in Berlin every 48 seconds and the roar of aircraft engines had become the symbol of survival. Over two million tons of supplies came in by air, a mighty achievement, and not only on the part of the US Air Force – the British ran one-third of the operation, though the French were tied up in Indo-China. The Berliners, managing on small, indeed minute rations, did not knuckle under, and there were hardly any signs of defeatism. In the election for the City Assembly, held in the middle of the winter of the blockade, when the last remnants of unified administration for Berlin disappeared, Reuter and the SPD won 64.5 per cent of the vote.

The first United Nations Secretary-General, Trygve Lie, whom I knew well from my time in exile, was not alone in thinking there was a serious danger of war. Now that some of the Soviet files have been made public we know that Stalin had taken purely defensive precautions in case of an American tank attack, a move that Clay had considered, but for which he did not have the President's blessing. Contact between Moscow and the Western capitals was not broken off during these critical months, but it was a curious kind of contact. On 2 August 1948 Stalin saw the three Western ambassadors and – according to the minutes of this meeting later published in Moscow and East

Berlin – told them that Berlin had ceased to be the capital of Germany 'because the three Western powers have split Germany into two states'. He repeated that the Western powers had forfeited the right 'to keep troops in West Berlin'. After the end of the blockade, he said, the mark which was the valid currency of the Eastern zone must be introduced into West Berlin as well. The Western zones could be economically integrated but could not have their own Government. And first, the Four Powers had to agree on the major issues affecting Germany. If they could not, he concluded, 'the Eastern and Western zones will develop in their different ways'.

The use of Berlin to exert pressure against the formation of the Federal Republic failed, like the attempt to dislodge the Western powers from the city and bring it within the Soviet sphere of influence. Stalin had underestimated the airlift, and had failed to take the measure of either his former wartime allies or the endurance of the people of Berlin. Whether because he saw that the venture was hopeless, or because he feared complications, Stalin lifted the blockade at midnight on 12 May 1949. There was great rejoicing. The unarmed struggle for independence had infused much energy into the new German democracy. Berlin had become the shield behind which the three Western zones could form the Federal Republic. But we had really wanted a different outcome; we had wanted more.

It became an article of faith with Reuter and me that the priority was for Berlin to be linked as closely as possible with the Federal Republic. We encountered resistance, and not just within our own party. Pundits in the foreign ministries of the protecting powers made pronouncements on status, ever ready to refute ideas that might have arisen from the confusion and illusory reality of their paperwork. They were soon in harmony with their colleagues in Bonn. In 1952, when even the American High Commissioner, John McCloy, agreed with Reuter in suggesting that Berlin should be given the status of a Federal *Land*, no one in Bonn would listen. And at the time of the building of the Wall, when I called for a fresh examination of Allied reservations against making Berlin a *Land* of the Federal Republic, I was again fobbed off with legal quibbles.

The Third Transition Law of 1952 at least established the legal tie with the Federal Republic, and West Germany's financial responsibility for Berlin. Reuter felt personal satisfaction, and I myself, by this time elected to both the Bundestag and the Berlin City Assembly, saw it as the reward for years of effort; but both of us thought that more could have been done, and that we could have faced the future with easier minds if Berlin had been integrated more completely with the Federal Republic.

The seventeenth of June 1953 brought the popular rising in East Berlin, with its dual demand for social liberation and national freedom. Stalin had died three months earlier. The new leadership in the Kremlin had dissolved the Soviet Control Commission and appointed a Supreme Commissar, with new instructions. He was Vladimir Semyonov, an expert on German affairs whom I had met briefly in Stockholm, and who was to be Ambassador to Bonn during the seventies. The exodus – 150,000 people had streamed into the West during the month of March – had set the alarm bells ringing. The SED, whether it liked it or not, was forced to redress certain grievances and watch people begin to hope. Appallingly high production norms set off the protest that led to such slogans as 'The goatee [Walter Ulbricht] must go' and 'Russians out'. The rising was suppressed first by the tanks of the occupying power, then by retribution from the security police. The West expressed sympathy. The rebels saw how isolated they were. Grave doubts about Western policy were entertained. The contrast between strong words and feeble deeds made a deep impression, and proved useful to the authorities. Finally, the people came to terms with their situation.

The rising of 17 June marked a watershed. People guessed it, but would not admit it. No one was prepared. I said in the Bundestag: 'The struggle for reunification in freedom takes precedence over all other plans and projects of foreign policy.' The eighteen million people in the Eastern zone, I said, must not be exposed 'by what we do or what we leave undone' to the danger of the further consolidation of a state of affairs which might perhaps be eased. 'There can be no solution but a peaceful one to the German question. There is no other way but to negotiate it.' But as to who would be ready to negotiate where and on what, no answer was forthcoming. Three months after 17 June Adenauer was on his way to an election victory influenced by West Germany's unexpected but impressive economic recovery, and his support for the Western treaties. Yet what had just happened in 'the Zone' must surely have shown everyone that there was no alternative to negotiation.

Who can count the long hours and many meetings that undermined Reuter's health? Who can assess the envy and futility that wore him down and broke his heart? Who can measure the disappointment he felt at the result of the second Bundestag election and the dogmatic attitudes at the head of his own party? After the loss of the election (in which the SPD had slipped to 28.8 per cent of the vote, while the CDU/CSU rose to 45.1 per cent), he had urged the leadership committees to start saying what the party stood for instead of what it was against, but in vain. It was obvious to him that his opinion was not wanted. Ernst Reuter was not a power politician, and certainly not a narrow party politician. It was not in his nature to set up a dynastic power, fighting and intriguing to get his supporters into key positions. He was more sensitive than he appeared.

On 29 September 1953 I was at home when the telephone rang. The call, from Oslo, asked me for an obituary of Reuter. A quarter of an hour later I was in his little house in Bülowstrasse. On the way back I saw a picture I shall never forget: candles were burning in the windows of every street I passed through. No one had been asked to light them. People stood in tears at the newspaper kiosks where the news of Reuter's death was on the posters. The city was mourning a mayor it had regarded as a father.

It seemed only natural for me to become leader of the Reuter wing of the Berlin branch of the SPD. I stood for the chairmanship for the second time at the Berlin party conference in the spring of 1954, and this time I lost by only two votes. Differences and indeed clashes of opinion had emerged more openly than ever. With one eye on the Federal Party, which still stood behind Neumann, I demanded a clear decision in favour of the West, and expressed my support for a security pact. I would not pretend, either to myself or to the delegates, that reunification could be achieved in the short term. An all-German policy, I thought, must be a long-term policy, and that included a German contribution to defence within the NATO framework. The wish for reunification, I thought, should cease to be a substitute for practical policies. In the mid-fifties, practical policies meant establishing the foundations of democracy and social security in the Federal Republic, and in Berlin they meant strengthening the economy so that the city could catch up with the west of the country.

At the Federal SPD party conference of July 1954 in Berlin, such 'reformist' ideas still appeared strange. So did my warning that the German Left still made a practice of ignoring the relationship between democratic order and armed might. The SPD, I concluded, could offer responsible and fruitful national and international policies only if it came to terms with power. The immediate reaction was yet another lesson in what party power meant: I gained just 155 votes in the election for the party committee, and was not elected, while Franz Neumann gained 270. I also failed to gain election the next time, in Munich in 1956.

My position in Berlin was not affected by this setback; if anything, the opposite. In the City Assembly elections in December 1954 the SPD won with a small majority, not of votes but of seats; the all-party coalition had broken up after Reuter's death and an alliance of the CDU and the FDP had taken over, under Walther Schreiber. It was therefore the SPD's turn to appoint the Governing Mayor, the title of the post now that Berlin had a new constitution and half a city had become a whole *Land*. The appointee was Otto Suhr; despite the opposition of the Neumann wing, I succeeded him as President of the City Assembly. This was an honorary post, and I continued to hold my seat in the Bundestag.

Otto Suhr had managed to maintain a position between the disputing party factions, although he continued Reuter's policies as long as he had the strength. He fell gravely ill in 1956, and representing the office of Mayor, both inside and outside the city, fell increasingly to me as the parliamentary leader. This shifted the power structure within the Berlin party further towards the 'American faction', as whose leader I found myself described in press and party jargon. But the climate of the times and coincidence were not the whole story: friends in the Federal Party supported me and believed that Berlin would become the focus of a regeneration of the entire SPD. Regeneration meant taking a clear look at facts – in Germany and in the world. At the *Land* party conference of 1955 I tried to explain to those who were flirting with ideas of neutrality why even a reunited Germany could not simply bow out of international politics. The axis of the balance of power ran right through the country, and the Great Powers, particularly the Soviet Union, would not take such risks with Germany as they were willing to take with Austria. Germany could not and should not assume the role of an isolated buffer-state. 'We must know that we cannot resign from Europe and the world, as if we were resigning from a bowling club.' I did not intend to stand for the Berlin party chairmanship again until I could be sure of election; defeats may steel the will, but only when there are not too many of them. So I contented myself with putting out a signal and, as before, filling the post of deputy.

Hopes of miracles from Moscow were drowned in the bloodbath of Budapest. On a gloomy November evening in 1956 100,000 Berliners had gathered outside the Schöneberg Rathaus to express their helpless anger at their inability to help Hungary any more than they had been able to help their own countrymen three years before. The speakers, Franz Neumann for the SPD and Ernst Lemmer for the CDU, were booed and shouted down. The crowd wanted action. All over the square, there were cries of, 'To the Brandenburg Gate!' 'To the Soviet Embassy!' and 'Russians out!' I am not sure how I came to find myself at the speaker's desk; there had been no plans for me to speak. I only remember that I warned my audience against slogans which would be as little use to our own cause as to the unfortunate people of Hungary. To prevent a violent march into the Eastern sector I asked the crowd to accompany me to the Steinplatz and gather around the memorial to the victims of Stalinism. Once we arrived there I found words that were at least partly adequate for the situation, and struck up the song 'Ich hatt' einen Kameraden'. They all joined in.

The final notes had hardly died away when alarming news reached me. A procession of several thousand young people was marching to the Brandenburg Gate, wielding torches. Some of them had been stopped by the police in the Strasse der 17. Juni, and there were clashes. It took me only a split second to realize that incidents on the sector boundary could mean war. Not only was the Volkspolizei [the East German People's Police] ready to fire, there were Russian tanks stationed in the side streets off the Unter den Linden.

I jumped into a car, switching to a police loudspeaker van with broken windows before getting to the gate. I could understand the feelings of those young people, many of them students, only too well. But they had not calculated the consequences of their actions, which I tried to point out in quite tough language. No sooner had this worked, and we were singing the song about the good comrade again, than I was summoned to the Brandenburg Gate. The police drove me there. I climbed on a car and explained, once again, that a bloody clash would not help Hungary but might well unleash war. Then I formed a new procession of demonstrators and led it away from the gate, with all its weight of symbolism, and to the Soviet memorial in the Tiergarten. Aggression melted away as we sang the national anthem − 'Einigkeit und Recht und Freiheit' − 'unity and right and freedom'. On the way back I met some English military policemen who had suffered rough treatment at the hands of young Berliners letting off steam in their impotent anger. When I spoke to the British a few days later I expressed gratitude for their forbearance.

Hopes can be dashed and then revive. The more strongly they are based on faith, the more tenacious they are of life, or such was the impression given by my party in 1957, the year when it picked itself up off the floor in more than one respect. Otto Suhr died on 30 August, and Franz Neumann, knowing he stood no chance himself, set out to find a candidate for mayor; a mass-circulation popular paper ran a headline announcing that Berlin wanted Brandt. On 15 September Adenauer and his party won the Bundestag election with an absolute majority of 50.2 per cent. Ollenhauer and the SPD, who dreamed of victory, won a moderate 31.8 per cent, and now the way to regeneration was opened up. Party Chairman Ollenhauer, from then on a friend of mine, was putting up no opposition to anything or anyone, and indeed I would not have carried the old, traditionalist party along with me so easily without his authority. After the Bundestag election, he called off Franz Neumann and gave unreserved support to my candidature.

On 3 October 1957 the City Assembly elected me Governing Mayor with 86 votes to 10, and 22 abstentions. A party conference was set for January, when I finally succeeded Franz Neumann as leader of the Berlin SPD. Once again, we did not pull our punches. No one in Berlin claimed that ours was only a personal rivalry. It was that too, but no one questioned what I said in an interview: 'If you are asking me how I differ objectively from Franz Neumann, then I have to say ... we are divided by a fundamentally different understanding of the nature of a political party.' In my speech, looking ahead to the likelihood of nomination as candidate for Chancellor, I spoke of 'a kind of natural contradiction between what Social Democracy represents in itself, and what it represents in power'. It was not very surprising that the people of Berlin repaid a decade of struggle for the identity of the Party with a magnificent vote of confidence. The Berlin election of December 1958 gave the SPD, of which I was now the leader, a clear absolute majority of 52.6 per cent; however, I continued the coalition with the CDU. Before this, in Stuttgart, I had also finally been elected to the party committee, at the same time as Helmut Schmidt.

Once again, the Berlin election had been no ordinary election, not simply a choice between parties or candidates. On 10 November, speaking in the Palace of Sport in Moscow, the Soviet Party leader and head of government Nikita Khrushchev had issued an ultimatum: West Berlin was to become a 'free city' within six months, the Occupation Statute was to be liquidated, and Soviet rights transferred to the GDR. As a precaution against any trouble, he announced a separate peace treaty with the GDR and threatened, more or less openly, to use force against the city and its access routes, to the use of which the Western powers had a basic right. After the blockade, in June 1949 the Four Powers had all agreed to return to the status quo ante and improve transport to and from Berlin. The question of how we were to go on from there was much on my mind. It could not be so hard to grasp that the formula of 'free access', which came under great strain in the months of the ultimatum, was inadequate – or could it? For the time being it took a great deal of strength to resist the ultimatum and weather the crisis, outside the city even more than inside it.

I never discovered what made Khrushchev suppose that the Berliners would flee from their city *en masse* and leave it to fall into the hands of the GDR like a rotten fruit. He let it be known through Halvard Lange, Norwegian Foreign Minister for many years, who he must have known was a friend of mine, that the West Berlin problem would solve itself: the people would run away and the city's economy would collapse. Years later a highly placed Soviet official still thought he ought to warn me that it was only a question of time before the Berlin problem was solved of its own accord. That never prevented the Kremlin from using the old imperial capital as a lever to promote its interests in other parts of the world.

I described the 'free city' [*freie Stadt*] announced by Khrushchev as more of an 'outlawed city' [*vogelfreie Stadt*], and spoke in favour of firm opposition. I felt sure of the support of the people of Berlin. When a situation became critical I used to visit a business firm or factory and find out for myself in conversation, or in people's reaction to a speech, what they would and what they would not tolerate. In Bonn, where a very militant tone was taken, opinions were divided. The head of the Eastern Section of the Foreign Ministry, Georg Ferdinand Duckwitz, sought me out in the Berlin mission and advised me: 'Accept the "free city" idea and extend it to the whole of Berlin; you won't get a better deal.'

This remarkable piece of advice was not official. The Government wanted nothing to do with an initiative involving Berlin as a whole, and this was still the case at the conference of Western foreign ministers in Paris at the beginning of the dramatic month of August 1961. Bonn thought poorly of initiatives in general. Accordingly, I made contact with the President of the Bundesbank on my own account and without involving the Government or the Allies: I wanted Karl Blessing to give me some idea of the nature of a possible currency which appeared unique to Berlin but was actually linked to the Western Deutschmark.

The ultimatum issued by the Kremlin in the form of a note on 27 November set a deadline of six months. On 1 May 1959, just before it ran out, some 600,000 people (according to police figures) assembled in the Platz der Republik. Speaking on behalf of them all, I told the world: 'Look at the people of Berlin, and then you will know what the Germans want!' The right to self-determination, I said, must apply to our people too. Brutal intervention in their internal affairs was intolerable. With colonial rule being dismantled in other parts of the world, we could not have a new colonialism established in the middle of Europe.

The twenty-seventh of May, when the ultimatum ran out, was a day like any other. Nothing happened – but nothing happened to ease the situation in the long term either. The scepticism expressed at the foreign ministers' conference that had been arranged was to prove only too well justified. I was angry when the Western powers unnecessarily let the subject of Berlin be treated in isolation, instead of putting up firm opposition to the Soviet attempt to separate Berlin from the Federal Republic. Bonn had previously emphasized to the Western foreign ministers that we were dealing not with *the* GDR, but the *so-called* GDR; Selwyn Lloyd, the British Foreign Secretary, thought this was amusing, and called the East German Foreign Minister, sitting in as an observer like Heinrich von Brentano, the 'so-called Mr Bolz'. In fact the Federal Government itself was not particularly pressing over the vital question of the ties between Berlin and the Federal Republic. In Bonn – not, as it has been claimed, in the Western capitals – pressure was put on the President of the Bundestag not to allow Berlin to participate in the election for the new President of the Federal Republic; the argument was that it would be wiser not to provoke the Russians. But Eugen Gerstenmaier stood firm.

Khrushchev withdrew the Berlin ultimatum when he visited the United States in 1959 and met President Eisenhower at Camp David. But it would have been unrealistic to hope for peaceful improvement in Berlin. Without the ultimatum the form of Soviet policy might change, but not its content. The tone was as shrill as ever. There was a widespread belief that some new action against Berlin could be only a question of time and opportunity. One day in May 1960, Defence Minister Franz Josef Strauss came to the Berlin mission in Bonn and privately gave me a military account of the situation. He concluded, 'Berlin cannot be defended.' I had to realize, he said, that Berlin would be an intolerable burden on Western policies in general and the Federal Republic in particular. We must look together for some 'half-way acceptable alignment of the front'. To understand Strauss's intervention, of which I have never made any use even by implication, one needs to know that the Americans had asked him what the Bundeswehr would do in an emergency. They had also mentioned the possibility of using tactical nuclear weapons if there was fighting for the access routes to Berlin. Sometimes the people who shout loudest are quite easily intimidated.

In those days, when things were going badly – and sometimes even worse by report than in actual fact – I received an entirely unexpected sign of encouragement. A Berlin doctor returning from Lambarene brought back with her a present for me: an elephant's tusk. Albert Schweitzer's accompanying letter said that he knew the Mayor of Berlin had teeth to show.

The Berlin crisis set in motion by Khrushchev in 1958 ended on 13 August 1961, with the barricading off of his *own* part of the city. The Kremlin had realized that it would not be able to touch the western part, or not in the short term. Everywhere I went, including the places I visited on a world tour undertaken for the Federal Government in early 1959, I explained that the Berlin crisis was the effect and not the cause of hostility in international politics. The fact that Berlin could not breathe freely until there was a thaw in the Cold War was the crucial realization of those years. Its reverse side was that Berlin was not going to shake the world to its foundations. We still had to assert ourselves in Berlin; the Wall had yet to be built. In 1959 I made a note of the phrase that was to be the maxim behind the Berlin Agreement of 1971: Berlin could not be seen as a down payment on détente, but as a touchstone of it.

The Old Man of the Rhine

Adenauer and I were separated by more than just the generation gap; he had been Mayor of Cologne for years when I was still at school in Lübeck. Our backgrounds had also shaped us differently in at least three ways.

He came from a lower-middle-class family and had made his way into the upper middle class. His fundamental convictions were deeply conservative, but not without liberal elements. He was firmly rooted in catholicism, although not in clericalism: he was not accustomed to speak of the kingdom of evil warring with the kingdom of God. But he needed no higher authority for his fixation on international Communism, or what he took for it, of which he was able to make considerable use. His thinking stemmed from the nineteenth century; he was a grown man by the time the twentieth began.

I came from a very humble background and had grown up in the labour movement. I was a democratic socialist and a Social Democrat, influenced in many ways by Lutheran Protestantism, although with a growing tendency to agnosticism. I was aware of the legacy of history but fascinated by the possibilities of the modern world.

He was very much a Rhinelander, considering himself more a West German than simply a German. The East, including the east of Germany, was foreign to his mind. He said himself that when he was President of the Prussian Council of State and was travelling by train to Berlin, he had always felt that Europe stopped at the Elbe, and once past Magdeburg he drew the curtains – 'so that I did not have to see the steppes of Asia'. He expressed himself in much the same way after the war, in a letter to Sollmann, the Cologne Reichstag deputy who had emigrated to the USA: Asia, said Adenauer, began at the Elbe. He never felt at home in the 'heathen' city of Berlin. The fact that people were more inclined to vote for left-wing than right-wing parties in Berlin and Saxony may have had something to do with it.

Growing up in a Hanseatic seaport, I was no Prussian either, or at most only as an acquired characteristic, but even today, when I am described as a West German, I protest that I was not born in 'West Germany' or 'l'Allemagne de l'Ouest', but in Germany, and, if more precise details are required, in northern Germany. Adenauer was closer to Paris, and not just in terms of space. To me, Europe was and still is incomplete without its East.

He was as firmly opposed to the Nazis as I was. He would not go along with them, and suffered for it at their hands. However, he could see no good coming of a radical break with the Nazi years. He favoured a considerable degree of continuity and the restoration of old traditions, and wanted to let bygones be bygones. To this end, the Weimar Republic's proliferation of political parties had to be overcome and a broad party camp established, extending from the old Centre Party and some of the German Democrats to the German Nationalists. Getting the support of the bureaucrats who (in a broad sense) had served the Nazi regime meant he could be sure of their gratitude as well as their professional expertise. He tended to evade the question of guilt, and relieved many people of a guilty conscience. In other words he was anxious to gain time, and contributed, with a certain amount of opportunism, to ensuring that the Germans were not hopelessly devastated by quarrels over the moral collapse they had just survived.

I was not in favour of the kind of denazification which called small fry to account and let the great go free. I hoped to help set the misdirected idealism of the younger generation on the right track and put it to the service of a better, democratic cause. There was a need for reconciliation, but the evil past had to be confronted unflinchingly. National rebirth, I thought, called for fundamental intellectual, political and social regeneration.

It did not work out quite like that: on the lower levels,

postmen and minor civil servants were solemnly if not altogether reliably denazified in the grand manner, while there was extensive reinstatement of the old staff in new positions on the upper levels. No sooner had bureaucrats in ministerial offices, judges, police chiefs and university teachers got off with a fright than they declined to look seriously at a regime that could not have existed without them. Some very able people went into trade and industry. The Allies had to rehabilitate officers with a suspect past when they needed new German army divisions. One particularly distasteful episode was the enlisting of Gestapo members and similar terrorists in the intelligence services of the victorious powers. Klaus Barbie, the 'Butcher of Lyons', was not an isolated case.

I was not Konrad Adenauer's opposite number until the early sixties, when I had a hand in bringing his final period in office to an end after only two years. Adenauer's principal antagonist when the Federal Republic was taking shape as a state, Kurt Schumacher, was fully his equal in strength of will and hostility to Communism. However, his style was very different, and so was the militancy that could turn to fanaticism. A powerful speaker, Schumacher became a national figure when Adenauer was hardly known outside Cologne and the Rhineland. This advantage, however, was only temporary. Schumacher's urge to usher in justice by means of radical social change was as out of tune with the people's need for peace as were his aggressive endeavours to achieve national unity. He lived to see only the first three years of the Federal Republic's existence. In 1952 his sick body could maintain his fighting spirit no longer. He left a far-reaching legacy to Social Democracy.

Schumacher was not anti-European, and indeed that would not have harmonized with the traditions of his party. There was an attempt to suggest that he and his followers were close to favouring a policy of neutrality even towards the Western democracies, but that was a misapprehension. However, there could be no question of persuading a population now sheltering thankfully under the wing of the mightiest of all earthly powers to like the idea of a special status for Germany, an idea which was not welcomed by anyone else in the West.

Adenauer was not an emotional man, and hardly ever allowed himself to feel disappointment. He took human weaknesses for granted and made good use of them. He spoke with even less complexity than he thought, and he had a remarkable talent for simplification – as when he suggested to his audience, at the time when the controversy over rearmament and integration with the West was just beginning, that a choice between East and West was involved: 'We will not go along with the East, ladies and gentlemen, and we cannot fall between two stools – not even the Social Democrats want that – so we must go along with the West!' A Scandinavian journalist, who had heard both Adenauer and me speaking one evening during the 1953 election campaign and with whom I was eating a late supper, told me bluntly, 'You can't win this argument.'

Adenauer's point could be put as simply as that, and that was how it was taken by the people who were now relieved, in addition, of the burden of weighing everything up. He could be ruthless where ruthlessness looked like being effective. He mingled cunning with obstinacy, used expediency to sanction a good many measures, and his wily patriarchalism could be disarming.

I visited him in the spring of 1961, at the beginning of the election campaign, when he was using some very dubious methods of attacking me, and asked if we really had to deal with one another on that level. He looked at me guilelessly and said: 'Why, Herr Brandt, if I had anything against you I would tell you so.' Adenauer was obsessed by the idea – or so he claimed, and it was an effective electoral device – that the Social Democrats would come under Communist influence. In June 1963, on the occasion of Kennedy's great success in Berlin, the President was rather surprised when Adenauer asked him for a private conversation before lunch in the Rathaus, and urged Kennedy not to let me get round him, because 'the Social Democrats are never reliable'. With Adenauer sitting on his other side, Kennedy whispered this information to me during the meal itself.

Adenauer was successful because most people wanted to hear what he told them. Moreover, his utterances were dictated by expediency, and were not always scrupulous with the truth. Such methods are nothing new in politics, although they are not always so skilfully and successfully pursued. He wanted to be the man whose word mattered, to clothe his composite political grouping with the dignity of a party in office, and to give a more or less exhausted society a firm footing in the European West, with American support. Worse could have befallen the Germans of the larger part of the country.

Recent impressions tend to be the strongest, but looking back on those early years I still have an impression that we did not get on too badly together. I was a not particularly influential deputy sitting on the Committee for Foreign Affairs when he began taking notice of me. After his visit to Moscow in 1955 he sent me a note commenting that Bulganin had asked him whether the Hotel Kempinski still stood in Berlin; the Russian leader seemed to have pleasant memories of it. When I was back from my 'world tour' early in 1959 he asked me over dinner one evening about the Japanese geishas. My comments on their place in cultural history did not satisfy him. Citing a Swiss art dealer as authority he announced categorically that: 'It's no different there from anywhere else.'

A certain intimacy arose from the relationship between mayor and mayor, particularly as he was sympathetic towards Berlin's financial needs and on several occasions overruled the Finance Minister and helped me to raise the money required by the city. On his visits to Berlin he spoke frankly and critically about his ministers; I learned more about his party's internal affairs than it might have liked. Speaking of a man who was sitting at the same table with us, and whose stance in German policies he did not like, he remarked that as I probably knew, the man had been 'dead drunk' when he delivered his last speech in the Congress Hall; in Bonn, he had forced his Cabinet colleague

Ernst Lemmer to move out of the Berlin mission, giving as his reason that 'Where he's living now, he tells the Socialists everything over cards.'

Did Adenauer take things as seriously as he let it seem? When I visited him in Rhöndorf after I had been elected Governing Mayor, Tito had just recognized the GDR. Suggesting that I knew my way around the East, he wanted to know what I thought of it. I did my best to tell him, but he had already reached his own conclusion: 'Never mind, I'll tell you how I see it: Tito is nothing but a brigand.' On another occasion, in my Rathaus, he had been joking about the President of the Bundestag, who had gone big-game hunting in Africa; he hinted, with a twinkle in his eye, that his relationship with Parliament was something that might be my own concern in the future: 'Those fellows need their rewards, you know; you want to let them go travelling a lot and give them plenty of leave.'

He was head of government for fourteen years. He had to cast his own vote to have himself elected on the first ballot in September 1949. Before his followers chose him as their candidate for Chancellor, at the age of seventy-three, he had assured them that the doctor had told him he could hold that office 'for at least a year'; in fact, Professor Martiny's opinion had been that he could hold office for two years. At least as important was the support of a young Bavarian deputy called Strauss. He spoke for that part of the Union [between the conservative parties in the Federal Republic] that called itself the CSU rather than the CDU, and said that should there be a grand coalition – something neither Adenauer nor his successor Ludwig Erhard wanted – the CSU would not form a single parliamentary party with the CDU.

Even after Adenauer had to resign as Federal Chancellor in the autumn of 1963, he and I did not lose sight of each other. He stayed on as Chairman of his party until March 1966; I became Chairman of mine early in 1964. Even later we had the occasional conversation, and I was among the guests celebrating Adenauer's ninetieth birthday at Godesberg in January 1966.

He stood there straight as a ramrod, speaking of his memories of 1888, the year of the three Kaisers, the Kaiser's visit to Cologne and events nearer our own time: it was a bravura performance. He had his own unique brand of wily charm.

Two months later, at the CDU Party conference of March 1966 – his last – he created a considerable furore when he said that the Soviet Union had joined the ranks of those nations who wanted peace; it had to be understood, he said, that the Russian people feared the Germans, for fifteen million of them had been killed (the Soviet figure gave it as twenty million). The harsh wounds the Russians had inflicted on Germany, he said, were 'retaliation for the harsh wounds inflicted on the Russians themselves under Hitler'. Around the same time, he told me: 'We have gone about things the wrong way with the Russians.' In particular, he said, 'the Foreign Ministry men' had adopted the wrong course, and had not known how to get along with the Soviet Ambassador.

Did this mean that the old gentleman had gone senile, as quite a number of his own party thought? I think not; I would call that too simple an interpretation. One of his few really close friends, Heinrich Krone, reported a remark Adenauer made at the end of 1961, the year of the crisis of the Wall: for the rest of his life, he said, the major task would be 'getting our relationship with Russia into some sort of order'. On the other hand, early in 1967 and shortly before his death, he inveighed vigorously against the nuclear arms non-proliferation treaty which the Great Powers were just concluding, calling it a 'super-Versailles' and a 'Morgenthau plan squared'; four years earlier, while still in office, he had rejected the test-ban agreement because the GDR had been invited to sign it too.

In 1955 Adenauer won much acclaim in the Federal Republic after his return from Moscow, when he had established diplomatic relations against the advice of his closest colleagues. The freeing of the remaining German prisoners of war and of Germans convicted of crimes under wartime conditions was attributed to his influence. For Adenauer himself, the most important political gain was a revelation made by Khrushchev. Privately, Khrushchev had told Adenauer of his anxieties over China. It already had a population of 600 million, and another twelve million were born every year. Adenauer, who preferred the more straightforward Prime Minister, ex-Marshal Bulganin, to Khrushchev, whom he considered 'a power-hungry, rabble-rousing Party man', drew from this revelation the hope that was to sustain him for years: he thought the Russians would not be able to stand up to pressure from both sides for ever, and must one day make concessions to the West.

Our search for common ground in foreign policy at the end of the Adenauer era did not change my belief that he had his eye firmly fixed on the Federal Republic's integration with the West rather than on the reunification of Germany. He proposed rearmament and carried it through, when it was by no means sure whether all the cards had been put on the table in the game currently being played with Germany as the stake. Had German unity fallen into his lap, he would have been confident of his ability to deal with it, but all his instincts had been against any slackening of ties with the Western Alliance and for a Western Europe led by France and Germany. He has been unjustly accused of separatism in the confusion that followed the First World War. The idea of a Rhineland republic with which he sympathized was anti-Prussian, not against a German federation. But there is no doubt that he wanted a hand in creating Western Europe, even if his image of it remained narrower than that of Charles de Gaulle, the friend of his old age. De Gaulle, historically speaking, took a wider view both retrospectively and looking ahead, and had a strong sense of that European dimension which extended far to the East.

After all that had happened, Adenauer did not really trust his own people. He did not believe they could find their way to moderation and a central position, and so he thought Germany must be protected against itself. Still much struck by the acclaim given to de Gaulle when he visited Germany in 1962, he told me: 'The Germans easily lose their balance.' He thought it undignified that when de Gaulle went to Bavaria he had been officially presented with a valuable engraving of Napoleon's entry into Munich.

It is a matter of record that Adenauer had made himself seem indispensable to the Allies; they would not be able to rely on a successor in the same way. It is also true that, for reasons of political necessity at home, he had kept the Western powers paying lip-service to German reunification, while assuring them that he was informed no such 'danger' need be feared. To Adenauer, neutrality and freedom of alliance, or however it might be phrased, meant playing into Moscow's hands, or at best opening the way to a dangerous policy of swings either to left or to right. He protested vigorously against the Soviet notes of the spring of 1952 not because he entertained any doubts that they were serious, but because he had no confidence in German independence to form alliances, and in no circumstances would he smooth the path for it.

However, he had no objection to proposing goals which could not be achieved, and which it was not part of his political timetable to achieve. When the Federal Republic had become a member of NATO I heard him say that, now we were a part of the strongest alliance in history, 'it will bring us reunification'. He did not hesitate to mock his critics by telling them, for instance in April 1960, that plans for reunification were making great progress – 'only the Soviet Union' was still against the idea. While he made public speeches promising that Silesia and East Prussia would be German again, he was saying privately in August 1953, of the territories on the other side of the rivers Oder and Neisse, 'They're gone.' And in a conversation in Hamburg, he said of the first twelve Bundeswehr divisions even before they were set up that it would be good to have them behind him when he was talking to the West. His interlocutor interrupted: surely he meant the East? 'No, Herr Ollenhauer, the West. That's where the pressure comes from. The other lot are much more realistic; they have enough on their own plates.'

He did not neglect to follow up the Soviet note in 1952 and

see what chances there were of allegedly free elections in the whole of Germany. He had not wanted to follow it up. A year later, after Stalin's death, when Churchill told him there might be an extensive change in Soviet policy, he regarded it as more of a nuisance than anything else. In a simple way he was fascinated by the strength of the USA. On his first visit – in the spring of 1953, still making the journey by sea in those days – he sat in the Consulate in New York early one evening, looked at the Manhattan skyline, and asked State Secretary Professor Hallstein: 'Can you make out why Herr Ollenhauer wouldn't want to be allied to such a powerful country?' This was Consul-General Riesser's version, a few months later. But his fascination with America never led him to lose sight of Paris.

He was attracted to France by his feelings as a Rhinelander and by the Carolingian tradition, and because he calculated soberly that nothing could thrive in Western Europe unless both the Germans and the French supported it. His coolness towards Britain was something he shared with de Gaulle, who resented the British, believed they had slighted him during his wartime exile in London, and also distrusted the special relationship between Britain and America.

In 1962 I urged Adenauer to use his influence with de Gaulle to open the door for the United Kingdom to join the EEC and avoid yet another division in Europe. He was not to be moved: he thought only France and Germany counted. There was Italy too, of course, and the 'small fry' of the Benelux countries. But if the two main participants, Paris and Bonn, were to become three with the addition of London, it was quite possible 'that the two others could tip the balance against us'. In order to keep the British at arm's length, and expecting no good of Kennedy, the two old men in Paris and Bonn placed an unnecessary burden on the Franco-German Treaty of Friendship of January 1963. The Bundestag and the Bundesrat sought to make a virtue of necessity – I was involved as a moderator – and added a preamble to the treaty paying tribute to the Atlantic Alliance and keeping open the way for an extension of the

European Community. Adenauer regarded this addition as interference with his life's work, and saw himself justified when Erhard employed neither vision nor determination in fostering the relationship with Paris, as would have been advisable. The preamble and its chilly reception in Paris were an additional encumbrance to him when he tried to use the treaty to prevent de Gaulle entering into relations with Moscow after all. Even before de Gaulle's visit to Germany Adenauer had told me, almost groaning, that he 'was not always like that'.

In fact Adenauer did not believe for a moment that he could choose between Paris and Washington. He tried devious ways of getting around the situation – guessing that de Gaulle wanted the Americans out of Europe but not out of Germany, and that he was thus acting very much against his own interests. Knowing that the Americans were in Germany was always the alpha and omega of Adenauer's policies.

On many issues 'the Old Man' was more flexible than he often seemed. In his home policies, he could go some way to meet the unions over worker representation in the coal and steel industries, and he could vote with the Social Democrats against a considerable part of his coalition on the issue of reparation payments to Israel. Nor was he always rigid over what was called all-German but was actually foreign policy, although – looking at it out of context – he was inclined to get bogged down in the tactical aspects. However, in 1958 he initiated discussion of a solution of the Austrian type for the GDR, first with Ambassador Andrei Smirnov and then in the Bundestag; such a solution would have presupposed recognition of the East German border. The same subject was broached to the Soviet Deputy Prime Minister when he visited Bonn in April 1958, but Mikoyan ignored it. I knew Ernst Reuter had hoped that something of benefit to Berlin and Germany could come of a solution for Vienna and Austria, but I thought he was over-optimistic. The geographical position and economic and military potential involved meant there could be no simple comparisons, particularly not at the end of the fifties.

In January 1959 Adenauer spoke of 'humanization' in the GDR, and in the summer of 1962 of a kind of 'truce': the existing situation might stay as it was for ten years if the people of the GDR could live more freely. In October that year he admitted to me, 'Things have not turned out as we expected in 1948.' He ventured a tiny step towards an official relationship with the other German state: a retired consul-general was to be appointed to the post of trustee for inter-German trade, but nothing came of it. In October 1962 the Chancellor told the Bundestag that the Government was ready to discuss a good deal if 'our brothers in the Zone' could live their lives as they saw fit – 'On this point, considerations of humanity matter more than national considerations.' This was clearly a bridge thrown out towards my own line of argument, particularly since the building of the Wall. Apropos of the Wall, much has been made of the fact that Adenauer did not go to Berlin immediately. Then and later, I did not feel it was particularly important. I was angry only when troublemakers around him spread the ridiculous rumour that he had stayed away for fear of provoking rebellion in 'the Zone'. And I could only shake my head help-lessly when he accused Khrushchev of giving 'intentional aid to the SPD in the election campaign' by building the Berlin Wall.

On 17 June 1963, a few months before his replacement, the Federal Chancellor was in Berlin, and made a speech suitable to the occasion although slight in content. The long and frank discussion we had afterwards in my office was in sharp contrast. Heinrich von Brentano took part in it: the former Foreign Minister was now once again Chairman of his parliamentary party. Adenauer asked what I really thought of the Hallstein doctrine, i.e. of the insistence that we must have no diplomatic relations with other states that decided to recognize the GDR. Why did he ask me, I inquired? He replied that certain con-cessions had to be made 'so long as you get something in return'. I said that I would visit him in a few days' time in Bonn, and indeed I went there next day, but he had lost interest in the subject he had broached.

In all that has been written about Adenauer much has been made of a 'Globke Plan': we still do not know whether the leader wanted to be identified with the text produced by Hans Globke, head of the Chancellery, or whether he simply gave him the go-ahead to draw it up. In any case, the Government had nothing to do with the plan, and the Opposition was certainly not taken into Adenauer's confidence. It was only much later that I myself learned of this footnote to the history of the time.

The so-called Globke Plan had two variants, one dating from the spring of 1959, the other from November 1960. In the original version, it suggested that the two Germanies should recognize each other as sovereign states; after five years there would be separate referenda to decide on the question of union, and there should be free traffic of people and information immediately. In the second version no recognition was proposed, but diplomatic and official relations were to begin at once – with a referendum after five years and demilitarization of the GDR; meanwhile, Berlin should have the status of a free city. In 1960, moreover, a (secret) plan was drawn up, probably at Adenauer's request, by Felix von Eckardt, head of the Federal Press Office: this plan envisaged a neutral, democratic GDR, with the whole of Berlin as its capital.

There was no shortage of projects designed to overcome the miseries of the division of Germany as the fifties passed into the sixties. Both the SPD and the FDP published Germany Plans in March 1959, aiming to achieve reunification by degrees, through negotiations between the Four Powers and the two German states. I did not think either of them took sufficient account of the facts, and had nothing to do with putting them on paper. At the end of June 1960 Herbert Wehner, Deputy Party and Parliamentary Party Chairman, took the Germany Plan he himself had drawn up from the table and made a brilliant speech in the Bundestag: to the considerable surprise of his closest colleagues in Bonn and even of the Party Chairman, he said that the SPD unreservedly accepted links with the West as the basis of future foreign and German policies. The previous year, I myself had drawn up a list of the issues on which I thought we were in agreement with the other parties; my friend Fritz Erler had put this résumé of our common ground to the Bundestag, but was unable to achieve any tangible results.

Would a serious, frank discussion between Konrad Adenauer and Nikita Khrushchev have changed anything? I must ask the same question of myself, with appropriate objectivity, for just as the Soviet leader wanted to meet Adenauer in 1962, he offered to see me in East Berlin in 1959 and 1963.

When a visit to Bonn by Khrushchev appeared likely, Adenauer had just retired from office. The Kremlin leader's son-in-law, Alexei Adzhubei, then editor-in-chief of *Pravda*, came to Bonn in 1964. I saw him both alone and with the conservative German editors who had invited him. Nothing now seemed to stand in the way of Khrushchev's visit to Bonn; Erhard was very ready to see him. But the burly Khrushchev's time ran out in October. His plan to visit West Germany had been a link in the chain of events leading to his fall. His erratic home and foreign policies, including his nuclear sabre-rattling at the time of the Cuba crisis, were other links in that chain; complaints from the East German leadership about Adzhubei and his comments on reunification seem to have brought it to breaking-point. When the invitation to the Russian leadership was repeated in early 1965 Kosygin – together with Brezhnev – showed no interest.

My own projected meeting with Khrushchev came to nothing either, but that was not of such consequence. In the argument over Berlin he had invested more in me than I had in him. His honest but inadequate attempt to overcome the abuses of Stalinism went hand in hand with a rather blustering, boastful attitude, not least towards the city of which I was Mayor. I sometimes think of an evening when I was watching a television transmission from Moscow, in the company of some American journalists. For his audience's benefit, Khrushchev made play with the fact that my name could be literally translated as 'fire'.

None the less, he still showed interest in a meeting later. Could I have dissuaded him from the incomprehensible project of the building of the Wall? I very much doubt it, yet I soon came to think I had made a mistake in avoiding that meeting and a second possibility of one.

In March 1959, on my flight back from India, I stopped off in Vienna. My friend Bruno Kreisky, later Austrian Chancellor but at the time still State Secretary in the Austrian Foreign Ministry, was waiting for me at Schwechat Airport, with an invitation for me from Khrushchev to visit East Berlin. To be precise, it was more of an indication of willingness to receive me; in Russian tradition, the guest is the one who should seem to have requested the invitation.

The background to all this was a lecture in which Bruno Kreisky had put forward his ideas on special status for Berlin – the whole of Berlin. The Russians thought I was behind it, and asked Kreisky to convey the suggestion of a meeting with Khrushchev to me at once, privately. I asked him to intimate my willingness in principle, and indicated that I would first have to put the plan to the Allied Powers and the Federal Chancellor.

Adenauer thought I should decide for myself, and left it to me to accept or refuse the Soviet offer. The American envoy in Berlin made an unusually sharp protest, supported by Günter Klein, a Senate member who was close to me. Moreover, there were indiscretions on the Soviet side which gave the general public a distorted and simplified view of the idea. I used this as a reason for declining. My friend Kreisky, who was in an awkward position in his relations with the Russians, was greatly disappointed; he had taken too much upon himself.

Independently of me, Erich Ollenhauer had made a date to meet Khrushchev in East Berlin, but nothing came of it. Also in March 1959, my friends Carlo Schmid and Fritz Erler visited the Soviet capital and came away empty-handed, or worse: not only were they given a flat 'No' to the question of whether there could be any discussion of steps towards German unity, but Khrushchev himself gave them a parting message – intended for me – that West Berlin should regard the Federal Republic as a foreign state. Carlo was even more disappointed than Fritz; he had been to Moscow with Adenauer in the autumn of 1955 and had got on very well with Nikita Khrushchev, not only because of his outspoken manner but because he held his drink so well (having taken plenty of cod-liver oil beforehand). His ability to hold his liquor, and his great girth, caused Khrushchev to address him as 'Comrade Greater Germany'. At home Carlo Schmid had to content himself with the nickname of 'Monte Carlo'.

Almost four years later, in January 1963, the second quasi-invitation was issued. The Kremlin leader had come to Berlin to take part in an SED Party conference. Through an official at his East Berlin Embassy, and the Austrian and Swedish consuls stationed in West Berlin, he let me know that he was prepared to talk to me, and indicated when it would be. This time, after and indeed because of the building of the Wall, everything seemed to me to speak in favour of accepting his offer of talks. Once again I turned to the Chancellor, by telephone, and once again Adenauer left the decision to me. He thought such a meeting would do neither harm nor good.

Not so Rainer Barzel, at a later date my opponent in the controversy over the Eastern treaties both inside and outside Parliament. At the time he was Minister for All-German Affairs. He called me from Bonn, in some agitation, advised me strongly not to accept, and appealed to the authority of a prominent Social Democrat to back him up. 'Herr Wehner is here at the moment, and agrees with me.' The Foreign Ministry gave advice which was diplomatic rather than clear. Consultation with the Allies produced no unambiguous results. I wanted to call Kennedy, but let the American envoy, new in his post, dissuade me. The decision was swung by my Berlin coalition partner. At an extraordinary meeting of the Senate, Mayor Amrehn, my deputy, stated in all due form, although the support of some of his CDU colleagues was hesitant, that his party would resign from the government of the city if I met Khrushchev. Berlin, he said, must not pursue 'a foreign policy of its own'. In the circumstances I decided at the last minute to decline the invitation. It did not seem sensible to meet the powerful Russian leader with a divided Senate behind me; moreover, we were on the brink of an election, and I should not have won such a resounding victory if I had decided the other way.

I was well aware that my refusal would offend Khrushchev. Pyotr Abrasimov, the Soviet Ambassador in East Berlin, told me later, when the thaw had set in, how upset his leader had been. Khrushchev was changing his clothes when news of my decision reached him, and he almost dropped his trousers. On that later occasion, in 1966, Abrasimov said that an opportunity had been missed: Khrushchev had 'wanted to give me something'. However, Abrasimov himself, in his book on the 1970–71 Berlin negotiations, remarked that had the Brandt–Khrushchev meeting taken place, it 'would not have led to a settlement of West Berlin affairs'.

Time has passed, leaving the question of the possible results of such talks behind. But my historical conscience tells me that I made the wrong decision. It was not wise to neglect the possibility of high-level talks to clarify the situation. Adenauer would not have minded. After his visit to Moscow he tended to believe what Khrushchev and Bulganin said. As he himself wrote, he felt 'that we might eventually find a solution to our problems together with the men in the Kremlin'. He elaborated this idea towards the end of his life, urgently advising us to get our relationship with our great neighbour not quite next door in the East into order as soon as possible.

I was drawing on my own knowledge of the records when I spoke, in May 1970, of Adenauer's courage and serious attempt to seek a settlement with the Soviet Union as well as other countries: he had seen the situation as it really was. But human beings are full of contradictions, often major ones, and are burdened with prejudices, some more, others less.

Adenauer's post-war aim was stability. At that time he feared nothing more than renewed rapprochement between the victorious powers. My own view was different. He rejected the chance of German unity and made use of the advantages that Western Europe could offer the West German state. So long as there was no alternative, there could be no objection to that. Although Adenauer was a very unmilitary head of government, he was supporting speedy rearmament of the Federal Republic as early as 1949; I thought this a mistake. I would have preferred us to concentrate on Federal border guards counterbalancing the militarized People's Police of the Eastern zone; I think the 'If it wasn't for us' view honourable but mistaken.

What the 'Old Man of the Rhine' said was often different from what he thought, but his robust realism predominated. It allowed him to do a great deal for the Federal Republic. Whether another approach – an all-German approach – could have achieved more remains an open question.

In November 1960, when my political friends in Hanover chose me as the party's candidate for Chancellor, I outlined the task from my own point of view: 'We need space, without endangering our own security, to put political forces to work to overcome stagnation and ideological trench warfare.' I thought we could allow ourselves 'a confident *Ostpolitik*', and added that I knew I was in agreement on this point with John F. Kennedy, the recently elected President of the USA. He was then just at the beginning of his three-year presidency, brief but brilliant if not without its anomalies, upon which such hopes were set.

Big Words, Small Steps

In August 1961 the division of Berlin was cast in concrete – against the nature of a city that had grown up in the course of many generations and, I was convinced, against the current of history. Twenty-five years later, in Washington, Ronald Reagan said that if he had been President at the time he would have had it torn down. When an American journalist in Berlin asked me, on 13 August 1986, what I thought of that statement I declined to comment. One may ask why I thought it inappropriate to engage in debate with a President of the USA to mark the Berlin anniversary. The reason is that I would have had to ask what military measures he would have taken. Would he have sent in the troops? To what end, and at what sort of cost? Even in retrospect, strong words were no use. Reagan certainly challenged Gorbachev publicly to tear the Wall down, but in negotiations with his Russian opposite number he laid the emphasis elsewhere, and he did not question the division of Germany established at Yalta in 1945. This was why I would not enter into discussion with him.

At the end of the war, Berlin received Four-Power status; it was to be ruled by a command of all the four victorious powers. But the rights and duties of the Four Powers had not been properly negotiated at a time when, understandably enough, no one was very much concerned with the future rights of the Germans. In principle, each commandant was authorized to govern his own sector as he liked or as his own government decided. The Russians withdrew from the joint Allied Command in 1948, and in the same year they had the elected governing bodies of the city as a whole – the City Assembly and the Magistrat – expelled from the old Rathaus in the Eastern sector. They installed people of whom they approved as administrators in their sector. Later on Four-Power status, so called – even in 1948 it hardly retained any substance – was made the excuse for political inactivity. In Bonn, lip-service paid to Berlin's Four-Power status often came close to support for the division of the city.

I had feared that access from the GDR to East Berlin would be made more difficult and that most of the crossing-points into West Berlin would be blocked off. Such a development could be foreseen, but not the timing of it or the form it would take, or I would not have been in Nuremberg on Saturday, 12 August 1961, to open the Bundestag election campaign at a major rally.

I had stopped off in Bonn on the Friday on my way to Nuremberg, and had a serious conversation with Heinrich von Brentano, the Foreign Minister, urging for the last time – and in vain – that the subject of Berlin should be extended to cover the entire city. In the Nuremberg Marktplatz, I tried to explain the increasing gravity of the situation: the refugee statistics had risen so dramatically because our countrymen in the Eastern zone feared that they would be cut off, trapped and left to their fate.

Almost three million people had left the Eastern zone and the GDR since 1945. There had been 120,000 refugees in the first half of 1961, but since the failure of the Vienna meeting between Kennedy and Khrushchev in June 1961 the stream had become a mass exodus. Thirty thousand people fled in July, and on 12 August alone two and a half thousand of our countrymen had arrived in West Berlin. They were voting *en masse* with their feet, as we put it at the time. Theirs was a vote of no confidence that the other side found unacceptable. It looked as if the GDR might be drained dry. The old alarmist catchphrases about people without space to live in might give way to the prospect of a state without any people to live in it. It was hardly surprising that the Soviets and the German Communists would spare no effort to stem this mass flight to the West. But I had not expected that East Berlin would actually be walled off and that the dividing line running through the city would be made a line of stone. I had forgotten or dismissed from my mind a project dating from 1959, when we heard that Mayor Ebert of East

Berlin, a son of the first President of republican Germany, had argued in favour of a 'Great Wall of China', but had met with a Soviet veto. That project, said to have been largely the work of Erich Honecker, Walter Ulbricht's eventual successor, disappeared into a drawer to be brought out again in 1961.

I did not keep my fears to myself. I tried to convey them to the Allies and the Federal Government and, cautiously, to the general public. On 11 August, when measures were announced in the Volkskammer against 'traffickers in human beings, saboteurs and persons enticing others', I spoke in forcible terms to Heinrich von Brentano of the danger of rigorous barriers. I told him it was likely that the GDR authorities – from pure instinct of self-preservation – would urge their Soviet masters to bestow their blessing on drastic action. At this point, although I did not know it, the Soviet Union had already given Ulbricht the go-ahead to cut off East Berlin completely; the signal had come from the Soviet Union and the other Warsaw Pact countries at an Eastern bloc conference held in Moscow from 3 to 5 August.

Only later did I learn the previous history of these events: in the middle of March 1961 Ulbricht had demanded the sternest possible measures before the plenum of his party's Central Committee, telling them that he was going to appeal directly to the Kremlin leader. I did know that on 17 February the Soviet Ambassador in Bonn had handed the Federal Chancellor two documents concerning West Berlin and the threatened peace treaty between the GDR and the USSR. They said that if the treaty was not accepted, and the rule of the occupying forces in West Berlin was not discontinued, we must expect 'all the consequences that would follow'. The Americans evaluated this threat correctly; the flames of the Berlin crisis had never really been extinguished after the 1958 ultimatum, but had continued flickering in 1959 and 1960, and now they had flared up again.

At the end of March the Warsaw Pact's Political Advisory Committee met, and Ulbricht explained why increased border controls and barbed-wire fences were not enough; a concrete wall and palisades were necessary. No one was really either for or against the idea, and Khrushchev kept his own counsel. However, on his return the SED leader felt confident enough to tell Erich Honecker, then in charge of national security, to procure materials and labour – in secret, and with the utmost caution. On 15 June Ulbricht announced at a press conference: 'No one has any intention of building a wall.'

Years later, I heard that at that conference Khrushchev had given permission only for barbed-wire fences, stipulating that no wall should be built until Western reactions had been tested. In fact the building of a wall in the literal sense did not begin until 16 August; on 13 August they were still erecting concrete posts linked by entanglements of barbed wire to block off the Eastern sector from West Berlin.

We were appallingly badly prepared. When the Wall had been built, all we could do at first was proclaim that it must come down. Counter-measures that might have been effective were not demanded of the Western powers. A severe crisis of confidence threatened, for objectively speaking this terrible day for the people of Berlin brought relief to the Western governments: their rights in West Berlin remained untouched, and the dreaded danger of war had been averted.

I may as well admit frankly that, with many of my fellow citizens, I was disappointed that 'the West' proved unwilling or unable to make Berlin's much-vaunted Four-Power status the justification for doing something to spare Germany and Europe the building of that monstrous and shameful Wall. At the time we had little leisure or inclination to put ourselves in the position of the Eastern side and assess Khrushchev's view of the Wall as an emergency measure, taken in desperation, to save the GDR. Nikita Khrushchev asked Ambassador Kroll, in the autumn of 1961, what else he could have done with so many refugees leaving. The German Ambassador recorded his exact words: 'I know the Wall is an ugly thing. And it will come down some day ... but only when the reasons for building it have gone.'

Only after the event did a significant, if not a very large, number of Germans realize that we could expect nothing from the Americans, or indeed from the Western powers as a whole, other than what they had promised besides the ever-precarious Four-Power status, namely the three 'essentials' adopted as principles by the Council of NATO at its spring meeting in Oslo in 1961: these were the Allied presence in Berlin, access to it, and securing the liberties of its citizens. There was no mention of Berlin as a community comprising the entire city, and when John F. Kennedy talked to the Soviet leader in Vienna in June 1961 he did not mention East Berlin. Limiting itself to West Berlin was the West's real concession. When Kennedy addressed the American and international public in a speech on 25 July 1961, during that summer of crisis, the conclusion drawn in Moscow, correctly, was that his guarantee stopped at the sector border. Conversely, according to the evidence of colleagues, the Americans thought that Khrushchev had 'given way'. Why would he have agreed to the building of the Wall if he intended to occupy the whole of Berlin? The Soviet side had repeated the Berlin ultimatum and the threat of a separate peace treaty in April 1961, before the Vienna summit; after it, there was talk on both sides of a possible slide into nuclear war. Kennedy's close colleague Arthur Schlesinger says that the President thought of hardly anything else that summer.

Kennedy had said, in the final talks in Vienna, that what happened to the GDR was up to his opposite number. The USA could not and would not get involved in decisions taken by the Soviet Union in its own sphere of interest. In a television interview at the end of July Senator Fulbright said what Kennedy was thinking: he could not understand why the GDR authorities did not shut up shop when they had every right to do so. In view of the outcry in the press he withdrew his remarks, but he could not unsay them.

It turned out that the Allies had been fearing the wrong crisis. What came as a cruel blow to us in Berlin, a disaster for our own country, appeared to others a relief or at least the lesser of two evils. Neither the Western European powers nor the Americans had undertaken to guarantee freedom of movement in a divided Germany. They did not feel responsible for the fate of the thousands of families torn apart, and many Western decision-makers were not without a certain sympathy for 'the Russians'. As honourable, influential and experienced a man as Senator William Fulbright, mentioned above, could be heard to say that the Russians might be acting brutally, but he could understand that they wanted to bring order to that area of Germany they controlled.

There was talk of counter-measures. But given the existing situation, with all the power politics and interests involved, what could they have been taken against – other than the fact that the Soviet side was transferring to the GDR powers which it had reserved to itself on the basis of Berlin's Four-Power status? And what conclusions were to be drawn from that? Reaction to the building of the Wall was a painful mixture of helpless fury and ineffectual protest. Vice-President Lyndon B. Johnson's lightning visit on the weekend following 13 August had a certain significance. The Texan went through West Berlin like a whirlwind for a day and a half and stabilized the mood. The Americans used the opportunity to convince themselves and us that another military unit could reach Berlin unhindered by road. Johnson was accompanied by Ambassador Charles Bohlen, an expert on Eastern affairs, and by Berlin's proven friend Lucius D. Clay, who stayed on in the city until the spring of 1962 as the President's special representative. The main message Charles Bohlen had to convey to me was that if I had any criticisms to make, perhaps I would telephone the President instead of writing him letters.

What criticisms had I already made? I thought we should not stop at the three 'essentials'. The guarantee of the presence of Allied troops, of their access to the city and of the city's liberties was inadequate so far as we were concerned because it left undecided the questions of whether Germans, too, had a right to free access, and of whether or not it was clear that the liberties of West Berlin were linked with its affiliation to the legal and economic structure of the Federal Republic. Moreover, everyone who had eyes to see and ears to hear knew how those 'essentials' were to be construed: the Soviet side could do what it liked to East Berlin, and could delegate its rights to the leadership of the GDR. This was exactly what happened, and it even received the blessing of Bonn. When Adenauer met Ambassador Smirnov on 16 August – even as I was assembling the Berliners for a great protest demonstration outside the Rathaus – he intimated that they had agreed 'not to extend the present area of dispute'. The Ambassador said that Soviet measures were not directed against the Federal Republic, and the Chancellor replied that the Federal Government would take no steps that might complicate relations with the Soviet Union and cause a deterioration in the international situation.

My suggestions to the Allies and the Federal Government before the building of the Wall had always aimed to extend the subject of Berlin and modify it as far as possible: why not negotiate over the reunification of the whole of Berlin? Why not accept the Soviet proposal of a peace conference on Germany? And if the subject must be kept within narrow limits, why not let the West Berliners vote on their ties with the Federal Republic? No one would hear of tackling the subject of Berlin as a whole; it was outside their customary terms of reference, and their habits of thought were too deeply ingrained to be rapidly changed now. Very likely any such endeavour would have run aground in the East as well. However, intermediaries indicated a cautious Soviet interest. The idea of a kind of referendum of the people of West Berlin, discussed by Adenauer with the Americans, had a dangerous drawback: the Federal Chancellor wanted the question to be whether the West Berliners wished to keep the protecting and (officially speaking) occupying powers in place. In my view that was not the right question to ask, and the point at issue should be membership of the Federal Republic.

I have never been able to understand why Bonn – and the Allied administrators – shrank from going to the United Nations. What I said in the Bundestag after the building of the

Wall, on 18 August, had been equally valid earlier: 'One cannot deny oneself access to the international forum in case a world begins to burn.' Nor was anything else seriously tried that might have extended the field of discussion. Preparations had been made, in an atmosphere of political apathy and the repetition of old legal clichés, for a crisis that did not come, and no one knew how to deal with the one that actually was approaching.

The crisis that did not come had revolved around a separate peace treaty and the presence of the Western Allies' garrisons. It conjured up images of the danger of war. I was unable to discover what the Allied intelligence services knew, and I received no helpful information from their German counterparts either then or afterwards. It still strikes me as rather a black joke that on the morning of 14 August a memo from the Bundesnachrichtendienst [the Federal Intelligence Service], appeared on the desk of Heinrich Albertz, head of the Berlin Senate Chancellery, to the effect that nothing in particular was imminent.

Western Intelligence had let itself be hoodwinked. Or did important details slip through the net because it was the weekend, or for some other reason? Or were they assessed as being unlikely to cause tension because they pointed to something that need not cause the Allied authorities any anxiety – less anxiety, anyway, than German families might feel? One of Kennedy's closest colleagues, P. O'Donnell, who planned his engagements, confirmed after some lapse of time that the American secret services – and those of all the other Western states – had not done particularly well, and Kennedy had been much annoyed. O'Donnell is also the source of the account we have of Kennedy's reaction: he thought that Khrushchev had given way, and would not have built the Wall if he meant to occupy all Berlin. Ted Sorensen, the President's brilliant speechwriter, has recorded how American Intelligence assessed the situation: the Communists would try to get control over their fast-disappearing labour force. However, Sorensen confirms that the intelligence services 'had offered no advance warning of this specific move'.

I have never cared for it when people act as if they were entitled to play with other people's weapons, particularly those of their powerful friends, or when propaganda replaces serious politics. So I never demanded that the Americans should tear down the Wall, and most certainly not for propaganda reasons. Kennedy himself recorded the fact that neither the Federal German Government nor the Mayor of Berlin asked him to do so. All concerned wanted to avoid the risk of any military confrontation, and we could not avoid asking, if that risk *had* been taken, then why and to what end?

Legally, it could have been argued that the Soviet decision to hand authority over East Berlin to the GDR left a vacuum in terms of international law. From that point of view it would have been legally justifiable to fill the vacuum, citing Berlin's Four-Power status. In practice that would inevitably have meant the military occupation of East Berlin. My answer was that it might be logical, but it was not practicable. Instead, the Allies could have taken energetic political action, accompanied by the conspicuous presence of their security forces at the sector border, thus forcing the Soviets to recognize their own responsibility for East Berlin. An absurd idea? It did at any rate take account of one of the other side's vital interests, for the Soviet leadership set store by continuing to have rights in and over 'Germany as a whole' as a victorious power, and thus over the whole of Berlin. It is possible that Khrushchev and his team could have been persuaded to reconsider the question of status.

There is a time for war and a time for peace; similarly, there is a time for taking small steps and a time for making great changes. After the event, many matters which at the time were the subject of heated debate and were carried through only in the face of strong resistance seem simple and sound obvious.

If it made no sense merely to protest about the Berlin Wall, it also made no sense to oppose the situation in Germany with nothing but legal protests and national defiance. That situation had been brought about by Hitler's war, and sanctioned by the agreement of the victorious powers – or rather, by their failure to agree. The only sensible course was to make the Wall less impenetrable, alleviate the worst hardships caused by the division, and help to overcome them where possible.

What else could be done? There were some who thought wounds should be kept open and not bound up: in Berlin, that would have meant not trying to make the best of the intractable facts, but letting them remain a thorn in our flesh. My view was and is that there is no point in policies which do not aim to make people's lives easier – whatever the principles behind them. Where a choice cannot be avoided, human welfare must come first: what is good for the people in a divided country is good for the nation too.

Proceeding by small steps meant, and still means, gaining ground for human rights. Human rights are less than democracy. But the alleviation of both human hardship and dangerous tensions helps to create a climate in which democracy can grow. At least it can be said that where human rights are not taken seriously, there can be no genuine democracy.

What has been called the 'small steps' policy was planned in advance, and was not just a reaction to the Wall. On 30 May 1956, after the twentieth Party conference of the Communist Party of the Soviet Union, and a central conference of the SED, I had to raise a formal question to the parliamentary parties in the Bundestag, pleading for 'the greatest possible degree of relations between the people in both parts of Germany'. I spoke in favour not of recognizing the present situation, but of 'making life easier in an arbitrarily divided Germany'. In 1958 I also spoke in favour of this idea at the Institute of International Affairs in London. In 1959 I made a speech in Springfield, Illinois, in honour of Abraham Lincoln, and said that there would be no quick solution to our problems, nor a solution in isolation, but that we must hope for gradual change and for progressive solutions as the result of tough confrontations.

In Berlin we had to fight hard to get visitors' passes for people on urgent family business. We also had to fight to reunite separated families with members in the other part of Germany, and to get permission for people of German origin to emigrate from the Soviet Union, Poland and Romania if they so desired. Our treaties policy and the Final Act of the Helsinki Conference did something to help these efforts forward, until an easing of relations between the various parts of Europe as a whole ushered in conditions of a less oppressive nature, if by no means satisfactory or entirely free of conflict.

There is indeed a time for war and a time for peace. When the Wall was built in 1961, and during the Cuban crisis of 1962, it looked as if neither small steps nor great changes would help those affected. But when a young President had determined to use both firmness and flexibility to ease the rigidity of the front lines, it could only be seen as a sign of the times in Berlin and in Germany.

Kennedy, or the Urge to Take Risks

In the Bundestag elections of September 1961 my party had a considerable amount of success, but I had hoped for more. Konrad Adenauer lost his absolute majority. The SPD gained a good two million additional votes, achieving its best result since the National Assembly election of 1919. Statistically, it won 36.7 per cent of votes as against its previous 31.8 per cent, and 190 seats instead of its previous 169.

The election had been overshadowed by the building of the Wall; I needed and indeed wanted to be in Berlin almost daily, and had to cancel a great many appearances. Hectic air travel in a tiny British chartered plane made matters only slightly easier. However, as SPD candidate for Chancellor I did succeed in setting new goals. I was campaigning on two major issues:

the great community tasks we faced at home, and realistic representation of our national and European interests. I had made these issues the heart of my nomination speech. To have proposed a candidate for Chancellor at all (in Hanover in 1960) was something new in the history of the SPD, and was part of a thorough process of renewal undertaken after the election débâcle of 1957, covering the organization of the party, its parliamentary party, its programme – drawn up at Godesberg in 1959 – and the choice of a candidate.

Purely arithmetically, our electoral performance would have been just good enough for a minor coalition of Social Democrats and Free Democrats to be formed in 1961, but the requisite political conditions did not exist – yet. This was confirmed at a confidential meeting at Mülheim in the Ruhr, to which an economist hostile to the Christian Democrats, Hugo Stinnes Jr, invited the Free Democrat Chairman Erich Mende and myself. I sounded out the possibility of an all-party Cabinet with my closest colleagues in the leadership of my own party – Ollenhauer, Wehner and Erler. Its main tasks would have included relaxing the rigid fronts of German foreign policy. An important partner in our discussion was the President of the Bundestag, Eugen Gerstenmaier, who would not have been unwilling to become Chancellor in a government concentrating our national forces. But the conservative Christian Democrats were not yet ready for a shift in the balance of power.

We talked to Adenauer too at this time, and despite all that had already passed between us, I myself approached Franz Josef Strauss. In March 1961, after a journey to the USA and a talk with John F. Kennedy, I had suggested that in the event of a new Berlin crisis the parties should show solidarity. After the October 1961 election, and again following a brief visit to America, I set down my recommendations in a memorandum which I placed before the Government and the Chairmen of the Bundestag parliamentary parties. I was not motivated by thoughts of party advantage alone; matters were too serious for that.

At the heart of all our deliberations was the question of how the East–West conflict could be transformed and coexistence made productive. In the year after the building of the Wall, Harvard University invited me to speak on the subject; interest in it was very great in October 1962. I gave the German version of my lectures the subtitle of 'The Urge to Take Risks'. Coexistence, I said, was not an invention of the Soviets nor their monopoly in argument; the difference between their concept of it and ours was caused by our very different understanding of the nature of the conflict.

At the centre of my Harvard lectures was the proposition that the interest of the Soviet leadership was clear, its theory wrong. There need not necessarily be conflict between states with different social and economic constitutions. Khrushchev's idea of peaceful coexistence was not a search for permanent stability, nor even a breathing-space in battle, but a new way for him to enlarge his own sphere of power and influence without running the risk of a nuclear war. Coexistence in the world of today, I said, depended on the interests, not the theoretical principles, of the Soviet leadership. I advocated a sensible division of labour between America and Europe: we must not forget that Europe was stronger than many people believed, and younger than many imagined. I saw more than a military alliance in the Atlantic partnership.

Further, I continued, our political strategy must assume that coexistence could be achieved only if we shook off our fear of Communist superiority, and the equally naïve and comfortable belief that things would automatically turn out all right in the end. The most testing task in history faced the Western democracies in the endeavour to bring about true coexistence. 'We must not be hypnotized by the defensive task of warding off catastrophe and holding our own; we cannot allow it to claim our undivided attention. To my mind, the East–West conflict is not the only, nor, in the final analysis, even the most important problem if we really want to win the future.' Our ideas should not be restricted to our relations with the

Communist East, but should extend to the relations between rich and poor nations. Coexistence as peaceful competition is largely won or lost in those countries.

Moreover, I said, we needed a policy of taking peaceful risks, a non-violent change in the conflict. History does not develop in accordance with dogmas, nor even consistently: 'The polarization of power between Moscow and Washington does keep the world in suspense today, but there is also a growing trend toward the diffusion of power. This trend will continue . . . New magnetic fields of power are emerging. We have to seek ways to surmount and to permeate the blocs of today. We need as many real points of contact and as much meaningful communication between them as possible . . . this is a programme and a posture that can encourage transformation on the other side. This is what I think coexistence calls for if it is to be an active, peaceful, and democratic policy.'

And finally, I said: 'Real political and ideological walls must be torn down stone by stone but without conflict. We do not need an anti-ideology, a counter-dogma. Our great political dream is that large areas of our society should be free of any political control or influence. Freedom is strength.'

From Harvard, where I was proud to be awarded an honorary doctorate the next year, I went on to Washington. One of the President's close colleagues, Professor Carl Kaysen, had given him the text of my speech and remarked how close the lines of our thinking lay. At this point the Cuban crisis was beginning to become acute. Kennedy showed me air photographs of the missile bases, and did not conceal his anxiety about the possibility of a serious confrontation; even my own city of Berlin, he intimated, could be drawn into it. I showed no nervousness, and when I was back in Berlin, and heard that the situation had become critical, I sent a message by night through the American envoy saying he must decide as he thought fit: we had no fears in Berlin. This expression of confidence impressed Kennedy and sealed our friendly relationship. Its beginnings went back to our first meeting in the White House in the spring of 1961. He had told me at the time that the subjects which concerned me struck him as familiar.

In retrospect, Kennedy's aides Ted Sorensen and Arthur Schlesinger have conjectured that with a hardliner as President there would have been a disastrous military conflict. Kennedy was indeed playing for high stakes, but he and his brother Robert were determined to avoid war. Later it became known that both of them, Robert working in close contact with Ambassador Dobrynin, were aiming for a secret agreement involving the withdrawal of Jupiter rockets from Turkey, which confirmed the existence of a softer line beneath the hard one. As with the dramatic building of the Wall, new perspectives were presented, and the crisis made them tremendously compelling. A new relation between the nuclear powers had been on the way for some time, but it took the Cuban crisis of the autumn of 1962 to make the necessity of avoiding confrontation starkly obvious. Kennedy had realized that he must spare his opposite number in international politics defeat and, in particular, humiliation. His associates said he did not want to drive the Russians a step further than necessary.

Professor Kaysen had remarked that the ideas I put forward in Harvard sounded 'familiar'; he would not have said the same of official Federal German policy, about which Kennedy's men were both uncertain and curious. In the garden of the White House – he did not want to have the Ambassador with us – the President asked me: 'What kind of Germany will I be dealing with?' I told him he could expect greater German independence and a growing interest of our own in détente.

Three-quarters of a year later, in June 1963, Kennedy entered Berlin like a conqueror. This was the climax of his visit to Germany, and a great day for the city. Never before had a guest been so acclaimed in the history of Berlin. The Wall had been standing for nearly two years. There was still great disappointment that frequent reference to Berlin's Four-Power status had not been able to prevent its being built. But Kennedy was in no doubt of his duties towards West Berlin. His widow told me, the evening after the funeral, that he often reran the documentary film of his visit to the city.

In his famous speech outside the Schöneberg Rathaus Kennedy praised the city's determination to assert itself, and at the same time indicated the prospect of a just peace. I shall never forget the moment before his speech when, laughingly, he rehearsed those famous four words in my office – '*Ich bin ein Berliner!*' The idea was thought up by Sorensen, who had told me about it the previous evening in Bonn. Speaking to the students of the Free University, their eminent guest went into further detail about future prospects: the wind of change, he said, was blowing over the Iron Curtain and the rest of the world, and the power of historical evolution would be felt in Eastern Europe too. Contacts between East and West could contribute, gradually, to overcoming the causes of tension. In the German question, similarly, progress could be made only if both sides played their part.

The President had set out his aims for international policy a few days before, in the Paulskirche in Frankfurt: the Atlantic community was to be built on two pillars – one North Atlantic, one Western European – with burdens and decisions divided fairly between them, and the European Community was to be constructed by the Europeans themselves as they thought fit. He advised us to engage in wholehearted co-operation with the developing countries as well as pursuing East–West policies. Even before Kennedy set off for Germany, on 10 June in Washington, he had made a speech on the strategy of peace. I thought it a significant and clear-sighted attempt to bring change into the relationship between East and West: an attempt to replace the balance of terror by the peaceful solution of problems. The aim of the peace strategy was to change the status quo gradually and thus overcome it. He knew that those who look only to the past will miss out on the future, and he warned against retreating into the period when we simply exported our own stagnation to each other.

Attempts were made soon after his death to cut him down

to size, emphasizing the fragmentary nature of his policies and concentrating on his shortcomings. And yet John F. Kennedy was a remarkable man with remarkable charisma. The fascination he exerted, despite the partial effect of this demythologizing, has remained alive. It stemmed not just from his frank expression, his clear wish for renewal, the freshness of the language he used so skilfully and the fact that he was always on the alert for new ideas. He opened a new chapter in the lives of black Americans. He encouraged hopes of greater justice in the world, and it would have been good for the world as well as America if he could have gone further along that road.

Kennedy had a great respect for Adenauer, but was unhappy about the doctrinaire rigidity of German foreign policy. He had noted a lack of constructive German contributions during the Berlin crisis. He thought a solution to the German question was possible only as the result of an historical process, and that at least a tactical recognition of the GDR was worth considering; like Eisenhower before him, he had long believed it essential to recognize the Oder–Neisse Line. In Vienna, Khrushchev had hinted to him that Adenauer did not want reunification at all. This information made its mark on him, exacerbating his impatience and that of his entourage. Washington expected more flexibility from the Federal Republic; I too was given that impression.

Kennedy did not engage in serious discussion of the future of Europe with the other nuclear world powers. The time was probably not ripe for a great gamble, and he would have needed a sufficiently imaginative and co-operative partner in such a venture. However, he did achieve some easing of the relationship with Moscow, particularly by the way in which the Cuban crisis was resolved. That easing was reflected as early as 1963 in the Test-Ban Treaty. Adenauer opposed it, because the GDR had been invited to sign as well.

Kennedy might have found a prickly but suitable partner in Charles de Gaulle, who saw the world from the European point of view. He was not on good terms with the arrogant

Frenchman, however, and urged Adenauer to make a clear choice between Paris and Washington. This was unreasonable, and inconsistent with his repeated demand for the Europeans to take more responsibility for themselves. Such anomalies nevertheless continued to surface in American policy over the years that followed.

On this subject, I have said that Kennedy made it clear that the United States hoped for a strong, united Europe, speaking the same language and acting with the same determination: a world power in a position to tackle problems as a full and equal partner. 'That is the most far-reaching American policy towards Europe ever formulated. I know of de Gaulle's belief that Europe should not assume a role which would make it inferior to the United States, either as a whole or in its separate parts. Kennedy's idea of Europe as a world power is entirely in accordance with de Gaulle's. Look at it in this way, and there is no need to fear that Germany might be faced with a choice between friendship with France and friendship with the United States.'

The assassination of Kennedy was a misfortune for the whole world. The rumours that grew up around it have never entirely died down. The judiciary found no conclusive proof of a conspiracy, but a House of Representatives investigatory committee later expressed the contrary opinion. Five years later the President's energetic brother Robert was also assassinated. He had been to Berlin in 1962, on a visit of importance to us and to himself, and I had followed his career, particularly his brave and far-sighted campaign for racial equality, with respect and liking. I had hoped for much, very much, if Robert Kennedy became President.

I think nothing of the shallow saying that no one is irreplaceable. In political as in personal life, some people are missed more than others.

What was to become of Germany and of Europe had been a matter of concern to me before Kennedy, and even more so after Kennedy. In July 1963 Egon Bahr created a furore with his Tutzing speech on 'change through rapprochement', in which he gave typically cogent expression to what we both thought. He had been going to speak after me at that July meeting, but in fact he spoke the evening before, thereby stealing the show – these things happen. By way of compensation, he attracted a certain amount of the criticism intended for me to himself. I myself had reservations about the phrasing; it might encourage the mistaken belief that we had in mind some kind of rapprochement to the Communist system as such. That was not what he meant, and the incident did not disturb our friendly co-operation.

Egon Bahr was not my only close colleague in Berlin and in the transition from Berlin to Bonn, but intellectually he was the most able. He was a highly esteemed radio journalist in the Federal capital when I asked him to head our press and information office in 1959. He went with me to the Foreign Ministry and the Federal Chancellery, became a Federal minister and a member of the top Social Democratic Party leadership. The drafting of the Moscow Treaty of June 1970, and of the subsequent treaties with the GDR, was mainly Bahr's work. A German patriot with a sense of international responsibility, he has gone far, but we have never lost sight of each other. Wherever plans are made for all-German co-operation and all-German security, his intellectual contribution is unmistakable. Much of what I achieved and attempted, from 1960 to 1980 and beyond, would not have been possible without such collaboration. It is not often that friendships survive the stress of politics for so many years.

My own speech at the Evangelical Academy of Tutzing was not confined to foreign policy, but aimed for critical appreciation of German policy as a whole. However, I was particularly concerned with foreign policy and the opportunities open to it. I took my cue from Kennedy and said I could hope, for the West, that 'our common policy might bring the Soviet Union to see that a change was in its own interests'. A change of direction such as that of which the American President spoke at the Free University required us to 'examine and reject earlier, unproductive ideas'. The question of whether the East really did or did not feel a need for security would be largely settled if we began to make – and even succeeded in making – a common interest in security the object of West–East agreements.

Such a policy stood or fell with confidence in the real state of Western strength and Western obligations: 'We could probably wait indefinitely for all Communists to abandon their ideological aims. However, there is plenty to suggest that though Khrushchev's grandsons may still call themselves Communists, they will no longer be real Communists.' It was possible, I said, that there could be no ideological coexistence, only ideological argument. 'However, we need space for it. Our alternative to the Wall is the capacity to engage in open, active argument, and our earnest desire to do our part to ensure peace.' That necessarily entailed Western unanimity, understood as unity in diversity. But Europe as a world power was still only a vision, and our relationship with the United States must remain the cornerstone of German policy. However, it was not too early to think in all-European terms. 'The best brains, the industry and the labour force of Europe, with the help of the United States, have brought a new flowering. We now have the essential preconditions for Europe to play a larger part, assume more responsibility, and grasp the fraternal American hand extended to us across the Atlantic.'

I spoke of an exciting period of change in international politics, one that opened up new horizons. What could only be guessed at a few years, even a few months ago, was now taking shape and coming within reach. 'It is quite possible that the years now lying ahead of us will bring new configurations. The Europe we know has the chance to play its part only in unity. If it does not do that, it will inevitably sink to being an assembly of third-rate structures in terms of international politics.' And I prophesied: 'At all events it looks as if in the year 2000 we shall not be looking back on either an American or a Soviet century.'

In a memorandum I sent the American Secretary of State,

Dean Rusk, a year later, in August 1964, and which was published in January 1965, I sketched out future relations with the countries of Eastern Europe, and the effects of the Common Market. My basic assumption was that a consciousness of being part of the whole of Europe had remained alive or been reawakened in the nations lying between Germany and Russia.

In saying this I also made it clear that I had no time for out-of-date theories of totalitarianism. By now there were at least hints that a Communist regime could change. Instinct told me that where there was room for a little change, more might come some day. Moreover, I had long taken it as a principle that everything is always in flux and nothing ever remains as it was, and that unpredictable interactions will have unpredictable results.

In Tutzing in 1963 I criticized the official attitude in Bonn that we were engaged in a race, and that we must 'always be swift and firm in rejecting any suggestion from the East just because it comes from the East'. My conclusion was: 'I think we should avoid giving any impression that we have not yet grasped two points: that disarmament is only the obverse of a policy of security, and that Germany is interested in détente, not in tension.'

Progress with the problems of Germany, I said, was unthinkable without détente, for 'the German problem has an international aspect, a European aspect, a security aspect, a human and a national aspect'. I agreed with Adenauer in giving the question of humanity precedence over nationality. 'If we are to serve the interests of our countrymen and bring humane relief, we must be ready to discuss a great deal. We cannot enlarge publicly on what those things might be, but we should at least come to a private understanding about them.' I mentioned the willingness of the German West to lend its economic strength to Eastern projects too, and suggested that in every case, various different aspects of the German question had to interlock. Initially, however, what mattered was the German policy on German questions. In 1963, I said there was no mistaking the fact that 'no solution to the German question can be found in opposition to the Soviet Union, only with it. We cannot give up our rights, but we must familiarize ourselves with the idea that to realize them we need a new relation between East and West, and with it a new relation between Germany and the Soviet Union. That will take time, but we can say that the time would seem shorter and less tedious if we knew that the lives of our people on the other side, and our own links with them, were made easier.' In 1963 I saw the Federal Republic not as holding the balance of power, nor as an opposite pole to America, nor as the spearhead of the Cold War; I thought it must play its own part in the concerted action of the West and make its own contribution – in accordance with its responsibility, of which no one would relieve it.

It was to be another three years before I was able to make my own contribution, from Bonn, to ensuring that the Federal Republic not only recognized its responsibility but used it on behalf of other people. However, my attempt to give foreign policy a new look, broadly based and rising above party politics, produced only modest results.

There were thus subjective limits to an objective need to take risks, and I was not the man to willingly shake the world and force it along an unknown path. In my public utterances, I followed the official policy of the Western governments even when I did not agree with them, and I showed forbearance to Bonn policies by openly saying I disagreed when sharper criticism would have been in place. However, I did not refrain from one action which, small as it was, opened a tiny crack in the Wall and pointed in the right direction, although it also taught me that even a path going in the right direction may turn out to be a blind alley. A year and a half after Ulbricht barred off the Eastern part of the city, I had become extremely impatient. The enormous confidence the Berliners had shown my party and me in the election of 17 February 1963 encouraged me to swerve from the beaten track. On 18 March I sketched the broad outlines of a possible interim solution to the City Assembly: 'We must alleviate the particularly inhumane hardships imposed by the Wall. West Berliners must at least have the same rights of access to East Berlin as anyone else. The restoration of arbitrarily broken links of family and friendship between the two parts of the city is a subject we cannot strike off the agenda, in the name of humanity and reason.' It was on the practical political agenda that very year.

West Berlin was quite well subsidized by the Federal Republic. Strengthening it economically and culturally was not entirely easy, but not impossible either. There had still been no serious attempt to bind it so closely to Bonn that it became a Federal *Land* of a special kind in the minds of the Allies, or at least, nothing of that nature had been achieved. The city's status was in danger of falling instead of rising. We had much to put up with. Only the bare remnants of Berlin's functions as a capital were left. After the building of the Wall, despite the city's Four-Power status, we had released the members of my party in the Eastern sector from the loyalty they owed. Many able people were attracted away to West Germany by the major positions they could hold there.

The Western powers did not stand in our way when we worked for economic and cultural expansion. They were more flexible than the Bonn Government over relations with the other German state. Even Dulles, the hardboiled Secretary of State, had advised his friend Adenauer to try increasing contacts with the GDR. Kennedy's Secretary of State Dean Rusk, like many others, was in favour of 'technical commissions' with representatives from both German states. Against this background, I decided to begin by venturing upon contact with 'the other side' in the humanitarian area.

Egon Bahr, Heinrich Albertz (then Senator for Home Affairs and Deputy Mayor), Klaus Schütz (then Federal Senator and later, for many years, Governing Mayor) and Dieter Spangenberg (subsequently State Secretary to Federal President Gustav Heinemann) all played a considerable part in the great achievement, as we saw it, of the modest agreement on passes concluded in December 1963. It came into force on my fiftieth birthday, and it meant that Berliners from East and West could visit each other again after twenty-eight months of separation. They made use of the facility to an extent no one had foreseen, fearing neither the bitter cold in which they had to queue for their passes, nor all the red tape, which was something we could not spare them.

I had persuaded myself that we had the Allied governments on our side in the fight for humanitarian relief. Kennedy had expressly told me, that autumn of 1962, that he wished me luck in our efforts to make the Wall less impenetrable. I had been assured by de Gaulle in April 1963, during a discussion at Saint-Dizier in eastern France, that he would look kindly on any sign of relief and encouragement for the people in the East, and I was not to hesitate to keep him informed. Nor did London give us any trouble.

Bonn was a different matter. Ludwig Erhard, who was now Chancellor, was well disposed, but exposed to the influences of people who thought we were deviating from the straight and narrow path of non-recognition, or assumed that we were being devious in Berlin for the sake of advantage in Federal politics. It was lucky for us that the FDP leader, Erich Mende, was at the head of the otherwise not very influential Ministry for All-German Affairs. We had to wait till the very last moment to get the green light from the Chancellor's office and conclude the agreement; it was out of the question without Bonn's co-operation. Afterwards Erhard let himself be persuaded once again that visiting permits were 'rather in the nature of a Trojan horse'.

I think it is fair to say that despite all Erhard's services to the German economy, he did not have a very assured command of politics. One day, during a drive through Berlin, he asked me seriously – and he was Economics Minister at the time – how much it would cost to buy the Eastern zone from the Russians! On another occasion, when he was acting Chancellor because Adenauer was out of the country, and I came to inform him of momentous and confidential talks between our Washington Embassy and the Poles (I was just back from the USA), it turned out that he did not know we had no diplomatic relations with the People's Republic of Poland. The Federal Republic immediately cut off our envoy Albrecht von Kessel from his Polish channel of communication. The reason given was that the American Government did not like the contact, although even conservative American politicians had long been in favour of normalizing relations with Poland. My relations with Erhard were always correct, and they remained correct when I was Federal Chancellor. He even undertook various missions abroad and discussed them with me as was appropriate.

A deciding factor, of course, was how the other German side would react to our efforts to get visiting passes. From all we could discover, Ulbricht was not happy to find that the Soviets had put their project for a 'Free City of West Berlin' on ice. He wanted formal recognition of the GDR by the Federal Republic and West Berlin. In February 1963 he said of our request for visiting facilities that the only settlement acceptable must 'conform to international law'. On another occasion he even accused us of intending 'aggression by stealth'.

All attempts to settle humanitarian issues other than through bureaucratic channels had been thwarted, or led to pitiful results. Now and then, in especially hard cases, the Churches were helpful, particularly through a representative of the Church of Sweden who lived in Berlin. The Committee of the International Red Cross, with whose members I was in close contact, could do no more than bring out a few sick and old people very occasionally. Lawyers had been working on the issue on both sides of the Wall: on our own Western side they tried to arrange urgent family reunions, with the help of the Ministry for All-German Affairs. An exchange of prisoners, overwhelmingly from East to West, was linked to generous financial settlements which were given humanitarian justification and were in the special interest of the secret services on both sides.

At the end of 1963 we learned that the other side was ready to talk; there had never been any lack of intermediaries of various kinds in such matters. On 5 December I received a letter from the Deputy Chairman of the Council of Ministers, Alexander Abusch, containing a restricted offer of passes subject to a time-limit. I jumped at it, and the Senate approved it the same day. Our negotiator had to take the utmost care that the settlement did not take on the character of an inter-state agreement. For one thing, that would have undermined our hopes of being linked to the Federal Republic, and for another the Federal Government would not have given the essential go-ahead. The agreement was to imply no recognition of the GDR, and was to avoid any East German acts of sovereignty (such as the checking of applications for passes) on our territory.

Long hours of negotiations brought modest gains: visitors' passes were valid only for the Christmas and New Year holiday period, only for West Berliners with relations in the other part of the city, only for the Eastern sector and not for the neighbouring suburbs. It is a mistake to think we were unaware of the precedent we were setting, but there was no point in talking about it. Let sleeping dogs lie, we thought. The immediate reaction was overwhelming. The GDR had expected 30,000 visitors; we thought that estimate far too low, but we never dreamed there would be 1.2 million visitors over the holiday period. Seven hundred and ninety thousand West Berliners took advantage of the opportunity, many of them several times. We could say, without exaggeration, that some four million people were reunited during those days.

The second agreement on passes was for the days around the last Sunday before Advent and Christmas of 1964, and for Easter and Whitsun 1965. Yet again there was a vast number of visitors. Yet again an office was set up for urgent family affairs, to which people could apply for visits outside the agreed times. In the course of a year 36,000 people made use of it. Married couples who had been separated could not apply, from East Berlin, to be reunited through the passes. A third agreement was for the New Year period of 1965 to 1966, and a fourth for Easter and Whitsun 1966. After that the GDR leadership would no longer agree to the saving clause, inserted by us so as not to imply recognition of the GDR, which stated that there had been no agreement on the description of the places, officials and offices involved. Only five years later, in 1971, when the Four-Power agreement on Berlin came into force, did the West Berliners get visiting facilities again – this time not just for relations, and the permits went beyond the city and could apply to the rest of the GDR.

In Berlin itself, and even more so in Bonn, the huge success of the pass scheme was covertly attacked by people who felt it endangered their own wishful thinking and their view of Berlin as an 'open wound'. I did not hide the bitterness I felt about such legalistically disguised anxieties while I was fighting for the fundamental requirements of the people of my city. These experiences were at the root of the contempt for 'pettifoggery' of which I was later accused.

At a Party conference in Dortmund early in June 1966, I described my view of patriotism as one that included European and international responsibility: German policies would gain influence and weight if we played an active part in détente. Compared with peace, I said, one's country was no longer the highest of all values. With all due respect for official policy, I recommended the modified and regulated coexistence of the two areas – I did not yet call the other one a state. I was aware that history is a dynamic process. Nothing in it is immutable.

In the summer of 1966, when the passes agreement ran out, a laboriously agreed exchange of spokesmen with the leaders of the SED in the GDR came to nothing. It turned out that the Russians were against the plan. The Soviet Ambassador told diplomats in East Berlin, 'This will not take place.' To me, he expressed his anxiety: 'Who knows what you might discuss behind closed doors?' He meant his remark as a joke, but I could see it was serious enough.

The limitations of even so well-meant an effort were brought home to me once again. There would be no point in drawing up a list of all the failed initiatives and missed opportunities, and it is a trying business to be involved in a task where there seems to be no prospect of success. But Berlin did more than teach me how to cope with a crisis. It also confirmed me in my belief that hardly any situation is hopeless unless you accept it as such, and that an urge to take risks can be a good thing.

2

The Discovery of the World

Uprooted in Youth

It was not hard for me to say goodbye to Lübeck on an early April day in 1933. If I was not to risk both body and soul I had to leave, and look outwards. I had no leisure to look back.

Five and a half years passed between that day and my introduction to Heinrich Mann in Paris in October 1938, a few days after the Munich Agreement. I was living in Oslo, I had spent some time in Berlin, I had learned in Spain how freedom can be crushed from without and destroyed from within, and now at last I felt the melancholy that makes saying goodbye so hard. 'I suppose we shall never see the seven towers again,' said Heinrich Mann, aged sixty-seven, with tears in his eyes and sadness in his voice, to his young countryman from Lübeck who was not yet twenty-five. At that moment, and I shall never forget it, the city with its seven towers found its way back into my heart again. My feeling that the Lübeck of the Manns, sons of a senator, was not my Lübeck vanished, although I could not forget it.

At the age of nineteen, when I fled from Nazi Germany, I knew what I was doing. If I did not protest vigorously at a later date against insinuations made against me for leaving, it was out of consideration for the feelings of my countrymen, who did not want to hear about the exception from the rule. I felt awkward, however, on the subject of my birth and the aspersions cast on it throughout a long political life: there was nothing I could do about it, but all the same it was thrown up at me. Why did I let it bother me for so long? Why did I not simply accept that there were plenty of other working-class children in Lübeck who did not know their fathers and bore their mothers' surnames? Why did I not hit back, bringing these meaningless personal details out into the open, even when Adenauer fought half an election campaign on the issue of my birth and referred to me as 'alias Frahm' the day after the building of the Wall? Or when the press speculated wildly about my father's identity? Names suggested ranged from Julius Leber – in fact I was eight when he came to Lübeck – to the conductor Hermann Abendroth, a count from Mecklenburg, a Nationalist district court judge, and a Bulgarian Communist called Pogoreloff. In 1960 Erich Ollenhauer, whom I was visiting in Bonn, took me aside and showed me a 'report' from London which 'revealed' the identity of my alleged Bulgarian father. A *Deutsche Nationalbiographie* [German National Biography] published abroad mentioned my book on the war in Norway and gave its author's name as: 'Brandt W.[ladimir, i.e. Wladimir Pogoreloff]'! Even well-intentioned people were far from helpful. The inhibitions I carried about with me went deep, too deep for me to be able to shake off my self-consciousness.

Neither my mother nor my grandfather, who brought me up, ever mentioned my father, and naturally I asked no questions. Even later I thought it would be wrong to try tracing him, since he so clearly did not want to know about me. Not until after the Second World War, when I was over thirty and thought I had better give precise personal details in applying to reclaim German citizenship, did I venture to ask my mother. I chose to employ the detached approach of a letter, and she immediately sent me a note with my father's name: John Möller of Hamburg.

On 7 June 1961 a cousin of whom I had never heard wrote to me; all the publicity had alerted him to my existence, he had pursued the matter, and now he had confirmation from my mother in Lübeck that my father, John Möller, and his own mother were brother and sister. I discovered that my father, who died in September 1958 in Hamburg, had spent his life as a bookkeeper; his memory had been impaired by a wound in the First World War. This information was probably intended to make me feel more kindly towards a father who – so my newly acquired cousin had heard from my father's other sister – had often expressed a wish to have news of his son in Lübeck but did nothing about it; I was entered in the Lübeck births register on 18 December 1913, two days after I was born, as Herbert Ernst Karl Frahm. My father had failed to notice that his son became Governing Mayor of Berlin in 1957; the campaigns that might have drawn me to his attention did not really begin until I stood for Chancellor. My cousin Gerd André was at least able to tell me that John Möller had been considered 'remarkably gifted' and would have liked to be a teacher, 'that he had great depth of humanity, and a character which impressed all who knew him, in spite of his relatively humble station in life'. When I was fourteen my mother, who worked as a sales assistant in a co-operative store, married a foreman bricklayer from Mecklenburg. I called him 'Uncle'.

My grandfather Ludwig Frahm was born in 1875. I grew up with him, called him 'Papa', and his name went down as my father on my school-leaving certificate. He came from Klütz, near Lübeck. When I met my Uncle Ernst, my mother's brother, in Copenhagen in 1934, he added to the confusion of our family circumstances by suggesting that Ludwig Frahm was probably not in fact my mother's real father. In old Mecklenburg – my mother was born in 1894 – it would not have been the first time a country girl working on the manorial estate had to submit to the *jus primae noctis*; the country girl in this case would have been the one who became the wife of Ludwig Frahm and died young. I never knew her. I did not get on at all well with his second wife, whom I called 'Aunt'. It was a great step up for an agricultural worker like my grandfather when he moved to the city to earn his living driving trucks at the beginning of the century. His ambition, which raised him far above his class, was to see me go further than himself and my mother Martha, whom he certainly brought up as his daughter even if she was not really his.

I learned to speak standard High German at the St Lorenz Secondary School for Boys, which I attended for seven years; we spoke Low German at home. I went on to the Realschule for a year in 1927, and then, with the help of a demanding teacher and a supportive grandfather, to the Johanneum. The Johanneum did not cut me off from the self-contained world of working-class culture – my home roots went too deep for that – but it enabled me to assert myself elsewhere when necessary; functionaries in the labour movement did not usually have to acquire self-confidence outside their own circle, and their reluctance to come into contact with the middle classes may have helped to explain their failures.

My grandfather and my mother had found their home in 'the Movement', as they called it. They felt at ease in the labour movement and sought their chance of recognition and self-fulfilment in it. They enrolled me in the children's section of the Labour Sports Club almost as soon as I could walk, and then in a Labour Mandolin Club. Before long I was also an ornament of the Labour Drama Club and the Labour Puppet Club. But it was not likely that these activities would satisfy a boy born with an urge to develop his abilities. I sought and found a home in the youth movement, first the Falken [Hawks], then in the Sozialistische Arbeiterjugend or SAJ [the Socialist Labour Youth organization]. At fifteen, writing in the Lübeck Volksbote of 27 August 1929, I announced that one thing should not be forgotten: 'that as young Socialists we must prepare for the political struggle, we must always work to improve ourselves, and not just fill our evenings with dancing, games and singing'.

Class-consciousness, not class hatred, I assured my readers, would be called for, if we were to see 'the state of the future'. I had learned that precept in my very early youth. 'The state of the future' was the name given to that community in which privileges derived from birth, possessions, education and culture would be swept away and equality and justice would prevail. This was what August Bebel, who died in the same year as I was born, stood for. I heard him spoken of like a legend, and like him, I thought justice and equality were one and the same thing. The legacy of Bebel's Social Democratic Party was a fine one, with all those organizations in which many others as well as Ludwig and Martha Frahm felt so much at home from the cradle to the grave, and with a faith in the future which could make one forget the gloomy present for quite long periods. It was fine, yet unsatisfactory, lacking the strength and will necessary for thorough democratic regeneration. I had no one to teach me at an early age that democracy is not a means but an end, and that freedom is not just a reflection of equality. By the time someone did try, I was at the age when young people are stubborn, and disinclined to reject what wisdom they have acquired.

My grandfather Frahm, a faithful and committed member of the majority Social Democratic Party, felt that the 1918–19 revolution was a great blessing. When he spoke of revolution he meant not just the transition from monarchy to republic, but also the eight-hour day and his rights as a citizen of the state. Had not much been achieved, and should we not be proud of it? The fact that reality seemed rather different was neither here nor there. He put that down to a higher power, or the class enemy, which he saw as more or less the same thing, and he expected that it would all come right in time. This was no kind of Social Democracy for the impatient young people of the Lübeck Party. We pitied those who thought that way.

By 1929, then, when I was fifteen, I felt politically adult and thought there was not much about the Republic worth defending. I had never forgotten, or wanted to forget, a childhood experience of August 1923, which seemed to show the true face of the Republic. I had seen the police attacking a demonstration of unemployed people, even beating Social Democratic stewards whose job it was to maintain order. Some of the demonstrators were badly injured, and the Lübeck Senate uttered not a word of blame. And where could I see improvement now? All I saw was increasing wretchedness, mainly affecting the weakest sons of the Republic, particularly during the economic crisis, and not stopping short of our own little household. However, for a long time my grandfather still had a job; the co-operative employed him as well as my mother, as a driver. In 1925 Hindenburg became Reich President, and the fact that those who vilified the Republic went unpunished added to the feelings that had Young Socialists in and beyond Lübeck shouting 'Republik, das ist nicht viel, Sozialismus ist das Ziel' [The Republic is not much, Socialism is our aim]. We did say 'Republic', not 'Democracy', as has often been claimed.

At the Johanneum, where there was not another working-class boy in sight, I was soon nicknamed 'the politician', and Dr Kramer, head of the English and French department, advised my startled mother in all seriousness: 'Keep your son away from politics! The boy has ability; it's a pity about him. Politics will be the ruin of him.' They were very nearly the ruin of my school-leaving Abitur examination. Not only was I spending my afternoons, evenings and Sundays debating, organizing, and writing articles for the Volksbote, but I soon found I needed the mornings too and played truant from school, writing excuse notes for myself. Not for the last time luck was on my side, and the forbearance of my teachers was almost inexhaustible. They looked kindly on me because I had read widely, if unsystematically.

Eilhard Erich Pauls, professor in my favourite subjects of German and History, was a conservative man and a tolerant and stimulating teacher. He made it easy for me to get a Grade One in History in my final examination; the written work was on August Bebel, and the oral examination required me to explain the difference between the immediate causes of wars and their origins. In my German essay I upheld the thesis, put forward by a final-year school student in Berlin, that we acquired none of the essential equipment for life from our schooldays: an arrogant and unjust assessment which can be understood only in the light of the times. I received my school-leaving certificate on 26 February 1932. Five months before that, I and some friends of my own age had broken away from the SPD. I believed that this was a significant move both politically and personally. In fact it led up a blind alley and into faction-alism, and from the personal point of view it initially barred my way to university. However, the struggle within and around the SAP, that small party situated between the SPD and the Communist Party, provided a much tougher testing-ground for a young man, not least in the matter of self-reliance, than was usually the case in the big parties. Without my detour into left-wing socialism I would hardly have got where I did. But more of that in good time.

I did not learn to take Hitler's supporters seriously in Lübeck, where they were still known not as the National Socialist Party but as the Völkische Partei [the People's Party], after one of their precursors. I could see nothing either national or socialist about them. I thought their tenets irritating rather than chal-lenging. However, it was probably exactly the confused and morbid element in their policy that attracted ever larger numbers in a nation which had nothing to hold on to. The Nazis kept rather quieter in Lübeck than in the neighbouring rural provinces or the Reich as a whole, and they were not particularly numerous in the city, but none the less their elect-oral tally shot up. The worse the situation became, the more fervently the Social Democrats hoped for better times to come, comforting themselves with that thought however loud the alarm bells rang. They thought they were still strong, or at any rate safe, and took refuge in their own world. People hardly ever mentioned any reasons for the increasing popularity of the Nazis, let alone took measures to counter it. But I and those who thought like me *were* concerned with such measures. It was obvious, I thought, that the National Socialists were making use of economic misery, and of the resentment fostered by defeat in the First World War, just because that defeat had not hit

Germany harder, and in my youthful arrogance I felt this could be countered – if only we went about it the right way. But what way was that?

I agreed with the answer given by the spokesmen for the left wing of the party, Max Seydewitz and Kurt Rosenfeld, who were expelled from the SPD on 29 September 1931; the formation of the SAP followed shortly afterwards.

You did not have to be particularly left-wing to feel that the SPD was a party of ageing people, and see that a great many of the young had no sense of direction and were following the brown-shirted Pied Pipers of the National Socialist Party. But you certainly did have to be left-wing to see the new party as a real change in direction. I thought that a new chapter would now be opened, and compromise would give way to a readiness to fight. The emergency decree 'for the securing of the economy and finance', which included making 10 per cent savings on unemployment benefit, already wretchedly low, had been enacted a few hours after the end of the Leipzig party conference of June 1931; this quiet piece of teamwork between Chancellor Brüning and the leadership of our own party had been too much for many members. It had become clear that at the last election the SPD had demanded money to be spent on feeding children and not on battle cruisers, only to settle the other way later, for reasons of state.

There was something else that made the new party attractive to me as well: my belief that it would help to overcome the split in the Left and among all opponents of the Nazis. The Communist Party, which had not grown to any significant size in Lübeck, had been alien to me ever since I learned anything at all about politics, and I could never have thought of joining it. The admiration I and those like me felt for Rosa Luxemburg and Karl Liebknecht, and also of course for Marx and Bebel, was another matter; we thought the Weimar Republic Communists had strayed from the path of their forebears, and saw ourselves as their true descendants.

Myself, I felt that I could not belong to a party which made so little of German needs and opportunities, and applauded the ridiculous catchphrase of 'Social Fascism' at Stalin's behest. In the SAP we thought that neither the Communists nor the Social Democrats could continue as they were, and if only they were shown an independent way they would understand their mistakes. We saw the dawning of the single, united labour movement of our dreams – or at least a united front, even including 'bourgeois' democrats, which would bar Hitler's way. Whether these were delusions of grandeur or blind faith, I too hoped that this new left-wing socialist approach might reunite the two older parties and bring the Nazis down.

Full of the magnificence of this task, I was not amenable to advice. Out of mingled resignation and respect, my grandfather Frahm, whose instincts were all against the breakaway party, did not even try to restrain me. Julius Leber, leader – not officially, but by virtue of the authority he had – of the Lübeck SPD did try: he summoned me to the editorial office of the *Volksbote*, of which he was editor-in-chief. I knew the office very well, since I wrote for the paper regularly – political articles and some lighter pieces too. I enjoyed it, and it made me some pocket-money. Leber, born in Alsace and inclined to look to the West, was a powerful front-line commander and a strong-willed honorary Lübecker. He tackled me with a line which I was disinclined to accept at the time. Only much later did I see the sense of it. He did not speak of the content of politics, which seemed to me their be-all and end-all, but talked about the weaknesses of colleagues in the Reichstag who had taken part in the left-wing secession. I knew how to appreciate a good glass of wine, he concluded, and he heard I was not averse to a pretty girl either. What was the appeal of an outfit led by failures who were always railing against life and quarrelling among themselves?

I was insufficiently aware that Leber was an outspoken critic of stalling tactics, that he preached militancy and the courage to take responsibility, including responsibility where the Reichswehr was concerned, or that he had no firm footing at all in the hierarchy of party and parliamentary party. Internal opposition did not bother him, and he was on very good terms with the Lübeck party and its functionaries. To me and my friends, he was just one of the Berlin politicians, all of whom we thought boring. Not until I had outgrown my youthful dogmatism did I appreciate his stature and realize what kindness he was showing in trying to keep me from taking the wrong path that early autumn of 1931. In 1933, when Julius Leber turned in the bitterness of his prison cell to investigating the 'causes of death of German Social Democracy', showing the falling curve of its inner force and criticizing the mediocrity and passivity of its leaders, he recognized that 'Great leaders almost always emerge from chaos; they seldom emerge from good order, and never by routine promotion.' Had he lived, he himself would have been a great leader, and he had certainly emerged from chaos: as a child he was adopted by a labourer, and he had a hard struggle to make his way in the world. How much further he would have gone remained hidden, even from the Nazi torturers. Although he had opted for Germany he had a great love for the French language and French culture; his children grew up with Napoleon's death mask, as was not uncommon in German families with a feeling for European culture.

My break with the old party cost me a grant which Leber had kindly been holding before me as a prospect for some time. When I applied to take the *Abitur* I had put 'journalist' as the profession I hoped to follow, adding that if possible I would like to go on studying German and History. But nothing came of the study grant, and instead of going to university I took a job in a shipping agent's office, dealing with formalities for the captains of small freight vessels. I found the work quite interesting, and at least it did not get in the way of my other activities. My evenings and Sundays were now entirely devoted to politics. I held small meetings – sometimes very small meetings – spoke in debates on many occasions, and discovered that public speaking came easily to me: I could speak with facility on any subject at all. I found it more difficult later. Although I was unknown to the general public, I had thus become a party leader on a small scale. When comrades from Mecklenburg asked me to stand for the Landtag in 1932 they were rather surprised to find I was not yet old enough. Although one was not of voting age at twenty in those parts, one could still be elected; but I was not even nineteen.

On 20 July 1932 Chancellor von Papen, availing himself of the President's emergency powers, dismissed the minority SPD–Centre coalition Government in Prussia on the pretext that the Altona riots had shown that it could not be relied on to deal firmly with the Communists. After a show of force by Papen, SPD Interior Minister Carl Severing, backed by the rest of his party and the trade unions, decided against even token resistance. I thought I was confirmed in my belief that I had done right to leave the SPD. Faith in the power to resist had been dealt a death-blow: you could sense it wherever news of the deposition of the Prussian Government and the silent capitulation of Braun and Severing was discussed. On the evening of that terrible day I spoke at a meeting in the city, replacing a speaker who was to have come from Berlin, but did not come among us again. Severing, a decent man from Bielefeld, had dressed up his abject surrender of power in fine words, giving as his excuse that he did not want to show defiance at the expense of his Prussian police officers. It could not have been known that timely resistance might have saved many human lives, and perhaps such forebodings had to be dismissed from the mind. But it should have been realized that God helps only those who help themselves. Not only would a show of democratic fighting spirit have deprived the Nazis of the certainty of victory, it would also have impressed Communist sympathizers, if not the Bolshevist leaders. The rising popularity of the Communist Party was not unconnected with the pusillanimity of their rivals.

Even today I am sure that my feelings did not deceive me: the great, indeed the overwhelming majority of the Lübeck labour movement was ready to strike, to fight, and to defend both the Republic, unloved as it was, and its own honour. And there is no reason why Lübeck should have been an isolated instance.

On the evening of 31 January 1933 Julius Leber was attacked by Nazi stormtroopers. One of the uniformed Nazis was killed in the scuffle; it was self-defence. When the news of Leber's arrest became known, there was unrest in the labour movement, and the workers in one large firm went on strike. I and a few friends tried to organize a general strike in protest. We all went to the head of the German Trades Union Federation. He lost his temper when we put our request: 'Take that off my desk. Don't you know striking is strictly forbidden now? They must know what ought to be done in Berlin. We're awaiting instructions, and we don't want any provocation.' All the same, there was a one-hour walkout in the city on 3 February, and on 19 February, in bitterly cold weather, Lübeck saw its greatest protest march since 1918. Leber had been released from prison on bail. He was not allowed to make a speech, but appeared with a cut nose and a bandaged eye and called out to the 15,000 people assembled in the Burgfeld, 'Freedom!' He went to Bavaria for a period of convalescence which was not to last long. He was rearrested on the way to the Reichstag on 23 March, the day when the Party Chairman Otto Wels, carrying a cyanide capsule in his coat pocket, set out the basis of Social Democratic opposition to the Enabling Act that conferred overriding powers on Hitler: 'We are defenceless, but to be defenceless does not mean to be without honour.' Leber's long ordeal began the same day, and it was the ordeal of a hero. Now that it was too late, many people were to suffer for the Party's timidity.

Initially the SAP benefited first by being few in number – only a few hundred in Lübeck – and thus attracting little attention, and second because officially the party no longer existed. After the Reichstag fire, the founding fathers had anticipated their own abolition by declaring the party dissolved. The leadership fell into the hands of 'right-wing' ex-Communists working with us young people. The party conference which was due to be held took place unofficially, on 11 and 12 March 1933, in a pub near Dresden; by way of disguise, I used a Johanneum school cap and the name of Willy Brandt as I travelled by train to Saxony via Berlin. Despite the factionalism that still marked this conference, despite the patronizing attitude to the older parties in which we continued to indulge, the job of resistance was our main subject. It was decided that some of us should go abroad to support the work going on at home. My own mission was to help the journalist Paul Frölich, biographer of Rosa Luxemburg, escape to Denmark; he planned to go on from Denmark and set up a base in Oslo.

Our venture came to grief on the island of Fehmarn, where Frölich was recognized. After that incident I was no longer safe in Lübeck. The SAP, now led by a Swabian metal-worker, Jacob Walcher, who had been expelled from the KPD at the end of the twenties, picked me for the Oslo mission. In view of the many murders and suicides of those days, I quickly saw that there was neither a moral nor a national duty to remain in Germany. It could not be incumbent on anyone to stay and perhaps get killed. Knowing that I had a job to do for the group to which I had committed myself made it easier for me to prepare for flight. Soon after I had left, a number of my friends were arrested in Lübeck. They got off lightly because they were able to suggest that I was to blame for their activities. Similar incidents happened over the next few years, making the Gestapo's list of my sins longer and longer. At least I did not have to reproach myself with cowardice at a later date.

My grandfather gave me 100 marks from the savings account he had opened for me. I was never to see him again. In 1934, sick and despairing, he took his own life. My mother did not hide her anxiety, but she was understanding. They both behaved like people who had grown up in the best traditions of the German labour movement. I went to Travemünde, where the son-in-law of a fisherman who sympathized with us was waiting to pick me up. Thoughtlessly, for all my precautions, I went to a pub in the evening and met an acquaintance from the previous generation of the labour youth movement. He had become friendly with the Nazis, but he let me go without raising the alarm. My briefcase and I went on board the cutter TRA 10, where I thought I was well hidden until a customs officer appeared; had it been a really thorough check and not just routine he would have found my hiding-place.

We set off soon after midnight and landed early in the morning at the Danish port of Rødbyhavn. The fisherman later described the crossing as calm, although I remember it as rough and extremely unpleasant. From the island of Lolland I went by train to Copenhagen, where I reported to the Social Democrat youth association and found accommodation in the home of the worker poet Oscar Hansen. I was registering the difficulty of giving foreigners any idea of what things were really like in Germany. My first impression was that Danish people thought I was guilty of gross exaggeration. I stayed for three days, and then booked a third-class ticket on the ship that took me to Norway. I was looking forward to arriving there, although I could not have guessed how much of a second homeland it would be to me.

The School of the North

Scandinavia was not new to me. I had been on a school exchange visit to Vejle in Denmark in the summer of 1928, and a friend and I had gone walking and hitch-hiking through Denmark, Norway and the south of Sweden in the summer holidays of 1931; I earned the money to cover our modest expenses by writing travel pieces for the *Volksbote* and various other provincial papers. In my application to take the *Abitur* I had noted that this Scandinavian tour 'familiarized me yet further with the beauties of the Nordic countryside and the character of the Scandinavian people'. It was not just the landscape I liked, but the reticent and taciturn friendliness of the people. I had no difficulty with their language, and their way of life attracted me. I did not expect my present visit to be a very short one, and Oslo, moreover, was a long way from the big *émigré* centres of Prague and Paris. It was not the kind of place where one would lick one's own wounds and become absorbed in *émigré* politics, so no sooner had I arrived than I decided that I should certainly do the work I had to do in exile, but I would not live the life of an *émigré*. Wondering how long my exile would last, I guessed at a period as long as the World War of 1914 to 1918. Acquaintances, Germans even more than Norwegians, thought this was an extremely pessimistic view.

My first call in Oslo was on Finn Moe, the foreign affairs editor of the *Arbeiderbladet*, the main organ of the Norwegian Labour Party (NAP). He provided me with a few kroner from the 'legal fund', and a further sum when I made myself useful in the office. However, I did not have to ask for such aid for long, only until my Norwegian was good enough for me to write and sell articles. By the autumn of 1933 I was standing on my own feet, and I was surprised to find that Norwegian socialism opened up prospects very different from those I was used to, and sprang from quite different traditions.

Norway had never known serfdom, and the ability to make decisions on his own fate was the breath of life to every individual, and every individual peasant in particular; patriarchalist ideologies were as alien to the Norwegians as concepts of historical necessity. I was impressed by the constitution of a democracy which the labour movement considered its natural home. It was clear that the rigorously conducted social struggles of those years did not question the internal constitution of the country, its democracy. Perhaps that was why an active crisis policy of creating jobs and assuring the farm labourers' standard of living had a chance of success. There was no need of the American example here: the policy had been drawn up from an understanding of Scandinavian needs. However, the simultaneous development of Roosevelt's New Deal policy showed me how far the German Left had fallen behind the times.

Question after question crowded in upon my mind, to be replaced by yet more questions. The impressions I received were fascinating but alien, too alien for me to be able to digest them all at once. Moreover, I carried a burden that was too heavy to be easily cast aside. It was the burden of the exiled German socialists, of their defeat and loss of a sense of realism, of their attitude of superiority and their factionalism, all of which, not wanting to live solely as an *émigré*, I now offloaded on to the Norwegian Labour Party. Full of zeal, and encouraged by my German Party superiors in Paris, I set to work. After all, the NAP looked particularly fertile ground: it was once so much attracted by the Russian Revolution that it had joined the Communist International. When enthusiasm wore off in 1923, and the nature of the abysses opening up became apparent, it had associated with that group of independent, i.e. left-wing socialist parties to which my own small SAP belonged. In view of these links we took support from the NAP for granted, including financial support.

But there was also the group known as Mot Dag – 'Towards the Day' – rather resembling a religious order, with its high priest Erling Falk. Mot Dag did not make it clear whether it wanted to work within the Labour Party or become the heart of a new party of the future, but it certainly showed that it wished to force the world into its own ivory tower, instil correct ways of thinking, and at least restrain the labour movement on its downward reformist path, whereas the NAP obviously aspired to governmental responsibility. I need hardly say that Mot Dag, with its gifted intellectuals, attracted and beguiled me, holding me under the spell of a kind of defiant reaction against the party's realism. I thus fell out of favour with the party itself, although its leaders were extraordinarily understanding. I put their magnanimity down to the fact that my affair with Mot Dag lasted barely a year, in 1933–4, and entirely cured me of factionalism. Expulsion from the party – for I belonged to its youth association and thus to the party itself – would have reinforced my political arrogance and caused me difficulties, material and otherwise; however, I went on writing in the party and trades union journals, gave lectures up and down the country, and organized refugee aid on behalf of the Labour Party, working in collaboration with a Norwegian lawyer. And above all, I could hardly have avoided the threat of deportation without the party's help.

Several requests for my extradition had been sent as early as the summer of 1933: although my temporary residence permit had run out, I was still in Norway. If Oscar Torp, Chairman of the Labour Party, which did not actually come to power until 1935, had not taken me under his wing at that point, making several applications on my behalf to the immigration authorities and the Ministry of Justice, I should have been lost. In the spring of 1934, with extreme political disloyalty, I wrote telling Walcher it was rumoured that the party would no longer help me to get a residence permit. In fact the immigration authorities applied to Torp, who summoned me and let himself be mollified. I could stay; neither I nor anyone else took any notice of the usual condition, to the effect that I was not to engage in any kind of political activity in future. The formalities were made easier when I followed Torp's advice and registered at Oslo University on 1 September 1934. I passed a 'preliminary examination' in philosophy with the comment 'Good', and attended a number of history lectures, but I did not have time to complete my studies, and I was not yet settled enough. My journey of discovery of the world – intellectually and geographically – was too exciting, attended by too many obstacles and too much coming and going; above all, I was too oppressed by the troubles of so many of my friends at home, which it was still my main endeavour to alleviate, and too anxious about the fate of Germany to find inner peace.

I went to Paris for the first time in February 1934. From Paris I went on to Laren in Holland, to an international youth conference which was broken up by the police before it even began. They surrounded the building where it was to be held, a youth hostel. Foreign delegates to the conference were arrested. Four German refugees, representatives of the youth association of the SAP, like myself, were taken to the German border in handcuffs and handed over – '*De duitschers over de grens gezet*', said the Dutch papers. Parliamentary protests led to intervention in Berlin; the four were not condemned to death, perhaps partly because they were able to put a good deal of the blame on me. One of them was my friend Franz Bobzien, a Hamburg teacher, who had fled to Copenhagen. He was interrogated in Berlin, sentenced in Hamburg, and served four years in jail before being moved to Sachsenhausen concentration camp, where he became one of the undercover camp leaders, in charge of a block of young Poles. One of them described him later as 'a true German'. Franz Bobzien, who had always argued along ethical Marxist lines, died in 1941 working in a bomb disposal squad.

Once again my own luck was in. My two Norwegian friends – one of them was the Labour Party member Finn Moe, another a young lawyer from Mot Dag called Aake Ording – made sure that I kept my German passport, issued in 1931 and still valid, in my pocket, and instead produced the document proving I had a Norwegian residence permit. It was suitably impressive and put the police off the track of thinking I might be an *émigré*. I and the rest of the 'foreigners' ended up in police cells in Amsterdam, where of course they discovered my identity, but there were no repercussions. We were all put over the 'green border' to Belgium, went to Brussels, held our conference there in rather a minor key, and set up an International Youth Bureau. It united members of factional groups from all countries, and gave me additional experience which was very useful when I turned my back on separatism a few years later.

The SAP leadership abroad held its first conference in Paris. Debates lasting whole days and nights on 'the future prospect' – how long would Hitler last? – kept coming back to the search for a single, pure, socialist doctrine. It was true of more than one group of *émigrés* that their inability to topple Hitler led them to fight substitute battles in their own ranks. I did not think all this out very thoroughly, but I had been feeling unhappy about it for some time. If I must remain essentially passive, I had told Walcher in November 1933, I would rather be working underground in Germany. I wanted to be linked to the SAP organization in Paris, but not dependent on either its ideological guidelines or its practical directions. Indeed, my links with friends in the Reich were even more important to me than before, despite my commitment to Norway and my growing interest in international affairs. I was not particularly conspiratorial by nature, but you can learn many of the tricks of the trade, particularly when your life is at stake – the use of invisible ink, suitcases with false bottoms, covers of books containing other material, false passes. It could be as crucial to collect money – there was little enough of it – and get it to the families of the persecuted or to any legal advisers they might have as to make representations to the German Embassy or the People's Court, only recently formed.

My tendency to political arrogance was restrained by my experiences of practical work and by my mingled emotions, with sorrow for what could not be done outweighing joy for what could. The passage of time and physical separation were also to turn me against factionalism. In 1935 the Norwegian Labour Party had become the party of government, something that had looked likely for quite a while. The fact could not but make a lasting impression on me. It aroused my desire to have a hand of my own in shaping events, to win majorities instead of thinking and acting only along minority lines. My commitment to resistance against the 'social-democratization' of my party and its youth association waned after 1935. Any relapses were rare, and finally ceased altogether.

Torsten Nilsson, later Swedish Foreign Minister, describes in his memoirs how I surprised him twice over in the Norwegian youth association in the spring of 1935: first because I spoke fluent Norwegian, second because my manner was 'of almost velvety softness'. He guessed that I must have been torn between contradictory feelings: 'In Norway he tended towards reformism, while as a German he was still a revolutionary socialist.' Had he not heard about my Norwegian political aberrations? It may also be that the legacy of the German labour movement in which I had grown up was still evident, leading me to use a traditional vocabulary, particularly in German. The Norwegian language did not favour such tendencies; the abstractions beloved of German do not come naturally to it.

Altogether, I may say that the example of Scandinavian Social Democracy also influenced my conduct as a German. Left-wing dogmatists had begun to suspect my firmness of principle as early as the beginning of 1935. In Paris, which I visited eight times before the beginning of the war, and where theoreticians of every kind liked to cross swords, I had become involved in an argument about the Norwegian Labour Party. It became particularly heated because it had been hoped that the Norwegians could be encouraged back to the path of literal radicalism. Now that they were doing the opposite, and adopting a Swedish type of reformism, disappointment was all the greater. I drew a comparison with the mountaineer who never dreams of taking the direct route to the summit. 'Comrade Brandt will never get there himself,' came the retort, 'because he is carrying the NAP in his rucksack.'

Naïvety and Reality

Late in the afternoon I regularly emptied the post-office box I kept, as a precaution, in the name of Norwegian friends. It often contained surprises, but the one I received in the middle of July 1936 was the biggest yet. An airmail letter from Paris told me indirectly but unmistakably to go to the 'Metro' for a time. The 'Metro' meant Berlin. Some more of our friends there had been picked up, and once again our lines of communication were threatened. I was to ensure that the two-way flow of information did not dry up entirely.

I was not enthusiastic when I had read the letter and realized what my marching orders meant. Of course no one could force me to go, but I never dreamed of refusing. I did not even ask for time to think it over, and immediately began preparing for the venture – not an *ad*venture; there was too much at stake for that. I needed to get a travel document prepared for me, a Norwegian passport in the name of Gunnar Gaasland, with a photograph doctored by a graphic artist; I had to learn a new signature and make another person's life my own. I did it so successfully that I could still remember all the dates of my supposed life history when I was Mayor of Berlin.

I set off a month after receiving this letter, in the middle of August 1936. I went from Copenhagen to Gedser, and from Gedser by ferry to Warnemünde. The customs official examined me, my passport, looked at me again, and it flashed through my mind that I knew the man from Lübeck. Whether he recognized me and let me go, or failed to recognize me and was simply feeling suspicious, I do not know. I had not yet recovered my composure when the train stopped in Lübeck. 'Hot sausages, cold minerals!' Who would get in? The minutes dragged out to an eternity – and nothing happened. The train went on. Nor did anything happen in Berlin when I got out to draw breath on my journey, or to bolster my courage. As Gunnar Gaasland,

I spent the night in a modest hotel on the Kurfürstendamm, and went on to our office in Paris by way of Aix and Liège. In Paris, I was given my directions. And in Paris I felt close to despair. It would not have taken much to make me call off my journey back to Berlin.

I had already met the exiled leaders and come to know the *émigré* society of Paris in 1934, 1935, and the spring of 1936, but I had also derived hope from the broad Socialist–Communist movement towards unity, as it seemed, in the face of Fascism. It was a wave that swept over France and rolled through the Paris of the exiled Germans. I spoke at large meetings, assemblies of German companions in misfortune, and like the otherwise rather cool Scandinavians who came to a trades union congress of unity in May 1936, and for whom I acted as interpreter, I let myself be carried away by the sense of a new departure. I was irritated by the dark, unrealistic spots on the bright picture presented by the French Socialists, but they did not overshadow the joy of the moment, not yet. As Hitler's German opponents, we thought we could withstand him. It was hard for us to gauge the importance of those voices waxing eloquent on the theme of the forty-hour week, failing to notice that people in Germany were working some sixty hours a week; or the influence of the dreamers who would not be shifted from their anti-militaristic stance, and unwaveringly demanded the dismantling of the Maginot Line. The speed with which Nazi Germany was arming did not move them at all. It was enough to drive you to despair.

And I could hardly notice what was wrong with the French without registering the mood among the Germans. We veered between optimism and depression. There was a threat of a new split in our own group. Walcher begged me to make sure that 'reliable' delegates from Berlin attended a conference planned for the end of the year in Czechoslovakia. Considering the alternatives, I agreed that the leadership should not find itself in a minority. But what did any of that mean against the background of current events?

The evening before I left for Berlin, still in August of 1936, I unburdened myself to my friend Max. Max Diamant came from Łódź, and was famous for his talent for bringing any deviation back to correct socialist lines. Did I know in my heart that he would set me right and exorcize the question of whether I was really going to risk everything for this sort of nonsense – was that what I actually wanted? It was not hard for him to restore my mental balance by dint of a combination of fruit brandy and clever reasoning, and to get me into the train to Berlin. I was only vaguely aware of the border checks.

I rented a room from a Frau Hamel in the Kurfürstendamm, on the corner of Joachimsthaler Strasse, and was sorry I could not respond to her anti-Nazi feelings. But I had assumed the character of a naïve Norwegian student, only moderately interested in politics and mainly concerned with studying history. Every morning I went off to the State Library, where I studied nineteenth-century sources and any amount of Nazi literature, including *Mein Kampf*. A perfect disguise? In the Reichsbank branch to which my Oslo friends sent my modest allowance, the counter clerk greeted me in a particularly friendly manner one day, telling me that another Norwegian student had just come in and could help me find my way around. There was nothing for it but to meet this 'other student' and keep the conversation short; my Norwegian stood up to the test, and my answers to his interested questions as to which Oslo grammar school I had attended, and which teachers I had studied with for my final examination, evidently moved him to turn up at my landlady's twice – luckily I was out both times – and invite me to a club of Scandinavian Nazi sympathizers.

And my disguise would not have been much use if luck had not been with me again when I was summoned to the Gedächtniskirche police station and asked for my passport. No reason was given. I got it back a few days later; again, no reason was given. Another time, at the very start of my stay in Berlin, I recognized a Social Democrat from Lübeck in the Moka Efti in the Friedrichstrasse, a teacher whom I had believed to be in a camp. Surprised, but unruffled, he indicated by glances that I should not approach his table. Did he think he was being followed? A year later he was dead.

Whether or not I admitted it to myself, my lack of hesitation in taking on the Berlin assignment, undeterred by any qualms or by any political nonsense, may have been partly due to an intense curiosity to find out something about the reality of life in Germany three years after the Nazis had seized power, the reality of post-Olympics Berlin. The Games had just finished when I arrived, and the gloss of prestige had not yet worn off. I saw that people had work again, and that the attitude to the regime was not effusively or emphatically friendly, but certainly not inimical either. I had to realize that even people who used to vote Left showed they were impressed. Full employment, the concessions granted by former victorious powers and their passivity – the Rhineland had been occupied only a few months before – all had an effect which was enhanced by fear and terror, pomp and propaganda, conformity and time-serving. But I did not agree with those foreign correspondents who thought that the Germans had either acquiesced cheerfully in the loss of their political freedom, or had become entirely a nation of Nazis. I did not fully realize how much the national factor worked in favour of the Nazis until I saw occupied Norway in 1940–41; there, a Resistance member was in his element.

I could not assess the situation more precisely. There was no reason for anyone to open his heart to a Norwegian student. I had to resist the temptation to look behind the façade, finding out who was a genuine Nazi, who was a half-hearted Nazi supporter and who was only pretending: the risk was too great. To ensure that I did not get too expansive in company, I did not allow myself a drop of alcohol, and I lived as inconspicuous a life as I possibly could. The one pleasure I allowed myself was going to Berlin Philharmonic concerts conducted by Wilhelm Furtwängler. Younger people who accuse him of serving the Nazis do not know what they are talking about. The paths between inspired art and deplorable politics are tortuous. I for one opposed banning him from performing directly after the war, and I was in the audience when the Americans first allowed him to make music again, in the Titania Palace in 1947.

I was therefore largely dependent for information on those friends I had come to help, and naturally all they had to tell me was about opposition, particularly among workers. My first meeting with a contact – at the Wertheim department store – was a great success. It was only later that I found out that the leader and organizer of our group, which still had 300 members – two years before it had been 700 – was a teacher from Brunswick. Where our people came from and where they were going was nothing to do with me; I knew only their cover names. The number of active members in the group had fallen; the Gestapo had made great gaps in its ranks, much larger than I had ever imagined, and it did not take much intelligence to realize that sticking together and preparing for 'afterwards' was all that counted now. Anyone not yet rounded up, holding out underground and intending to go on holding out, had to concentrate on mere survival, at least after 1935. That had been the case with the overwhelming majority of Social Democrats from the start. There was no theoretical political discussion or talk of 'doing something' at the choral societies and bowling clubs where like-minded people met, or at the funerals of old comrades to which thousands of party members flocked, as if led by some ghostly hand. People pinned their hopes on internal disintegration, on the Wehrmacht, or on nothing at all any more. However, there was already much talk of war in Berlin in 1936, and anyone with eyes to see and ears to hear could not help realizing that the country was rearming at great speed.

The handful of young activists with whom I mixed – always out of doors, on principle – and who called me Martin, still wanted to 'do something', whether that meant working to create a strong organizational structure and preparing for 'afterwards', or vehement discussion of the future – and what would the German Resistance have been without such people's heroism?

I met the organizer of the group several times a week, and others, who brought information and carried messages to those trustworthy people who remained, only once. They worked in cells of five, with only one member of each cell having contact with the next level up. The idea was to decrease risk if anyone was arrested. A few times I walked with several trusted people, although never more than three or four at once, in the woods north of Berlin. Controls were becoming stricter, and I impressed it upon my companions that I was a student: they had only just met me, and they knew nothing more about me. In a real emergency this would have been little or no use. But at least we realized that individuals must be kept in the dark about anything they did not need to know, and which indeed they should not know in their own interests. Thus I myself did not know which official from which embassy was helping our leader to channel documents through. Later I discovered it was the Czech Embassy that was involved. And I had no idea how contact was made with the crossing-point in the Erzgebirge on the Czech border; however, our people had just succeeded in getting one of themselves out of the clutches of the Gestapo by dint of clever deception, without resort to violence or bribery, and over the border to Prague.

I myself made contact with the outside world using invisible ink; I wrote my reports between the lines of a private letter or of the printed page of a book. I kept the equipment hidden amongst my shaving kit, along with the cotton wool that I needed to help me decipher the news I received before I destroyed the letters. My reports on the general situation stated, for instance, that I had reminded our friends not to forget one thing: for most people, life consists not of any kind of 'isms' but of eating, drinking, making love, going to football games. We must learn, I said, not to talk abstract politics all the time, but to make our way towards them 'with whatever tea-making water lies to hand' (a reference to a remark made by Lenin in his days as a conspirator). I also reported that personal lines of communication were still open between the groups in various towns, but that there were no permanent contacts left, and each group had to be self-sufficient. However, I indicated that contacts were being made with new groups which opposed the regime, such as the Roter Stosstrupp [Red Combat Troop] and the Volksfront [Popular Front], of which Fritz Erler became a member in 1937; he had been expelled from the SPD in April 1933 for engaging in conspiracy against the party's will. When the Gestapo picked him up he was in the middle of a short training course with the Wehrmacht, and if an army officer had not exerted influence on his behalf he would certainly have been condemned to death. He was sentenced to ten years' penal servitude, and survived.

I reported no views on or discussions of the character of the National Socialist state. There were none to be heard, except in an inadequate and fragmentary form. That may have been because the reality would have been too depressing, or would have led people's minds too far from their own horizons. Or was it that they simply could not comprehend it, or that the clichés were too powerful? Or did fear and the sense of oppression, physical and mental, weigh too heavily to allow them to think about the matter freely? I was immensely glad and greatly relieved just before Christmas when I went to Anhalt station, caught the train to Prague, and passed the border controls three hours later. Prague, still a golden city, enchanted me and let me breathe freely for a brief moment that enabled me to forget the strain of the last few months.

Why make myself out stronger than I was? The thought 'what if?' had been my constant companion in Berlin. Again and again, I had promised myself I would not succumb to the temptation of committing suicide to protect other people. This was not on religious grounds; it was more of a down-to-earth belief that you could never know what way out might suddenly appear. I used this notion to make others see reason, in particular a friend deeply involved in underground work who was determined to kill himself if he was arrested. As he had been a courier between Scandinavia and the Reich for years, he knew a great deal, and was not sure what the Gestapo might get out of him. My advice proved useful, and Walter Michaelis, cover name Sverre, took systematic precautions for the worst, in case it happened.

He began by making a curious collection of press cuttings and faked notes. The idea was to give the impression he had been going through a severe psychological crisis and was just coming to recognize the true worth of National Socialism. From week to week he painted his admiration for the Third Reich in ever more glowing colours, in the form of a memoir. When the moment actually came, some time around the end of 1938 or early 1939, he put on a bravura performance. On his way back from Paris he fell into the clutches of the police, and insisted on appealing direct 'to the Führer'. He said he had come back from Scandinavia – his assumed identity was that of a Norwegian music student – because he could no longer bear to live in exile, or anywhere but Germany. Having no chance of returning in the normal way, he had used a false passport. The Nazi press reported that 'he fed his masters in Paris worthless "information" and kept them sweet by telling trifling political jokes'. To all appearances, he had become a fervent supporter of the new Germany. A Ministry of Propaganda man thought this story worth retailing to foreign countries, particularly the Scandinavians, but the war intervened. Excerpts from the court report appeared in the Berlin *Morgenpost* of 21 May 1940. The accused, in a letter to Hitler, had given a detailed account of 'the wonderful story of his conversion' and asked for leniency 'so that he would not be deprived of the chance to serve his newly discovered fatherland under arms'. The bitterness of the *émigré*'s life, he claimed, had revealed itself all too clearly. 'The voice of blood triumphed in him over the prejudices of Marxist error.' The court must have been much impressed. Shortly before the end of 1939 he received an incredibly mild sentence of one year's imprisonment; it was even suspended. Sverre was one of the most remarkable people I have met, and I shall never forget him. He was posted missing on the Eastern Front in 1943. I visited his parents in the Eastern sector of Berlin in 1947. His mother was still hoping he might come home, like so many other mothers, and not just in Germany.

The conference we thought so important was held around New Year 1937. It was to have taken place in Brno, but the Gestapo had got wind of it and intervened. So we went to Ostrava in Moravia, on the Polish border, found accommodation with poor but proud Sudeten German workers, and called the conference the Katowice conference, in order to mislead. 'We' meant first and foremost thirty steadfast representatives of SAP groups based abroad – in all some 300 souls exiled in Paris, Prague and London, as well as in Scandinavia, Palestine and elsewhere. One of the Oslo deputation was a girlfriend of mine from Lübeck who had followed me into exile. In the second place 'we' were the faithful of the German underground, including my friend Sverre as one of the Bremen delegates and four people representing Berlin as the most important German-based organization. I myself was one of the Berlin delegates, and perhaps that was why I felt particularly sympathetic towards a young woman from Berlin who had risked her life crossing the border, whose fiancé was in jail, and who was now expected to listen patiently to the squabbling of the socialist delegates from abroad, which always revolved around the question of presenting a united front with the Communists. We did not even succeed in settling the argument, and one-third seceded and set up an organization of their own. The Berliners could not understand why I was allowed to risk my neck but was still too young to be elected to the party executive. One elderly lady said straight out that 'the time for twenty-three-year-olds' had not come yet. In fact I had lost favour with some of the old leaders because I did not guard my tongue and could be disrespectful. The lady, who became much mellower when she was even older, was the former deputy Rose Wolfstein-Frölich; she lived to be ninety-nine, and I visited her shortly before her death in a home for the elderly in Frankfurt.

At the time of the 'Katowice conference' I had expressed my willingness to go to Spain for a time. We all wanted first-hand reports from the scene of the defensive action and of that war within a war which was discussed surreptitiously, and still with some incredulity. It was as hard to believe that the Communists had begun a kind of extermination campaign within the Left as it was to believe the news of the Moscow trials that sometimes reached us, and was increasingly depressing. However, when I visited Otto Bauer, the Austrian Marxist, in exile in Brno, he told me that there was indeed a bitter struggle going on within the labour movement in Spain, proceeding, he said sadly, 'with uncanny speed and thoroughness'. There could hardly have been a more credible witness. Otto Bauer, leader of the Austrian Socialists, had always been distinctly to the left, and had always had great hopes of co-operation with the Soviet Union. Now I was hearing this news from his lips. My feelings about my new mission, which looked like being yet another confrontation with reality, were mixed, to say the least. Was not Spain the hope of all European anti-Fascists? Was not Franco to be defeated, and Hitler with him, as it were, on Spanish soil?

But first I had to go home to Oslo. I went by train to Danzig – I had acquired a Polish transit visa in return for some banknotes hidden in my Norwegian passport – and thence to Copenhagen on a Danish freighter. I settled several personal affairs in Oslo. My main concern was to get journalistic commissions as a correspondent; as an SAP contact in Spain I would have an important job, but nothing to live on. At the end of January 1937 I set off once more, by ferry to Jutland and Antwerp, then by train to Paris, where I obtained a travel visa for Spain, paying cash again, and boarded the train to Perpignan. My journey proceeded by laborious stages to Barcelona.

The situation in Catalonia was confusing. You soon got used to having hardly anything to eat, and taking the edge off your hunger with red wine or at best with olives; you quickly found that it was not good manners to give tips or summon waiters by clapping your hands; you found that a 'socialism of direct producers' was highly thought of. But what else? It was some time before I began to understand. I found it was true that the workers and peasants had opposed Franco's revolt of July 1936. Germany and Italy were fighting for Franco. England, with France in tow, observed neutrality. The Soviet Union was biding its time.

In October Stalin began delivering some antediluvian weapons for which he wanted payment in gold, and which he subsequently used as a lever. When the Madrid Government asked Moscow for military assistance, it had no Communists in it; the Communists were still regarded as a *partido microscópico* or splinter group. That soon changed. Three thousand Soviet 'advisers' occupied key positions and set up a secret service which made itself a state above the state, and firmly opposed social revolution on the grounds, correct enough so far as they went, that military requirements must come first. The International Brigades, units in which anti-Fascists of all countries and all political colours came together, and without which the cause of the Republic would have been lost much sooner, were also the subject of 'communization'. Moreover, the Moscow Communists favoured social revolution only if they could control it, not an easy thing to arrange in Spain. The labour movement in Spain was more heterogeneous than anywhere else in Europe, comprising anarchists, syndicalists, Trotskyites or those held to be Trotskyites, and socialists both orthodox and independent. My SAP was linked to the POUM [Partido Obrero de Unificación Marxista, Workers' Party of Marxist Unity] in Catalonia, a similar left-wing socialist party, with more influence than the numbers of its members led one to suppose. George Orwell had joined its militia.

As chance would have it, I was not far off when Orwell was severely wounded, as he describes in *Homage to Catalonia*, in the middle of March 1937. I had gone to the front in Aragon to observe and to listen. The Republican units had been trying for weeks to take the hill of Huesca mentioned in Ilya Ehrenburg's memoirs. By night I moved to an observation post in a deserted farmhouse: the hill was taken, but then came the counter-attack. Enemy artillery, supported by aircraft of the

Condor Legion, fired on the troops I was with. I had just given up smoking; I started again between the second and the third rounds of fire. Orwell accused his country of handing Spain over to the Fascists, and castigated the Communist terror that inspired his visions of totalitarian horror and taught me once and for all that there is no greater good than freedom, and that it may be attacked from more than one quarter. I learned, not only from third persons but from those directly involved and from my own experience, how easily the last inhibitions fall away once you have started down the road of contempt for human dignity and for basic constitutional standards.

I had made friends with Mark Rein in Barcelona. He was the son of Rafael Abramovich, the Russian Social Democrat who went into Western exile in 1920. His son, growing up in the Berlin labour movement's youth association, and full of left-wing but not Communist hopes, had gone to Spain and placed himself at the disposal of the Catalan Government as a telegraph engineer. We exchanged opinions and experiences and went to many meetings together. One of them was on 9 April 1937. Late that evening we crossed Las Ramblas, and I said good night outside the Hotel Continental, where he was staying. Two days later a common acquaintance turned up at my hotel, the Falcon, and told me in anxious tones that Rein was not at his hotel and his bed had not been slept in. I was surprised, but what could be done? A few days passed before the acquaintance came back and told me that Mark had written him a letter in Russian, and sent a message in French to the hotel proprietor. Apparently he had gone out for another breath of air on the evening in question, met a comrade and accepted his offer of a lift to Madrid by car; he would be away some days. In view of the difficulty of getting any transport to the capital, this was not an unlikely story. But why had he taken nothing with him, not even his toothbrush? And we could not help feeling that the handwritten date had been tampered with. So had he been kidnapped? Why? By whom? Had the Communist secret service struck, perhaps because of his father Abramovich, who was friendly with prominent European Social Democrats?

Some of the large parties stepped in, particularly the French, and so did the office of the Socialist International. I did what I could with my own modest means to solve the puzzle, forcing my way into the Casa Carlos Marx as far as the office of a high-ranking Comintern representative: I could not yet know that he was Karl Mewis, who would rise high in the GDR. Keeping calm only with difficulty, I argued that the Communists had taken leave of their senses if they were behind the abduction. They must shake off unworthy suspicions and help to find the guilty parties. 'Comrade Arndt' pretended not to understand me: might there not be a lady in the case? Or perhaps anarchists? Soon afterwards Rein's father, who had already suffered so much, came to Barcelona. I shall never forget it. He did not want theories, he just wanted to know where his son was.

It turned out, with probability bordering on certainty, that Mark Rein was among those abducted on the orders of the Soviet party machinery: imprisoned, mistreated, and liquidated when there was too much of an outcry, or perhaps put on board a Russian ship.

The case made me very angry. Should I stay any longer? I was torn this way and that when another abyss opened up. Because of all the tension in the air – tension within the Left, that is, for Franco had no footing in Catalonia – all May Day meetings were forbidden. It was a useless gesture. An additional and crazy civil war began on 3 May, claiming hundreds of victims within a few days. The regional Government, now run by the Communists, took over the *telefónica*, the telephone and telegraph switchboards, run by the syndicalists, and with it control of the city of Barcelona. People who did not go along with this arrangement were slandered, persecuted and murdered. They included the members of POUM, at the time allied with the anarchists; their leaders, such as Andrés Nin, were now at the top of the Soviet secret police's blacklist. Albert Camus called the torture and murder of Nin 'a milestone in the tragedy of the twentieth century'.

During May the situation seemed initially to be calming down, but by early June I no longer dared to spend the night in my hotel. I packed my case, went back to Paris and spoke and wrote about 'A Year of War and Revolution in Spain'. I described, with as much exactitude as I could, 'the crazy aims' of the Comintern, which wished 'to abolish all forces that will not toe its line', and gave reasons for my doubts about the further course of the war.

It had been quite an experience. Jeanne Maurin, sister of the firmly anti-Stalinist Boris Souvarine, was at a meeting of the London (left-wing socialist) Bureau, to which the SAP belonged, held in Letchworth in England in the summer of 1937. We thought she was now the widow of the murdered POUM leader, but in fact Joaquin Maurin had managed to go into hiding. She stood both by and for her husband. At the same time, she tried privately to persuade me to abandon the dubious business of politics and take to some proper career. I told her – and myself – that leaving politics was only one of two possible alternatives for me. If there was ever a time after Hitler, would not the struggle to establish a great and free Social Democratic movement in Europe be very much to the point? I recognized, in a survey of 'The Comintern and the Communist Parties' published in 1939 in Oslo, that the organizational system of the Comintern contradicted 'the most elementary principles of the labour movement'. Was it not important to help to establish those elementary principles?

When I had my feet on Norwegian soil again, after my journey back via England and Sweden, nothing was as it had been. I became active in the Spanish Aid organization, which was mainly supported by the trade unions and organized deliveries of medicines and food. In 1939 the Spanish Aid committee changed its name to People's Aid, now supporting the brave Finns against the Russian aggressors; the organization became a successful cross between a labour welfare movement and a humanitarian foreign aid scheme. I had now shed all my inclinations towards party intrigue and factionalism. In 1938 I wrote to Martin Tranmäl, officially chief editor of the Party journal but actually the most important man in the Party so far as influence went, on his birthday: 'Thank you for giving many of us hope again.' I could now unreservedly welcome the new Norwegian Labour Party programme being prepared; it was adopted in 1939. Marxism was no longer obligatory; it was no longer to be a class party, but a great democratic party of reform. Strange as it may seem, I felt more confident after my months in Berlin and Barcelona, and was no longer in search of myself.

'We should therefore keep our eyes firmly and clearly on the goal of amalgamation with active Social Democratic forces,' I said in a circular sent out at the beginning of 1938. This angered many SAP members, for 'active Social Democratic forces' included the representatives of the mother party we had once left. That year I visited Erich Ollenhauer in Paris, and we discussed ways of bringing the youth organizations together again. The death throes of Heinrich Mann's German Popular Front hardly troubled me. A few years before, amidst general enthusiasm for the Popular Front, German literary and political émigrés had met in Paris; manifestos had been drawn up, and I thoroughly approved of them, even during the time I was in Berlin. The manifestos sounded good but were just paper. Trying to set up a Popular Front without the people bordered on hubris, like the assumption that the German nation was only waiting to get rid of Hitler and the 'German system of autocracy'. It was naïve to think we could make common cause with the Communists around Walter Ulbricht. Heinrich Mann did not realize what was going on and allowed himself to be used in 1938, when almost all the adherents of the Popular Front were Communist party-liners or hangers-on, and the venture failed.

The situation was becoming clearer elsewhere, too. On my return from Paris towards the end of that fateful year of 1938, I found a notable communication awaiting me: the *Deutscher Reichsanzeiger* had published a notice stripping me of my citizenship, as an acquaintance who analysed the official German publications informed me. I was not particularly bothered – to be stripped of German citizenship, as Bert Brecht had said, meant to be de-Nazified. Indeed, I felt almost relieved. Of course I wondered why it had been done now, all of a sudden. Were there spies involved? What would it lead to? But like others deprived of their German citizenship, I thought that once the Nazi nightmare was over its loss would be invalidated.

Spies had indeed been at work, and had got access in Paris to a post-office box kept by friends of mine under French names, and containing such papers as my expired German passport; just how they got at it I still do not know. I had travelled on that passport in 1934–5, on my false Norwegian passport in 1936, and since then I had been using a proper alien's passport. A report on the Paris documents was drawn up at the Foreign Ministry in Berlin, and everything else flowed automatically from that. I was now stateless, and thought it better not to remain in that condition, so I applied for Norwegian citizenship. I could produce evidence that I had been in the country for five years, but not that I had paid taxes, or at least not regularly. Without a work permit, I could not officially earn the fees I was paid, and so they were not taxed. The Ministry of Justice told me to apply again in a year's time. In 1939 no one anticipated the German occupation.

Thoughts in Time of War

I promised myself that the year 1939 would be less hectic. I would not travel around so much, certainly not so strenuously as I had over the last three years. I intended to be sensible and impose some regularity on my life. I continued giving lectures for the Educational Association, preferably on issues of foreign policy. I devoted much time and energy to working for the People's Aid organization, which was actually my employer, and finally, as usual, I was writing a great many newspaper articles and helping in the editorial offices of the *Arbeiderbladet*.

As chance would have it, I was on stand-by editorial duty on Sunday 3 September. My knowledgeable Norwegian colleagues were far from sure that the attack on Poland two days before would set off the war. We had become too used to appeasement by the Western powers and were too deeply shaken by the pact between Hitler and Stalin for anyone to have counted on decisive action, particularly from London. When I had heard the British Prime Minister Chamberlain speaking on the radio and knew that war had been declared, I called the editor-in-chief, Martin Tranmäl, and Finn Moe, who was in charge of the paper's foreign desk, asking them to come into the office. I was surprised by the casual manner in which they both took it. We brought out a special edition, soothing – or perhaps annoying – our readers by assuming that this was a new kind of war of nerves. I did not share that view. However, it looked as if I would soon have to accept that I was wrong. Life went on much as usual, no acts of war worth mentioning were announced; there was no sense of danger, and I even went skiing as usual over Christmas and again at Easter of 1940.

There had been an enormous amount of discussion of 'the war question' among exiles. German socialists of every political hue had been declaring war on Nazi Germany in their own way for years; we could not want it to win, nor could we wish to see Germany collapse as a result of the war. But now the war had come, and beyond all the old high-principled nonsense still being propounded by some die-hards, to the effect that we should at all times and in all places keep out of imperialist wars, the fronts were clearly drawn. In the political though not the military sense, a German opponent of the Nazis was now at war with Nazi Germany. That September of 1939 I set down on paper the views held by my friends and me. We thought that even if co-operation between Hitler and Stalin went yet further, it would not be decisive. It was more likely, I wrote, that there would be 'confrontation between Germany and Russia' in some future round.

We did not believe they could remain allies permanently; it took no great penetration to see this, whether you were looking at German Fascism or Russian Bolshevism. The fascination exercised by the Soviet Union on even the non-Communist Left had melted away. Spain and the Moscow trials had great influence, Finland and the pact with Hitler even more. No calculation, even the gaining of time, could be any excuse for the goings-on whose details we did not even guess in 1939 and 1940, from discussions of the carving-up of the world to secret agreements which included the surrendering of several German – and Communist – opponents of Hitler. The diabolical pact between Hitler and Stalin helped to clarify the situation for *émigrés* on the left. The Communists had fallen silent, as directed, and had no credit left at all. In our paper we wrote that anyone who defended Stalin's policies could not be a partner of ours. Grandly spoken, and of significance for the more distant future, but other concerns were more pressing in the hours of the German invasion.

On 8 April 1940 the reports in the *Dagbladet* were more confusing than alarming; they told us that 100 warships and transport vessels had passed through the Danish straits, heading north. At midday I was pleased to see the first copy of my book on my desk: *Die Kriegsziele der Grossmächte und das neue Europa* ['The War Aims of the Great Powers and the New Europe']. It never reached the public; the small edition was impounded when the Gestapo turned its attention to the publishers. (They were the firm of Tiden Norsk Forlag, which published prominent writers such as Maxim Gorki. The uneducated Gestapo men promptly demanded Gorki's address.) In the evening – the beacons in Oslo Fjord had just been extinguished and the coastguard had been put on a state of heightened alert, nothing more – I spoke to a meeting of German, Austrian and Czech refugees. I said we must not be surprised to see

German aircraft in the sky over Oslo. But I could hardly believe it myself. I went home to bed.

The Government had buried its head in the sand and was anxious to preserve the country's neutrality, which it regarded as endangered by the Western powers and their offshore mine-fields. In notes delivered in Copenhagen and Oslo on the morning of 9 April the German Government referred to an imminent attack by the British, who in fact had progressed little further than some rather vague plans to cut off the northern route whereby Swedish mineral ore reached the Reich. However, Hitler needed no pretext; his 'Weser Exercise' plan [of aggression against Scandinavia] had long been worked out in every detail.

Early on the morning of 9 April a German acquaintance called me. For two hours he had been trying unsuccessfully to get through. In great agitation, hardly able to speak coherently, he told me that German warships had entered Oslo Fjord and troops had landed at several places.

Within hours, as a result of combined operations by the German navy, air force and army landing troops, the main Norwegian coastal towns had been taken and airfields and troop assembly points occupied in surprise attacks. The one consolation, from the point of view of the Norwegians and their protégés, was that the *Blücher*, one of Germany's most modern battle cruisers, was sunk in Oslo Fjord by an old artillery battery almost ripe for consignment to a museum, and a spoke had been put in the wheel of the occupation plans – to my personal advantage, as well as other people's. The 1,600 men on board the *Blücher*, almost all of them drowned, had included a staff of some size, armed with the relevant files, which was to put the thousand or so German opponents of the Nazis in Norway out of action. As it was, no SS action group arrived until most of their prospective victims had already escaped to Sweden.

Norway declined to surrender. The King, the Government and the Norwegian Parliament fled to Hamar and shored up the nation's sense of unity from Elverum. There was never any doubt about the exercise of governmental power from outside the country if necessary. On the 9th I myself, with Martin Tranmäl and other leading Labour Party members, had left Oslo, where the occupying power had set up one Quisling as Prime Minister. On arriving in Elverum, we discovered it already deserted again; in a hotel further east I found nothing but some government files left behind in the heat of the moment, which I gave into the safe-keeping of the police. King Haakon had rejected the German ultimatum for the second time, and the place was being bombed. I took refuge with acquaintances until I had worked out what to do: I decided not to part from my Norwegian friends. I could have crossed into Sweden, but at the time I did not know if that would have meant safety.

On my way back into the interior of the country I came upon colleagues from People's Aid – and some rather unhappy British units in retreat. The hope of Allied defence was gone, and I was faced yet again with the question of what to do. I found myself with some colleagues in a valley on the west coast when the British put to sea and the Norwegian armed forces surrendered. We might expect Germans checking up at any time, and there was only one way out of the valley. I followed my friends' advice, which sounded rash but turned out to be very sensible. I borrowed a Norwegian uniform from Paul Gauguin, grandson of the painter and himself a painter. His mother was Norwegian; I had met him in Oslo, had come to know him better in Barcelona, and now I chanced upon him again in this lonely place. He was with a volunteer unit – a 'lobscouse' unit, they called it. I enrolled before it was captured, and found other reliable friends there. Paul Gauguin intended to try to get through to friends on his own initiative.

Things turned out as we had expected: we were all taken to Dovre by lorry, and put in a camp located in a country school I already knew. Through intermediaries, I managed to make contact with Oslo. My problem was that the Red Cross might make well-meant inquiries leading to the discovery of my identity. The guards had been told to treat us well because Norwegians were 'Germanic'. For the same reason, the prisoners were released after a few weeks; first the farmers' sons, and in my own case in the middle of June. Armed with a document issued by the camp commandant, Captain Nippus, certifying that I had received a prisoner's pay and board and lodging until the day of my release, I was allowed a free journey 'home' to Oslo. No sooner was I in the train than I went to the lavatory, put on a trench-coat I had kept as a precaution in my rucksack, and packed away my military uniform cap. When I arrived at Oslo station I was a civilian again, but the future was unclear. Again, the question was where to go.

I and the mother of the child we were expecting – a daughter – sought and found refuge with friends, a married couple called Stang, but I knew I must not be a burden on them, and moved after a few days to a remote summer chalet beside the fjord. It belonged to a good friend of mine from People's Aid. The organization made my back pay available, so I was not in financial difficulty, and I changed my appearance to avoid attracting notice on such public forays as I had to make, but otherwise I lived like a hermit for some weeks, in a state of great uncertainty. Only a very few friends knew where I was and visited me. When they did, our conversation always revolved around the question of future prospects. Since the invasion of France they had become even gloomier. I knew from the radio that Winston Churchill had taken over the helm, but one could draw no conclusions from that for the time being. He himself promised his countrymen nothing but 'blood, sweat and tears'. I also learned from the radio that Roosevelt had been re-elected President. However, the hopes to be derived from the fact were muted. I had to bring an assessment of the war situation directly to bear on my decision: a German stripped of his citizenship and now a stateless Norwegian, where could I turn, and where could I be useful? I could not simply go underground; I was too well known, and might easily have put those around me in danger.

At the beginning of August 1940 I went to Sweden by fjord

steamer, car, rail, and on foot for the last part of the journey to a farm on the border. The farmer, who had advance notice of my arrival, gave me food and set me on the right track. I crossed the Swedish border without running into any German patrols, gave myself up at a Swedish post near Skillingmark, was taken to a military assembly camp and handed over to the police in Charlottenberg next morning. I sent word to August Spangberg, one of the two Swedish deputies who had been with me at the time of the May riots in Barcelona in 1937, and he promptly arrived to vouch for me. I was soon in Stockholm. I was a free man who had lost his homeland for a second time, was going into exile for the second time, and for the first time facing the prospect that Hitler might win the war. I was a German who had fled to Norway and a Norwegian who had escaped to Sweden. It was a great relief to my mind, as well as for practical reasons, when the Norwegian Government in exile confirmed from London that I had Norwegian citizenship, and instructed the Embassy in Stockholm to issue me with a passport.

At Christmas 1940 I returned from Sweden to occupied Norway; I was getting quite used to illegal border crossings by now. I soon discovered that the Norwegians who had accepted Nazism felt ill at ease in Norway, unlike those who resisted the hated occupying Power. One did not feel like an enemy in one's own country, and I had no qualms about getting information from railwaymen who knew when and where controls could be expected. That summer the Norwegians, for whom King Haakon (declared by the Germans to have been deposed) spoke from exile in London, had gone through a resigned phase, but they resisted the temptation to conform or adjust unduly to the situation; at the end of 1940 I heard that all members of the High Court had resigned, publicly stating that all the decrees issued by the Reich Commissar were contrary to Norwegian law. Nothing united the Norwegians more than the conduct of the Reich Commissar and his aides; the fact that the German occupation was less oppressive in Norway than elsewhere, because of the alleged Germanic relationship and because the country was not at the centre of military activity, made no difference. A great many separate actions merged into a broad popular movement, the 'Home Front', more a state of mind than an organization, which was in contact with the Government in London and in which no one took much account of political party membership. People did not talk about their convictions, but they were all ready to work for the common good. The occupation and the war cost Norway 10,000 human lives.

If Hitler had been set on it, Sweden too would have been overrun in 1940. However, the military made it clear to him that the battle would have been costly: Sweden, the governing Social Democrats not excepted, had a long tradition of defending itself. Now that its two neighbours had been overrun, efforts were redoubled and the country was criss-crossed with a network of fortifications. In 1942, however, the situation appeared very menacing again, and no one in Stockholm would have wagered on the country's being spared. With a heavy heart, I registered at the American Embassy so that if the worst came to the worst I would have the chance of a visa. However, a visa in itself would not have meant an opportunity to travel, and I was prepared to retreat to somewhere in the country where I could make a living as a forester.

The Swedish policy of neutrality – maintained during the war by a coalition government of all parties except the Communists, and headed by the legendary Social Democrat Per Albin Hansson – has often been criticized, sometimes harshly. Not only Norwegian and Danish refugees, who were entitled to talk, but many Swedes themselves thought their Government too complaisant. Did it have to let German soldiers travel across Swedish territory by rail? Did the occasional Austrian-German soldiers who had deserted in Finland have to be sent back to their deaths? Items on the list continued to mount up until the end of the war, when refugees from the Baltic states were repatriated against their will. And yet who would venture to say that the price of neutrality was too high? Pressure from

Berlin was very strong indeed, and in retrospect it seems to me miraculous that the Swedes managed to resist it so well.

There was no reason why various conflicting interests should not have been at work in Sweden. Some forces would have been only too glad to see a policy of complaisance. There were civil service departments where the right hand did not know what the left hand was doing; there were departments busily frustrating the efforts of other departments. This I found out for myself a few months after my illegal visit to Oslo, when I reported to the police supervising aliens and asked for an extension of my residence permit. From being a routine call it became an interrogation lasting for days: where had I been in Norway, and whom had I met? Who had helped us on the Swedish side? I could not and would not answer any such questions. Did I take any interest in airfields or troop strengths? With the best will in the world I could hardly answer that; heaven knew I had nothing to do with military information. And I had nothing to hide that might have harmed the interests of my country of asylum, Sweden; on the contrary, Swedish officers had helped me over the border. So what was all this about? Had someone informed on me, even denounced me? If so, who? Question after question raced through my mind.

The police cell was spotlessly clean and brightly lit, by night as well as day. I ignored the threat of deportation to Germany – I was not going to be impressed by bluff. I did not know that some of the Swedish security officers were co-operating with the Gestapo. During the days I spent behind bars three officers of the security police had returned from an 'exchange of views' with Heydrich. Hitler had many admirers. There was no reason why what was happening everywhere else should not happen in Sweden. In December 1944 an inspector was arrested; next April he was convicted of giving the Gestapo information about German refugees. Fortunately it was not until after the war that I discovered that I had not only been followed by Nazi agents in Stockholm, but that the Swedish authorities had tapped my phone.

My guest appearance in the police cell passed off without unpleasantness. Firm intervention by the Norwegian Embassy and a visit by a high-ranking official may have had something to do with it, but the deciding factor was the protest raised by Martin Tranmäl, who had an office of his own in Stockholm and lodged a complaint with the Minister of Social Affairs, Gustav Möller. Möller and his state secretary Tage Erlander were officially concerned with refugees, and they had me released at once. There was a sequel to this incident in the summer of 1941, when a security policeman ran me to earth in a café opposite the main post office and inquired guilelessly whether, as an editor, I was acting with true neutrality now.

In their own bitterness, Norwegian and Danish refugees sometimes forgot what Sweden was to them – not just a refuge, and a reasonably pleasant one, but a base for resistance and a source of help in the work of reconstruction; the Swedes proved particularly generous to their much-tried Finnish neighbours to the east. On the whole Swedish foreign aid, per head of the population, was higher than American foreign aid at the time of the Marshall Plan.

I did not need to reacclimatize myself to Scandinavian life. I had immediately and eagerly plunged into journalistic activity, writing mainly about the fate of Norway. Countless articles in Stockholm papers and provincial journals, and a number of shorter pieces, were devoted to the situation in the occupied country of which I was a citizen. In 1942 a Swedish friend and I opened a press agency, which made my work even more effective. I continued writing and as a rule speaking Norwegian, using Swedish expressions only when I had to be sure of avoiding misunderstanding. Closely related languages have their pitfalls.

In Swedish Social Democracy, even more conspicuously than in its Norwegian counterpart, I saw an undogmatic, free, popular and confident movement. My observations made an impression on me which was all the deeper because by now I was quite experienced and had seen a good deal of the world. I did not mix a great deal with other *émigrés*, and my attention was less and less occupied by my own political group, although after the invasion of France and Walcher's flight to the USA I had been given full authority to mange the party's affairs. I had made no use of it; on the contrary, to the best of my ability I encouraged the efforts of the Stockholm SAP group to merge with the local German Social Democratic group. The amalgamation went through in autumn 1944. I was thus once again a member of the SPD myself. The individual groupings that had arisen to rebuild the labour movement had outlived their usefulness by the time Hitler's fall began to show on the distant horizon. It was as if it took that prospect to bring unity into being, unity this side of the Communist Party. London had been the main centre for left-wing *émigrés* when they had to flee from Paris, and matters there were much the same as in Stockholm. Erich Ollenhauer was at the helm of the London group.

What would become of Germany? That was the crucial question as soon as it became clear that an Allied victory was only a question of time, so it was a question that had been asked since the beginning of 1943 at the latest. I was still much concerned with the aims of war and of peace, and kept rewriting the book that had been impounded in Oslo. The first revision was in the summer of 1942, for an international discussion group arranged by the Norwegians for Social Democrats from a dozen countries, occupied as well as neutral, from Allied countries as well as from Germany and its own allies. The last remnants of provincial narrow-mindedness and national pettiness were shed in the fruitful discussions of this group; no one was interested now in anyone's membership of any particular branch of the labour movement. The Communists took no part, and did not ask to attend. After this first meeting in July 1942 we called ourselves the International Group of Democratic Socialists, and I became honorary secretary. My friendship with Bruno Kreisky dates from the early days of this 'Little International'. The pressing task, a sad but a grand one, that those of us who came from Germany set ourselves was to try, with the help of contacts in politics and the Churches, to save the lives of those socialist leaders who were now in German camps: the Frenchman Léon Blum, the Dutchman Koos Vorrink, the Norwegian Einar Gerhardsen, whom I knew very well. In the summer of 1944 he was transferred from Sachsenhausen to a camp near Oslo, and in the hours immediately after the liberation he took over the premiership of Norway.

The faster the end of the war approached, as I said boldly at that first meeting, the clearer it became that national resistance and the fight against the Nazis did not of themselves provide answers for the problems of 'afterwards'. Our subsequent discussions revolved around three subjects: the dangers of a reversed policy of occupation, European unity, and the role of the Soviet Union. Only recently we had been deep in gloom at the thought of the victory of Nazi Germany; now the prospect of a future without Hitler lay ahead. How could we have seen this future other than in the rosiest of hues? However, the ideas I set down on paper and put to the group in the summer of 1942 were not far from reality: a break between the Soviet Union and the Anglo-Saxon democracies, I said, could conjure up the danger of another war. On 1 May 1943 we ventured to publish the 'Peacetime Aims of Democratic Socialists': Sweden no longer took the ban on political activity by refugees seriously. What worried us now was that the war might be won on the battlefield but lost politically. We still hoped that the promises of the Atlantic Charter might become reality: freedom of opinion and conscience, freedom from hardship and fear. We wanted peace to be built on reason: post-war politics, we believed, must not be dominated by a wish for revenge, but must depend on the will to common reconstruction.

News of what was being done in the misused name of Germany in occupied countries did not make it any easier to defend the 'other' Germany. In Sweden, attention was focused primarily on Norway, and in the second half of the war on Denmark as well. But news of extermination operations in Poland, the Soviet Union and the south-east also reached us. Shocked Norwegian friends had shocking tales to tell of Yugoslav and Russian prisoners taken to the Arctic and slaughtered there. The name of Germany meant unspeakable shame. I had a foreboding that it would be a long time before that shame was lifted from us.

Outside our own circle such horrors, although their full extent was not known, were a heavy burden to objective discussion of peacetime aims. An emotional hostility to the Germans began to spread. There was even an inverted form of racism which found eloquent expression through the Englishman, Lord Vansittart, who said that the 'supposedly' democratic forces of the German people were no better than the others. My own future was not necessarily going to be in Germany, but I felt it was my natural duty to put up firm opposition to the idea that Germany should have no future at all. The argument I propounded, in a number of variants, was that there was no inevitability about the way things had turned out; no one was born a criminal; a nation may have particular characteristics, but they are not immutable; a heavy historical legacy is a hard burden to bear, yet it can be overcome. I wrote that we opposed 'Vansittartism' not because it denounced the crimes of Nazis, militarists and imperialists, but because in real terms it meant penalizing ordinary German people while sparing the reactionary strata; neither collective guilt nor collective innocence existed. But I did not neglect the other side of the doctrine: we must not let despotism compel us to act like scavengers or settle for living a life unworthy of us.

Not surprisingly I gave offence, and soon acquired the reputation of being 'only a German' after all. Trygve Lie, then Foreign Minister of the Norwegian Government in exile, said in 1941 that I was 'too friendly towards the Germans'. He wrote a letter to Stockholm containing a dig at me: blood, he said, was obviously thicker than water. The Communists felt called upon to join in the attack, describing me as a 'German of dubious origins' and a 'bitter enemy of the Soviet Union'. I replied in an open letter printed by several Swedish newspapers printed in August 1943: 'I am bound to Norway by countless ties, but I have never given up Germany – the "other" Germany. I am working for the destruction of Nazism and its allies in all countries, so that the Norwegians as well as the Germans and all other nations can live freely.'

Were we simply chanting mantras when we spoke of the right of nations to self-determination, taking it for granted that that included the Germans, and of the unity of the Reich? The closer the end of the war came, the more the grounds of discussion shifted. I could not rid myself of the fear that Germany's future might be clouded just as liberation from the Nazi yoke seemed near. When I heard the news of the Allied landings in Normandy on 6 June 1944, tears came into my eyes. On the same day Thomas Mann, in distant California, noted the depth of his own emotion: after all the incidents of preceding years, he recognized one of the moments of true 'rightness' in his life. Yet I still could not quite imagine the total collapse of the Nazi regime, so that the premises on which I based another document, 'On the Post-War Policy of German Socialists', written in collaboration with German friends in Stockholm, were to some extent illusory. We thought we should warn the future occupying Powers that a revival of nationalism might be a major problem. 'Against nationalism – for national unity', was our catchphrase. I produced variations on it that year in my book *Efter Segern* – 'After Victory'.

Our links with Germany had grown ever more tenuous during the war years, but they were never entirely broken. Swedish seamen whom we knew through the transport workers' union took great risks to keep open lines of communication with the underground movement in Bremen until the end of the war. We thus not only had sources of information but were able to provide help for a number of people. Bremen was not our only point of contact inside Germany.

A German businessman who had fled from Oslo to Stockholm invited me to meet a number of prominent people in the German Resistance; this was around 1942 or 1943. One of them was Theodor Stelzer, who was in charge of transport on the staff of

Major-General von Falkenhorst, the German Supreme Commander in Norway. Formerly a *Landrat* [district administrator], Stelzer belonged to the Kreisau Circle formed by Count Helmuth James von Moltke. Like von Moltke, he was not in favour of assassinating Hitler, a plan supported by other members of the opposition, but supported the resistance movement with courage and without regard for his own safety. He told me at the very outset, on a memorable evening in Stockholm, that he did not want to discuss anything that might bring him into a conflict of conscience as an army officer, an attitude I respected. He made no secret of his basic attitude or of his close connections with the Norwegian Church. I knew that he had done much in his efforts to alleviate the harshness of the occupation policy. When he was arrested after the 20 July plot and condemned to death, he was saved by the intervention of influential Scandinavians, using Himmler's Finnish masseur as their go-between. Himmler himself commented: 'We'll hang the whole lot later.' Theodor Stelzer, a very fine man, was a co-founder of the Christian Democratic Union in Berlin after the war, and became the first (appointed) Prime Minister of Schleswig-Holstein.

Stelzer had told me the lines along which important opposition forces in the Reich were thinking. For the first time in ten years I had news of Julius Leber and his central place among the Berlin conspirators. I asked Stelzer to give Leber my good wishes, and soon had evidence that the message had got through.

The emissary who visited me one June morning in 1944 was Legation Councillor Adam von Trott zu Solz. A Swedish churchman had telephoned me in advance and asked if he could call, with a friend. He came, recommended his companion to me, and left at once. My visitor, a tall, self-assured man in his mid-thirties, almost bald, introduced himself and said, 'I bring you good wishes from Julius Leber. He asks you to trust me.' Could I be sure of that? Leber had added something which meant nothing to me, about a glass of red wine drunk in the Lübeck Ratskeller on a certain day of 1931 when I apparently had a nasty cold. It was thirteen years ago, I couldn't remember the occasion, and I felt I should follow it up to make sure I was really dealing with the man thus twice recommended to me.

Adam von Trott, the cosmopolitan son of a Prussian Minister of Culture, who used to vote for the SPD without, as he admitted, wanting to be identified with all its tenets, filled in my picture of the German Resistance and its members: people who, despite their differences, shared a conviction that an end must be put to German shame and European misery. His hints of an imminent assassination attempt were exciting and new. The structure of a new government, he said, had been largely established, but there could still be 'progressive alterations', and Leber might yet be allotted an even more important task than the post of Interior Minister intended for him. Leber had spent four years in prison and concentration camp before settling in Berlin in 1937 under cover of running a coal merchant's business. Trott did not tell me that after the arrest of Count Moltke he himself had become Colonel Stauffenberg's adviser on foreign policy, and that his future post was to be State Secretary for Foreign Affairs. But with thoughtful, concerned frankness, and referring to opinions expressed by Leber, he wondered aloud whether the Allies would give a new German government any chance.

Like Leber – and unlike Carl Goerdeler, who was to have headed the new government – Trott supposed that the occupation of the whole of Germany could hardly be avoided, and there would be no point in pursuing the war in hopes of an 'equitable' peace. At our second meeting he gave me the impression that he no longer thought it would be wise to attempt anything: surely 'the others', the Nazis, would have to take all the blame for total defeat. Afterwards I worked out that this was his reaction to some disheartening Allied, or more precisely British, news which he had received in Stockholm, to the effect that if the Resistance rid the world of Hitler and set up a provisional non-Nazi government, negotiations might perhaps begin, along more accommodating lines than those foreseen in Casablanca. Casablanca, since the meeting there between Roosevelt and Churchill in early 1943, stood for unconditional surrender.

Why had Trott come to see me? First, he asked if I would place myself at the disposal of the new Government, and remain in Scandinavia for the time being, to carry out a task yet to be defined. I could feel sure that this question came from Leber himself, and I had no hesitation in agreeing. Second, in agreement with both Leber and Stauffenberg, he wanted me to get him an interview with the Russian Ambassador, Alexandra Kollontai, to discuss the Soviet reaction to a coup in Berlin. I thought I could do so, and consented. I had only met that strong-minded lady once, but Martin Tranmäl knew her well, and at once agreed to act as intermediary.

It is one of the many legends that have grown up around the plot of 20 July that the officers who had determined to revolt, and the politicians allied with them, wanted to make a separate peace with the Western powers, so that subsequently they could all carry on the war together against the Soviet Union. Not only would no one in the West have agreed, but Leber and Stauffenberg were determined that Germany after Hitler must not oscillate between the powers of East and West, and most certainly must not play games with them. Leber had told Trott when he left for Sweden not to do anything to make it look as if there were any wish to split the Allies. The only chance was to bring the tyrant down and then offer an armistice. For the very reason that Germany lay in the middle, said Trott himself, it could not come to an exclusive agreement with the West and against Russia.

Both Leber and Stauffenberg would have welcomed a faster and more decisive breakthrough by the Western powers after their landings in France. Then the war would have been lost, and the only remaining question would be whether Europe and the Germans themselves could be spared suffering and destruction. Leber's closest friends in the Army, so his widow Annedore told me, had toyed with the thought of passing information to the Allies to bring about a quicker end to the war.

When I met Trott again two days after our first meeting, he urgently asked me not to follow up any contacts with the Soviet mission. He had heard – through his contact in the German Embassy, I suspected – that there was a leak by way of the Russians in Stockholm. He was also uneasy because of the rumours that were circulating about his visit. We know now that a civil servant from Ribbentrop's ministerial office had been taking soundings in Stockholm, holding discussions with Legation Councillor Vladimir Semyonov, and that to cap it all Himmler's outfit (as one colonel put it) was looking for 'a loose establishment of contact with Russia' through Stockholm. I knew nothing of any of these rumours, but I immediately acceded to Trott's request.

Five days after 20 July Adam von Trott was arrested, and a month later executed. Julius Leber had been captured on 5 July after a conversation, authorized by Stauffenberg, with two Communist Party members; Leber and Stauffenberg had worked out the shape of the future Government and thought that if the Communists were not to be included they should at least be reassured. Annedore Leber learned from Colonel Stauffenberg that his friend's arrest spurred him on to attempt the assassination at any price.

Despite brutal maltreatment, Julius Leber said nothing. Only when his wife and his two children were taken into custody, on grounds of joint family liability, did he make a statement, and then he avoided incriminating anyone but himself. The vicious Nazi judge Roland Freisler, who presided at the trial of the conspirators, called him the 'most firmly fixed star in the political firmament of the Resistance.' Leber was condemned to death in October 1944, but the hangmen spared him, perhaps with some idea of holding him hostage. The decision to execute him came only with the Ardennes offensive and the erroneous belief that Hitler might yet win the war. In Lübeck, early in 1933, he had said, 'When you are fighting for freedom you do not ask what will happen tomorrow.' Before the hangman ended his life on 5 January 1945, he sent a message to his family: 'The risk of one's own life for so good and just a cause is the fitting price that is asked. We have done what was in our power. It is not our fault that it turned out as it did and not otherwise.'

Less than four months later, Julius Leber would have been a free man, and a Social Democrat Party leader who – cosmopolitan, bold, charismatic and assured as he was – would certainly have had it in him to become Chancellor.

On the Brink of Life

On the evening of 1 May 1945 our International Group was celebrating with Swedish friends. Speeches were made by Sigurd Hoel the Norwegian writer, Vilmos Böhm, very soon to be Hungarian Ambassador, and Professor Gunnar Myrdal. I proposed a resolution: 'We, the socialist refugees, wish to thank the Swedish labour movement and the Swedish people for the hospitality we have received here. We would like to express our gratitude for the help given by Sweden to victims of the war.'

I had not quite finished when a news agency report was handed to me. I passed its contents on to the assembled company. 'Friends, it can't be more than a matter of days now. Hitler has evaded justice by committing suicide.' We parted in a mood of deep emotion.

The Stockholm Government and the Swedish Red Cross were responsible for a last-minute operation which saved 20,000 prisoners in German camps: 7,000 Danes and Norwegians and 13,000 French, Poles and Czechs, many of them of Jewish origin. The scheme involving the now legendary white buses which brought the rescued prisoners to Sweden had been planned in February by Count Folke Bernadotte and Himmler, trying to provide himself with a safety net. Bernadotte, who died in Jerusalem in the autumn of 1948, employed the Finnish masseur as a go-between. By the end of April the Norwegians had arrived in Sweden. I was glad to see my friends again: Arnulf Överland, Trygve Bratteli, Halvard and August Lange, Olav Brunvand. Those who had suffered most were the first to advocate the dictates of reason and the necessity of co-operation. Ordeals endured beside German companions in misfortune had done away with any desire for revenge.

Himmler had a final meeting with Folke Bernadotte in Lübeck on 23 April. He wanted, so he said, to let the Western powers know he was ready to capitulate. I heard about this some days later, in a confidential report from the Foreign Ministry. Could there have been any more encouraging news than a hint from Germany itself that the end was near? My friends and I were much concerned with the question of the fate of Norway. Were the occupying forces sufficiently demoralized, or would they hold on for a final and terrible battle? Much depended on the answer. Anxious to know it, I adopted an unorthodox method of finding out.

On the evening of 28 April, a Sunday, we booked a call through from the press agency to the Reich Commissariat in the Parliament building in Oslo. Remarkably, we got our connection, and I came on the line. 'I want to speak to the Reich Commissar. At once, please.' Whereupon I was reconnected to Skaugum, the Crown Prince's residence on Oslo Fjord, which Terboven had taken over. I heard someone ask who wanted him; then a voice said, 'This is the Reich Commissar's residence,' and added, 'Obergruppenführer Rediess speaking.' My record of this conversation runs as follows:

Brandt: 'Half an hour ago we were talking to Consul Stören (a kind of Foreign Minister in the Quisling Government) and we asked if any discussions about a change in the current situation in Oslo were in progress. We'd like an opinion from an authoritative source.'

Rediess: 'I can tell you that that's not correct.'

Brandt: 'Not correct? There are no such discussions in prospect?'

Rediess: 'You'd better wait for an official announcement.'

Brandt: 'We've also heard rumours here of the imminent release of political prisoners in Norway.'

Rediess: 'In so far as the SS Reichsführer and Count Bernadotte have discussed it, preparations are under way for that.'

Brandt: 'But it needn't be expected to go through directly?'

Rediess: 'Oh yes. Yes.'

Brandt: 'May we expect an announcement from the occupation authorities in Oslo as a consequence of events in Germany?'

Rediess: 'No. Well, is that clear, then?'

So saying the Obergruppenführer put down the phone, and we knew our answer. Norway would be spared a final battle. On 8 May Terboven blew up his bunker, himself, and the corpse of Rediess, who had put a bullet through his head. On 9 May Norway was free. The next day I was among the first people able to travel by rail to Oslo. I was reporting for the Swedish press on their liberated neighbour. I found that many members of the occupying forces had continued signing off with 'Heil Hitler' when they issued orders, and in general acting as if nothing had happened.

From May to August I travelled back and forth between Oslo and Stockholm. In September I agreed to report on the Nuremberg war trials for several Scandinavian papers. I jumped at this commission: it was an excellent early opportunity to get to grips with the reality of Germany.

Leaving Oslo was not easy, even with a Norwegian passport and Allied authorization. I received accreditation as a 'war correspondent' for Nuremberg, obtained travel documents from the British Embassy, and booked on an RAF transport plane carrying diplomats and other civilians. We broke the flight in Copenhagen and went on next day to Bremen, where I was put up at the American Press Club.

Bremen was a city on the brink of life. 'A burnt-out minefield', its mayor called it, and its harbour was a harbour no longer. Who could have imagined the extent of the destruction, the unparalleled nature of the collapse now nearly six months in the past? From the American enclave on the Weser I tried to grasp it all. However, not all that I saw was depressing. Visible progress was being made with the job of clearing up. Transport and the public utilities had begun working again, if on a small scale. The people I met, shabby and undernourished, did not act as if they had no will to face the future. Bremen was a city on the brink of life, with life and the will to live stirring in it again. That September I realized how close together human wretchedness and human greatness can lie, and saw that the ability to forget is both a curse and a blessing.

Mayor Kaisen asked me to the Rathaus, and I gave him an account of what had been going on outside Germany, the present international situation, and what Germany might now expect. Then he said without more ado: 'It's a long time since you saw your mother. You'd better go home.' How, though? My travel order was valid only for Nuremberg, not the British zone. Kaisen said I could leave that to him; he would speak to the American Commandant, would lend me his own official car, a Horch, and the Americans would provide petrol.

The drive took a day. When I arrived in Lübeck it was dark. I could no longer find my way around the bombed city – I thought of Heinrich Mann and what he had said to me in Paris – and it was some time before at last I was standing at my mother's door on the Vorrad housing estate. No one was expecting me. It was ten years since I had last seen my mother, in Copenhagen, and what a ten years they had been! Years in which, moreover, she had suffered much harassment because of me; her home had been searched, and once she had been arrested. During that time we had exchanged some letters – I had mine to her posted in Germany – and I had been able to send her messages now and then, but that was all. The phlegmatic nature of the Mecklenburgers eased a reunion that could not have stood up to too many words. Only when our first emotion had died down, giving way to the joy of seeing each other again safe and well, did we compare notes – on our experiences, the crimes of the Nazis, and what people in Germany had known about them.

My mother and her husband, both of them undoubted and staunch opponents of the Nazis, said they had had no idea of the mass extermination programme. It was not difficult to sense what was going on in their minds. The imputation that all Germans were murderers was a heavy burden, and they did not want to shoulder it. I was confirmed in my belief that the theory of collective guilt is merely destructive. Horrified by the extent of the crimes, many people took refuge in excuses and sought to play it down. Or perhaps they were afraid to ask what should have been done if they had known more, or if they had admitted what they did know to themselves. Once people's fears had receded it all came pouring out of them: things they had seen themselves, tales told by soldiers on the Eastern Front.

Human ability to turn a blind eye is almost infinite, and not confined to those Germans who stayed in the country under Hitler. This is one of the essential insights we have gained from Nazism, and in a rather different way from Stalinism. We in Stockholm did not know everything either, not by a long way, but we did know some of it. We spoke out about the rising in the Warsaw ghetto, and indeed the Warsaw rising itself, when the Soviet troops halted on the right bank of the Vistula. Towards the end of 1942 or the beginning of 1943 the Polish socialist Karniol, an envoy of the Government in exile, had given me a brief account of gassings in motor vehicles which had reached him via the underground. I prepared a report for a New York news agency and circulated it to our small group, in which everything was openly discussed. But there was no discussion of this. Fritz Tarnow, the prominent trade unionist, formerly leader of the woodworkers' union, and in the end a voice crying in the wilderness demanding a programme of job-opportunity creation, firmly rejected the report: he simply would not believe it was true, because 'Germans don't do things like that'. His view, only too eagerly accepted, was that the story was a revival of the horror propaganda of the First World War. A book by our mutual friend Stefan Szende, *Der letzte Jude aus Polen* ['The Last Jew from Poland'], written and published just before the end of the war, contained the essential facts; the title says it all. It did not go down well.

What was guilt? What was responsibility? When does the knowledge of a crime become complicity? The Nuremberg war trials helped to clarify our ideas. I said the Nazis were guilty, or more precisely the Nazi hard core comprising about a million people. I wanted guilt to be individually established. I said the opponents of the Nazis were not guilty, nor was the great mass of people who were more or less indifferent. But there could be no doubt that they all bore responsibility, and must bear it into the future: 'Those who feel that they are innocent and had no part in Nazi crimes, if they want to work with this nation and improve it, still cannot dodge the consequences of a policy which far too large a part of that nation was willing to accept.' I was particularly lenient in my judgement of young people who had grown up in the Hitler Youth movement: the worst Nazis, I said, were not among those 'who grew up with Nazism, as it were, but among those who were already Nazis when Hitler came to power'. Generalizing, I thought 'it would be terrible, but simple, if the Germans as a whole were criminals of that kind'. But special circumstances had made them both tools and victims of Nazism. I thought these issues over during the months of the Nuremberg trials, and published them in Oslo in 1946 as *Forbrytere og andrej tyskers*. The title – 'Criminals and the Other Germans' – caused a good deal of perplexity. The book itself was a defence of the majority of Germans against the minority of criminals.

I had gone to Nuremberg from Bremen by way of Frankfurt, and like all other accredited journalists I was put up on a camp bed in the castle of the Faber-Castell pencil-manufacturing dynasty. The trials, which I thought were valuable for all their flaws, began on 20 November 1945 and ended on 1 October 1946. I wrote tirelessly, but more than once I felt like an

American colleague who cabled home to say he couldn't go on; he had no words left. The appearance of the accused aroused additional horror; only Albert Speer admitted his own responsibility. In his final remarks he explained something of the mechanism that makes a technocrat a tool of absolute evil.

The horror that was brought home to us in Nuremberg took the strongest minds to the edge of mental collapse – and beyond. But how else could we have looked to the future? Antagonism between the Western powers and the Soviet Union cast dark shadows over the trials and fascinated the observer. What would become of the Germans if the anti-Hitler coalition fell apart? I had become increasingly convinced, that winter, that they would work and work to survive, but would they get the chance? Or must we reckon with a third war? I put that question down on paper in Stockholm, in a kind of effort at exorcism. Preventing such a development, I wrote from Nuremberg to friends in Scandinavia, was in 'our most fundamental interests'. I added that orientation solely towards the West was incompatible with the restoration of German unity; a united state could emerge only by agreement with all the victorious powers. Was this another attempt at exorcism? Few could still believe that the Allies were united. The credit of the Soviet Union had fallen rapidly. Fear of 'the Russians' was growing among the population at large, and was constantly refuelled. Forcible communization within their zone was no secret to anyone with eyes to see and ears to hear. Then there was the struggle for freedom of the Social Democrats in Berlin, which I followed with both indignation and fascination during that spring of 1946, and which turned out to be a very valuable lesson in post-war realities.

And what would the United States do? As early as 1944, in *Efter Segern*, I had said that the Americans had given the clearest definition of what the struggle against Nazi Germany was about: 'It cannot be that America will withdraw from Europe.' In the months of the Nuremberg trials many lines intersected, intellectual and emotional, political and very personal, ideas of how the past could be overcome and the future contemplated. I felt my ties with Germany to be very close, closer than I had ever thought. But that spring I would have taken no bets on whether my own future was to be Norwegian or German. A Norwegian friend with whom I was comparing notes predicted that I would go to Berlin. He knew me well enough to realize I could not live without politics. As I had not been born in Norway, I would have had to spend several years living on the land to prove myself a peasant before I went into politics there, and even then I could not have got very far.

On 20 May 1946, in Lübeck, I spoke in a meeting on the subject of 'The World and Germany'. I reported back to Oslo that I had been warmly welcomed 'and the comrades would like me to go there. Perhaps I will.' I discussed it that summer with Theodor Stelzer, now living in Kiel. He asked if I was available for a post in Lübeck; if so, he would make the acting mayor Otto Passarge police chief of the *Land* instead. Social Democrats from Lübeck went to Hanover, where Kurt Schumacher had revived the SPD, bringing it back on course with an iron hand and the aid of devoted assistants. I had been there myself for the party conference in May 1946, but no prospects had then been held out to me, and I did not get the feeling that the Party was waiting for me.

Did the left-wing socialism of my past count against me? Hardly, since other members of past factions had become highly regarded in the party and were doing good work. As early as 1945, moreover, Schumacher had agreed with three deviationists – Otto Brenner, Willi Eichler, Erwin Schoettle – that membership of such groups and the SAP was to be regarded as membership of the Social Democratic Party. And indeed, no one was ever inclined to make pointed remarks about that past. There was no common ground between Social Democrats and Communists now, and no one cherished illusions. We had gone one way or the other, like Jacob Walcher, who had decided for the East while still in exile in America, and consequently ended up in the SED. He tried to persuade me to do the same, but I turned the notion down firmly after the forcible merger of the SPD and the Communist Party in the Soviet zone. I wrote to him saying that I felt the deciding factor was the attempt to impose unity 'by undemocratic means and even, in part, by force'. Basic democratic rights, and democracy within the labour movement, I said, were 'not questions of expediency. They are fundamental issues of the utmost importance.'

The well-intentioned Lübeckers wanted the leadership to give its blessing to 'Julius Leber's successor'. That should have been left unsaid. Leber and Schumacher never got on well together, even before 1933. After the war Schumacher, who had survived, took steps to ensure that the name of Leber, who had not shrunk from death, was not unduly remembered. Kurt Schumacher, scarred by his own sufferings, derived his power within the party from that great majority of Social Democrats who had adopted the policy of a waiting game in 1933, neither complying nor rebelling, and who did not want to be constantly reminded of the heroes of the Resistance. Nor were they willing to accept that a Social Democrat could also have sought an alliance with conservative forces. Schumacher's friend Andreas Gayk, the energetic Mayor of Kiel and leader of the Social Democrats in Schleswig-Holstein, had a hand in this. I heard him say that democratic socialism must be reborn of distress and suffering. It was hardly surprising that we were not on the same wavelength. At the end of my thirteen-year journey of discovery of the world, I was convinced of the opposite. I did not mind too much; Lübeck seemed to me rather narrow now, and I felt no overwhelming desire to go back.

I travelled all through the Western zones. In the editorial offices of the Hamburg *Echo* I met Herbert Wehner for the first time. I did not receive the offer of the chief editorship from Hugh Carleton Greene, Controller of dpd, which became dpa [the German Press Agency], until I was back in Oslo at the end of October 1945, and had decided to continue in the employment of Norway for a while, as press attaché to the Norwegian Embassy in Paris. The post was offered to me by Foreign

Minister Halvard Lange, and I thought it was a way into one of the international organizations, telling myself I could be useful to both my countries at once.

When I called at the Foreign Ministry in the middle of October to clarify details, Lange had a surprise for me: he and Prime Minister Gerhardsen had changed their minds and wanted to send me to Berlin, not Paris. They needed someone to keep them reliably and promptly informed of what went on in Germany. I jumped at the chance. The only snag, if it was one, was that Norway's mission in Berlin was a military one, and even a press attaché had to hold a 'civil military' rank; I was described as Civilian Officer on the left arm of the uniform jacket which I very seldom wore in Berlin. I insisted on the rank of major instead of captain, as originally planned, only because of the salary scale.

At Christmas 1946, then, equipped with a Norwegian diplomat's pass, I returned to Berlin once more. I travelled by way of Copenhagen, where I waited a fortnight for the British to stamp my entry permit, and then via Hamburg to the city that was not to let me go for twenty years. Ernst Reuter had returned from his Turkish exile a few weeks before. I met him early in 1947 at Annedore Leber's home in Zehlendorf, and I may have guessed that it was a meeting of great importance for my future. My feeling for Reuter certainly had nothing to do with the wish to find a father-figure, as has sometimes been imputed to me.

The atmosphere of the Norwegian mission in Berlin was pleasant, as pleasant as anything could be that year in a city which had ceased to be the capital of Germany. I made contacts and dropped them, made many new friendships and sent daily reports to Oslo. Routine news and dramatic incidents alternated. I saw the growth of the Cold War. One of my tasks was to observe developments 'on the other side' and smooth the way for Norwegian guests. Accordingly I took a conservative editor from Oslo to see Wilhelm Pieck in the spring of 1947. Pieck, chairman of the SED, had agreed to give an interview. Tedium soon set in; Pieck lived up to his reputation as a

Communist Hindenburg. But then the Norwegian mentioned the fact that concentration camps in the Soviet zone had been 'brought back into operation', saying he had heard that Social Democrats who opposed communization were being put back in the prisons they had occupied under the Nazis. Pieck did not see the point, and groaned: 'Oh yes, if you only knew the kind of letters I get – from comrades whose sons have gone missing – but it's nothing to do with us, it's entirely up to the Soviet authorities.'

I did my Norwegian tasks as was expected of me, but my sights were set on German affairs: it did not take me long to realize that. When Erich Brost of Danzig came to see me late that summer, suggesting that I might succeed him in the post of special representative of the SPD to the Berlin party committee, I was not unwilling. I went to Hanover and discussed the post, which would fall vacant on 1 January: Erich Brost had been given the licence to publish the *Westdeutsche Allgemeine*. Early in November I told Halvard Lange, my boss and my friend, that I wanted to turn to political work in Germany and intended to give up my Norwegian citizenship. I told him and other friends in Oslo that I had made my decision to take this step under no illusions, and was prepared to experience 'the greatest defeat of my life' in Berlin. 'It is nothing so simple as choosing Germany instead of Norway. It seems to me that I can and should do something more active to promote the ideas I profess, and that such action is particularly necessary in Germany.'

My decision became known, and intrigues immediately began. Two days before Christmas Brost came and told me there were doubts in Hanover: would it be right to give me the job? I sat down and wrote Schumacher a note dated 23 December 1947, and saying bluntly: 'Let me explain myself clearly: I stand by the principles of democratic socialism in general and the policies of German Social Democracy in particular. I mean to puzzle out for myself any new problems that may arise. And I will never agree in advance to any one formula, even if it is drawn up by the leader of the party.' Tradition means much, but respect for tradition, I said, should never go to such lengths that one may not admit to past mistakes and errors. 'How else can a party grow from within? And how can it win over the younger generation?' I reminded him that I had given up my Norwegian post 'and more too', but that I was not pushing myself forward, and saw no reason to vindicate myself.

The letter worked. Early in January 1948, at the age of thirty-four, I took up my new post, feeling a great urge for action, and even more optimism that it would all be worth while. I gave not a thought to the fact that I had exchanged the quite comfortable life-style of a Scandinavian citizen for the life of Berlin before currency reform. The *Land* government in Kiel accepted my application for renewed German citizenship: I applied there because I had been born in Lübeck. It was at this point that I legally took the name of Willy Brandt, under which I had worked almost continuously since the age of nineteen, and which was on my Norwegian diplomatic passport.

On 1 July 1948 I was officially a German citizen again. What would become of Germany was still a mystery.

3

Terminus, Peace

What Unity?

How long ago is it that Oxenstierna, Chancellor of Sweden, asked his son if he knew with how little wisdom the world was governed? The sum of knowledge has greatly increased since Oxenstierna's time, but what about good sense? It is no new discovery that people are easily fobbed off with wishful thinking, or will delude themselves rather than look reality straight in the eye.

Hitler and his accomplices had laid waste Europe and devastated Germany, and now clever legal tricks were brought into play to prove that what should not be, *could* not be. The Reich had not perished after all. It lived on and would rise again – purged, purified or however you liked to put it – in the unity decreed by natural law. Not everyone believed what was said on that subject. And not everyone intended to act as they said they would. But the majority allowed themselves to be taken in to some extent.

I thought the theory that, in principle, the German Reich continued to exist undiminished was nonsense, but I did not want to enter into argument with its supporters. That would have kept me from more important work. However, I had no doubt that the division of Germany was unreasonable and indeed dangerous as a burden on European peace. It was not easy for me to acknowledge that even in a divided state, the essential German contribution to prosperous development in Europe could still be made. Yet whatever answers the future might still hold to the question of Germany as a nation, it would have been flying in the face of history, so far as I could tell, to reject or refuse even to entertain that thought. The German cause could not be promoted by loud proclamation of arrogant legal claims, or by taking the Allies' assurances too seriously. It was a grave error to suppose that only despotic rule, not the state itself, had been defeated in 1945.

But had not the Allies – the Three Powers at Potsdam, the Four Powers (with the admission of France to their circle) in the Allied Control Council – indicated that they intended to restrict and remodel the structure of the German state, but not to dismember or replace it? Was there not explicit talk of a 'provisional' state of affairs three years later, when work began on drawing up the Basic Law in Bonn? And could we not deduce from the preamble to the Basic Law that 'reuniting' what the occupying powers in East and West had divided was all that had to be done?

It was pure wishful thinking to suppose that either before or after the victorious powers met in Potsdam they had pledged themselves to preserve or restore our state unity. They felt under no obligation to Germany. But many will have wondered why they did not at least pay lip-service to that unity which German politicians from left to right of the spectrum declared their highest aim.

In the mid-fifties I was visited in Berlin by a Norwegian friend who had become a state secretary in the Oslo Foreign Ministry, and wanted to know what I thought of the prospects for German unity. When I had explained the difficulties, frankly and sceptically, my friend Jens summed up cheerfully: 'Then we can just go on agreeing with what everyone says.' A witty if unkind saying started to go the rounds among the French: they loved Germany so much, they wanted more than one of it.

Early in 1959, when I had been Governing Mayor for a year and a half, John Foster Dulles, Eisenhower's Secretary of State, impressed me with his honest but deflating observation that though the Americans might differ from the Russians on a hundred questions, they agreed on the hundred and first: there would not be a single, neutral Germany, perhaps rearmed, which could swing back and forth between the two fronts. Around the same time Khrushchev told the French Foreign Minister that he would rather have twenty million Germans on his side than seventy million against him. On another occasion the Kremlin leader said that both Prime Minister Macmillan and President de Gaulle had left him in no doubt that they were not working for a reunified Germany, although they had not liked to say so to the Federal Government and would not confirm it publicly.

It was error or self-deception to try to derive a legal title to state unity from the declarations and decisions of the victorious powers. In point of fact a different set of conditions might have been created if there had been central administrations run by German state secretaries, as was originally envisaged. But that idea foundered first on French objections and then as a whole. After all that had passed, it was not surprising that the victorious powers were content to keep the idea of reunification merely as a propaganda point.

Sooner than the Germans, their neighbours recognized that the assignment of the two German states to opposing alliances, and their subsequent rearmament, could not be reconciled with demands for the restoration of state unity – unless a military roll-back was on the cards, but to expect that would have been neither realistic nor in accordance with the German nature. Nevertheless, it is still interesting to muse – without dogmatism or excessive enthusiasm, of course – on circumstances from which something better might peacefully have emerged.

History has no last word. But we had to recognize – some of us sooner, others later – that rearmament and reunification were mutually exclusive. Was that, as was sometimes said, the real price for what Hitler's Germany had done to the world? The great double illusion of German post-war history – that the prevailing state of affairs was only provisional, and that the division would not last long – was neither here nor there. So far as the provisional nature of the circumstances was concerned, it is a fact that the German leaders of the *Länder* told the Parliamentary Council of 1948 to draw up a 'Basic Law' – not a 'constitution', as envisaged by the occupying powers; more had come of it than some wanted and others expected, but that was part of the logic of an unpredictable development. The military governors had to be warily talked round; they said the world was expecting a 'constitutional work'. On the German side too, and not just among conservatives, there were objections to an interpretation of the 'provisional order' that 'shrank from responsibility'.

For a long time an alleged duty to work for reunification was deduced from the Basic Law. In fact, its preamble speaks of the duty of the entire German people 'to bring about the unity and freedom of Germany in free self-determination'. That was a different matter, and one that was not just imaginary. For it should be said that the German people, split by Hitler's war and the occupation, found themselves at one in sharing a fate from which state unity might emerge again. However, ideas were very confused. Unity was interpreted as reunification – as if history and European realities meant we could carry straight on from Bismarck's Reich, or as if the whole problem could be reduced to discussion of how the amalgamation of the GDR with the Federal Republic of Germany could or would be brought about. Even the Federal Constitutional Court adopted the idea of a Reich that was only temporarily 'unable to act'. The border with the GDR was unrealistically equated with the borders between the Federal *Länder*. A year and a half later the Court carefully corrected its misapprehension.

The aim of putting the west of Germany in order and making it strong was not confined to Konrad Adenauer's adherents. Opinions differed over finding actual ways whereby the two parts of Germany might be brought together again after all – other than by *Anschluss*. Instead of coming to terms with the new realities of international politics, people preferred the fictions of national policies of the past. The theory that the German Reich still existed – my friend Carlo Schmid spoke of 'all-German jurisdiction in West Germany' – made it much more difficult for us to deal with the problems of German unity. Encouraged by the Cold War and its repercussions, 'reunification' became the peculiar illusion of the second German Republic.

There was more talking than thinking about reunification in the Federal Republic of Germany; either that, or people did not speak as they thought. My own views were more complex than might be supposed from the verbal formula with which I opened meetings of the Berlin City Assembly: I regularly used to ask its members to demonstrate our 'firm determination' to see 'Germany, with its capital of Berlin, united again in freedom'. One hardly liked to admit to oneself that there would be no 'again', let alone make it the subject of public discussion. Dogmatic dispute which was almost verbal civil war on the subject of Bonn's policies left no room for judicious assessment. In the Cold War, the sledgehammer was preferred to the magnifying-glass. People who advised patient confidence were speaking to thin air.

In the discussions of those years in small, indeed very small groups, we naturally tried to work out how Germany could be brought together again, other than by pointlessly citing an alleged legal status, or by linking the operation, perilously, with military roll-back. I had cast in my lot with the West long before – in that I supported a constitutional state, a democratic constitution and freedom of the cultural heritage – and I was ready to pay the price for it. I had long hoped that Europe might come together as a great political force. I had very little doubt that Stalin would neither subdue Europe nor determine the Russian future. Russia would come up against America, Western Europe, other constellations of power in other parts of the world, and would have to come to terms as best it could.

At the SPD's party conference in Dortmund, the first to be

held after Schumacher's death in 1952, I put it like this: 'We do not necessarily support every project that is labelled "Western", but I believe we have always stood with the West, and still do, in support of freedom and human dignity; and for the sake of peace and freedom we also stand ready to defend democracy in a world where there is so little peace.' I added: 'Suppose that today or tomorrow there was a chance, in the context of world politics, of reunifying Germany on a basis of freedom, then we ought to agree even if such a Germany, reunited in freedom, could not – and I would like to add the rider "unfortunately" – be a part of the military policy of the Atlantic Alliance. Such a contingency would be far removed from playing around with ideas of neutrality, and I do not approve of the Federal Government's trying to discredit every idea proposing possible answers to the German question by calling it neutralism.' Finally, I urged the party to resist the inclination 'just to go on in the same old way, when we should be examining, changing and renewing our ideas'.

In the early years of the Federal Republic there was virtually no question of German *Ostpolitik* except in speeches such as this, which attracted little attention. It was to be years before any new German foreign policy was permissible and possible. Moreover, the whole concept of *Ostpolitik* was so loaded that one had to be very much on one's guard against mis-understandings; I for one never guessed that the word would be taken over some day into other languages, in the same way as *Weltanschauung* and *Gemütlichkeit*.

The term was loaded not just because of the murderous orgies of the recent past, but because of unthinking reversion to the attitudes of 'the good old days'. These were now reinforced by fears of revenge and the terror aroused by the peculiar features of the Soviet occupation. Even if all the poison of Nazi propaganda had been eliminated, which was improbable, fear of the Russians turned to a dour anti-Communism which became a part of early West German state doctrine.

We realized that nothing positive had come of the Potsdam

Conference of the late summer of 1945. The participants did indeed say, on paper, that Germany was not to be destroyed, was to be given the chance of returning to 'the comity of civilized nations', and was to be treated as a single economic unit. But the central administrations envisaged for this purpose had never been set up.

The victorious powers did not agree on whether they should help the Germans to live together in one state again; at Yalta the Three Powers, including Stalin, had still been in favour of partition. But then Stalin decided, from a position of great military success, to grab what there was to be grabbed. One thing was certain: the eastern border of Germany would not remain unchanged.

Looking back, it seems very strange that the Federal Government, like the political parties before it and contemporaneous with it, insisted on the borders at least of 1937, although they must have known that they would get no support for that demand anywhere in the world. The United States and Britain had agreed *de facto* to the new western border of Poland at Potsdam, and the subsequent French agreement was all the more amicable. Small adjustments did not seem out of the question, and I thought in the immediate post-war years they were quite possible. The passage of time made the whole question a subsection in that book of the past which so easily becomes a stumbling-block to the future. The lost rights of residence of millions of Germans were superseded by new rights of residence of millions of Poles who had moved to the West or were born there.

The combination of an abstract legal claim and concrete electoral opportunism prevented most of us from taking proper notice of these new facts. Even a man like Ernst Reuter seemed to have forgotten that at his last council meeting as Mayor of Magdeburg, in March 1933, he had predicted that Hitler meant war, and war meant the loss of the eastern part of Germany. I had been more cautious about what I put down on paper during the war, and I was persuaded to keep my ideas to myself. Very few of us knew that the conservative Carl Goerdeler – Mayor of Leipzig until 1937, when he began working against the Nazis – had written in 1938 that if war came, Germany would lose its territory east of the Oder.

Instead of the reunification of those territories that had not been otherwise disposed of, we saw rearmament on both sides. What seemed to some the most natural thing in the world was, to others, a move setting the seal on the division established in the Cold War. Or was it the payment of another debt for what the Hitler regime had done to Europe?

In those post-war years the Eastern zone – later the GDR – was treated as if it bore much more liability; as if the people there had lost the war even more comprehensively than their countrymen in the West. The Federal Republic had an easier time. People worked hard in both German states, but the results were much greater in the West because the economy was able to develop and had American aid available in the early stages. The Federal Republic was soon able to stand on its own feet, and to some extent paid for that with its self-appointed status as successor to the Reich, but it became a sovereign power only by stages. It was described as an economic giant and a political dwarf. Was it likely that striving for equal status in the West would go hand in hand with the wish to be able to protect our own interests in the East?

Not everyone thought that wish expedient or appropriate. In 1952, on behalf of the Foreign Affairs Committee of the Bundestag (still known as the 'Committee for the Occupation Statute and Foreign Affairs') I said that we all agreed German policy must be based on a special interest in peace and must try to establish normal relations with all states. However, the majority of the committee, colleagues in the coalition Government of the time, wanted it put on the record that a non-aligned position was always to be avoided. They wanted reunification through strength, and were convinced that the Soviet Union would retreat.

The Social Democrats, whose minority vote I also had to

record, were more sceptical. They thought a German *Ostpolitik* would be made more difficult, even impossible, by the forthcoming treaties with the victorious Western Powers. However, my political friends were anxious not to be labelled neutralists. In July 1952 I said in the Bundestag that the Social Democratic Parliamentary Party did not consist 'of people under an illusion and advocating total disarmament in this sadly imperfect and strife-torn world'. I stated my support for solidarity with the democracies, for equal participation in European and international co-operation, and for 'constant and earnest endeavours to solve the all-German question and the European crisis'.

I thought early rearmament a mistake, and would have preferred to counter the East German militarized Volkspolizei [People's Police] with a corresponding body. I was not guided in this by the pacifist dreams of my early youth; indeed, I was regarded as one of those Social Democrats who were quite well disposed towards the Army, and I took an interest in the conditions under which the Bundeswehr was to be built up. Some of us had learnt that you must be able to handle armed force if you do not want it to handle you.

Federal German policy made a straitjacket for itself. The Government expected the world to accept the theory of its identity whereby Bonn was the only legal successor to the German Reich, the Federal Republic alone was empowered to represent Germany, and 'the Zone' must be forced to hold free elections, as a consequence of which it would be bound to disappear.

Federal President Heinrich Lübke, a decent man, was allowed to go travelling around Africa and other parts of the Third World and to feel he had scored a success if he could get every communiqué to report, first, that the government he visited recognized only the Federal Republic as Germany, and second, that the Federal Republic could be expected to provide development aid, or more of it.

As Mayor of Berlin I was sent travelling half-way round the world to promote my city's cause, but at the beginning of the trip I was not supposed to visit Dag Hammarskjöld, Secretary-

General of the United Nations, at his office. Instead, Hammarskjöld came to my hotel. The idea was that if I visited the United Nations glass palace I might seem to have accepted the proposition of making Berlin a 'free city'. And who knew what might happen if the unpredictable members of the United Nations at large were encouraged to concern themselves with German affairs?

On another visit to New York soon afterwards, I was told by the Consul-General's deputy when he met me at the airport that a concession to the three-state theory had just been successfully defeated. Had I understood him correctly? Yes, they had induced the head porter of the Waldorf Astoria, where I usually stayed, to lower the Berlin flag. Alas, the former Berliners now living in New York had always been so pleased to see the flag with the Berlin bear flying!

In the conversation we held with Konrad Adenauer in my Berlin office in 1963, Heinrich von Brentano opined that the Hallstein doctrine should really have been called after him. The doctrine was formulated by Professor Wilhelm Grewe after various leading GDR functionaries visited Egypt, Iraq and India in 1957 and met with a friendly reception. It was first brought to bear on Cuba, early in 1963, because Fidel Castro had recognized the GDR. Diplomatic but not practical relations with Yugoslavia had already been broken off in 1957; Tito had allowed the GDR to send an ambassador to Belgrade instead of a mere envoy. Of course the doctrine did not apply to the Soviet Union. Adenauer had agreed to exchange ambassadors with the Soviets in the autumn of 1955. The Bonn Government that preceded the Grand Coalition had finally decided to establish diplomatic relations with other states in the Eastern bloc. Departure from doctrine was justified by the argument that the Federal Government could do nothing about the basic error of those states in accepting East German ambassadors.

The real issue, of course, was not one of protocol. And the real question remains: was there any genuine opportunity to find an all-German solution after 1945, and if so, why did it fail? A good deal written on this question was based on the assumption that no serious intentions could be expected on the Soviet side. Will this ever be satisfactorily cleared up? For the moment, we must be patient. Much still lies hidden in the archives. But do they or did they ever contain all the crucial points?

It is clear that there was no chance of avoiding the division of Europe at the end of the war; there could certainly not be any positive German influence. But why did no one draw conclusions in 1949 from the weathering of the Berlin blockade, and why were its lessons not learnt? The events of 1952 remain an open question. I did not and do not believe Stalin was prepared to give up 'his' part of Germany. But I thought and still think that the West would have been well advised to discover the facts of the matter as clearly as possible, and that it was incumbent upon the Federal Government to do so. It seems to me that it would have been in line with the general, overriding European interest to take vigorous measures at the time to counteract the manner in which the continent was drifting apart, and the consequent threat to peace. But such an attempt would have been vain unless the representatives of the newly founded German democracy had believed that they had the power for freedom of alliance, including military freedom of alliance, and unless the determining external factors had permitted the Germans to have their own way. Neither precondition existed.

In the note of 10 March 1952, and the second which followed in April (diplomats describe these, slightingly and incorrectly, as 'the Stalin notes'), it was proposed that a 'neutral' Germany should be set up and 'free elections' held. We now know that Ulbricht considered these proposals a threat to him and his regime, but fortunately the opposite side turned them down. In fact those in the West who did not want even to entertain the idea of freedom of alliance for Germany were automatically bound to reject anything, even the testing of the ground to see how the land lay.

WHAT UNITY? 149

Naturally there was a connection between Soviet soundings and the forthcoming treaty on the European Defence Community, to which the Federal Republic was to belong, vetoed by the French and replaced in 1955 by the Federal Republic's admission to NATO. In January 1955, before that admission, the USSR announced that it would permit 'free elections under international supervision' if all parts of Germany remained free of military ties. The outcome of this episode is well known: in May 1955, the Federal Republic joined NATO and the GDR joined the Warsaw Pact. Both German states had their sovereignty confirmed in principle, and many people felt that everything was now settled. A Four-Power conference held in Geneva in July 1955 produced no results. On his way back Khrushchev said, in East Berlin, that German reunification could come, first, only if it were linked with a system of collective security in Europe; second, if appropriate contacts developed between the two parts of Germany; and third, if the 'political and social achievements' of the GDR were not abandoned.

In 1955 I was spokesman to the German Bundestag on the treaties with the former Western occupying Powers, as I had been three years before. In the meantime important events had occurred of which those like me were hardly aware. Their significance was not properly understood at all until much later. I refer to the events in Moscow after Stalin's death and in connection with the 'East German' rising of 17 June 1953.

There is much evidence to show that it was this revolt which prevented the possibility of a major change in Soviet policy towards Germany. It is in the nature of spontaneous movements that deliberations on high-level policy cannot plan for them. Stalin was dead. In the group comprising his successors, the notorious secret police chief Beria, in contact with opposition German Communist politicians, attempted to steer a new course. In return for state unity, the East German SED was to make the sacrifice of going into opposition with the West German KPD. There was also talk of replacing Ulbricht, but it was nearly another twenty years before that happened. Vladimir Semyonov, previously at the Russian embassies in Berlin and Stockholm, subsequently one of the Soviet deputy foreign ministers and later still Ambassador to the Federal Republic, was then at the head of the Soviet Control Commission in the GDR. He went to Moscow and came back with new instructions.

Interested Germans – including people as deeply involved as I was – had no idea what was going on. Adenauer knew more, but he was not going to impart his knowledge to those who might ask questions. Winston Churchill, whom he visited in the middle of May, had passed on information from Moscow which would have been of a sort to bring about serious consideration of tendencies towards change in Soviet policy; the old Englishman had found no support in his own bureaucracy. The Americans, with whom Adenauer instantly communicated, also thought the hint should not be followed up. And yet it became clear – after some time, and at least to insiders – that something serious actually had been in the offing: after Beria's fall and execution at the end of June Ulbricht accused him, before the plenum of his Central Committee, of planning to sell off the GDR. Later on, Khrushchev also brought the charge of the intended 'sale' of the GDR against Malenkov.

Was this, perhaps, a chance which would not come again, one that arose because of a serious examination of the interests of Soviet security? An inexhaustible subject for analysis and speculation! It will surely surprise interested Germans of later generations that a parliamentary deputy like myself, involved in foreign policy, remained in the dark about tensions which – stirring enough even from the perspective of policy towards Germany – concerned the relationship of his own head of government with forthcoming alliance partners and what might be presumed to be tough long-term opponents.

There may be argument about dates and the assessment of statements and information. Discussion of Stalin's attitude in 1952 and the feuding of his successors in 1953 will go on for a long time. But there can be no disputing the fact that the year

1955, when the two German states were formally incorporated into their respective military alliances, was the real watershed. The so-called Germany Treaty of 1954, which established sovereignty, described the status of a reunified Germany as 'integrated into the community of Europe' (not, at that date, the European Community!). However, the years 1955 to 1958 still saw many attempts to keep talks going, even to bring about a certain détente.

One such attempt was the Eden Plan, called after Churchill's Foreign Secretary and successor, and proposed at the Geneva Four-Power Conference of 1955; the idea of zones of military inspection on both sides of the line dividing Europe failed because there was no hope of getting agreement on Germany. Adenauer prevailed on the West to discuss the border between a reunified Germany and the Eastern European countries. The content of this initiative was taken up and extended in the plan called by the name of the Polish Foreign Minister Adam Rapacki, which envisaged a nuclear-free zone in Europe; the first draft was put forward in October 1957, the second in February and the third in November of 1958. I would be exaggerating if I were to suggest that German policy, and not just the policy of the Government in office, had paid more than fleeting attention to the Warsaw initiative. It was so easy and so cheap to suspect Soviet influence behind it. But plans for a disengagement kept re-emerging, in altered forms.

George Kennan, the leading American diplomat and an expert on European affairs, explained in January 1957, to a Senate subcommittee on disarmament, that reduction, regrouping or withdrawal of the American and Soviet fighting forces stationed in Europe was advisable; so long as they faced each other in Germany there could be no progress on either the disarmament question or the question of German unity. In November 1957 Kennan's lectures for the BBC attracted considerable attention. He recommended the withdrawal of the Russians from Eastern Europe and freedom of alignment for Germany.

Khrushchev had struck a similar note early in 1957 in Delhi:

he said he would agree to a simultaneous withdrawal of the Soviet Union and of NATO from Central Europe. The previous year, the twentieth conference of the Soviet Communist Party had taken place in an atmosphere promising not just de-Stalinization but peaceful coexistence; the belief, attributed to the Chinese, that wars could not be avoided was firmly rejected.

On the last day of 1956 Ulbricht, certainly not without discussion with Moscow, had called for a conference between the two German states – as an interim solution leading to possible reunification. In 1958 Moscow made its bid for a German peace treaty linked to the prospect of a European conference on security. Khrushchev also urged a summit conference of the two alliances and the neutral powers to discuss the Rapacki Plan and the peace treaty. Early in 1959, although by then it was overshadowed by the Berlin ultimatum, he followed this up with the Soviet plan for a peace treaty with both German states or a confederation.

On the Western side, the last joint proposal for 'reunification' was a plan named after Dulles's successor Christian Herter, put forward at the Geneva conference of the foreign ministers of the Four Powers in 1959. I went to Geneva twice, in the middle of June and the end of July, to no avail. The talks broke down.

As a consequence, those who deplored German inflexibility, particularly on the American side, expressed their impatience. There were loud accusations that the Germans were trying to assert their outdated positions by playing games with the means of nuclear destruction held by the powers that were protecting the Germans themselves.

Should the SPD's 1959 Germany Plan be classed with these abortive efforts? Was it the last link in that chain? It worked on assumptions that were not actually false, just not wholly valid. Again, although there was a difference between confederation plans that came from Germany and those that came from the think-tanks of the victorious powers, past years had shown that none of them bore fruit. Herbert Wehner swept that last plan off the table even faster than he had put it there.

Nothing could disguise the fact that a new policy was needed to overcome the obvious loss of any sense of reality. Furthermore, the Western powers were expressing increasing dissatisfaction with the sterilities of Bonn. However, the change of course that almost everyone thought natural a few years later was not easy to make. Everyone could see that the claim for the Federal Republic alone to represent Germany was invalid. But how could it be superseded? What could take its place? At a later date I said of the new *Ostpolitik*: 'Like the rest of us, I did not want to let unresolved questions from the past prevent us from shaping the future.' I was speaking of ideas that had been in my mind before they were actually given expression.

Insistence on German legal claims – sometimes purely imaginary ones – and a faith in Allied guarantees which was often mocked for its naïvety, did nothing at all to promote the German cause.

Five years later I became Foreign Minister, and asked the outgoing state secretary – Karl Carstens, later President of the Federal Republic from 1979 to 1984 – to acquaint me with various confidential matters. He had prepared some notes which dealt not with any steps towards state unification, but with the ending of attempts to deny the GDR international recognition; it had become increasingly difficult to object to its membership of international organizations. As a result, the Federal German claim to 'sole representation' could at best be maintained for a while only if military expenditure and funds for development aid were much increased. Two months before, the state secretary had told the Federal Cabinet, then still headed by Ludwig Erhard, that the time for what was called an 'active policy of reunification' was past.

Demands for a different policy could no longer be rejected point-blank. But changing course turned out to be very difficult.

The Difficulty of Changing Course

Early in December 1966 Bonn had a new government – a coalition of the two main parties. I was Federal Minister for Foreign Affairs and Deputy Chancellor. I had to leave behind the Berlin job I had grown to like.

I had not aspired to the position in Bonn at that time or in those circumstances. I did not like the idea of the Grand Coalition, but no better solution seemed available. When I was persuaded to join it, the Chancellor-designate had already promised the Foreign Ministry to his fellow Swabian Eugen Gerstenmaier. Gerstenmaier said later that he should not have released Kurt-Georg Kiesinger from his word, but ought to have put some tough questions about 'the formation of that Government'. He became increasingly bitter during the Grand Coalition, when his friends in his own party forced him out of office as President of the Bundestag, on the grotesque grounds that he – a July Plot veteran – should not have claimed the compensation to which he was legally entitled.

The alliance in government of the two main parties worked quite well in home politics. In foreign politics it creaked, since a considerable number of Christian Democrats, and the Bavarian Christian Socialists in particular, did not relish the task of sweeping fictions and illusions aside. There was no great gulf between Kiesinger and myself, merely that distance created by our different lives and careers. 'King Silver-tongue', as Kiesinger was called behind his back and by some organs of the press, was ten years older than I was. He had distinguished himself in the Bundestag by his verbal skill in interpreting his Chancellor's intentions while always leaving room for potential common ground. Adenauer is said to have borne him a long-standing grudge for pleading in September 1949, at a meeting of the CDU Parliamentary Party preceding the first Federal Parliament, for a presidential candidate whom they could elect in unanimity with the Social Democrats. When he was passed over in Bonn in the various government reshuffles, he accepted the premiership of Baden-Württemberg in 1957. In the years that followed we had more than fleeting contact through the Bundesrat [the Federal upper house] and in meetings of the leaders of the *Länder*.

Kiesinger was too intelligent and too cultured to have had more than token Nazi party membership. He never hid the fact that he had once fallen prey to delusions, like many another, and he did not claim to have worked in the Resistance. His post-war expressions of democratic feeling were not to everyone's taste, but there was no reason to doubt the intellectual basis of his political commitment. Kiesinger, a Swabian committed to the idea of Europe, agreed with me that Federal foreign policy needed modification, correction and further development. Something had to be done to ease our relationship with Washington, which still dominated our foreign policy and was rather the worse for wear, and not simply because of an argument about compensatory payments for the fighting forces stationed in Germany. Our relations with Paris, which were under severe strain, had also eased. Erhard was not at all on the same wavelength as de Gaulle, and he let the Texan in the White House poke fun at him. He also had to face a home-grown recession, the first since the war. Adenauer, who had predicted Erhard's failure, did what he could to promote it, although his powers were now fading.

Foreign affairs at this time were subject to a multiplicity of small changes rather than major upheavals. The presidency of Lyndon B. Johnson sank in the morass of Vietnam; at the end of 1968 Richard Nixon was elected by a very narrow majority. In the Soviet Union, the conservative leadership group around Brezhnev consolidated itself after the fall of Khrushchev in 1964. Relations between Moscow and Beijing were fast deteriorating. In France, the May riots of 1968 convulsed de Gaulle's presidency. The General retired the following year and Georges Pompidou took over, guiding the country along moderately conservative lines.

The Cold War had passed its peak. The world situation had changed. Legitimate national interests required a spring-cleaning of Federal German policy towards Moscow and its allies. We knew where we belonged, and we realized that loyalty to and friendship with the West must be complemented by adjustment to and co-operation with the East.

While the Social Democratic side argued strongly for 'recon-ciliation', and wanted the consideration of measures which would limit arms, such as the inclusion of the GDR in legally binding non-aggression pacts, our coalition partners raised objections, and were unwilling to accept the idea of a new policy. In the statement of government policy, old right-wing positions – or what were seen as old right-wing positions – reappeared, but to many people's surprise the Soviet Union was given priority in the section on foreign policy. Europe was again regarded as more than a fossilized product of the East–West conflict; hence, over and above the question of Western Euro-pean union, our readiness to co-operate to the best of our ability and search for new points of departure towards the creation of a peaceful European order.

It was said that the aim of peace and understanding was the beginning and end and the whole basis of our foreign policy. I added that European politics must be a never-ending attempt to investigate areas of common interest, extend them and make them fruitful, and to neutralize distrust and finally over-come it through material co-operation. I thought that improve-ments in the lives of people in a divided Germany could be achieved if we made the active securing of peace the common denominator of our foreign policy. We hoped that such a course would contribute to the preservation of our essential nationhood.

My colleagues in the Foreign Ministry, the vast majority of them extremely able and loyal, helped me to define German interests more clearly. When I went to Paris in December 1966 it was understood by the French and by the Council of NATO, meeting there for the last time before its move to Brussels, that we were setting to work without arrogance but with new self-confidence. On my first visit to Washington as Foreign Minister in early 1967, I made it very clear that we intended to represent our own interests not arrogantly but with determination. I would not accept any mistaken ideas of continuity, or that faith in miraculous legal formulae whereby Hitler's war was ostensibly consigned to oblivion or its consequences rescinded. Not everyone was pleased, of course, when I stated my conviction (and now I stated it with the authority of my governmental office in Bonn) that Nazism, even repackaged Nazism, indeed any kind of poisonous nationalism at all, was a betrayal of both one's country and one's people.

Kiesinger did not lack for good intentions, but he did lack the resolution necessary if the leopard is to change his spots. It was difficult for many of his entourage to admit publicly all the crimes of the Nazi leadership, and the necessity of taking new realities as the point of departure. 'My' Federal Chancellor did bring himself to answer letters from the other Germany, which was something, but he would rather have had half the world laugh at him than dignify the GDR by the name of a state; he insisted on calling it a 'phenomenon'. In the Foreign Ministry we found it helpful not to have to speak of 'the Soviet zone' all the time; when I spoke of 'the other part of Germany' [der andere Teil Deutschlands] it immediately though briefly became known by the initials ATD. Those whose view of things was solely black and white – or perhaps I should say black and red – refused to see that major changes were coming in the East, changes with much potential for conflict, but changes which might be helpful. To that extent, Kiesinger was in an easier position than I was when the Prague Spring failed in 1968. He felt confirmed in his view that Communism (others said socialism) and freedom could not be reconciled, and that that was the end of the matter.

The foreign policy of the Grand Coalition did not revolve solely around the transition to a new Ostpolitik. By far the greater part of our work was concerned with relations with the protecting powers, NATO and the EEC, and our numerous old and new trade partners in many parts of the world. However, such affairs no longer concealed the blank spaces on the map: from the Federal German point of view, the blank spaces were the Communist-ruled states.

Just how difficult it would be to catch up with the new realities became evident at the turn of the year in 1966–7, when the Americans, the British and the Russians were reaching agreement on a nuclear non-proliferation treaty. Secretary of State Dean Rusk gave me the text of the first two articles of the draft treaty when we met at the Council of NATO in Paris in December 1966. Kiesinger, influenced by prejudices not all of which were his own, agreed with de Gaulle in suspecting 'nuclear complicity' between the super-powers. Adenauer was reminded of the Morgenthau Plan. Franz Josef Strauss painted a picture of the dangers of 'a new Versailles of cosmic extent'. People were led to believe that their security would be threatened and that the economy would be bound to suffer.

At the turn of the year I went to Sicily for a week, worked my way through the files, and wrote an account of what our policy in this area should be. At the Foreign Ministry they thought this an odd way of working, but they were glad to have someone marking out the road ahead.

The non-proliferation treaty threatened to become a kind of psychological test of tension within the Grand Coalition. In fact it was not until we had a new government that the treaty was finally signed, in November 1969. Ratification had to wait several more years. This was not the only project that had to be put on a back burner.

The fear of a 'Versailles of cosmic extent' was wide of the mark. But the belief that it would be difficult to keep the number of nuclear states down to five proved correct, and so did the view that the great majority of states would not consent to permanent renunciation of nuclear weapons if the minority, so clearly set apart from them, was not willing to take the first steps towards arms limitation and disarmament.

In 1968 the nuclear states had to be shown the moral and political necessity of disarming; they had to be persuaded to run down their arsenals of nuclear weapons and if possible dismantle them entirely – such ideas were already being formulated at the time. The non-nuclear states were expected to make a contribution to world peace by renouncing nuclear arms. The non-proliferation treaty was thus conceived as a bridge on the way to arms control and arms limitation; however, no one thought that disarmament could be a quick process. Article 6 of the treaty did mention a kind of duty to disarm, but it was many years before attempts to make any progress bore fruit. The nuclear arsenals were even topped up, causing non-nuclear nations to express their impatience distinctly at the review conferences held every five years. In the end, the number of states possessing nuclear arms grew no fewer over the years, and the number of those on the verge of possessing them most certainly did not. It was generally recognized that, from the global perspective, this terrain was a very difficult one to survey. Treaty or no treaty, more nuclear means of destruction were stationed on German soil than in any comparable area.

It looked as if the Kremlin leadership was anxious for friendly contact with the Grand Coalition government, but then the Ambassador, Semyon Zarapkin, was called off. There seemed to be some fear in Moscow that we wanted to play off the Soviets' Eastern partners against them. Ulbricht made difficulties for reasons of his own. An exchange of notes between Germany and the Soviet Union on the subject of non-aggression remained nothing but paper. However, attitudes did not harden any further.

With Consul-General Sven Backlund, later Ambassador to Bonn, acting as intermediary, I had several meetings in Berlin with Ambassador Pyotr Abrasimov between May and November 1966, some of them at his Embassy in the Unter den Linden; at a dinner in October he introduced me to the world-famous cellist Slava Rostropovich, who was still living in Moscow at that time; we have been friends ever since.

The discussions of those years touched on subjects – with reference to the chairmanship of my party – which went far beyond the problems of Berlin and included various aspects of the future German–Soviet relationship. It was as if we guessed there were complications in the air.

In the late autumn of that eventful year Abrasimov invited me to Moscow, and I did not decline the invitation. A little later the Soviet Ambassador to Bonn, Smirnov, repeated it at a dinner with Berthold Beitz, and even told me where I would be staying in Moscow. However, the Moscow visit never took place because I became Foreign Minister. Abrasimov did not hide his dissatisfaction with the formation of the Grand Coalition, but he managed to adjust to it.

I had thought kindly of Smirnov ever since 1960, when he sent me an interesting memorandum which went to the Federal Government at the same time, but was not deemed worthy of further consideration. It suggested that West Berlin, as a 'free city', could have closer ties with the Federal Republic, and become a forum of contacts between the two parts of Germany.

At the time, in the summer of 1960, the Soviet Foreign Minister Andrei Gromyko had tried to take matters further. When he visited Vienna he gave Bruno Kreisky a document urging me to enter into negotiation with the Government of the USSR. That was impossible; I was not empowered to do so, and Kreisky's idea that Adenauer and I might be able to go to Moscow together ignored the difference between German and Austrian conditions. Perhaps we did miss an opportunity then, but subsequently the situation changed anyway.

That was obvious when – rather unconventionally for a Federal German Foreign Minister – I visited Abrasimov at his embassy before the summer break in 1968. It was a long and interesting evening, and successful in a limited way. While we were eating, the Ambassador received a call from Leonid Brezhnev, and he was very anxious to emphasize that his side did not want any aggravation of the situation in and around Berlin. Abrasimov therefore reacted positively to my suggestion of making a lump-sum payment for autobahn costs; when I mentioned this to the Foreign Ministers of the Three Powers a little later, Dean Rusk said that such an agreement would make matters much easier. I also persuaded Abrasimov to look more closely at the issue of a non-aggression treaty, and we began a very useful discussion. I summed it up in the Bundestag by saying that 'after a conversation the importance of which had been greatly exaggerated' I had no reason to think that the Soviet Union did not recognize the real importance of our proposals.

In 1968 I made another Soviet contact outside the circumstances of ordinary routine, with Andrei Gromyko in New York. I had been taking part in the first conference of the non-nuclear states held in Geneva, and went on from there to New York; there was an 'informal' meeting of the NATO foreign ministers at the UN General Assembly, and my conversation with the Soviet Foreign Minister was also 'informal'. It had been arranged by a journalist – Otto Leichter, an Austrian friend who represented the dpa agency in New York – and it took place in the USSR's United Nations Embassy. Gromyko was accompanied by Semyonov, the old expert on German affairs. I was accompanied by Egon Bahr, who was soon to spend many days in Moscow with Gromyko, working out the essential features of the treaty that I signed in August 1970.

I found Gromyko more agreeable than the picture I had formed of a caustic 'Mr Nyet'. He seemed friendly and relaxed, and reserved in a pleasant, almost British way. His skill made itself unobtrusively felt; his memory was said to be phenomenal. My impressions were reinforced when we met again in the autumn of 1969. I had flown to New York especially for this meeting, although – or perhaps because – Bundestag elections were imminent. This time Gromyko was accompanied by Valentin Falin, whose task in the Foreign Ministry was to work on the issues connected with our forthcoming treaty. Later he was a highly regarded Ambassador to Bonn, and indeed a friend of some of us. Gorbachev brought him into the inner circle of his advisers.

The content of both conversations largely anticipated matters with which we would be concerned in drawing up the Moscow Treaty. Gromyko was inflexible on the matter of the frontiers established after the Second World War; he said the issue was 'a matter of war and peace'. On the other hand, he said, he did not see the Germans as 'the eternal enemy', and they had no need to fear, in connection with the non-proliferation treaty, that the Soviet Union would keep open its option of invoking the enemy states clause of the UN Charter and derive therefrom a right to intervene. The improvement in the German–Soviet climate in 1969 seemed to be connected with Moscow's problems in the Far East. Ambassador Zarapkin had already visited me that spring, to inform us on his government's behalf – and in some agitation – of the tense situation with China; there had been skirmishes between border troops on the Ussuri River in early March.

In the first half of 1969 I had half a dozen long conversations with the Soviet Ambassador, who also visited me at Bühlerhöhe, where I was recovering from pleurisy. After the summer break we continued our exchange of opinions, and in September Moscow reacted officially to our initiative on non-aggression, offering to negotiate. I thought that the Soviet interest in economic co-operation would be the crucial factor now, and I believed the difficulties of Russia's relationship with China had also played a part.

Or was the Soviet leadership chiefly swayed by the possibility that it was dealing with a future Federal Chancellor? Directly after the elections, on 28 October, Zarapkin came to see me and conveyed the Kremlin's hope that the new Federal Government would normalize relations with the Eastern European states and pave the way for détente in Europe.

A special significance, one that almost everyone could recognize, was attached to relations with the Soviet Union. It was no use trying to conduct relations separately with the states lying between Germany and Russia; the Foreign Ministry had tried it before my time. In agreement with the Social Democrats, trade missions had been set up in 1963–4 in Warsaw, Bucharest, Budapest and Sofia. Prague was opposed for a long time to the involvement of Berlin, but we set up another trade mission there in the summer of 1967. In the spring of 1966 Foreign Minister Schröder, again after agreement with the Social Democrats, had sent a 'peace note' to all states including those of Eastern Europe, expressing willingness to exchange declarations of non-aggression. The Kiesinger Government put the offer in such a way that the GDR too could have been included.

Diplomatic relations with Romania were an exception. I had agreed to their establishment with my colleague Corneliu Manescu in Bonn early in 1967, and in the summer of that year I myself went to Bucharest. Nicolae Ceausescu was still capable of rational communication at the time.

During my visit to Bucharest, one of those storms in a teacup not uncommon in Bonn politics broke, over a tiny addition I made to a pre-written after-dinner speech. The text said that in working for European security we agreed on the necessity of setting out from existing realities. My addition was that this applied to the two political systems at present existing on German soil. We had to relieve people of their sense of insecurity and their fear of war. This addition was a consequence of questions I had been asked during dinner. The near-hysterical reaction in the Federal capital was hard to understand, and showed that inclusion of the other German state still met with much resistance.

Others had also let it be seen that they were interested in normalized relations, but when they asked permission they failed to get it. The Warsaw Pact sealed itself off again – at the behest of East Berlin in particular – although not for long. Ulbricht persuaded Warsaw and Prague to form an 'iron tri-angle' once more, pursuing a counter-doctrine: full diplomatic relations with us only if the GDR and the Oder–Neisse Line were recognized in international law, West Berlin accepted as an 'independent political unit', the Munich Agreement declared 'invalid from the outset', and an undertaking of permanent renunciation of nuclear weapons given. A matter peripheral to our endeavours to normalize relations with the Soviet Union and its allies, but still one of importance to European politics, was the restoration of full diplomatic relations with Yugoslavia. I went to Belgrade in the early summer of 1968, and went on to see President Tito in Brioni. Once again I had the assistance of a journalist in making contact; in this case a Yugoslavian correspondent who was a friend from Berlin days.

A hint of movement had entered our relations with Poland a few months before the Prague crisis of 1968. At the Nuremberg party conference in March of that year I had spoken in favour of 'the recognition and respecting of the Oder–Neisse Line'. I was convinced that the same historical rank had to be accorded to reconciliation between Poles and Germans as to the friendship between Germany and France.

Although my speech could hardly have surprised anyone, it still created a stir. Kiesinger, with whom I spoke on the phone, said correctly that there would be trouble with those who spoke for the people who had been driven out of their old territories. I pointed out to him that the Federal Chancellor was responsible for the guidelines of governmental policy, but not for those of the Social Democratic Party. The party conference backed me, and Gomulka picked up the ball thrown in Nuremberg. My narrow electoral success in the following year was achieved, despite the ever-present efforts of demagogy, in the context of the border question.

As Foreign Minister and indeed before, I was in no doubt that our *Ostpolitik* must be firmly safeguarded in the West. The ghost of Rapallo loomed ominously, although nothing worse had happened at that coastal resort near Genoa in 1922 than the ending of a state of war with Russia and agreement on most-favoured-nation status in economic co-operation. On the other hand, I saw more clearly than some that détente between the Great Powers – fragile as it was – would be bound to fail without us. German policies had considerable influence at the all-European level and beyond.

The NATO ministerial conference of December 1966 was the first in which I took part as Foreign Minister. What I had to say was heard with some curiosity and a good deal of friendly agreement. The Federal Republic, I said, was determined to play its part with a policy that aimed for détente without endangering security. It had often been suggested that we could make a contribution to overcoming tension: 'And so we will – in line with our own interests and our duties within the Alliance.' The subject on hand was described as the 'reform of the Alliance', and the double function of defence and détente defined as a new task in international politics.

The same subject was discussed in June 1967 in Luxembourg, and next December in Brussels. The Belgian Foreign Minister Pierre Harmel had done the preliminary work on the definition of the Alliance's future task, and for this reason the report adopted at the end of 1967 bore his name. I was in the confidence of the Christian Socialist Harmel. During the 1969 election campaign, after I had made a brief detour to visit Brussels, he took me to the airport and told me that my friends and I must remain in power – for Europe's sake.

The NATO ministerial conference in the Icelandic capital at the end of June 1968 was a particularly important one. It was to have been the turn of Couve de Murville to chair it, but he was kept at home because of the May riots in France, and passed the chairmanship on to me. The 'Reykjavik signal' formulated there entailed asking Moscow and the Warsaw Pact to consider negotiations on a proportional reduction of armed forces. The 'signal', which I helped to draft, spoke of a 'process'. I argued for beginning the reduction of forces where it was most needed, in Central Europe. Exploratory discussions by the Allies with Moscow and the Warsaw Pact at an early date would be desirable, and I also made it clear that the other part of Germany could not remain excluded from such considerations.

This initiative led to the Vienna talks on balanced troop

reductions, but before anything could be done it foundered on the Soviet invasion of Czechoslovakia. This was a severe blow to our neighbours, and a serious setback for our policy.

The month after the Soviet punitive action against Prague, I spoke at the League of Nations Palace in Geneva at the first conference of the non-nuclear states. I referred to the shattering blow of the Prague tragedy: 'We do not countenance anyone's right to intervene.' And I added that 'those who have power, particularly nuclear power, do not thereby have either morality or wisdom on their side'. Moreover, I said: 'The great dangers for mankind proceed from the great powers, not the small ones.'

The Czech delegates, who were bound to silence, had tears in their eyes – as they did a little later at the UNESCO conference in Paris when I said: 'Let every nation determine its own path.' Everyone knew, I said, that nations feared for their independence. What seemed to have become the normal standards of international coexistence in the years after the Second World War were now endangered again. Our policy was to replace threats backed up by force, or a balance of terror, with a peaceful European order; even a show of strength by others ought not to be answered in such a way as to increase tension yet further.

If some of my Cabinet colleagues, such as Defence Minister Schröder, had had their way, the Federal Republic would have been conspicuous in Geneva by its absence. But I made it clear that I considered it dereliction of my official duty not to represent our interests there, and no one, not even Franz Josef Strauss, ventured to oppose that argument.

The Prague events were discussed in New York in the autumn of 1968, on the periphery of the UN General Assembly – we Germans remained only observers for a few more years – at a special meeting of NATO foreign ministers. We agreed that the terrible incident we had been unable to prevent was to be regarded as a relapse into evil forms of aggression, but that none the less we must continue on course to reduce East–West tensions. Discussion of some slight additional military precautions was purely for show; no one believed that the West was threatened any more or any less than before the Russians marched into Prague.

In April 1969 the NATO ministerial conference in Washington celebrated the Alliance's twenty years of existence, and sounded notes that were not only new but calculated to make a German Foreign Minister above all prick up his ears. President Nixon was inviting us to a meeting attended only by the ministers, with one colleague each: as we were approaching a time of negotiations, he said, it was important for us not to enter into a 'selective' form of détente determined by Moscow. Put more plainly, this meant that Washington wanted to have the last word; it was not difficult to recognize Henry Kissinger's handwriting. Nixon also told us about the present state of strategic nuclear arms. Six or seven years ago, during the Cuban crisis, the ratio of American to Soviet nuclear arms had been ten to one; that was no longer the case. Another six or seven years would see the two powers standing level. Finally, the President told us about the negotiations which later came into international terminology as SALT.

Despite or perhaps because of the Prague crisis, I used my influence at that 1969 NATO conference in Washington to urge that ideas of a European security conference should not be left to the propaganda of the Eastern side, but that we should discuss them constructively; to my mind, that entailed the desired Europeanization of *Ostpolitik*. The aged Italian Socialist leader Pietro Nenni, briefly Foreign Minister of his country, took my ideas a step further and said that the West should itself take the initiative for a security conference.

At their conference in Budapest the previous year the governments of the Warsaw Pact had issued a statement which looked worth examining – and not just because it omitted the usual attacks on Washington and Bonn. I thought we should take soundings to see what was in it, but without any preconditions, and with insistence on the participation of our North American partners. This would establish their presence on grounds going beyond those of a victorious power. Henry Kissinger took exception to this idea as an impertinence. Moreover, I thought, the conference should take place only if there was a reasonable prospect of making progress. Meanwhile, we should begin public discussion of partial aspects, at least, of European security. That was in fact the route pursued – if not with special ardour, but still pursued – by the Western Alliance.

The Italian Communists gave us some hints about the Budapest meeting of the Warsaw Pact countries and other events in Eastern Europe. My ex-Communist friend Leo Bauer, who had returned from the Soviet Union after years of suffering, had made friends with the Italian Communist leader Pietro Longo during their internment together, and he now put the contact to good use. What he told us of his talks in Rome was extremely interesting, and it seems likely that the contact was of some significance in forming opinion on the Italian side as well.

At its December conference in 1969, which took place without me because I was no longer Foreign Minister, NATO made its support for a European security conference dependent on the achievement of progress over Berlin and in the negotiations between Bonn and Moscow. A few months earlier, the Finnish Government had circulated a memorandum intended to help with investigation of the prerequisites for a conference. On behalf of the Federal Government, I reacted with caution but not hostility. As Federal Chancellor I helped President Kekkonen to have Helsinki picked as the site of the conference. It took place in the summer of 1975.

I repeated both to the Bundestag in March 1969, and to the USA and NATO in Washington in April 1969, in the clearest possible terms, that we could not dispense with the participation of the United States and Canada at such a conference. At the same time, I left no one in any doubt that Federal German participation in a European security conference would have no point, or very little, if the relationship between the two parts of Germany had not been settled first. I did not overestimate the leverage I could gain from this point, but I could not prevent myself from hinting that if one of the bridal couple failed to turn up at the altar, the other partner would not be very happy about it.

Our Western partners in the Alliance took the hint. They availed themselves of our practical experience, and added a demand that a satisfactory Four-Power agreement on Berlin should be concluded first.

I was very keen that this initiative should not become just a routine exercise. Why should we leave this part of the peace process to the 'other side'? Why not use Federal German beliefs and interests to work out the internal connection between European security, arms limitation and nuclear non-proliferation? All three elements aroused the suspicion of the SPD's coalition partner. Kiesinger himself encountered considerable resistance on the right wing of his party, and I heard that the Bavarian CSU had threatened to leave the coalition. However, no one had expressed open opposition when I said, in December 1967, that we intended to work for a treaty which, as a result of proportional reduction in all fighting forces, would also lead to the progressive removal of nuclear weapons from Europe; in my Geneva speech I also brought up the subject of biological and chemical weapons.

Then, in the spring of 1969, Cambodia in distant south-east Asia precipitated a West German governmental crisis. With what was undoubtedly considerable Soviet influence being brought to bear, Prince Sihanouk – like the governments of Egypt and several other Arab states before him – recognized the GDR. Consequently, we were supposed to break off diplomatic relations. The dpa report on this reached me during a visit to Turkey; highly coloured descriptions of my angry reaction – 'This is too much!' – were quite correct. It was even assumed that I had made it clear, that evening by the Bosporus, that I would not be available for office in a second Grand Coalition Government.

I could not think it sensible to haul down our flag wherever our German rival's was hoisted. And it was hardly possible to keep the GDR out of important international institutions, starting with the World Health Organization. During a night-time Cabinet meeting a 'solution' was found, and became known as the Cambodian solution: relations with Phnom Penh would not be broken off but simply frozen. An inaccurate version of events would have it that Kiesinger had gone half-way to meet me in May 1969 through that freezing of relations. In fact I left the nocturnal Cabinet meeting before it finished, contemplating resignation, but it seemed an inappropriate move at the time, and moreover elections were imminent.

Altogether, I was not displeased with my brief three years as Foreign Minister. I considered the regional ambassadorial conferences that I headed in our Bonn headquarters, in Japan in 1967 and in the Ivory Coast and Chile in 1968, a great gain. I also remember with pleasure the helpful attitude that prevailed in the 'Foreign Ministers' Trade Union'. Later, I did what I could for some of its members who found themselves in difficulties at home. When it came to opening closed doors I myself found the support of my Scandinavian colleagues particularly valuable.

Détente – Whose Doing?

In September 1969 I thought the election result made govern-ment by a Social Democratic–Liberal coalition possible. During the election campaign the FDP Chairman Walter Scheel and I had been saying that the advent of a new government was desirable, even necessary, particularly for reasons of foreign policy.

The CDU had opened the champagne too soon at the Schaumburg Palace. The first projections of the result were wrong, and also misled the American President in Washington – or his security adviser, well versed as he was in German affairs.

Nixon telephoned Kiesinger and congratulated him on a non-existent election victory. Although Nixon was not without his prejudices, he did not mean to snub me. When we met at the White House for the first time after my election as Federal Chancellor, he said quite disarmingly that he had been given a wrong number that autumn evening. I answered that to err is human, particularly at such a distance.

The Social Democratic Party had good reason to feel satisfied with the election result. In spite of considerable reservations about the Grand Coalition, our share of the vote rose from 39.3 to 42.7 per cent. We had 224 seats, as against 202 last time; for the first time the number of directly elected Social Democratic deputies was higher than for the CDU/CSU. But the Free Democrats had dropped to 5.8 per cent of the vote, and had only 30 instead of their previous 49 seats. An interesting feature of the election was that the extreme right NPD, with only 4.3 per cent, had failed to get the 5 per cent of the vote needed to qualify for proportional representation; those votes were distributed to the other parties in the allocation of seats. If the NPD had got more than 5 per cent I should not have become Chancellor in 1969.

On the evening of the election Walter Scheel was so disappointed that we made no definite arrangements. But in a telephone conversation, he did not object when I told him what I intended to do: our two parties had a majority, and I would try to form the new Federal Government on that basis. The proposition received lukewarm support at best in the inner circle of the SPD leadership, but they agreed that I could try. I was not inclined to let anything prevent me.

Even on the night of the election I spoke of my feeling that now Hitler finally *had* lost the war. I did not hesitate to add that if I were elected I would consider myself Chancellor not of a vanquished but of a liberated Germany. I would be a reliable partner, but I would not follow in the footsteps of those who felt at ease in the role of time-servers and disregarded yes-men. I had to set out from the assumption that the world powers wanted to stabilize their interests, but would neither make our peace nor our contribution to a peaceful European order for us.

Many years before I became Chancellor I had to ask myself: what can your state do, what can the Federal Republic of Germany do, to make peace more secure? What can it do, what can you do, to overcome the consequences of the Second World War, reduce tension, and surmount the antagonisms that will no doubt continue to be felt, in order to construct a system of security and co-operation in Europe? A peace policy had to mean more than talking about peace, and it still does. It must entail more than applauding or criticizing others. In the Federal Republic of Germany, above all, it had to mean action and not just verbiage. We had to avoid getting bogged down in generalizations, and had to try to be equal to our country's specific role.

In other words: we should not expect others to find the answers we had to find for ourselves. We had to start out not from any imaginary situation, but from the real one as it had developed a quarter of a century after the war. We had to overcome a widespread propensity to self-delusion, and avoid confusing quasi-legalistic formulae with reality. Then and only then could we be capable of action on the international stage.

I was not happy about the concept of *Ostpolitik* as it was first ascribed to me and then identified with me. But how can you capture a term which has acquired a life of its own and been swiftly adopted into foreign languages? Why did I dislike the label? Because I was afraid it suggested that I regarded foreign policy as a chest from which you might pull out now one drawer, now another. Together with my colleagues, and not least my Foreign Minister and Deputy Chancellor, I assumed that we needed two things at the same time, and co-ordinated with each other: reliable partnership with the West, and the understanding with the East that was laboriously taking shape and must then be extended. I was aware that our national interests simply would not allow us to oscillate between West and East.

Reduced to basics, this meant that our efforts in *Ostpolitik* must be attuned to our Western partners and rooted in the political structure of the Atlantic Alliance. Even more simply: our *Ostpolitik* had to begin in the West. But developments since the Western treaties of 1955 meant that relations as normal and productive as possible were also called for with the Soviet Union and the other Warsaw Pact countries. Normalizing those relations was necessary for the Federal Republic to be able to protect its own interests in European co-operation on anything like an equal footing. We were therefore determined to do what we could to encourage peace on a basis of the utmost possible security – 'in awareness of our special responsibility in Europe and to the best of our ability, which we do not, however, overestimate'.

At the time, in the autumn of 1969, a West European summit conference of the six Common Market countries was imminent. It took place in The Hague at the beginning of December. We said that this conference could and perhaps would decide whether Western Europe took a brave step forward or plunged into a dangerous crisis. My government assumed that the European Economic Community would have to be made deeper and broader, and needed both the United Kingdom and the other countries that were willing to join. It must also find appropriate forms of co-operation with those European states which could not or would not join. We determined that German and French unanimity could be the deciding factor in this process. We would try to give our close contractual ties with France a steadiness which would be a model for the nature of relations between European partners. We declared our readiness to encourage closer co-operation in foreign policy, with the aim of helping the Western European states, step by step, to adopt a common stance on international political questions.

Another important point of departure was our assumption that the North Atlantic Alliance would continue to guarantee our security. Its firm coherence was the prerequisite for the kind of solidarity of conduct which could lead to détente in Europe.

Safeguarding peace was the first essential, whether we were concerned with a serious and tenacious effort to bring about proportional arms limitation, or with the guaranteeing of our own security policy. As part of the Western Alliance, we wanted to help bring equilibrium between West and East. We saw our contribution as defensive, which was how the Western Alliance soon came to see itself. The Bundeswehr, we said, was not suitable for offensive strategy, by virtue either of its training and structure or of its arms and equipment. At no price would I be moved from the defensive principle that lay at the heart of our defence policy.

It has sometimes been suggested, not always kindly, that my policies may have been motivated by doubts about the intentions of the United States. They were not. However, it is true that I took an evaluation of the interests and special problems of the United States into consideration, and assumed that American commitment to Europe would be reduced rather than increased over the years. But I stated with the utmost clarity that our close ties with the United States excluded any doubt about the binding nature of the duties they had undertaken towards Europe, the Federal Republic and West Berlin. Our common interest required neither additional assurances nor repeated declarations. They supported a more independent German policy in a more active partnership.

And what about keeping the Western powers informed? What about consulting them, in so far as their rights in connection with 'Germany as a whole' were affected? It is true that we wanted to represent ourselves – that goes for the East as well – and to that extent we wanted to be 'more equal' than before. We did observe the principle of regularly furnishing accurate information. However, Henry Kissinger was correct in saying that Brandt had not asked for permission, but for American co-operation in a political course whose direction was already determined.

You do not need to have read Kissinger's memoirs to know that there was ill-concealed suspicion in the Western capitals –

as far as I could see, it was least felt in London; in Paris, there were marked swings between friendly understanding and wild speculation; the Washington attitude was quite simple – Nixon's security adviser told my eminent colleague Paul Frank in 1970 that any détente with the Soviet Union would be America's doing.

Before our meeting in April 1970 Nixon invited me to spend a few days of relaxation at Camp David; I had come from El Paso, where I had been visiting Bundeswehr units and had heard, with helpless anger, the news of the murder of the kidnapped Ambassador Count Spreti in Guatemala. Henry Kissinger turned up at the President's retreat, and did not trouble to hide his suspicions. In later years, however, he set the record straight by several times 'congratulating' me on the achievements of German *Ostpolitik*. He was once heard to say that all we got in return for accepting the division of Germany was 'improvements in the political atmosphere'. Kissinger, powerful as a security adviser, and later Secretary of State under Presidents Nixon and Ford, thought in terms of the Concert of Powers and the classic secret diplomacy of the nineteenth century. He saw Europeans as pawns in the great game of the superpowers.

There have been all kinds of speculation, but some serious consideration too, as to whether the Government in Washington supported our *Ostpolitik* or simply accepted it with an ill grace.

In broad outline it could hardly dissent, for Nixon, advised by Kissinger, described his policy towards the Soviet Union as 'co-operation, not confrontation', thus picking up where Kennedy had left off. The US Government knew that we never dreamed of ceasing to co-operate with the West; indeed, we could not have done so.

The version of the story which says that we only followed the dictates of the USA is not true. German *Ostpolitik* had its own roots and its own reasons, but where I and my governmental policy were concerned it was never influenced by any illusion that we might go back and forth between the 'camps'.

I had no need to make up for any lack of loyal co-operation
and friendship with the United States.

As Mayor of Berlin, I had always found support and a
friendly welcome in the USA – including a ticker-tape parade in
February 1959 at the height of the Khrushchev ultimatum
period. I knew the presidents and a number of influential
senators; there had been a special friendship between
John F. Kennedy and me, but my meetings with Lyndon B.
Johnson were also marked by trust. Only when the Vietnam
war overshadowed American politics did Berlin show some
reservations.

I had known Richard Nixon since 1954, when he was Eisenhower's Vice-President. At the time, and later, he used to appeal
to the fact that we were born in the same year, and we got
along easily with each other. However, I have never been able
to forget that he was eager and active when the witch-hunts
of the McCarthy era were nearing their end, with all their
demoralizing effects in Germany and Europe as well as the
United States.

In our conversation of 10 April 1970 Richard Nixon said
point-blank that he had confidence in our policy, and knew we
had no intention of risking tried and true friendships. However,
we would have to expect that there might be some uncertainty
in France and England, and indeed in some quarters in the
USA. He would fully understand – was this a request? – if we
recognized the Oder–Neisse Line; after all, it was a fact by now.
The main point was the understanding between us that we
would keep in close touch over all East–West questions.

When I was back in Washington in the early summer of 1971
I was very pleased to see that doubts about German *Ostpolitik*,
as expressed by various people who either were or set themselves
up as experts on German affairs, had been dispelled. In any
case, neither the President nor his Secretary of State Bill Rogers,
who was succeeded by Kissinger, nor my old friends of the
Senate Foreign Affairs Committee, had ever entertained such
doubts.

However, men like Clay, McCloy and Dean Acheson, and in particular the elderly trade union leader George Meany, did express some anxiety, and took their fears to others as well as to the President. Acheson, who had been Truman's Secretary of State and had a great reputation, even spoke of a wild race towards Moscow.

I was well aware that there were considerable reservations in the Pentagon and the State Department, even if its spokesman repeatedly expressed his confidence in the Brandt Government. These reservations were encouraged by lobbyists and by the Bonn Opposition, which was bent on anything but a national consensus.

Rainer Barzel said, of his visit to Nixon in San Clemente in September 1970, that he saw little indication of support for Brandt. In January 1972, after a discussion with Kissinger, he struck another blow: it was the Soviet Union's intention, he said, to 'Finlandize' Western Europe, starting with the Federal Republic. The rumour of 'Finlandization' was remote from reality, and an insult to a brave little nation. The next day, Nixon was said to have told him: 'We stand by our old friends. My regards to Kiesinger and Schröder.'

It has often been claimed but never proved that what Henry Kissinger said to my face was not quite what he said behind my back. There were many who envied Kissinger his knowledge and skill – and envied, even more, the extraordinary career of a German Jewish lad from Fürth who had risen to become the second most powerful man in the most powerful country in the world.

I was never one of Kissinger's uncritical admirers; he was too old-fashioned for my taste, his borrowings from Metternich and Bismarck too noticeable. I will grant that he thought I went to work with too much speed and too little patience. He feared the Germans might fall back into their old ways of German nationalism (from Bismarck to Rapallo?). It was a fear that affected others too, yet one I thought and still think was unfounded. At heart, we were too independent for Kissinger's taste; he would have liked to keep us – and others as well – on a shorter leash. Henry Kissinger did not like to think of Europeans speaking with one voice. He preferred to juggle with Paris, London and Bonn, playing them off one against another, in the old style. And if his comment that he would rather have fourteen dwarfs than one giant is *trouvé*, then it is *bien trouvé*.

However that may be, in 1973 he managed to declare a European Year without consulting the European governments. His opposition to European–Arab dialogue fitted into the picture only too well. Kissinger wanted to ensure that there was a distinction between Europe's independent regional responsibility and its international co-responsibility. This was not the way to win the future. For the rest, he annoyed the French more than us Germans; we were cooler-headed, and used to putting up with a certain amount. He was not pleased when I indicated that the Helsinki Final Act would give additional grounds for the American presence in Europe: the USA, he intimated, had no need to legitimize its role in Europe.

I was relieved to find that President Nixon looked on our *Ostpolitik* with increasing favour. In the early summer of 1971, during my visit, he took a particular interest in the forthcoming Berlin Agreement. On 17 June, the anniversary of the Berlin uprising of 1953 and the 'Day of German Unity', I spoke to the American Council on Germany at the Waldorf-Astoria; those former friends of Germany McCloy and Clay were present, and seemed to have shed their own scepticism. I had spoken frankly of our aims and our responsibility and had given a sober and by no means exaggerated assessment of the situation, and perhaps that approach aroused sympathy. At the end of the year, when I visited Richard Nixon in Florida, he gave the provisional go-ahead, saying the USA would not tell the Germans what they should or should not do, but would leave them full freedom of action.

The fact that this could not be the last word was in the nature of the interests of world powers, and was only partly to do with the specific nature of *Ostpolitik*. At the beginning of March

1973, when the shadow of Watergate had fallen over the White House, Nixon expressed reservations again: he feared, he said, that détente might lead to euphoria. That would encourage movements in the USA supporting isolationism or unilateral disarmament. The Soviet Union did not want war, but would keep trying to drive a wedge between Europe and America. How far beyond our attempts at *Ostpolitik* this anxiety went, and how little it was actually founded on any distrust of myself and my government, was made clear in a letter written to me by Richard Nixon dated 8 May 1974: whatever the future might bring, he said, I was to be sure of his close personal friendship.

After my election as Federal Chancellor, I had said to anyone who would listen that the German people needed peace, in the full sense of the word, including peace with the peoples of the Soviet Union and all Eastern European nations. We were ready to make an honourable attempt at communication to overcome the consequences of the disaster brought on Europe by a criminal clique. However, I continued, we entertained no false hopes: interests, power relationships and social differences would not be dialectically resolved, nor should they be obscured. Our partners must know that the right of self-determination set out in the United Nations Charter applied to our nation too; we would not be talked out of our intention of claiming that right. However, I said, it was clear to me that only all-European rapprochement would enable the two parts of Germany to move towards each other.

I knew, therefore, that I cherished no illusions, and I did not think the work of reconciliation could be done easily or quickly. I thought it was time to start it. There were certain points at which we could pick up from the attempts of earlier Federal governments. An instance was the endeavour to conclude a binding agreement on the renunciation of armed force or the threat of it. We were convinced that a policy of non-aggression respecting the territorial integrity of all partners concerned would be a great gain for détente in Europe, and would be further encouraged by trade, technical co-operation and cultural exchange.

At a distance, it is hard to understand why the struggle for an *Ostpolitik* took such bitter forms. At the time I was surprised that some people who thought themselves conservative showed little interest in gaining more independence. At the beginning of my chancellorship, on 14 January 1970, speaking to the Bundestag, I said that those who were asking what we would get in return for *Ostpolitik* were faint-hearted and insufficiently patriotic. Addressing myself to them, I said: 'Is it nothing to make peace more secure for all our people? To take friendship with the peoples of the West, the North and the South, and add to it trust, conciliation and then friendship with the peoples of the East as well – is that nothing? And will not Germany itself then have more security and a better peace? Will not every one of its people profit? Put it like this: they will profit because there will be less fear; because burdens will be lighter; because people who have been unable to meet for years will be able to see each other again; because two people from the two states in Germany who are now parted by inhumane compulsion may perhaps be able to marry.' These, I said, were the criteria my government faced soberly, in clear awareness of the difficulties ahead, of the length of the road, of the calculated risk. This was the task we could set ourselves 'because we have confidence, and because we have good friends'.

In the Kremlin and the Crimea

Like many less prominent Russians, Leonid Brezhnev was inclined to overestimate the Germans. One reason may have had something to do with Marx and Engels, but for whom Lenin would have had no antecedents, so to speak. Another and more important reason was that the hated Germans had nearly captured Moscow even while they were simultaneously fighting the British and Americans. How far might they not get another time, with American equipment? And their post-1945 reconstruction was no small achievement...

There is no doubt that the Russian people and its leaders shared much the same feelings about the dark legacy of the Second World War. To quote Brezhnev: 'To change for the better is not a simple or an easy thing. A terrible past lies between our states and our peoples. The Soviet people lost twenty millions in the war unleashed by Hitler. Such a past cannot be erased from human memory. Many millions of Germans died in that war, too.' And memories, he said, lived on. Could the Soviet people be sure that foreign policies would lay a new foundation?

He made these remarks on the afternoon of 12 August 1970. He had been standing behind me in the Catherine Hall of the Kremlin as I, Alexei Kosygin and the two foreign ministers signed the Moscow Treaty. My presence had not originally been envisaged, but at the prompting of his Soviet counterpart, Foreign Minister Scheel had called me while I was on vacation in Norway and urged me to go to Moscow. It was a momentous date, and a significant treaty. In view of the burden it must still mean for many, I could not and would not decline to go. What Hitler's war had done could not be undone, but to alleviate its after-effects was as much a duty of patriotism as of European responsibility. Speaking in Moscow, I told my countrymen that the treaty endangered nothing and no one; its aim was to help open up the way forward.

Since I was going to commemorate the building of the Berlin Wall next day, 13 August, my hosts thought it prudent to claim that there were technical difficulties in transmitting my speech to Bonn. Speaking very loud and clear in the Embassy – in the safe assumption that I would be overheard – I announced that if necessary I would have an aircraft fly in from Bonn to take home the tape of my speech. The reaction was prompt: a high-ranking official whispered to me, on my way to lay a wreath at the Kremlin wall, that everything was now in order for the transmission. A fully fledged minister was mobilized. He accompanied me to the recording and never took his eyes off me.

My first impressions of Brezhnev in his gloomy office in the Kremlin that August afternoon were rather tedious. They could hardly be otherwise when he sat reading from a text for two hours or so. After I had replied, a second reading followed the first, and that left hardly any time for another answer, although we had had four hours at our disposal. Before inviting me to talk with him the General Secretary, without prior notification to our side, had turned up for the signing of the treaty. He also attended the drinks party afterwards but not the dinner, explaining that he had just been in hospital. When his poor health was not visibly troubling him, and if he did not happen to be reading a text at the time, the thickset Brezhnev appeared lively, almost restless. He loved telling and hearing jokes. He was curious about prominent people in other countries. 'You know Nixon. Does he really want peace?' Again, in June 1981 on the way to the airport, he asked me what he should think of Mitterrand. In between these occasions, a man had come to Bonn to question me about Jimmy Carter: the Muscovites found access to Carter's mind even more difficult than understanding Ronald Reagan at a later date. Small, cheap tricks were part of the repertory: at the end of that first discussion in the Kremlin Brezhnev said he hoped I knew that not everyone in my own party's leadership was my friend, but at least – so 'someone' had informed him in a note – I could rely on X (the name of a certain *Land* prime minister, incorrectly pronounced). A mixture of party apparatus and secret service can produce some strange results.

What did depress me about that first conversation was the lack of any really serious line of argument, and the obvious clinging to Stalinism. Firstly, Brezhnev really expected me to believe the official Party and Government version of the facts whereby 99.99 per cent of the population went to the polling booths in the Soviet Union, as in no other country, and almost without exception voted for the 'candidates of the Communist Party and independents'. Even the more sophisticated Kosygin, when I told him that I felt I had a clear majority of my countrymen behind me, did not blush to say that 99 per cent of the Soviet Union's population favoured the treaty. At the same time he mocked Social Democrats such as the Scandinavians: you could never tell whether they were still in power or out again, he said.

Secondly, Brezhnev was anxious to make it clear to me from the start that he did not want to be identified with Khrushchev's anti-Stalinist ideas. Stalin, he said, had achieved much, and after all the country had finally won the war under his leadership; he would return to favour. Leonid Ilyich certainly did not claim to be a reformer. I was never able to see him as a revolutionary either, more of an extremely powerful conservative administrator. However, I did not doubt his interest in peace, and I do not doubt it now. One of the most sobering feelings I had in the Kremlin was that Brezhnev would have been glad to see Stalin rehabilitated, for all his mania for extermination. Today Brezhnev, leader of the Soviet Union from 1964 to 1982, has been more or less demoted to the status of an unperson, accused of serious political omissions as well as nepotism and other weaknesses. For that very reason I thought it proper to tell Mikhail Gorbachev why I would not disown Brezhnev so far as the serious nature of our common efforts was concerned.

Americans like Henry Kissinger have come to similar conclusions in their assessment of co-operation with the Russians
at that time. I found Brezhnev not unsympathetic in personal
conversation, although talking to him was a rather unsettling
experience because of his selective grasp of reality and his
dependence on written notes; he probably relied on them in
other contexts too. However, I could hardly have chosen my
opposite number or have waited for Gorbachev to come along.
In 1970 I certainly did not expect to be welcomed to Moscow
by an intellectual giant or a great moralist.

Officially, my host in 1970 was not Brezhnev but Kosygin,
who as Chairman of the Council of Ministers ranked equal to
the General Secretary of the Party in the pecking order of the
time. A year later that had changed, with the General Secretary
now Number One in foreign policy as well; he bound the
Foreign Minister Andrei Gromyko to him more closely, partly
by making him a member of the Politburo. There was not much
more to be said in Moscow about the treaty. Kosygin, cultivated
and reserved in manner, an engineer from Leningrad who had
worked hard rather than successfully, spoke of 'a political act
to which the Soviet leadership and the whole world ascribe
great significance'. I replied that the text was important, but
what was made of it was even more important. Kosygin picked
the ball up. The morning after the treaty and the inevitable
official dinner he said he was in favour of 'less noise and more
results'. I assured him that I thought the contents of a bottle
mattered more than its label. He replied, varying the theme to
refer to the prospects of a European security conference: 'The
length of a meeting is no sign that progress is being made.' For
the rest, he said that war was no longer a political method, and
that the central problem of détente in Europe lay in relations
between the Soviet Union and the Federal Republic of Germany.

On 12 August 1970 both parties to the treaty promised to
solve any future disputes exclusively by peaceful means. This
pledge of non-aggression included an obligation not to violate
any existing European frontiers, including the Oder–Neisse

Line, and to make no territorial claims; we recognized the principle of the inviolability of borders. I did not see this as being at all inconsistent with making it as easy as possible to cross those borders. The very idea of our attacking the Soviet Union was pure fantasy! However, one could not very well say, out loud, that the Soviet promise of non-aggression carried a good deal more weight on that point. Explicit recognition was given to the validity of treaties and agreements concluded at an earlier date, thus including those between the Federal Republic and its Western allies. The preamble referred to the aims and principles of the United Nations. The aim of German unity through self-determination was not affected. In a special letter, endorsed by the Soviet Government, our Foreign Minister stated 'that this treaty does not contradict the political aim of the Federal Republic of Germany in working for a state of peace in Europe in which the German people regains its unity in free self-determination'.

The Opposition had been particularly anxious that European union should not be affected by the Moscow Treaty, and we took this into account. The expected extension of the EEC was discussed, and it was suggested that experts should have talks with Comecon. In Bonn in 1973 Brezhnev took the line that the Soviet Union was against bloc policies in economic questions. He did not see, he said, why you should go to Brussels when you wanted to buy something from Krupp in Essen; it would only complicate matters. On the other hand, the Soviet side did not ignore the existence of the EEC. Perhaps, he said, it would be a good idea to seek co-operation between the EEC and Comecon, whatever form such co-operation might take. However, one of the main consequences of the treaty nego-tiations was the dropping of reference to the enemy states clause of the UN Charter from the relations of the Soviet Union towards the Federal Republic.

The path to the conclusion of the treaty was a short one if the formation of the new Federal Government is regarded as its starting-point. I had entrusted the preliminary discussions in

Moscow to my experienced colleague Egon Bahr, now State Secretary in the Chancellery. However, the Ambassador felt slighted. There were others, both well- and ill-intentioned, who felt sure they would have done a better job and would not have acted under what they claimed was pressure of time. In fact, every position had been fought for and every phrase was carefully polished. When I visited Gromyko eighteen years later, before he vacated the position of President to which he was appointed at the beginning of the Gorbachev era, he had clear memories of the fifty-five hours of his time Bahr had taken up in February, March and May of 1970. Andrei Gromyko erected a small memorial to me in his memoirs, mentioning the great part I had played 'personally' in working out the treaty.

The result of Bahr's negotiations was approved in Bonn, and the Foreign Minister took over the final discussions; these brought some alterations providing the treaty with additional safeguards for those with misgivings and for serious critics.

There is a monument that stands a few kilometres from the airfield where I landed on 11 August 1970 (rather late because of a bomb scare before take-off – hence my comment on landing that 'We have arrived late, but we have arrived'). It marks the point where the German tanks were forced to turn back in 1941. But the trauma of mortal danger had roots going even further back. On the drive from the airport to the residence, Kosygin had the car stopped on the Lenin Hills and led me to the place where Napoleon had taken a last look back at the burning city of Moscow. He was evoking yet another piece of history.

What I would not take from Brezhnev were the personal reminiscences he served up of the day of the attack in June 1941. There had been a pact between Russians and Germans, he said, and good economic relations; he himself had seen a goods train laden with wheat on its way to the western border when the Luftwaffe began bombing. On the first day of the war it was his job as secretary of the district committee of Dniepropetrovsk to stop the transports bound for Germany. He recalled all this, he said, only to show how positively the Soviet people had felt towards Germany – and how unsuspecting their leaders were. The press had been full of pictures of Soviet–German co-operation! He also referred to co-operation with German firms in the old days and the inter-war period. Not a few of his colleagues, he said, had been trained in such firms as Krupp and Mannesmann. And then such treachery! (He implied that it was not the kind of thing you expected of an honourable partner.) He went on to reminiscences of the front, with melodramatic appeals to the 'comrades on the other side'. I was startled rather than impressed by this access of sentimentality. Truth and falsehood lie very close together when war reminiscences are exchanged. In the spring of 1973, when I gave a dinner for Brezhnev at the Venusberg in Bonn, Helmut Schmidt described his mixed feelings as a young officer on the Eastern Front; at the time, he said, he would not have thought it possible that there could be any chance of discussions between Germans and the Soviet leader after that terrible war. Brezhnev replied, proposing some highly emotional toasts. My Russian hosts too had tears in their eyes when, during my after-dinner speech, I read a passage from a letter written to his parents by a German soldier who never returned home after the invasion of the Soviet Union.

Early in the summer of 1970 Brezhnev had picked up a saying of Nixon's, to the effect that we should move from an era of confrontation into an era of negotiation. I could accept that, as well as some comments by the General Secretary in a speech about Communists and Social Democrats made in June of that year: principles should not be set aside, but there should be concrete examination of what might be done for peace and in the interests of the nations.

Brezhnev was always vague in discussion of the military elements of the peace policy. In our first conversation he actually stated, and probably meant in all seriousness, that arms limitation was 'not a subject of cardinal importance'. The Soviet Union and he himself, he said, supported full disarmament. He did not respond, even by implication, to the 'Reykjavik signal' with its ideas, developed by us through NATO, of proportional troop reductions. In the Crimea in 1971 I tried in vain to make him realize that there must be serious negotiations on reciprocal troop and arms reductions, and that these reductions must be balanced so that the global equilibrium was not upset. But Brezhnev did not see the point, either then or in Bonn in 1973. His advisers at home cannot have explained the problem of military imbalance in Europe to him, or the fact that there were two areas – co-operation and the building-up of trust on the one hand, and the reduction of military forces on the other – which had to be dealt with separately. The former issues were eventually discussed at Helsinki and its follow-up, the latter in Vienna.

Even later, when concrete steps were being considered, I could not see that Brezhnev expected any new thinking from the military leadership. This was particularly clear in the field of missiles. But once, when I spoke to him about the naval armaments race, I was surprised by his cheerful reaction: the Americans were well ahead, he said, 'but not so far ahead as before. And now,' he added, gesturing like a child playing pat-a-cake, 'we are baking a new submarine every week.' It was characteristic of the Brezhnev era that further armament and constant 'modernization' continued full speed ahead, irrespective of political détente. NATO did not weaken its forces during those years either, of course, and the American service concerned with such matters had to admit that it had over-estimated the rate of increase in the Soviet military budget by half.

In terms of military pragmatism, Brezhnev and Khrushchev were not so far apart. The latter said at the time of the Cuban crisis that the Soviet Union was making rockets like sausages coming out of a sausage-machine. At a New Year reception in 1960, after consuming a good deal of vodka, he even 'divulged' to Western ambassadors that there were fifty rockets ready for France and fifty for Britain, and thirty for the Federal Republic. When the French Ambassador's wife inquired how many were set aside for the USA, the jovial Khrushchev replied that that was a military secret.

The memoirs ascribed to him attacked those military leaders 'who seek, in their speeches and memoirs, to whitewash Stalin and put him back on his pedestal as the father of the people'. Brezhnev, as I have mentioned, thought differently, but both Russian leaders shared an alarming ideological narrowness in their thinking. After a few years of *glasnost* the top generals protested that responsibility which was not theirs had been laid at their door: it was the political rather than the military leadership that favoured the invasion of Afghanistan at Christmas 1979. In the fourth year of the Gorbachev era, moreover, it finally became possible for those in charge of foreign and military policy in Moscow to criticize a course which had placed too much emphasis on the military balance of power and propaganda successes in the seventies and early eighties.

The Kremlin leader was realistic about the Federal Republic's links with the West: there was no wish to separate us from our allies, he said, and no intention to make us pursue our future relations with the Soviet Union at the expense of relations with other states. Brezhnev said – so unctuously that it would have been bound to make one suspicious, had one not been suspicious anyway – 'We did not and do not have any such devious plans, and I believe this is an important factor.' Kosygin too emphasized that there was no desire for the treaty to distance us from our Western allies. 'We have no such aim in view, nor would it be realistic.' There was no gainsaying that last point.

In Moscow in 1970 we were concerned, over and beyond many small details, with the transition to a new period in European post-war history. At the same time I had an opportunity to set the parameters for settling certain practical questions. In the first place, there was Berlin: I said we would ratify the Moscow Treaty only when the Four Powers had concluded their negotiations on Berlin satisfactorily. If we wanted détente, Berlin could not remain a factor in the Cold War; it must play a part in peaceful co-operation instead of being an apple of discord. This package deal annoyed Brezhnev. He thought my attitude implied giving the USA a right of veto. In fact many points were not settled, but the misuse of the Berlin question as a means of making trouble was reduced, although unfortunately not eliminated. At the end of October 1970 Gromyko let it be known indirectly, at a meeting with Scheel in the Taunus before the Hessian Landtag elections, that the Soviet Union could live with our package deal on Berlin.

We also had our sights set on human rights, which we described as 'humanitarian questions' to make them sound more innocuous. We were concerned for the repatriation of people in the Soviet Union who were German citizens when the war broke out, and with actual cases of the reuniting of families. Kosygin said that the two Red Cross associations should continue to deal with the matter (as they had been all along, although not with much success up to that time); I managed to lend a hand here, even when I was no longer occupied with government business. In the years after 1970 many people of German origin were able to emigrate from the Soviet Union, and eventually better general living conditions for Soviet citizens of German nationality even seemed a possibility. Without wishing to boast, I can say that over the years I was able to intervene in a number of cases involving the fate of so-called dissidents. The results were modest; in some cases intellectuals who would rather have stayed at home emigrated, in others they found that their conditions became easier.

Thirdly, of course, there were economic interests at stake: I wanted a clear statement by the Russians from the start that further reparation payments – in addition to those imposed after the war – would not be expected of us. Brezhnev took his time over responding; next year in the Crimea he said, briefly, that the question did not arise in the Soviet Union. Intelligent commentators could have discovered that this was the only point where comparison to Rapallo was in the least relevant.

Both Brezhnev and Kosygin spoke of 'great, indeed mighty prospects' in the economic, scientific and technological spheres;

above all, they were eager to sell us the idea of co-operation in exploiting the mineral wealth of Siberia. This was and remained a constant factor in German–Russian discussions. I looked the subject up and found that Karl Radek, the Bolshevist expert on German affairs, who was of Polish origin and died in one of Stalin's camps, told the leader of the Eastern Section in the Foreign Ministry as early as 1922 that: 'Germany has the advantage of being able to exploit the great Russian stocks of raw materials. German labour will now find support in Russia.'

Many castles in the air were built in the years that followed. Kosygin was not inclined to exuberance: 'We are not a charity and nor are you; co-operation must benefit both sides.' He also knew that there was vociferous complaint from interested German parties about the cumbersome and often unproductive procedures of Soviet economic administration. Trade with the Soviet Union, however, did come to develop very satisfactorily by comparison with trade figures at the start.

The Moscow Treaty was of importance both in principle and in practice for the Government I led. It was significant for European politics as a whole, and not just for us in Bonn, to see the spectre of the eternal German threat disappear from Soviet utterances and the political indoctrination of the Soviet fighting forces – and in the same connection to see the anti-German card removed from the inter-Communist game.

The next year, during the summer break of 1971, I was asked if I would visit Brezhnev for a few days in the Crimea in mid-September – without protocol or a 'delegation'. The Soviet leader was so anxious to dispense with protocol that he was standing entirely alone at Simferopol airport when I landed on the afternoon of 16 September. I had come in a Luftwaffe plane, in itself a new departure. The crew was looked after most attentively, which was not something that could be taken for granted.

There was a reception in the airport building, which dragged on for a long time; the stock of jokes into which we both dipped seemed inexhaustible, and the atmosphere was suitably unbuttoned. If it was part of the plan to see if I could stand the pace, quite literally, then I passed the test well. Brezhnev was clearly the top man in the Kremlin now, and was in better form than when I had met him the year before in Moscow, or when I saw him later in Bonn in 1973.

Official Bonn and indeed officious Bonn, complementing each other and intermingling, felt challenged: was what was going on in the Crimea really something quite outside government business, 'just' a meeting of party leaders? Could this, asked Franz Josef Strauss, be an 'assignation'? There were further difficulties later over the Soviet General Secretary and his protocolary rank. Although he was received in Paris with all the honours due to a head of state, the Bonn bureaucracy was disinclined to allow him the mandatory gun salutes when he arrived, and I did not feel like insisting on them.

As for Oreanda, where the Soviet leader had a property at his disposal and to which he invited guests from near and far in summer months, was it not near Yalta, or actually a suburb of Yalta, where in early 1945 Stalin had made those decisions with Roosevelt and Churchill which were now seen as having sealed the division of Europe once and for all, as one of the not uncommon shorthand versions of history would have it? If prejudice is going to be brought to bear on actual localities, however, where could we have gone in Germany after 1945 if we were bent upon sparing others – and ourselves – some very uncomfortable memories?

Some other questions were equally beside the point. Why was no 'official' press entourage provided for Oreanda? The fact that many journalists and cameramen turned up anyway without difficulty did not silence this criticism. The photographers captured not only my casual attire – no tie – when I went out for a boat trip on the Black Sea with the Russians, but the occasion when I went swimming with Brezhnev. Was this, they implied, really responsible behaviour?

And did I have on-the-spot expert advice from the Foreign Ministry? In fact as well as Egon Bahr, State Secretary in the

Chancellery, I was accompanied by an expert from the Foreign Ministry who later served twice as Ambassador to Moscow. Naturally there was also an interpreter with me, and he made notes of the proceedings.

On my return I told Opposition representatives, though not as a point of major importance, that Brezhnev had asked me about Communists in the Federal Republic, and I had confirmed their legal existence. This made a considerable stir. The Soviet leader had wanted to know in what way 'Herr Bachmann's party' was active. He meant the German Communist Party, the DKP, set up in 1968 with the advice of Justice Minister Heinemann on formalities; the Federal Constitutional Court, acting for the Federal Government, had banned the old Communist Party, the KPD, in 1956.

Brezhnev seemed to want to get away from an unwelcome subject. There had been much argument about it during my visit to Moscow the year before. Kosygin said that revanchist powers were able to surface in the Federal Republic while Communists were driven underground. I merely confirmed in Oreanda that the DKP was active, and legally so. It was not exactly friendly towards me, but I did not expect it to be, and I resisted those who wanted it banned like its predecessor. All this was twisted to make it appear that I had expressed my goodwill towards the Communist Party. In the summer of 1988 Gerhard Schröder, my predecessor as Foreign Minister, was still asserting what he imagined he knew: that I had told Brezhnev, on that fateful boat trip, that the German Communist Party was 'constitutional'. This account of the matter was wrong about both the occasion and the subject. So was Schröder's conclusion: 'Since then we have had a DKP.'

More serious than this petty argument at home was a storm in a Parisian teacup. There were those in Paris who suggested to President Pompidou that I had forced my way into Brezhnev's timetable of engagements before he visited France and had even met him for secret talks. That rumour was easily dispelled, but it was a reminder of the French suspicions latent whenever

Germany and Russia met to discuss matters of mutual interest. For the rest, I could see no harm in the Soviet leader's asking for German opinions on Europe. European development, said Brezhnev, would depend to a great extent on the relationship between the Soviet Union on the one hand, and the Federal Republic and France on the other. He was not so wide of the mark.

Pompidou, who entertained Brezhnev in Paris early in December 1971, will not have contradicted his guest when the latter told him he trusted the Federal Chancellor more than he trusted Germany. It was hardly my responsibility if such distinctions were still drawn in Paris, Moscow and elsewhere.

We had several discussions at Oreanda lasting some hours, mainly about our bilateral relations and opportunities for European co-operation. Also about China, which I had proposed as a subject for discussion, although nothing constructive came of it. Naturally Soviet–American relations and the German question loomed large. I was impressed by the way Brezhnev, after the hours of sociability in the reception room at the airport and when we were on the way to the Crimea, immediately mentioned the German question and removed it from the sphere of discussion. When the car started, he put his hand on my knee and said: 'I understand you, Willy Brandt, so far as Germany is concerned. But it's not our responsibility, it was Hitler's.' He may even have said there was nothing we could do to change it now.

'Entirely between ourselves', he wanted to know if the Moscow Treaty would really be ratified; failure could mean a setback lasting for decades. My readiness to speak openly about the fragile majority of my coalition was not without its effect; I added, 'I have linked the fate of my government to the treaty, and I shall stick to that.'

Brezhnev seemed to want to get the subject of Berlin out of the way. He could not and would not understand our anxiety that West Berlin might be even more distinctly separated from the Federal Republic than ordained by the special status negotiated by the victorious powers. The new Four-Power Agreement had been signed two weeks before, on 3 September. There had been trouble over the German translation – a Western or an Eastern version? At first Brezhnev did not want to hear anything about it, but then he thanked me for my explanation – adding that this thanks bound him to nothing.

After Oreanda, opponents tried to accuse me of negotiating with the General Secretary over German unity, offering neutrality. This was not the case, and indeed it would have been unrealistic. I told the Bundestag, time and again, that progress in German unity would be made only in so far as there was a general and fundamental improvement in East–West relations. After my resignation in 1974 some of my more implacable opponents even murmured that they would prosecute me for treason if I 'stuck my neck out too far'. The reason given was that with Brezhnev, so they claimed, I had discussed security status for Germany other than that provided by NATO.

Brezhnev's visit to Bonn in May 1973 was a hectic affair. The Russian was not in good form. He appeared tired and nervous, and did not seem at ease on what, to him, was very unfamiliar terrain. But that was not the whole story. We both felt that American–Soviet relations were deteriorating again. A year before, Nixon had signed a declaration of principle on relations between the two powers. This meant, basically, that America recognized the Soviet Union as an equal power in world affairs. But the hope of the President and his Secretary of State that they could more or less keep the Russians out of the Third World proved illusory.

Our policy on the treaty made distinct progress while Brezhnev was in Bonn: the Bundestag had just approved the Basic Treaty with the GDR, and some of the Opposition deputies had voted in favour. Membership of the United Nations was approved with an even greater majority, about half the Opposition voting for it. A considerable upswing in trade with the East was perceptible. We signed a ten-year treaty on the development of economic, industrial and technical co-operation. Brezhnev struck up a tune I now knew by heart: would we not participate in developing the mighty natural resources of the Soviet Union, particularly in Siberia? Not just natural gas and coal but considerable quantities of metal ore awaited us there, and such rich supplies of timber as were found nowhere else. Of course, said Brezhnev, our systems were different: 'We can give orders, it's otherwise with you. But all the same, if the leaders say the word, the businessmen will begin to think in new ways. I and my people are ready to take a bolder view.'

I met Brezhnev twice more – in 1975 and 1981 – in the Soviet Union, and had lengthy discussions with him, and I also met him when he visited the Federal Republic in 1978. My travels in the summer of 1975 took me not only to Moscow and Leningrad but to Novosibirsk and Uzbekistan as well. The General Secretary's colleagues had tried to get an even earlier date. They were very keen for me to hear, from their leader, that he had had nothing whatever to do with the spy who was the occasion of my resignation.

Kneeling in Warsaw

In 1970 and also later, I was asked why I did not give precedence over the treaty with the Soviet Union to the treaty to be concluded with the Poles, who had suffered so unspeakably. This was a purely academic question, and the Polish leaders shared my view. We had no choice; the key to normal relations lay in Moscow. Nor was Russia to be seen only as the seat of power; its own people had suffered terribly as well.

I will concede, though, that the Polish people and their leaders alike would have preferred our declaration on the Oder–Neisse border to be on the agenda in Warsaw first; it seemed worth only half as much as a 'present from Russia'. The leaders, however, knew what the general public could not: a government I headed would be ready to accept the new western frontier of Poland contractually. I had signalled as much during the 1969 election campaign, and thus before it was clear whether I would be able to form the new Government. In 1970 I accepted the Polish proposal to make the establishment of the border the prime concern in the Warsaw Treaty, and let non-aggression follow.

When I was talking to Władysław Gomulka, Polish Communist Party leader and *de facto* head of state, after the signing of the treaty, on the afternoon of 7 December 1970, the problem of the order of precedence surfaced again. Well-meaning Polish journalists had expressed a wish for us to ratify the Warsaw Treaty before the Moscow Treaty. Gomulka asked me not to lose sight of the facts. Any attempt to pry Poland away from its alliance or even drive a wedge between Poland and its great neighbour to the east, he said, was bound to fail. Moreover, the Moscow Treaty had been concluded first; both should be ratified at the same time, or very close together.

Of course the Poles did not want to be treated as a mere appendage of their masters' power. And of course they did not like the idea that the Russians and Germans might make issues affecting their own lives the subject of exercises in wording. The Poles did not hide the bitterness that marked their relations with the Soviet Union; Stalin had had their officer corps annihilated, the Red Army had stopped on the east bank of the Vistula in 1944 and watched Warsaw bleed to death, the Poles had lost their own eastern territories, and though these things were never explicitly mentioned, they were frequently hinted at. Consequently the Poles were very anxious not to seem dependent on the Russians. When I met Brezhnev in the Crimea in September 1971, I received an invitation to stop off in Warsaw on the flight back. I said I was unable to accept it because of other engagements. Later I wondered, and not just in connection with this occasion, whether I had not been too much of a slave to my engagements diary.

Josef Cyrankiewicz, a survivor of Mauthausen, a member of the Social Democratic wing of the PVAP, the Communist Unity Party, and Prime Minister, said at the start of the Warsaw talks that our two governments should undergo a kind of psychoanalysis, digging up everything that was wrong first, and the therapeutic talking would follow. Various forms of co-operation would be a help, he said, and time, the great healer, would take care of the rest. On the eve of the signing of the treaty, Gomulka said that we should envisage taking at least a decade over the process of rapprochement. Even so, his estimate fell short.

Gomulka fell from power that December over protests against food shortages. Demonstrating workers, not least in Gdańsk, forced him to resign. His character had been hardened in the Resistance; in the early fifties he had been imprisoned as a Titoist, but in 1956, against the will of Khrushchev, he had risen to be party leader. Like all Communist leaders, he was a master of the ritual of long speeches that were a substitute for proper discussion. 'Between the two of us' (four, including the interpreters) he held forth for two hours; if only for reasons of prestige, I had to spend at least one hour over my reply before the rest of the programme could go ahead.

The Warsaw Treaty clarified 'the basis for normalizing relations' and showed on what thin ice we were skating. None the less, it was important for us to establish that, as with the other Eastern treaties, the validity of treaties concluded earlier was unaffected and that no international agreements were set at issue. The Polish head of government did not hesitate to say that his side knew that the man signing in the name of the Federal Republic was one who 'saw, as soon as the Fascists seized power, the boundless misfortune it would bring on the German people, the peoples of Europe and the peace of the world'. In my reply I said I was aware that rifts brutally torn open could not be filled in by any paper, however important.

Understanding, even reconciliation, could not be ushered in by governments but must come to maturity in the hearts of people on both sides. I told my opposite numbers of talks I had had with General de Gaulle about Germany and Poland. He and I, I said, had agreed that the nations of Europe must retain their own identities, and that indeed that would open up great prospects for the whole continent. I knew, I said, 'that there are no answers in isolation, only European answers. That, too, has brought me here.' In my speech on the signing of the treaty I said: 'My government accepts the lessons of history: conscience and insight lead us to those conclusions without which we would not be here.' But no one would expect me 'to undertake more in political, legal and moral respects than dictated by insight and conviction'. Above all, I said, borders must 'be less divisive and less hurtful'.

It was a great burden I carried with me to Warsaw. Nowhere had a nation and its people suffered as they did in Poland. The routine extermination of Polish Jews took bloodlust to lengths no one would have thought possible. Who can name all the Jews from Poland, and other parts of Europe, who were annihilated in Auschwitz alone? The memory of six million murder victims lay along my road to Warsaw, and the memory of the fight to the death of the Warsaw ghetto, which I had followed from my observation post in Stockholm, and of which the governments fighting Hitler had taken hardly any more notice than they did of the heroic rising of the Polish capital itself a few months later.

On the morning after my arrival, my Warsaw programme contained two wreath-laying ceremonies, the first at the grave of the Unknown Soldier. There, I remembered the victims of violence and treachery. The screens and newspapers of the world featured a picture that showed me kneeling – before the memorial dedicated to the Jewish ghetto of the city and its dead. I have often been asked what the idea behind that gesture was: had it been planned in advance? No, it had not. My close colleagues were as surprised as the reporters and photographers with me, and as those who did not attend the ceremony because they could see no 'story' in it.

I had not planned anything, but I had left Wilanow Castle, where I was staying, with a feeling that I must express the exceptional significance of the ghetto memorial. From the bottom of the abyss of German history, under the burden of millions of victims of murder, I did what human beings do when speech fails them.

Even twenty years later, I cannot say more than the reporter whose account ran: 'Then he who does not need to kneel knelt, on behalf of all who do need to kneel but do not – because they dare not, or cannot, or cannot dare to kneel.'

At home in the Federal Republic there was no lack of questions, either malicious or foolish, as to whether the gesture had not been 'overdone'. I noted embarrassment on the Polish side. The day after the incident none of my hosts referred to it. I concluded that others besides ourselves had not yet digested this chapter of history. Carlo Schmid, who was with me in Warsaw, told me later that he had been asked why, at the grave of the Unknown Soldier, I only laid a wreath and did not kneel. Next morning, in the car on the way to the airport, Cyrankiewicz took my arm and told me that the gesture had in fact touched many people; his wife had telephoned a friend of hers in Vienna that evening, and both women shed bitter tears.

Over the question of the border, some thought had been required to bring legal and political facts and political and psychological necessities down to a common denominator. In my statement of Government policy at the beginning of 1970 I had said that: 'What our fathers lost will not be won back by rhetoric, however fine, or legal tricks, however clever.' Yet it was still difficult, in Germany, to adjust to the changed realities of the present. In Poland, the Oder–Neisse Line had become a question of absolute national importance. It was not enough that the Russians had made the GDR recognize it in 1950. The word of the Federal Republic carried more weight with the Poles, although they had no common border with us. They would have welcomed it and felt it helpful if the Federal Republic – in any peace treaty – had given a prior undertaking to respect the Oder–Neisse Line. No one put this to me, and indeed I could not have outmanoeuvred the legal objections to it.

It had been established at Potsdam that the German–Polish border should be finally settled 'in the peace treaties'. But the American President and the British head of government had sanctioned the compulsory resettlement of Germans in 1945, and they had not opposed the determining of the new border. De Gaulle bore the other Western leaders a grudge for keeping him out of the Potsdam conference, not for their conduct there.

The right of residence of millions of Germans was replaced by a right of residence for Poles who had moved west or been born there. There was not a government in the world that would have been prepared to support German border claims. It was some time before leading representatives of the Western world publicly and clearly indicated to the Germans that they had to come to terms with the drawing of the new borders. Adenauer and his close colleagues knew how matters stood. But there was much outcry from refugees and displaced persons, and loud protest from those professionally engaged in looking after their affairs. It was quite late in the day that the Social Democrats decided to swim against the stream. I always remembered what Ernst Reuter had said the year he died: we should meet the Poles half-way – Poland could no longer be expected to be a state on wheels. But my guiding principle was that *Ostpolitik* should not be pursued 'behind the backs of those expelled from their homes'. That meant they must be taken into our confidence and decide for themselves what was acceptable and what was not. We were also bound to such a course because of the great contribution to the work of reconstruction made by the Eastern and Sudeten Germans who had been expelled or fled from their homes. In 1965 a memorandum from the Evangelical Church did much to ease the discussion; it was harder for the Catholic bishops of the Federal Republic to move towards their Polish counterparts. However, Federal Chancellor Kiesinger could smell the wind of change in the second half of the sixties when he spoke of his understanding of the Polish people's desire 'to live at last in a national territory with secure boundaries'.

There were practical questions connected with the treaty of December 1970 which could not be answered satisfactorily: one concerned giving ethnic Germans the opportunity to settle in the Federal Republic, or indeed in either of the two German states. Another was the Polish wish for material reparation, either directly or in the form of more and cheap state credit. The modification of school textbooks and youth exchanges, which we asked for and promised to encourage, also proved to be major factors.

The Polish side did not want emigration and resettlement agreed by treaty; they insisted on the form of a unilateral 'information': 'Several tens of thousands of persons' (this was explained as meaning 60,000 to 100,000) 'of undisputed German nationality' were to be allowed to emigrate; considerably more had already reached the Federal Republic with the help of the national Red Cross organizations in the 1950s. The Red Cross now had to be approached again and told that the number mentioned by the Polish side was not to be understood as a fixed upper limit, particularly as the number of those who would like to emigrate was undoubtedly higher. Easier family visiting was promised. Our wish that those Germans who stayed behind should be given cultural consideration, particularly through language teaching, met with little or no response.

But this was by no means the end of the chapter. When some 60,000 people had emigrated, considerable resistance by local and regional bureaucracies was felt in Poland. Figures were juggled in Germany. How many people really wanted to emigrate? How far could the reuniting of separated families be used as a justification. And what about cases where Germans and Poles had intermingled for generations? Often enough, reunion on one side meant new partings on the other.

In Warsaw Gomulka had told me that Poland had refrained

from demanding reparations in 1953, but that some ten million people would be legally entitled to them if the West German reparation laws were taken as a basis; on that basis, experts had worked it out as a sum of some 180 billion D M. Could we not forget that large sum and instead agree on a more modest but sizeable ten-year credit – either interest-free or at a very low rate of interest? In principle, I was not against an 'indirect' solution which favoured economic development. At the time, however, the Finance Ministry was unwilling to accept rates of interest kept down artificially by the state, although that was usual in other countries. The price rose later. The linking of factors which strictly speaking had nothing to do with each other – credit, indemnity from pension claims by Polish forced labourers, and emigration permits – overshadowed German–Polish relations for years and put up the price the Federal Republic had to pay; it had claimed legal inheritance from the German Reich, and now it could hardly avoid being presented with the bill.

Just as in my talks with Tito in Yugoslavia, I never concealed the fact that I thought heavy material burdens were psychologically oppressive, and I did not like to think of their effect on future generations. It should not be overlooked, after all, that the Germans expelled from their homes had lost much other property as well as land.

The turbulence of Poland in the two decades following the Warsaw Treaty had little to do with its relationship with the Germans. However, normalization did not make as much progress as had been hoped. There was much negotiation and a good deal of argument about emigration applications and permits: no one yet suspected that emigrants of more or less German origin were no longer sure to find open arms awaiting them in the Federal Republic. It was true, and still is, that relations between Germans and Poles are of particular European significance.

And what about Czechoslovakia? Over the years I have often been asked why normalizing of relations with Czechoslovakia took three more years, to the end of 1973, and why the Prague Treaty did not come into force until the summer of 1974; meanwhile, like the GDR, we had become members of the United Nations, and the foreign ministers of East and West had met in Helsinki to work towards the all-European conference. Had I or anyone else forgotten what was done to the Czechoslovak Republic as the Second World War approached, and what sufferings its people had to endure during the Nazi occupation? Certainly not. It is true that the legal or quasi-legal arguments about the Munich Agreement took up a great deal of time. But although objectively speaking that is a fact, it was only half the truth. The repercussions of the events of August 1968 continued to cripple the policies of Prague, and made their mark on my visit to that city in December 1973. The cold weather seemed to reflect the mood. But I listened attentively when my hosts spoke of the sufferings and hopes of their people; when Prime Minister Lubomir Strougal, less wooden than most of his colleagues in the leadership, who held office until 1988, spoke of 'the crown of thorns of Lidice'; when General Svoboda, nearing death, head of state in 1968 and still in office, spoke in very friendly terms of 'good-neighbourliness'; and when Gustav Husák, party leader and soon to be President, agreed to my request for clemency for some Germans in prison. He would see what could be done, he said; after all, he knew what it was like to be in prison himself. He had been a prisoner for a long time, even when his own party came to power. He would obviously have liked to be in a position similar to that of Janos Kadar in the difficult years after 1956, but what was at least partly successful on the Danube could not succeed on the Moldau. Husák and his group failed, above all, because they could not overcome the suspicion of their countrymen.

In my speech in Prague I recalled my visits in the winter of 1936–7 and the summer of 1947; what Prague had meant to a German exile; the major elements in a history that linked us – the coexistence of Germans and Slavs in Bohemian territories, the tragedy of the German occupation under Hitler, that other tragedy of undiscriminating expulsion: I had been one of the first to report it.

The Prague Spring of 1968 had fascinated me, like so many others. And like them, I was mentally unprepared to see the efforts of the reforming Communists countered by the Warsaw Pact invasion. Any claims that the invasion had been provoked by the interference of the Federal Republic, or by actual military precautions on German soil, were pure invention. The insinuations were not just made in the East, but believed by many in the West. When I visited Paris, not long after my visit to Prague on 21 August, Michel Debré, who had succeeded Couve de Murville as Foreign Minister, accused me in all seriousness of supposedly damaging activities. His intelligence service had provided him with hair-raising information; such things do happen. The French Foreign Minister was right to warn NATO against unthinking reaction, but he fell very short of the mark in playing down this new Prague tragedy as an 'accident on the road to détente'. Even de Gaulle struck the same note, complaining to Kiesinger that the Federal Republic had encouraged the Prague reformers and must thus take some of the blame for the tragedy, and – as a kind of confidential aside – that Brezhnev had previously ascertained from President Johnson that the United States would do nothing.

The presence of a leading German liberal in Prague shortly before the violent climax of the crisis may have been unnecessary, but it could not actually have harmed relations between Prague and Moscow. The readiness of the head of the Bundesbank to discuss the extension of bilateral relations immediately after trade missions were finally set up in the summer of 1967 did not evince a trace of hostility towards other parties. Egon Bahr, my head of planning in the Foreign Ministry at the time, met Foreign Minister Jiři Hajek during a stopover in Frankfurt for legitimate purposes of information and nothing more. However, the worst possible construction was put on all this. The SPD itself had to put up with a welter of absurd accusations. It could hardly surprise anyone that Social

Democrats in my country, as elsewhere, felt deeply sympathetic towards the attempt to give socialism a human face. Of course the secret services knew how strictly German Social Democrats stuck to the principle of non-interference: we gave no encouragement to endeavours to resurrect Czech Social Democracy (over 300 local organizations had formed within a very short time). Social Democratic solidarity had to be withheld where European responsibility for peace took precedence, even if that was not to everyone's liking.

News of the military intervention of the Warsaw Pact had reached me on board ship off the Norwegian coast. I flew to Oslo and then in an army aircraft to Bonn. My colleagues in the Foreign Ministry and at party headquarters, and everyone else I met over the next few hours, were shattered by the crushing of the Prague Spring and its aspirations to freedom. It saddened and shamed me to think that German soldiers of the GDR People's Army had been employed in the punitive action. Numerically they were not very many, but the thing itself horrified me more than my conservative colleagues, who said nothing else was to be expected of Communists.

The Romanian Party leader Nicolae Ceausescu, who did not become deranged and begin to rule tyrannically until later, showed to some advantage at the time. He had refused to participate and kept the Romanian army in barracks; on 21 August he condemned the invasion at an open-air meeting. His ambassador knocked at many doors asking for concrete help in this emergency. The Czech opposition came to the conclusion that Romania was spared intervention because it showed it was ready to defend itself. Not surprisingly, the reformers were unable to agree on the practical application of this theory.

By chance, I met a Prague friend from my Stockholm days soon after the Russians rolled into the city. Valter Taub had resumed his career as an actor, and was appearing successfully on stages in Germany and Austria. Like most other intellectuals, he was on the side of the reformers. With tears in his eyes Taub, an ex-Communist, asked if no help could be expected from anywhere in the world: was Europe going to put up with such things? I understood how people could feel like that, but I could not help them when, in their distress and despair, they expected something of the Western Alliance which it had not been created to provide.

There was much discussion in those days. But was there any sensible alternative to the course of détente? In Bonn we told ourselves, and not just within the leadership of my own party, that a retreat into the period of tense confrontation would help neither Czechoslovakia nor anyone else. I did not allow myself to be drawn into criticism of the methods adopted by the Prague reformers. It was not for the Germans to discuss the question of whether their strategy had been adequately thought out and their tactics sufficiently adroit, and it is rare for any great good to come of such discussions. Which of us would like the job of steering a broad reform movement and channelling such a complex urge towards freedom? Particularly in a nation which had such long traditions of freedom?

The Slovak Party Secretary Alexander Dubček, who succeeded the Communist Party leader Novotný in Prague in January 1968, and who had been involved in the fascinating cultural awakening of the two preceding years, knew that he was borne up by a wave of sympathy and confidence. Treacherous colleagues, in league with their Soviet counterparts, brought him down and silenced him. He was thrown the sop of a post as Ambassador to Turkey, and then lived in seclusion in Bratislava. I was impressed by his steadfast dignity. He remained a Communist, but could not be moved to deny what he had stood for. When he was accused of dubious political connections he pointed, quite rightly, to me; he too would have worked for fair agreements and material co-operation had he been allowed to, as he was not.

After Gorbachev's third year in power there were signs that Dubček was to be rehabilitated. But the Czechoslovak Republic had now taken a back seat in East–West politics. Ion Gheorghe Maurer, the stimulating and witty Prime Minister of Romania,

said of Czechoslovakia, with some malice, that it was the most
neutral state in the world – it did not interfere even in its own
affairs.

Normalization of relations with Czechoslovakia proved particularly difficult because the lawyers were seeking to crack the
hard nut of the Munich Agreement of 1938. Schröder's peace
note of March 1966 said that that treaty had been torn up by
Hitler and now had no territorial significance. At the end of
1966 I supported Justice Minister Heinemann in his demand for
the Grand Coalition's statement of Government policy to settle
the matter. The statement said that the agreement 'made under
the threat of force' was now invalid. This meant from now on,
but in Prague they insisted on its retrospective application.

How could we draw up an official declaration of invalidity
without incurring harmful legal consequences for the Sudeten
Germans? We could not have them retrospectively branded
traitors. Nor, despite the years that had passed, could we dis-
regard the fact that German citizens of old Czechoslovakia had
also suffered severely under the Nazis – and had still been
victims of the savage expulsions of 1945–6.

The Prague Treaty says that the Munich Agreement was
forced upon the Czechoslovak Republic by the Nazi regime
'under the threat of force'. Both sides wanted to break with the
dreadful past, in both countries a new generation had grown
up, and it had 'a right to a secure and peaceful future'. The
fateful agreement was therefore described as 'invalid . . . in
respect of their mutual relations under the terms of this treaty'.
This was the compromise formula. It was for this formula that
the brilliant State Secretary Paul Frank had toiled for three
years! The treaty did not touch on the legal consequences which
had been felt in the autumn of 1938 and in May 1945, apart
from those measures which both states regarded as invalid
'because of their irreconcilability with the fundamental principles of justice'.

The treaty was also impeded and delayed even further by a
petty quarrel about legal aid for West Berlin and its citizens. I

could not rid myself of the feeling that Ulbricht and his men had a hand in this.

Brezhnev and Gomulka had predicted to me, in 1970, that it would not be difficult to come to the verge of agreement with 'the Czechs'. In May 1973 the Kremlin leader repeated, as if to encourage us, that the situation now looked favourable 'for getting rid of the damned Munich Agreement'; Husák, he said, had twice confirmed that he was ready to meet us half-way. There was no doubt that the intransigence and devious behaviour of the Prague negotiators had to do with the difficulties the Government and the Party were having with the Czech people.

Whether in Warsaw or Prague or any other centre in Central and Eastern Europe, Federal German policy was able to take almost none of the burden from those who bore responsibility there, but it did not lay any further burdens on them.

The Two Germanies and the Old Capital

In my statement of Government policy in October 1969 I said that though two states might exist in Germany, they did not regard each other as foreign countries – 'their relations with one another are bound to be of a special kind'. This was a necessary farewell to outdated notions. Many had expected it, many were surprised.

I could take that step, without which *Ostpolitik* would have got nowhere, only because I did not propose to discuss it any further. It was important, naturally, for me to get the consent of Walter Scheel as Foreign Minister and leader of our coalition partners, and the President of the Federal Republic had also agreed. Egon Bahr thought the statement came too soon, h[ ] he expressed no reservations except to me. Horst Ehmk[ ] new Chancellery Minister, had assured me that it was con- stitutionally correct. The stir it created was enormous.

Recognition that the GDR represented a second state on German soil went hand in hand with readiness to negotiate on the settlement of practical questions. I had learnt that when I was Mayor of Berlin. As Federal Chancellor I offered nego- tiations – without discrimination and without preconditions. The GDR leadership reacted with some constraint. In December 1969 Walter Ulbricht, in his capacity as Chairman of the Council of State, sent Federal President Heinemann a draft treaty the aim of which was recognition in international law, and which was to serve the purpose of establishing equal relations. But the offer contained grave stumbling-blocks. The Soviet side offered help – after all, it did not want to see unnecessary encumbrances on its treaty with Bonn – and sig- nalled its readiness to accept our viewpoint, although the Soviets thought it would be illogical to refuse recognition in inter- national law. A communiqué recommending negotiations unim- peded by preconditions could not be misunderstood. I was given a discreet hint: as no doubt I remembered, the weather in Berlin could be very good in March.

On 22 January 1970, therefore, I wrote to Willi Stoph, Chair- man of the GDR Council of Ministers, and suggested nego- tiations on non-aggression and on an agreement to settle practical questions; we could also then exchange views on equal relations. Stoph invited me to visit East Berlin in February. But nothing came of it because the other side wanted to dictate my means of getting there: by air to East Berlin. My own plan was to go by rail and stop off in West Berlin. We sought a compro- mise, found one, and agreed to meet in Erfurt in Thuringia on 19 March. Before I boarded the special train I confirmed that politics meant something to me only 'if they serve humanity and peace'.

As for that day in Erfurt – can there have been any other in my whole life charged with more emotion? On the other side of the border between the Germanies, the road was lined with people waving, although the People's Police was supposed to have stopped them. Women waved from windows; their husbands waved from or outside their work-places. I was travelling through the heartland of German Protestantism and of the labour movement. Willi Stoph was waiting at the railway station, and we went to the Erfurter Hof hotel. A large crowd outside the hotel was expressing its pleasure with shouts of welcome. When I had gone in they shouted in chorus for Willy Brandt to come to the window. I did not comply at once, but then I did go to the window, gesturing a request for restraint. I was moved, and felt these were one people with me. How strong their sense of kinship must have been to express itself in such a way! But I wondered whether they were not expressing hopes which could not be fulfilled, or not very quickly. I would be back in Bonn next day. Could I be sure that I had enough influence to benefit people here whose demonstration of sympathy might bring them into conflict with less sympathetic authorities?

During the day a number of people who toed the party line were summoned, to restore some order to the square outside the hotel and gratify the other Willi, Herr Stoph, by shouting plaudits for him now and then. In the afternoon the GDR Foreign Minister Winzer accompanied me to the former concentration camp of Buchenwald. Here we were singing the same song once more, even if not quite in tune. On the way there and back, through the outer districts of Weimar, many well-wishers waved again.

I was not particularly impressed by the Chairman of the Council of Ministers. What was actually said at the negotiating table, or rather most of the time read out, was hardly worth the effort. Stoph appeared to be pervaded by a sense of the infallibility of the Socialist Unity Party. He actually called the Wall 'an act of humanity'. And West Germany, he said, had to answer for relieving the citizens of the GDR of 100 billion marks.

We did agree that 'no war shall ever start again from German soil'. This was to become only too familiar a cliché in the years ahead. We also agreed that we needed no interpreters, for as my colleague from the other side remarked, 'We both speak German.'

Willi Stoph acted as if he were solely interested in recognition in international law, and as if we need think no more about relations of a special kind. That blocked the way to the humanitarian relief we ourselves urgently wanted to talk about, or at least postponed discussion of it. On the other hand, he did not hide his strong interest in a flourishing development of trade, nor did he shrink from discussion of the EEC when we were on our own. Thanks to Federal Republican urging, the GDR had already become a silent participant in some areas of the Economic Community, a fact regarded with some envy elsewhere in the Eastern bloc.

However, the instructions Ulbricht's envoy had brought to Erfurt with him were merely to get recognition in international law, and to gain more time. In East Berlin, as well as in Bonn, they knew that negotiations over the Moscow Treaty had begun in the Soviet capital. Would they be steamrollered, or would they be able to get something for themselves first?

In our private conversation in the morning, and again in the evening, the Chairman of the Council of Ministers asked why we should not agree to exchange ambassadors at once. In the evening, he added: why not also declare that we would apply in unison for membership of the United Nations? Our own timetable was different. We had to ensure, after all, that the Federal Constitutional Court did not disown us on account of the nature of the relations to be agreed with the GDR.

Late in the evening of that day, 19 March, Stoph and I had another short conversation in private. This was to obviate any impression that the meeting had been a complete failure; however, we had already agreed on a second one, on 21 May in Kassel. Stoph's report to the Volkskammer said that little had changed in the Federal Republic. And indeed, the East

German press continued to claim that the Brandt Government had aggressive intentions.

The Kassel meeting was not a promising occasion. The police were not up to the job demanded of them. Several thousand Nazis – and others who acted like Nazis – had assembled in a protest demonstration; the slogans on their posters – 'Brandt an die Wand' ['Execute Brandt'] – had been added to in such a way that our guest from East Berlin need not feel left out. He also allowed a number of Communist Party members to greet him. The car in which we drove from the station to the Schloss Hotel was actually attacked. Fanatical youngsters hauled down the East German flag in front of the hotel.

A wreath-laying ceremony at the memorial to victims of Fascism had to be postponed until evening. When the rowdy demonstrators had left, Kassell showed itself in its true, pleasant colours. But the GDR used outward appearances as an excuse to say as little as possible on the subjects of the meeting as submitted. We had drawn up twenty carefully phrased points of principle and practice – including elements of the treaty – adding two proposals of a special nature: permanent representatives should be exchanged, and both East and West Germany should apply for and take up membership of international organizations.

At the negotiating table, although not in private conversation with me, Stoph took a rather sharp tone and insisted that we could conclude a treaty only if it were drawn up on principles of international law. As in Erfurt, he asked if we could not at least agree on simultaneous application to join the United Nations. References to him as a public enemy, he said, had made preparing for Kassel difficult; in fact, with touching German naïvety, the principle of 'exemption from prosecution' had been applied to him. On the other hand, he did not want to prejudice any practical matters, particularly trade. There must be no impression, said Stoph, that Kassel meant 'an end to our relations and our efforts. Perhaps a pause for thought will be a good thing.' At home he said, as we were immediately told, that

I was the one who had suggested the pause for thought. In public he said we needed time to come up with some better ideas. Such shifts in emphasis are easily brought about, and not only when they are the work of one's Communist partners in discussion.

Some of our private talks in Kassel had been out of doors. These were opportunities for Stoph to speak without constraint; the certainty that we were not overheard seemed to help him. He was now quite clear about the key role of our negotiations with the Soviet Union. In the evening, before we went over to the meeting hall, he repeated that co-operation in the spheres of the economy, transport communications and postal services should not be jeopardized. He thanked us for making the wreath-laying ceremony possible after all, and for the distinctly friendly attitude of the local people, in contrast to that of the trouble-makers.

While new agreements with the GDR were not concluded until 1971, after Ulbricht's departure from the centre of the stage, at the end of March 1970 the ambassadors of the Four Powers – the Soviet Ambassador in the GDR, the ambassadors of the Western powers in Bonn – had begun those negotiations on Berlin for which we had long been working.

As early as 1968, while I was Foreign Minister, I had persuaded my colleagues of the three Western controlling powers to enter into negotiations with the Soviet Union to get improved conditions in Berlin and for the Berliners. Among other things, I was able to tell my colleagues that Ambassador Abrasimov had reacted positively to the idea of a lump-sum reimbursement for the use of the access routes to Berlin. At the NATO ministerial conference in Washington in April 1969, the foreign ministers agreed, when I urged it yet again, to prepare official exploratory approaches to the Soviet Union by the Three Powers. The sole subject was to be improvement of the situation in and around Berlin. The ambassadors in Moscow made their approach in July 1969, telling the Soviet Government that the Federal Government was ready to hold talks with the GDR on questions of transport and traffic and wanted to improve the situation in and around Berlin, particularly with regard to access. They also outlined Bonn's (or rather, the Grand Coalition's) willingness to compromise on Soviet complaints about certain Federal German activities in Berlin; at the end of February 1969, before the election of Heinemann as President, Chancellor Kiesinger had told the Soviet Ambassador we were ready to renounce Berlin's right to be the scene of the election of the Federal President if the Soviet Union, in return, would use its influence to enable West Berliners to visit the Eastern part of the city. Gromyko replied before the Supreme Soviet on 10 July, and supported the readiness of the Soviet Union, in principle, to talk to the 'war allies' about precluding future 'complications over West Berlin'. The realization that the Moscow Treaty, or rather its ratification, would not come about without a Berlin agreement also worked wonders.

An unofficial but extremely effective trio in Bonn helped to get the Berlin agreement off the ground: the American Ambassador Kenneth Rush, who also functioned in his official capacity in Berlin and who had the personal confidence of Nixon; the Soviet Ambassador Valentin Falin; and Egon Bahr, State Secretary in the Chancellery. Henry Kissinger, who had set up a direct telephone line to Bahr and was in contact with Ambassador Dobrynin in Washington when appropriate, has given a detailed account of this interesting piece of crisis management in his memoirs.

However, the negotiations made no progress until West and East had agreed to exclude questions of status and legality from discussion: the Soviet draft of March 1971 spoke only of 'the area concerned'.

We wanted access to West Berlin guaranteed, and its links with the Federal Republic confirmed; this included the right of the Federal Government to represent West Berlin and its citizens abroad. And we wanted visiting rights for East Berlin and beyond. The GDR leadership was keen at least to assert its sovereignty over the access routes and keep Federal institutions out of Berlin; it had to moderate its demands considerably.

The Four-Power Agreement, initialled in September 1971, marked important progress, even though it could be brought into force only step by step: traffic to and from Berlin went smoothly on the whole, and visiting opportunities went far beyond what we had achieved with the agreements on passes. Almost at the last moment, I managed to clear up a point which mattered a lot to me. In the summer of 1971 I sent Brezhnev a handwritten letter: I requested that his ambassador should make no more difficulties over West Berliners holding Federal passports. Non-recognition of such passports in Eastern bloc countries had been a particular thorn in my flesh while I was Mayor. The French and the British were surprised when Abrasimov gave way; the Americans, who had tried in vain to get the same concession, had been told about the step I was taking and were not surprised. The new ruling was that if a Federal passport held by a West Berliner was used for travel to Moscow or Prague, it had to be stamped 'Issued in conformity with the Four-Power Agreement of 3.9.1971'.

In Berlin itself not much recognition was initially given to our success. Abandoning the image of the city as a capital on standby was not easy. Instead of being confirmed in that view of itself, Berlin now had to accept that it was not explicitly regarded as a 'constituent part' of the Federal Republic. However, the curtailment of an ostentatious Federal presence was not a particular source of annoyance, and there was compensation in the form of generous Federal aid for Berlin as a cultural metropolis.

Walter Ulbricht, who had opposed the Soviet urging for better relations with the Federal Republic, had to quit his post at the head of the Socialist Unity Party in May 1971. I never met him, but he was described to me more than once, sometimes by people from the East, as arrogant and overbearing. For all his oddity, however, I was rather impressed by his doggedness, and I thought it to his credit that under his government there had been no show trials with death sentences passed on dissidents, such as there had been in Prague and Budapest. Erich

Honecker succeeded Ulbricht, and after the latter's death in the summer of 1973 Honecker also became Chairman of the Council of State.

The Four-Power Agreement on Berlin had to be complemented by agreements between the two German sides. A transit traffic agreement was concluded in December 1971 and a lump-sum payment for road costs was finally made. The Berlin Senate concluded a visiting agreement. Particular importance attached to the transport treaty with the GDR of May 1972, the month in which the Moscow and Warsaw treaties were passed by the Bundestag. Before the prematurely dissolved Bundestag adjourned in September the transport treaty was passed with no votes against and nine abstentions.

The same month, May 1972, Brezhnev and Nixon set their sights on much further-reaching projects. In June the representatives of the Four Powers in Berlin signed their concluding protocol, thus clearing the last hurdles, and the agreement came into force; the Soviets had delayed this last move until it could coincide with the ratification of the treaties. At the end of the year the two German states concluded the Basic Treaty, mostly negotiated by State Secretaries Egon Bahr and Michael Kohl, which ruled on the setting up of permanent missions and eased humanitarian tasks. To many people, this seemed to set the seal on détente in Europe. In the same way as the blockade had once symbolized the Cold War, the ruling on the coexistence of the two German states and the prospects of their future partnership ushered in a new period of post-war European history. That did not mean there would be no sudden chills.

The opposition objected to the fact that – so it had persuaded itself – the negotiations had been 'over-hasty'. Strauss induced the Bavarian State Government to appeal to the Constitutional Court. The Court ruled that the agreement could be reconciled with the Basic Law, though for reasons some of which were surprising.

The two governments had brought the treaty into force on 20 June 1973. The next day, both their applications for membership lay before the Security Council of the United Nations. At the beginning of July the foreign ministers met in Helsinki to get the all-European conference off the ground. The improved visiting opportunities were particularly welcome to the public – and good for national solidarity! Soon, people had taken advantage of them a million times, although mainly in the West-to-East direction.

It is certain that no more than we had achieved *could* have been achieved at the beginning of the seventies. We could not cause the Wall to disappear by magic. A solution for Berlin as a whole had not suggested itself. Would the attempt have been doomed to failure? We could not be sure how German questions would be answered in a process whereby the two halves of Europe were beginning to come together. But I was in no doubt that both German states had a duty to reinforce peace and stability at the heart of Europe. Rendering Europe such a service might be a tardy reparation for the harm that had sprung from German soil. There can be common responsibility even in division, and it no longer seemed impossible to make that division more tolerable.

Recognition – Resignation or a New Start?

I have often been asked if it was really necessary to recognize the division of Germany and the borders that came into being by right of conquest. Such questions often rose less from a genuine wish for enlightenment than from cheap polemics or contentious dogmatism. I did not see that any wrong had been done in either past or present. I could not give away what was no longer ours, or to put it more clearly, what had long ago been forfeited. I linked non-aggression in the abstract to the concrete facts resulting from Hitler's war. Adenauer said he was ready to discuss a great deal if it would ease the situation of 'the people in the Zone', and we must seek to abandon the Hallstein doctrine so long as we got something in return. All that was lacking from that idea, surely, was its realization?

I did not want – we did not want – a bitter heritage to prevent us from shaping the future. Therefore, the outcome of history had to be accepted, not in a spirit of mere resignation, but so that we could jettison the ballast that prevented us from helping to bring about a peaceful change of the situation in Europe and in Germany. My criticism was also directed at myself.

Our efforts to make ourselves understood bore no fruit, or very little. 'Politicians preaching surrender' were regarded as legitimate quarry. In 1967 Kiesinger had used the phrase 'the party of recognition', which he did not mean kindly, applying it first to a certain trend in journalism and then to my own party. Over the following years neo-Nazis, and others who would not have called themselves neo-Nazis, demonstrated against people whom they accused of treacherous surrender or immoral acceptance of injustice. Even in 1988, before a visit from Gorbachev, I received letters asking whether I intended to 'sell off' any *more* of Germany.

It is sometimes claimed that the GDR was not officially recognized until the autumn of 1987, when Erich Honecker visited Bonn. If this theory were correct then the political battle at home over my visit to Erfurt seventeen and a half years before would have been a figment of the imagination. Even in the autumn of 1987, however, people were ready to split hairs over protocol. Half amused, half astonished, I saw the Chairman of the Council of State being received by the Chancellery with slightly downgraded military ceremonial: the guard of honour was a little smaller than usual; its deputy commander performed the ceremony instead of its commander; there was playing of 'anthems', not 'national anthems' (which made no difference to the tunes).

By way of excuse for the directors of this spectacle, it may be said that the legacy of a period when protocol was a substitute for politics cast a very long shadow. The Federal Republic had been caught up in the ritual non-recognition of the other German state too long for it to free itself all at once. In my own time in Berlin I had seen how difficult, even impossible, it could be to explain to foreigners the thinking behind non-recognition. Harold Wilson, when British Prime Minister, made a joke involving comparison with a visit to the zoo: he said he did not recognize the elephant even though he recognized him, playing on the double meaning of 'recognize' in English.

I emphasized, not least in parliamentary discussion of the Eastern treaties, that to accept a certain state of affairs with the hope of improving it was very different from inactivity accompanied by grand words. In Moscow, as in Warsaw and elsewhere later, we made it clear beyond all doubt that we were serious about non-aggression and our contribution to a peaceful European order, but we did not intend to regard the other part of Germany as a foreign country or credit it with a democratic nature which it could not claim. From our point of view there could be no question of putting a stamp of finality on all the accidents and absurdities of the post-war situation – and of the Cold War. However, I will cheerfully admit that there was a certain grim fascination in the sight of Marxists, or those who liked to be thought Marxists, competing with conservatives of other kinds to show maximum inflexibility in the face of existing circumstances.

The Moscow Treaty neither prejudiced a peace treaty nor undermined the rights of the Four (!) Powers. It is nonsense to claim that the Foreign Ministry should have clarified these points: nor did we need to be told that the inviolability of borders is not necessarily identical with their finality. In concrete terms, Egon Bahr's acumen went furthest when he countered the demand for recognition of the GDR in international law with our readiness to conclude an agreement 'that will have the same binding power usual between states as other treaties concluded by the Federal Republic and the GDR with third parties'.

For good reasons – and with an eye on millions of our East

German countrymen – I placed particular emphasis in Warsaw in December 1970 on what we intended to recognize and what we did not. The treaty, I said on television, did not mean that we were legitimizing injustice or approving of expulsions. What had been lost hurt us, and I could be sure that the Polish people, tried in suffering, respected our pain. In Bonn I also addressed myself to the Germans who had been expelled and asked them to look to the future. None of us had resigned ourselves lightly to the loss of a quarter of German territory (within its borders before Hitler's expansion), districts which had meant so much in Prussian and German history and for German culture. But in the logical light of what I had learnt I added, once again: 'You cannot give away what you do not own any more. You cannot have the disposal of something when history has already disposed of it.'

After our relationship with the GDR had been settled within the framework of what was possible, and the Four-Power Agreement on Berlin had been completed, we established diplomatic relations with Hungary and Bulgaria, which in practical terms meant turning trade missions into embassies. The contact with Hungary was to prove especially fruitful: from time to time Janos Kadar and I had informative and confidential exchanges of opinion. I think that he really did do something for his people before the great changes in the East began; at least he was able to avert any worse fate that might have befallen them after the 1956 revolt.

In 1968, as Foreign Minister, I had been able to resume relations on a modest scale with non-aligned Yugoslavia, and exchange ambassadors; our co-operation had developed quite well since then. As a consequence I met Tito on a number of occasions, at Brioni, in Dubrovnik and in Belgrade, and several times in Bonn. Despite all his idiosyncrasies, which he seemed to have borrowed from the feudal age, I thought very highly of him, and not just because he appreciated my efforts to achieve détente and co-operation in Europe. Tito deserved great respect for the brave battles he had fought – first against the occupying

power, then against Stalin's attempted imposition of the Soviet
Russian style of Communism – and for his vigorous efforts to
create a modern federal state, to the advantage of Mediterranean
stability. Unfortunately the fear that many difficulties still
awaited a multi-national state was fulfilled.

A particularly significant rearguard action of *Ostpolitik* was
won with the establishment of official relations with the People's
Republic of China. Walter Scheel went to Beijing in the autumn
of 1972 and made it clear beyond all doubt, against much other
advice, that we had no intention of taking part in any attempts
to play off the Communist-ruled Great Powers against each
other. I was invited to China in 1973, and was to have gone in
the autumn of 1974; Helmut Schmidt went a year later and
brought greetings from Chairman Mao to cheer me. Almost
another decade was to pass before I myself, in another capacity,
visited that important area of the world.

Once the frame had been decided, the picture almost painted
itself: diplomatic relations (without either side having an
embassy of its own) were established with the People's Republic
of Mongolia in 1974, and the relations that had been broken
off with Vietnam and Cuba were resumed in 1975. Albania
long remained a special case, but that had nothing to do with
Ostpolitik; normal contacts were not resumed until 1987, when
the country began to normalize itself at home as well.

Only understanding of the actual situation on the one hand
and of German responsibility on the other made us capable of
that realism that went further than the balancing of interests,
and made our share in responsibility for Europe more than mere
routine. The doctrine adopted late in the day by many, and
never by some, said that you must set out from the status quo
if you want to alter it; refusing to recognize altered realities is
a long-term option open only to those who are not affected by
them.

In December 1971 I received the Nobel Peace Prize in Oslo –
an honour that affected me deeply. I said that a policy for peace
was the true *Realpolitik* of this epoch: 'If the balance-sheet of

what I have been able to do could say I helped to open up the way to a new realism in Germany, then one great hope of my life would be fulfilled.' I added: 'A good German knows that he cannot deny his European destiny. Through Europe, Germany comes home to itself and the constructive forces in its history. Reason commits us to our present Europe, born of the experience of suffering and failure.'

I also mentioned change when I spoke to the General Assembly of the United Nations in New York in late September 1973. I had not come, I said, to make use of the UN as a Wailing Wall; instead, I would like to interpret the admission of both German states to membership as an invitation to 'spell out peaceful coexistence in German'. Perhaps this would be seen some day as a significant experiment. 'If it actually succeeded in reducing the sheer waste that results from distrust between antagonistic systems, by taking steps to build up trust, then we would have set an historical example.'

When, in the summer of 1975, we finally achieved that 'Conference for Security and Co-operation in Europe' for which I had sought to smooth the way since my first days as Foreign Minister, declaring myself for Helsinki as the venue when most people were against the idea, there was still no sign of any far-reaching change. The parallel negotiations in Vienna on arms reduction in Central Europe were taking a particularly unsatisfactory turn; they became a diplomatic and military dry run which lasted for years. Many questions also remained open in Helsinki.

It had been especially difficult to reach agreement on what was known as 'Basket Three', comprising issues of humanitarian relief and the exchange of information. I would have preferred a slimmer document to one permeated by so much argument about interpretation. Several of the inevitable inkslingers wrote as if Brezhnev and the Eastern bloc had agreed to deprive themselves of political power, which of course they had not, but co-operation between East and West was making progress.

It was also of some significance that campaigners for civil rights and other dissidents could now cite Helsinki. The fact did not smooth out differences between systems, but it did help to break down taboos. Subsequent conferences gradually began to run more smoothly, although no real results were achieved, particularly in problems of military security, until new framework data arising from altered relations between the Western Powers could be evaluated.

Those who had thought that the Helsinki conference was designed only to help the Soviet Union secure the status quo in Europe were proved wrong, and were more and more inclined to keep their mouths shut. The fact was that a phase of change, albeit one full of inconsistencies, was on the way.

Europe was no longer merely either beneficiary or victim of dealings on the larger scale between East and West. Torn apart as it was, the old continent began to see itself in a new light and to influence world events. This was the sequel to the results of German *Ostpolitik* at the beginning of the seventies.

Charles the Great and Europe the Small

Anyone asking about Germany's place in Europe had to realize that the answer involved France, and the man who said of himself that he had to carry France on his shoulders while he was virtually unknown. The influence he exerted from London and Algiers has been compared to a beacon light that never went out during the long night of Hitler's war. I was greatly impressed by this Frenchman who, although a conservative, fitted into no categories, and I have felt sorry that I was unable to attempt more with him in European politics.

At the beginning of February 1968 Federal President Heinrich Lübke had gone to Paris to inaugurate the new (or old) German (or Prussian) Embassy in the rue de Lille. De Gaulle, who attended the reception that evening, had returned us the building, which had been confiscated as a matter of routine. The gift was considered extremely valuable, and not just by the Finance Ministry; a new embassy would have cost only half what restoring the old one did. Frederick William III of Prussia had acquired it from Napoleon's stepson Eugène de Beauharnais. Bismarck had spent a short time in it. The French did not spend their money in vain; they had a shrewd idea of the German historical consciousness.

But no reminiscences were exchanged that February evening. For a press agency report had alarmed my Cabinet colleagues; it claimed that at a gathering in Ravensburg in Upper Swabia I had said that the President of the French Republic was out of his mind. Next morning the President's deep displeasure and his decision not to attend the lunch given for Lübke were conveyed to the two Federal ministers and the State Secretary of the Foreign Ministry who were present, all of whom had omitted to telephone me at once. The Federal President thought he would just have to put up with this and went to the lunch along with the Ambassador, although he had been told that nothing would have induced me to say anything in the least like the alleged insult.

So what had happened? Kiesinger and I had been on a state visit to Rome, where we yet again discussed the French veto on Britain's entry to the European Economic Community. I then flew on from Rome to southern Germany for an SPD party conference in Baden-Württemberg. In my unscripted speech I said, with reference to the EEC and its extension: 'Good-neighbourliness is the ruling principle of co-operation between Germany and France. And friendly, trusting co-operation does not mean that one partner simply repeats what the other says.' I went on to say that the reconciliation between the French and the Germans and the friendship that had grown from it were firmly rooted in the hearts of many people on both sides. We might therefore hope that those roots were so strong 'that not even unreasonable governments will be in a position to affect them'.

I greatly respected the General, and had never dreamed of describing him in such terms as the former American Secretary of State, Dean Acheson, who had spoken of 'that fool in Paris'. Nor did I share the view of an experienced diplomat in my own ministry who saw him as a mixture of Don Quixote and Parsifal. I saw the tall army officer from northern France as the great symbol of the French Resistance. It had been the most natural thing in the world for me to address him as '*mon général*', like his companions of wartime days. His achievements in giving the colonies, including the North African departments, their independence in the face of much opposition could only increase respect for him.

My mildly critical remark that Saturday morning in Swabia referred to what might be taken for granted: we would say what we thought and stand up for our own interests in Paris and anywhere else. Even more than twenty years later, it is hard to explain how this could have become what was known as 'the Ravensburg telegram'. It was not even as if a journalist ill-disposed to me had been involved. In fact the source of the report was a reporter who had no malicious intentions at all, and was even described as a supporter of mine. Perhaps he had not slept well and just wrote down what he thought might have been said.

Matters were made worse because I did not take an alarmed phone call to my home seriously; it was from a friendly journalist who wanted to point out the possible effects of the incorrect report. Once I had finally realized what was going on I set everything in motion, which was easier said than done. There was no one in the local Party office, it took some time to track down the man who had the key, and then it was hours before the authentic text of my speech was transcribed from tape in Bonn and sent to Paris. The unfortunate effects of a multiple breakdown of communications could not be undone, only mitigated.

Shortly afterwards, when I attended one of the regular consultations in Paris, no one wanted to be reminded of the agitation the incident had caused. When I met the General before lunch, I looked him straight in the face and asked if he could understand how hard it could be to know one was not to blame. He did not bat an eyelid, but sought to disarm me by showing the greatest amiability. At table, where I sat on his left, he made sure I was particularly well served.

I visited the Élysée Palace for the first time in June 1959, when de Gaulle greeted me in German. Each of us, as in all our later conversations, used his mother tongue. His interpreter, a doctor from Berlin who had been in the Resistance, recorded what we said and helped out with the translation of any 'difficult' phrase if we wanted to go particularly carefully. The General asked me, with great affability but rather like a military supreme commander requiring information from a divisional officer:

'What can the Mayor tell me about the state of affairs in Berlin?

'And how are things in the Federal Republic?

'And what about the position in Prussia?'

It took me a moment to realize that by Prussia he meant the GDR. I made a remark setting his terminology right, but the only result was that next time he spoke of 'Prussia and Saxony'. This reflected his understanding of the historical context. He thought nothing of social systems and supra-national groupings, and everything of states and nations; he always spoke of the Soviets as 'the Russians'.

Finally he asked what the SPD was doing. This fourth question was the one I had least expected. After my brief account, the President remarked that he thought the Mayor of Berlin was one of those Europeans of whom more would be heard. Next year he returned to the theme. I recorded it in a note: 'He referred to remarks made to me in 1959 on the role of various people in further European development.'

He politely but firmly turned down several invitations to visit my city which I made him over the years. At first, in 1959, he explained his hesitation by saying that he did not have such means at his disposal as the Americans did. Decoded, this meant he would not guarantee anything which the major power in the West might not back. At the end of that year he told Harold Macmillan, the British Prime Minister, who still thought the Berlin risk a very high one: 'You don't want to die for Berlin, but you may be sure the Russians don't want to either.' Some while later he told me, unconvincingly and with positively disarming cynicism, that he could not come because he did not want to recognize the Wall. It was to be feared that the Americans might get involved in the wrong sort of compromises, he said. Furthermore, the West had plenty of opportunities to answer Soviet pressure on Berlin with counter-pressure somewhere else. The people of West Berlin must not doubt France's goodwill, but France did not stand alone and was not the strongest of the Western powers – which of course was no understatement. The French attitude to Berlin in 1963 was beyond doubt, he said. French policy was not to abandon what the free world possessed, and if there was any chance of heartening people in the East and bringing them relief, he was in favour of it. The Americans' talks with the Russians worried him; you always had to fear for the Western position, he said. You had to be particularly wary of the United Nations, especially those neutral states that were inclined to take a stance pleasing to the Soviet Union. Consequently, he wanted no change in the status of Berlin; let it last another eighteen years, and then we would see where the Russians stood. It was hardly likely that the city's Governing Mayor would find these views constructive.

In the mind of Charles de Gaulle, the East had never ceased to be a part of Europe. But he sought to draw political conclusions from this only in the last years of his presidency, and they were inextricably linked with his attitude towards the United States. He did not favour the nuclear protection of Europe by the USA, but he did not want separation from the

USA. The independence to which he aspired, in any case, was incompatible with membership of an integrated NATO.

Once France, giving plenty of notice, had left the integrated Western defence organization in 1966, when NATO had moved from its headquarters in Fontainebleau and set up in Brussels and the French troops in Germany had left the command structure of the Alliance, the President was sure of his ground: the Federal Republic of Germany would be neither willing nor able to imitate France. It was easier to support the demand 'Americans out of France' when he was sure they would stay in Germany. The theme song of the time was 'Americans out of Europe', but not out of Germany.

The General had already withdrawn the French fleet in the Mediterranean from the NATO Supreme Command in the spring of 1959. Previously, in 1958, he had clashed with Lauris Norstad, the American Supreme Commander in Europe, who could not tell him, because he was not allowed to, how many American nuclear weapons were stationed whereabouts in France. De Gaulle said that a leader of France would not accept such a reply a second time. In addition, President Eisenhower would not go along with his wish to bring France and the United Kingdom into a kind of Western triumvirate; shortly afterwards, in December 1962, Kennedy gave Polaris missiles to the British. The new President's concept of the Alliance resting on two pillars was not at all to the liking of the French leadership. To what end had France, without overwhelming material means, managed to achieve the honorary rank of a Great Power? De Gaulle's idea was to try combining the means of the Federal Republic with France's own, as a basis for a renewed claim to the leadership of Europe.

Germany might have made more of this than it did. In any case, it knew what was to be expected of its partner and what was not. In 1962 de Gaulle told Austrian Foreign Minister Bruno Kreisky: 'We have brought Germany the friendship of France, and that must be worth at least as much as reunification.'

He had said frankly and undiplomatically to Adenauer in the

summer of 1960 that France's position in NATO could not last much longer 'in its present form'. To me, a little later, he said he did not want to be thought foolish; naturally he also believed that the Atlantic Alliance should continue, but the details were open to discussion. To my indication that neither did many of us like the role of satellite or spearhead of the USA, he replied that he could appreciate Germany's situation. He added, with some sarcasm, that in the Dulles period Western policy had been to overcome the Soviet Union and then solve the German question. Now the idea seemed to be that the German question might be solved by the occasional presentation of a petition to Moscow by the Western powers. Although France's experience of a united Germany had not been particularly happy, he was in favour of our national unity. However, we should know that there was no chance of that without recognition of our borders with Czechoslovakia and Poland (and in passing he added Austria!). Furthermore, we could not expect to have nuclear arms. He briefly considered the idea that the Germans should 'have a say' in the use of such arms, and then asked if any intelligent person could seriously think a nuclear power would let others 'have a say' in the use of their nuclear weapons.

He also told me, in 1963, that 'If we want Europe, then it must *be* Europe, and not America plus individual European states.' Either there would be war, he said, or the Soviet Union would find itself facing new problems. He thought Communism as a doctrine and a regime in Russia and Eastern Europe 'much less convincing than in Stalin's time'. He had let the other side know what crucial questions must be included in a peace settlement, he said, but he was not sure if the Germans were really interested in that – he was thinking of the borders. France could live with a divided Germany if need be.

The French head of state thought well of the policy of small steps that I had employed in Berlin. Foreign Minister Couve de Murville said his government had viewed the procedure with reservations at first, but soon saw that it did not infringe legal positions; it was in the general interest for this policy to be continued successfully.

A group had now formed among conservative politicians in Munich and Bonn which saw itself as 'Gaullist' or 'European' – as distinct from the 'Atlantic' supporters predominant in the Government (and in the SPD). The controversy bypassed reality in two ways: the German 'Gaullists' overlooked the fact, or wished to overlook the fact, that the General would never entertain their dreams of European nuclear arms, or sharing in French nuclear arms. They also failed to see that de Gaulle did not want too much German influence in the EEC, and moreover was on the point of inaugurating his own détente policy, one which would benefit rather than detract from a German *Ostpolitik*. The 'Atlantic' group in Bonn, in its own turn, pursued the phantom of a special strategic relationship with the USA, something for which none of the prerequisites existed. Nor did they take adequate account of the fact that the Americans paid only lip-service to European union. Washington viewed the presumed internal dynamics of Western European integration with anything but enthusiasm; it was anxious about stronger economic competition from Europe, and growing political independence there.

Consultation talks in the summer of 1964 showed up the dry and unimaginative state of Bonn policies of the time; the contrast between a friendship treaty signed in the Élysée Palace at the beginning of Adenauer's last year of office and an abrupt French veto to the extension of the EEC had been rather clumsily brought into play. The President came with all the important members of his government, and was rather disappointed when his idea of European independence, including a military component, fell flat. The Federal Foreign Minister had no opinion on the subject, the Chancellor had neither understanding nor feeling for it. Erhard made a remark which became all too notorious: 'We'll put it on the agenda.'

During that week in the spring of 1964 I had told a New York audience that I thought it neither sensible nor just to hold de Gaulle responsible for all the difficulties of the Western world. Many of his decisions were not easy to understand, but I would not say anything against him, certainly not in the USA. Rather, we should be aware 'that de Gaulle has thought the unthinkable and begun to draw conclusions, boldly and independently'. The balance of terror gave room for manoeuvring to bring some movement into the rigid fronts. The French President made use of that fact in his own way, and sometimes, as a German, I asked myself why he should be the only one. Building bridges from the past to the future did not necessarily mean losing sight of the present.

In a lecture to the German Society for Foreign Policy, I recalled the old platitude that there are some aspects of political reality which cannot be covered by a simple pro or con. It is rightly said that movement is not good in itself, I said, but 'lack of movement is not good either. Particularly not when a frozen sheet of ice does at last break up and the blocks of ice begin moving.' Not only the French but the British and others, and of course the Americans, I argued, made use of relative freedom of movement in their own way: 'And what are we doing? The Federal Republic cannot appear to have no interests or will of its own. The Federal Republic too must face the question of the uses of mobility.'

Early in 1965, before the Bundestag elections, when I was again in Paris speaking to the assembly of the Western European Union (its members included the United Kingdom), de Gaulle expressed his fear lest the Europeans should become victims of a mistaken American strategy: a 'strategy of flexible deterrence', which might be pursued with conventional and so-called tactical nuclear weapons on the backs of both parts of Germany and probably of France too. The Europeans would bear the brunt of it. American determination to make a full-scale retaliatory strike with nuclear weapons was necessary, but we had to assume, said de Gaulle, that the Soviet Union and the USA did not want war with each other. In case that should not be so, France was building up its own nuclear defence potential; the decision had been taken in 1956 under the Socialist Prime Minister Guy Mollet.

When I took over the Foreign Ministry in December 1966, my first foreign trip – I saw it as the way into the traffic system of Europe – was to Paris, on the last occasion that the Council of NATO met there. We had to make a serious effort – Kiesinger and I were entirely agreed on this point – to ease and encourage German–French relations. They had suffered, and it had not done our relationship with America any good, indeed quite the opposite. France's pursuit of an empty-chair policy in the EEC Council of Ministers since the summer of 1965 had been an additional disappointment and obstacle to us.

De Gaulle and his colleagues had realized that there was clear emphasis on German–French relations in the Grand Coalition's statement of Government policy. Kiesinger had said, in agreement with me, that in the present circumstances European geography and European history were bringing about a particularly high degree of consensus between the two nations and their peoples. The co-operation we desired was not inimical to any other nation or its people; instead, it was the crystallization of our policies, the aim of which was European union. The Europe which spoke with one voice, as American statesmen demanded, required increasing co-ordination of German and French policy. Co-operation between the French and the Germans in as many areas as possible was also of the utmost value for improving relations with our Eastern European neighbours. For all these reasons, the Federal Government wanted to use the opportunities provided by the treaty of January 1963 to co-ordinate our policies in as concrete a form as possible.

However, we did not conceal the fact that both nations would continue to have different interests and opinions; friendship, we said, does not mean neglecting your own interest or slavish imitation of your partner. We had therefore tried to explain to our French neighbours why we did not agree with them over the extension of the EEC, and why we valued the alliance with America more highly than they did. Yet it was certain that

Europe could not be built up against France and Germany, only with them. Reconciliation between the two nations had become a fact of post-war life, perhaps the most important and certainly the happiest fact of all.

Couve de Murville, referring to Kosygin's latest visit to Paris, was concerned with 'what the Russians call European security', seeing it as including the problem of Germany's future. The Soviet side, he said, had understood that France was in favour of improved relations between Bonn and Moscow, and with Central and East European states. In fact they knew very well at the Quai d'Orsay that there was little to be gained from going it alone in policies of détente. I explained how we intended to bring together questions affecting German unity and integrate them with our policy for ensuring peace. As long as there was no political solution we wanted to concentrate on holding the two parts of Germany together as firmly as possible – through trade, cultural exchanges and the easing of travel restrictions – and we were glad to think we could count on French understanding. A serious attempt should be made to breathe more political life into the Franco-German treaty. Couve reacted positively. Later he remarked, accurately, that I had distinguished myself clearly from Kiesinger but 'worked just as hard for Franco-German relations'.

De Gaulle too had a private talk with me that December of 1966. I explained why that serious attempt to give more content to our work, in the spirit of the Franco-German treaty, was in our own interest. De Gaulle said he was glad I had become Foreign Minister, and hoped he could also work well with the new Federal Chancellor. He had no unfriendly feelings towards Ludwig Erhard, whom he also esteemed, he said, and with whom he had always co-operated 'as far as possible'. He had found our statement of Government policy interesting and even encouraging. Now we must all see what could be done. France would do nothing to make our situation more difficult. The range of the treaty should not be overestimated; it was primarily a document of goodwill and reconciliation. That, said de Gaulle, was important. The aims of the two sides were not very different. France understood the German wish for reunification, and not only did not object, but shared that wish – out of friendly feelings for Germany and because it was the only way in which the consequences of the war could finally be overcome. But coming closer to that goal in the climate of the Cold War would have been possible only if we had been willing to make war on Russia. No one wanted that, though, said de Gaulle – 'not even Germany, and not America'. Consequently, there had never been a position of strength from which German unity could have been achieved. Now was the time to seek another way: 'As you know, France recommends the path of European détente.' No movement would come into the German question if relations between the European states were not given a new basis. Of course, de Gaulle said, France too must proceed cautiously, for Russia, although a very great power, had not gone beyond what was conceded to it at Yalta. There was no reason to suppose it intended to attack. Russia's main anxiety was China; moreover, it had to develop its own territory, and to do that it needed Western aid. It was peaceful in its own way, with a strong, totalitarian regime, although its ideology was in decline. France – that was to say, de Gaulle himself, who had been to the Soviet Union in June 1966 – had expressed approval of a policy of German–Russian détente to the Soviets. That was assuming Germany wanted such a policy, of course, and would do something to encourage it: 'I said to Mr Kosygin, if Herr Brandt comes to Moscow – as no doubt you will – I suppose the Russians will receive him well?' Kosygin had said yes, perhaps.

De Gaulle continued: if Germany liked, France would help it along the new road – had already begun to do so – particularly in Moscow, and would not pursue its own détente policy in any way that might injure Germany. He had also said, in Russia, that in the final resort there were not two German states but a single people. One day, perhaps the Russians themselves would realize that. At any rate, France did not intend to recognize the

GDR as a state, although its views on the borders 'to the east and the south' would not change. It wanted friendship only with a non-imperialist Germany: 'It cannot be Germany's friend if Germany should ever wish to recover what it lost because of the war.' Germany would have no chance of pushing back the eastern frontier, 'for the Russia of today cannot be compared with the Russia of the past'. In Brezhnev's view it looked as if 'our relations in all areas were able to improve when de Gaulle became independent in foreign policy'. The General repeated that whenever the Federal Republic wanted to strengthen practical contacts with the people of the Soviet-occupied zone, France would consider such attempts 'satisfactory to all parties and particularly the Germans themselves'. Further: 'Above all, everyone must have his own policy. France must have a French policy, and it does. Germany must have a German policy, and it is up to Germany to construct one. A French or German or English policy that was really an American policy would not be a good one.' Not that France was in any way anti-American, he emphasized; France was America's friend. But nothing could be worse for Europe than 'an American hegemony which extinguished Europe and prevented the Europeans from being themselves'; American hegemony would stand in the way of European self-confidence.

There is no doubt, then, that de Gaulle wanted more than the mere prevention of conflict, and agreed with my concept of 'regulated coexistence' – people existing side by side so that they might then come to live *with* each other. This proudest of all proud Frenchmen thought the German question one of great historical importance – to be 'studied, settled and guaranteed' in front of all the nations of Europe. Washington and Paris seemed to agree on that point when they turned their attention to European and German unity (in that order).

I did not fail to point out that matters looked more complicated to the Germans than they did to the authorities in Paris and Washington, although I agreed that Russian aggression did not enter into German calculations either. After de Gaulle had spoken more than once about Austria, I felt obliged to point out that there was no one with any authority in Germany who entertained the notion of another *Anschluss*. De Gaulle said that our proposals struck him as reasonable, if a little too timorous over the alteration of psychological factors.

After several long conversations over the years – with the General himself and with his closest colleagues – I was not surprised to find myself achieving close agreement with the French side over *Ostpolitik*. I clearly remembered the treasure-hunting metaphor used by de Gaulle on his visit to Bonn in the summer of 1967, his last visit but one: he said he hoped that together Germany and France would unearth the treasure of a policy that overcame the division of Europe.

By now Adenauer had been out of politics for five years, but the effort to forge a special relationship with France remained alive. It was nonsense to suggest that Adenauer and de Gaulle had been just waiting for each other and went together like right and left shoes. In fact they had little more in common than advanced age and a basic conservatism; you could have said they were two right shoes. But that was only half the truth. The Frenchman, who thought the German provincial, was more firmly rooted in the past and looked further into the future.

In his extreme old age Adenauer said he (still) trusted no one but de Gaulle to unite Western Europe. Yet the Chancellor had initially not been very enthusiastic when the General resumed the helm in Paris in 1958. Adenauer had reacted with suspicion. Considerable persuasion had to be brought to bear on him when de Gaulle invited him to his home at Colombey-les-Deux-Églises in September 1958. However, that visit melted the ice and was a success. The 'Old Man' was not as guileless as the ingenuous Ludwig Erhard. When I met the Vice-Chancellor at Cologne–Bonn airport that May of 1958 – he was deputizing for Adenauer, I was President of the Bundesrat – Erhard seriously and naïvely thought that the hour of Fascism had come in France. This was nonsense, but I was not without fears myself, and I felt they were confirmed when friends in Paris – sometimes in what I felt was a distinctly doom-laden mood – complained that de Gaulle was making a desert of the political landscape at home; now and then they made comparisons with Berlin at the beginning of 1933.

When the war and its humiliations were over, France had to look hard at itself. De Gaulle succeeded in getting it to do so only sporadically before he withdraw in annoyance. When he returned to power at the end of the fifties, he undertook – and who else would have had the authority? – to end the war in Algeria by 'peaceful cunning'. Even during the war, word had got around that he was not an easy man; Churchill once said de Gaulle was the heaviest cross he had to bear, and Roosevelt spoke even more sharply. François Mitterrand told me how he sought out de Gaulle at his headquarters when he was on a secret mission from the French underground to North Africa, travelling by way of London; the General's first suspicious question was whether Mitterrand had flown in on an English aircraft.

I suspect that it cost de Gaulle – like other French people, not all of them conservatives – a good deal to face the Germans with even a degree of ease; the French post-war Government had favoured the idea of central administrative bodies with German state secretaries even less than others did.

So why would Paris back the Germans and German unity? De Gaulle, like others, had hopes of making the left bank of the Rhine, including the part north of Alsace, into the western border of Germany and putting the Ruhr under 'international' control. When the matter came up on the agenda he was against a 'supra-national' Europe and had a hand in the French veto which scuttled the European Defence Community. His adherents in the French Chamber of Deputies voted against the EEC, but he backed it when he came to power. However, he did not want the British in it; their links with the USA were too strong for his liking. Moreover, there was a danger that they might dispute the French claim to leadership in Western Europe.

He finally concluded the Treaty of Friendship of January

1963 with Adenauer. Five days before it was signed in the Élysée Palace, at one of those press conferences which resembled a *mise-en-scène* for the issuing of proclamations, the General once again put his objection to Britain's membership of the EEC on record. Adenauer was not worried. When his Foreign Minister Gerhard Schröder telephoned from Brussels, rather irritated by the timing, Adenauer asked whether he would have preferred de Gaulle to make his statement *after* the signing! I happened to be in London, and witnessed the dismay of the German Ambassador as well as the calm and composed bitterness felt by the British Government. The Ambassador's colleague in Paris, Blankenhorn, who had worked with the Chancellor for years, called the treaty 'something I can regard only with mixed feelings'. In addition, the Federal Government had neglected or not thought it necessary to get full backing for the treaty. As a consequence Kennedy, who had not been adequately advised, asked the Federal Chancellor if he was thinking of preferring Paris to Washington.

However, none of this diplomatic awkwardness affected reconciliation, and there was not a living soul who could claim that he suffered as a result. The new relationship between the two countries, a friendship rooted in the minds of the next generation, became a basic component of a peaceful European order. In September 1962, the year before the Treaty of Friendship, de Gaulle had paid a sensational visit to the Federal Republic and had spoken of 'the great German people'. He had been wildly applauded – it was almost as if people saw him as a kind of substitute Führer and wanted to relieve their feelings by acclaiming him. He remarked to me that the trip had been 'more emotional' than he expected. After a meal to which he invited me at Godesberg, he thanked me privately for a sympathetic statement I had made to the Berlin City Assembly.

In April 1963 I went to Paris for the Berlin Cultural Festival. With André Malraux, I opened a Watteau exhibition in the Louvre. Marlene Dietrich came to an evening reception. Couve gave a dinner for me, and for the first time I visited Georges

Pompidou in the Prime Minister's official residence. The President was on one of his provincial tours, and had me brought by military helicopter to Saint-Dizier in eastern France, where he had stopped off at the *sous-préfecture*. De Gaulle said Bonn's reactions to the treaty concluded with Adenauer had 'rather disturbed him'. Now we must wait and see, he said; we ought to know that he thought even more of practical co-operation than of the black and white print of the treaty. I urged him, with due respect for his historic role, not to cause the German people unnecessary conflicts. I referred in particular to our relationship with the United States, which had been and would continue to be so important for our post-war development. The treaty had been ratified by the Bundestag and the Bundesrat with a huge majority; I asked him to be understanding if we made it clear, in a preamble or by some other means, that we did not want anything to impair either our relations with the Atlantic Alliance in general and the USA in particular, or the obligations entailed upon us by the EEC. I did not find it easy to speak like this, for I was far from happy about the preparation and the parliamentary handling of the Franco-German treaty. De Gaulle remained displeased, and so did Washington. Inconsistent behaviour was bound to cause doubts as to whether German foreign policy was really serious.

In 1965 de Gaulle told me he had the impression that he agreed with Adenauer on the basics of a common policy, but the preamble we had added to the treaty largely devalued its content and made co-operation dependent on others. He felt the treaty had become more sentimental than political. I suggested that people could speak openly about their different ideas – on the concept of defence, for instance – while at the same time they worked closely together in practical matters. He said that such opportunities had not been taken on the German side, or hardly at all, and we had stuck almost entirely to the USA over arms contracts.

In all these arguments, of course, there was more involved than contracts – although the French Government wanted contracts too, and did not shrink from employing diplomacy and pressure to keep the Germans from turning to third parties for them. De Gaulle and the men of his generation also bore the Americans and British a grudge for preventing France from making good all its claims after the First World War. Now the leadership of Western Europe was at stake. Paris would have it if London was kept at a distance; no one wanted German leadership. German economic interests seemed to favour an economic community incorporating Britain's commercial traditions and international experience. In addition, those who shared my view wanted the partnership of other Social Democratic and Protestant areas over and beyond Britain.

De Gaulle came to Bonn for consultations in the September of 1968, later than usual. A sense of resignation marked this meeting, like the final one he attended in Paris in 1969. The exposés in which the General summed up the Franco-German meetings without the prompting of a written outline were as masterly as ever. But it was obvious that he was feeling the effects of the French crisis of May 1968. I had spent the eve of that crisis in cheerful company in Dijon; Couve and I had just been made *chevaliers* of a Burgundian wine-tasting order when my colleague was hastily recalled to Paris. The General was still away on a state visit to Romania when the student revolts gathered momentum, bringing with them strikes and leading the country to the brink of revolution.

On 29 May the head of state and his family flew by helicopter to Baden-Baden to see General Massu, the fire-eating former commander in Algeria; de Gaulle had recalled him from that country, and as Mayor of Berlin I had met him when he became commander of the French troops in Germany. It was not so much a real flight as a momentary panic. When his ever-loyal commander, who had been given no previous warning, faced him in Baden-Baden, de Gaulle said everything was over, the Communists had blocked everything: 'Massu, tout est foutu. Les communistes ont tout bloqué. Alors je viens chez vous. Pour voir.' The question was whether he could go to Strasbourg. He agreed to be flown to Colombey, and next day he was back in Paris. I believe the version of the incident which says that de Gaulle was planning a *putsch* was incorrect; he had simply lost his nerve. Massu said later that if the President had stayed in Baden-Baden it would have been a catastrophe – another Varennes (a reference to the arrest of the fleeing Louix XVI during the French Revolution).

Imagine de Gaulle, of all people, in some kind of German exile! It is unthinkable. By way of a tragi-comic sequel, the head of the Soviet military mission in Baden-Baden told General Massu that Moscow would look favourably on the upholding of the regime.

In Paris, where the Communists were trying to calm things down rather than working for revolution, large conservative counter-demonstrations helped to turn the tide. New elections were announced. Prime Minister Pompidou, whom de Gaulle dropped after his cool-headed conduct had saved the regime, was replaced by Couve de Murville; it was a last and briefly held post for that brilliant technician of state before he left the Government. His successor in the Foreign Ministry was the Gaullist Archangel Michael – Michel Debré, with whom I got on rather well, to many people's surprise. The referendum held in the spring of 1969 on decentralization and the reform of the Senate obviously made de Gaulle feel that it was time to go. When the result was known, he left for Colombey without a word of farewell. One of the last great figures who had shaped European wartime and post-war history and preserved national self-respect left the helm. He had reminded us that we meant something. Irrespective of the disappointment he had caused us and all other Europeans, he had ventured to think Utopian thoughts of a permanently peaceful Europe.

It might have been guessed that de Gaulle would not long survive his farewell to power. I was deeply moved by the news of his death in November 1970. I was unwell at the time, and unable to go to the funeral. On my next visit to Paris, in January 1971, I said: 'On the way here this morning, I visited the grave –

not far from the battlefields of unholy wars – of the man whose awareness of the painful experiences of our common history was greater than that of almost any other statesman, and who, for that very reason, was able to assist the process whereby understanding between our peoples became friendship.'

I had come to this Franco-German consultation by train. On a gloomy winter morning, still in twilight, I stood by a simple grave in Colombey-les-Deux-Églises. Years later that road also led to the great Cross of Lorraine that stands above the village, a memorial to the remarkable Frenchman who stood, so unmistakably a European, between the past and the future. In his perceptions, he came closer to a *whole* Europe than any of those who wanted to adapt too fast and too permanently to the post-war landscape.

4

Power Struggles

Who Dares, Wins

In parliamentary democracy as elsewhere, a large majority is not always an advantage, and is no guarantee of success. Furthermore, you can seldom choose the circumstances in which political responsibility is to be undertaken. It is my experience that you can strike out in a new direction even with a very small majority.

Early in December 1966, when Ludwig Erhard had resigned as Chancellor, a government formed by the two large parties took office. The Grand Coalition was better than its reputation; I set aside my own original reservations at the moment of its formation. It dealt with a recession which was overestimated at the time, worked reasonably well at home, and prepared the way for a realistic and imaginative approach abroad. But it was a remarkably laborious business to do away with a number of fictions and illusions.

As regards content, my party was well prepared on the important subjects of home and foreign policy. We were personally weakened by the fact that Fritz Erler was dying. I had a less serious health problem of my own, and played only a marginal part in the preliminary talks. Ever since I had found myself unable to breathe one early autumn morning – the condition is known as the Roemheld syndrome – and knew what it must be like to be dying, I had felt very fatigued and without ambition; I recovered both strength and ambition all the more slowly because the wounds of the 1965 election campaign had not yet healed.

Another campaign which sought to show my anti-Nazism in an unfavourable light as painfully as in the campaign of four years earlier seemed to me increasingly objectionable. A prominent Bavarian (though not Bavarian-born) member of the Bundestag had contrived to link my change of name with Hitler's, and in the heat of the campaign Erhard, whose later behaviour was perfectly correct, thought fit to taunt me with the fact that directly after the war I was 'not even a German citizen'.

The morning after the election, which Erhard had won as expected but which had brought the SPD close to the 40 per cent mark, I spoke to the press without telling anyone what I meant to do. I told them that I would not even stand for the office of Chancellor. An important factor in this decision was that various mostly unhelpful reports led me to conclude that I could not expect grass-roots Social Democrats to back me again in the face of venomous nationalistic pressure; however, most of them did thereafter support me for over two more decades. I had no cause to complain of lack of support and assistance there. But the long road from my candidature in 1961 to the great success of 1972 was not a straight one, and was full of temptations to swerve aside from the path. There were moments when I wavered, and some of my companions along the way also wavered now and then.

The party I had officially led since the beginning of 1964, and which had just re-elected me its Chairman almost unanimously, expected me to take part in the experiment of the Bonn coalition Government. It is true that friends in the party who were especially close to me would have preferred a 'minor' coalition – with the Free Democrats who, in a rather confused manner, had caused the fall of Erhard's government; that would have slightly speeded up the process of correcting course in foreign policy.

I discovered in the course of discussions of the situation – I had been able to take part in some of them – that this would not work. A former Finance Minister seriously went on record as saying that the words 'worker participation' should not appear in a statement of Government policy. Quite apart from questions of content, such a coalition would not have sufficed in the secret ballot for Chancellor. My respected Berlin Free Democrat colleague William Borm had given me the reasons against, and concluded, 'Don't do it.' I did do it three years later, and it still entailed some risks.

In 1966 I thought that if I was to be part of the Government it should be in the Ministry for Scientific Research. I should be able to put the department to the service of long-neglected tasks and still have time for the party. Research was a high priority at the time; the ministry was regarded as the department of the future. But in the inner circle of the party leadership there was strong feeling that the Party Chairman should hold the 'second most important' post in the Government, the most classic of all the classic ministries, the Foreign Ministry.

I felt at home in the Foreign Ministry, and was quite readily accepted there. I found access to my opposite numbers in other countries easy. I knew most of what the post entailed. There was some difficulty when Kiesinger's staff in the Chancellery thought they should act as my superiors. That tendency became more marked, and was increasingly tolerated by the Chancellor as the date of the 1969 election came closer. Kiesinger also entertained a suspicion which cannot have been a comfortable one: that I might not only want to succeed him as Chancellor, but might actually have my wish granted. I did not try to persuade him of the opposite, although I calculated that other Government members indicated as much to him. Others as well as his friends in his own party were telling Kiesinger he would carry on as Chancellor.

Objectively, it was a good thing for German honesty to have both a 'time-server' and an '*émigré*' of the Nazi period working together at the head of the Government. But there was a price to be paid for this evidence of reconciliation, indeed a double price, since parliamentary democracy came under pressure from two sides at once. On the left, the movement that called itself the Extra-Parliamentary Opposition emerged, and in the short term weakened Social Democracy rather than reinvigorated it; on the right, people whom I did not consider it particularly helpful to describe as *neo*-Nazis, since there was nothing new about them, made their way into the Landtag parliaments. Fortunately they had no chance to rise to positions of power or actually get elected to them. The majority electoral law announced in the Government's programme did not materialize; it would have meant the end of the right-wing radicals but of the liberals too, and would have made it impossible for new groups like the Greens to enter parliamentary life. Considerable misgivings had been expressed by both the large parties, mine even more than the Christian Democrats. In the early post-war years, thinking of the experience of the Weimar Republic, I had thought about electoral reform, but I never saw it as a universal panacea; object lessons from abroad were not wholly convincing.

Change of power was the order of the day in 1969. Most of the conservative Union thought the adjustments indicated in foreign and home policy either unnecessary, indeed harmful, or something from which they could dissociate themselves despite better judgement. This was at the expense of credibility at home; the intelligently critical public – then as later – was not to be confused with the majority. Ignoring its mood could not benefit a party pledged to progress.

A new Federal President was to be elected in March 1969. The SPD could find no candidate that our coalition partner could support, so I had to look for a candidate acceptable to the Free Democrats. This was Gustav Heinemann, a member of my governmental team in 1965 and Minister of Justice in the Kiesinger Cabinet, who was duly elected. Now the question of the consequences arose. Would matters still be the same after the next Bundestag election, due in September? At that time FDP leader Walter Scheel and I met only once, for lunch in a

Düsseldorf club in early May 1969, when we agreed that at least we would not reject the possibility of a coalition in the autumn out of hand. I did not conceal my opinion that I could envisage a good co-operation between us, with Scheel as Foreign Minister.

25 September 1969: three days before the election, in the television debate between the leading candidates, it became clear to anyone not already aware of it that, in the controversial issues of foreign policy, Scheel and I would suggest solutions which were at least similar. Nor did there seem to be any gaps that could not be bridged in home policy. I said, for all to hear, that the SPD and the FDP were closer to each other than either was to the CDU and CSU. Walter Scheel, when explicitly asked, said he was in favour of a coalition between us if we got enough seats.

And that was a big 'if'! According to first projections, a small absolute majority of seats for Kiesinger (and Strauss) could not be discounted; Scheel's candidates seemed to have fallen at the 5-per-cent hurdle. There was celebration in the Chancellery. The Young Union waved torches. Nixon phoned congratulations.

It turned out that the Free Democrats would be all right after all, if only just; they had slipped from 9.5 to 5.8 per cent of the vote and from 49 to 30 seats in the Bundestag. The SPD and FDP together now had twelve more seats than the CDU/CSU, and only five more than were needed to elect the Chancellor. Could we build on that? Could we suppose that the tiny majority would hold for the four years of a legislative period? I was not sure, but I thought the risk was justifiable. Otherwise, we would have dashed many hopes. Above all, we did not want to be back on the Opposition benches unnecessarily; there was so much to be done in German politics.

So on 21 October 1969 I was elected the fourth Chancellor of the Federal Republic of Germany, with 251 votes to 235, only two more than absolutely necessary. I had become head of government at my third attempt, and a watershed had been passed. It was almost forty years since March 1930, when the last Social Democrat Chancellor of the Reich, Hermann Müller, resigned. Ever since the end of the war I had been determined to show our ability to govern not only in cities and *Länder*, but in the state as a whole. The Federal Republic had passed the test of democracy in showing itself capable of change. And for the democratic outside world, the significance of the shift of power also lay in that capacity for peaceful change.

On the evening of that September election and in the days that followed there was much uncertainty and yet more excitement. I telephoned Walter Scheel during the evening and said I was going to tell the press simply that the SPD and FDP had more seats than the CDU and CSU. Almost casually, Scheel said, 'Yes, do that'. His own party's poor showing had rather depressed him; he felt unable to make concrete arrangements. The disappointment went deep. We did not meet until next day.

The executive committee of my party had dispersed before the situation became clear. Wehner and Schmidt could not make much of my plan for a government; they would both have preferred to continue with the Grand Coalition, which Kiesinger had already written off at least as firmly as I had. Wehner spoke angrily of the oscillations of the Liberals, while Alex Möller, nicknamed 'Comrade Chairman of the Board', who became my first Finance Minister but unfortunately did not remain in the post for long, began discussing practical matters with FDP colleagues that very night. Those who thought as he and I did included Professor Karl Schiller, the Economics Minister who had already helped me in the Berlin Senate in his own idiosyncratic and brilliant way. There were also younger people who were in a position to help with decision-making, and there was Gustav Heinemann behind the scenes. Next day even our opponents in the party leadership agreed that I should try the Social Democratic–Liberal coalition. It was clear to everyone that I was not going to be stopped now.

Meanwhile Kurt-Georg Kiesinger had become nervous and active. Late that same evening he had sent his protégé Helmut Kohl, the young Prime Minister of the Rhineland-Palatinate and his heir presumptive as Chairman of the Federal CDU, to his friend Hans-Dietrich Genscher, manager of the FDP parliamentary party and Scheel's Deputy Chairman, to win the Free Democrats over.

Kohl came away from his exploratory talks with the impression that there were enough opponents to a Social Democratic–Liberal coalition among the Free Democrats to prevent my election. Twenty-four hours later, on the Monday night when he and the CDU General Secretary Bruno Heck met ten FDP deputies in Erich Mende's home in Godesberg – deputies for whom the new coalition was 'not yet a settled thing' – he felt confirmed in his assessment. On Tuesday a delegation of Free Democrats ready to negotiate went to have an 'informative discussion' with Kiesinger.

A rather vaguely formulated proposal was conveyed to Scheel by Kiesinger on 3 October, but by then the Chancellor could be cherishing no more illusions. That Friday I had been to the Federal President with Scheel to tell him that we had agreed in all essentials on the formation of the Government. When the alliance was sealed Olof Palme said he had been wrong to say Willy Brandt could be elected head of government in any country of Europe but his own. (Later he added, in his occasionally impish manner, that he had been right after all.)

I was not showing over-confidence when I said that now Hitler finally *had* lost the war, and I would consider myself Chancellor not of a conquered but of a liberated Germany. The world would be dealing with a government that was not always easy-going but was loyal. I did not feel I had said more than I should or undertaken too much. The revival of policies for peace was as necessary as resolving the stagnation of reform. I wanted to be a Chancellor of renewal at home. I have always felt the accusation that I neglected home policies to be unjust.

Debit and Credit

With Adenauer the watchword was 'no experiments'. It answered the need for calm felt by a nation glad to have the aberrations of the Nazi period and the war behind it and as yet unwilling to look back. A preference for looking forward was good for economic reconstruction. Change was not indicated until that watchword had found independent life, and post-war society threatened to be stifled as if by a layer of smog.

I said, 'Don't be afraid of experiments. Let us create a modern Germany.' I said, 'If we want to live in security tomorrow we must fight for reform today.' These were effective slogans. But unlike some of the slogans of later years, they had a philosophy behind them: hitherto, German citizens had been rather afraid of reform, but now it dawned upon them that you could not have long-term security without it.

We may smile now at the urge for modernity of the late sixties, but it was better than the anxiety in the face of progress that was felt a decade later. Those who helped to shape the Social Democratic–Liberal coalition could not be happy to see a reforming, forward-looking policy under double pressure – from naïve neo-conservatism and a fundamental rejection of progress. Not everything was well enough planned, and much turned out differently from the way it was intended, but that is another matter. Perhaps we had simply undertaken too much for the short period of a legislative term.

I had seen in Scandinavia what it means for state and society to be involved in a constant process of shedding outworn concepts, and where it can lead. I had also seen that material want can be banished, and the democratic idea carried beyond the civic and state framework into wide areas of society. However, I never thought that all areas of life should be officially and bureaucratically 'democratized'. Later, the strange growths that flowered in many universities taught us that where democratization is part of the programme, it cannot always be assumed from the start that there is a will for tolerance and efficiency. But we had set sail on the right course; we had to make it possible for a growing number of people to know freedom, and we had to ensure that the basic values of democracy permeated the major areas of society.

This was not an exclusively Social Democratic view. It had intellectual links with Liberal ideas, and with elements of Catholic social doctrine and the Evangelical social ethic. It is one of the unfortunate – and objectively unnecessary – burdens on post-war Germany that forces for regeneration did not come together to a greater extent, surmounting the old party boundaries. It was not to be regretted that the adherents of the traditional bourgeois parties found their way to a new form of party, the 'ecumenical' CDU/CSU. However, it *was* regrettable that the Union perpetuated Konrad Adenauer's patriarchalist although by no means unsocial approach. Perhaps that was the very reason for his success in post-war Germany.

When the bulk of the work of reconstruction had been done, and the need for calm began to slacken, a predominantly moderate Social Democratic Party urged putting the social justice rooted in the Basic Law into practice and making the responsible citizen a model. It was an expectation shared by many notable representatives of the intellectual life of Germany, and found its first expression in legal reforms; they were begun during the Grand Coalition and under the stern eye of Gustav Heinemann. The era of reform was ushered in by the rescinding of the old criminal law on sexual conduct, which in part still stemmed from the Kaiser's Reich. There was wide approval of the fact that the state could no longer lay down the law on sexual morality and that the old clichés about guilt and sin had died away.

Is it inevitable for moderation to fly out of the window when movement comes into a society? Only too often, the new departures of restless student youth and the 'Extra-Parliamentary Opposition' which was largely their creation were destructive rather than helpful; they could hardly help matters forward by trying to impose immoderate programmes on society. However, there is no denying that some of what the young people of the 1968 protests were saying had a stimulating influence in the medium term.

I observed the student revolts closely, outside as well as inside German frontiers: in France at the beginning of May 1968, then in Belgrade, in the USA, in Rio, even in Iceland. I was moved by the events in Berlin: the death of the student Benno Ohnesorg during the Shah's visit in June 1967; the attempted assassination of student leader Rudi Dutschke at Easter 1968; the uproar in Frankfurt in the autumn of the same year when the Senegalese President Léopold Senghor was awarded the Peace Prize of the German Book Trade. I felt angry: I did not wish to be Foreign Minister of a country to which it was impossible to welcome a foreign guest with due propriety. There was also trouble with gatecrashers at the 1968 SPD party conference. A youth congress I had supported in Godesberg at the beginning of 1969 foundered on the obstinacy of groups who wanted to disturb proceedings rather than listen.

My advice to the Government to which I belonged and the party of which I was Chairman was to listen to the criticisms of the young. I was not particularly successful. I certainly did not mean accepting everything these young people said. Without actually doing anything in particular to earn it, I have acquired a reputation for being ready to talk and able to learn rather than cutting myself off from the young. That may have been a change from the general ignorance, but I did not understand what was really worrying the younger generation, and by no means its worst elements. Perhaps I did not want to understand; the language of vapid radical slogans made communication difficult. However, I said to UNESCO in Paris in November 1968: 'None of us should be too old to pursue these questions. It is not particularly surprising if young people rebel against the discrepancy between outworn structures and new opportunities; if they protest against the difference between appearance and reality; if they despair of a policy that sets itself goals but proves powerless to do anything about law-breaking, the use of force, oppression and bloodshed. I am not in favour of going along with everything the young say. I am against concessions to intolerance and violence. Here, responsibility and respect for posterity urge us not to give way. But I think we should not shut ourselves off. Listening is not enough. We must take up the challenge and be willing to question ourselves and learn something new.'

I had seen which long-standing tasks had been neglected when they ought to have been tackled. Only gradually and with some qualifications did I come to see what new tasks faced us; a good many people were upset by my going at least a little way ahead of the bellwethers of society.

I had made environmental problems part of my platform in my first Bundestag election campaign, thereby providing amusement for pragmatic politicians of all shades. When I spoke before the election – supported by American data – of the hitherto almost entirely neglected community task of protecting the environment, my principal argument was that the health of millions of people was at stake. Demands for pure air, clean water and less noise should not be left merely on paper.

Later, when I spoke as the party's leading candidate in North Rhine-Westphalia, I concluded by wishing that the sky above the Ruhr might be blue again; this was made to sound ridiculous by lowbrow critics. It is hard to understand why people were so slow to perceive the great ecological threats of our time, although we in the Federal Republic were slightly ahead of a number of our European neighbours. Not until the autumn of 1969 did protection of the environment become an independent part of the work of the Ministry of the Interior; at the time I tried to make it clear that this was a subject of very great urgency in home politics.

Despite the still explosive crisis of the Wall as it dragged on, a congress on German Community Tasks met in Berlin in 1962; it drew public attention to the neglected community components of welfare, from the urban infrastructure to the crisis in education and the health service. In 1964 I looked around me in the USA and sought ideas for the 1965 election campaign. Scientific advice was not hard to find at home, but expert political advice was not sufficiently valued. However, the Club of Rome had some influence. We guessed rather than actually knew that ideas of automatic growth must be jettisoned. Drawing conclusions was a slow process, first because so much had been left undone, and second because the prime concern for a Social Democratic party standing at last on the threshold of governmental power was to honour its own pledge to promote social security.

In 1966, and even more in 1969, we tried to reintegrate into the community those who had been marginalized not by any fault of their own but by the accidents of life. We took the initiative in continuing to pay wages when workers fell sick, and then in ensuring that first pensions and then health insurance received more consideration than prescribed by narrow ideas of obligation. Many employees had had no reliable system of social security co-financed by their employers. It sounds a technical point, and yet the chance for self-realization would have been worth only half as much without such partial reforms. Health insurance for agricultural workers comes into this category.

Healing the cracks in the social state was one of our first concerns; by bringing in compulsory accident insurance for schoolchildren and students – without great administrative or financial expense – we came a little closer to that aim, and new provisions for the rehabilitation of the severely handicapped and accident victims brought it a great deal closer.

It had become impossible to speak of a new social policy and ignore the issue of equal rights for women. That was on our agenda, and above all it had to be implemented by social legislation, or equal rights would have been only for the better-off. We set about getting fixed minimum rates for women who received ridiculously low pensions – in spite of long working lives and because of their low incomes – and we won equal treatment for war widows.

A special landmark was reached with the pensions law of 1972; as well as material improvements it brought flexibility of retiring age. Vigorous action on pensions for war victims also proved a prudent step. I had long felt it was shameful that the victims of war, of all people, had to organize demonstrations to complain about the adjustment of their benefits.

Social legislation had to clear the hurdle of the Bundesrat, where it was not easy to find a majority for the Government. Social reforms remained incomplete because one cannot do everything at once, or because they could not command the necessary majority, or because even if they did there was no extra money available. However, when unemployment figures shot up in 1974–5, as a result of the state of the world economy, it was important that the net of social security had been drawn tighter.

Superficial criticism has accused the governmental policy of the Social Democratic–Liberal coalition of neglecting the interests of the economy and laying a heavy burden of debt on the state. Neither accusation is correct, and both are clearly refuted by the statistics; no evidence to the contrary is required for an objective assessment. I never believed that as much as possible ought to be settled by the state. Private initiative in society and the economy deserves encouragement, not repression.

Dependence on the international economic situation gave us much food for thought at the beginning of the seventies. Inadequate United States responsibility for the world monetary system, and co-operation in the world economy where financial policy was concerned, were both problems. We did not approve when the dollar came off the gold standard in the summer of 1971, or when exchange rates were decontrolled in the spring of 1973. At the end of that year the first oil-price crisis was a heavy blow, causing panic where a more appropriate German and European reaction was called for.

In my first statement of Government policy in 1969 I had said I wanted to 'take a chance on more democracy', and I added challengingly that we had not come to the end of our democracy but were 'only just beginning'. That remark brought both committed support and opposition. A hostile campaign – insinuating that we would throw democracy overboard – had only limited effect; it contained a confused mixture of objections to our policies both at home and abroad.

We certainly intended to give our work as high a profile as possible and meet the need for shared information. But inexperience meant that we greatly overestimated the weight carried by forward planning.

We assumed that worker representation and participation in management would generate a force for mobility in the country from within. The amendment of the Labour Management Act in 1971 (giving workers co-determination on the shop floor), and with it of the law governing the status of the Civil Service Association, did not satisfy the unions, but they did recognize it as a 'great step forward'. Nor did worker representation on the boards of large firms – a law passed in 1974 but not enacted until 1976, after managerial associations had appealed to the Federal Constitutional Court – come up to the expectations of the trade unions. It proved to have been a serious shortcoming, particularly after our great election success of November 1972, that we did not make it sufficiently clear what could be achieved with a given parliamentary majority and what could not.

I still regret that we did not succeed in making a breakthrough in the acquisition of assets by employees. Two different positions in the trade union camp blocked each other. One feared 'mini-capitalism', and with it a weakening of the workers' fighting spirit; it was particularly active in the metal-workers' union. The construction workers' union took the opposite position. The SPD allowed this conflict to cripple it, omitting to take the step the Swedish Social Democrats had, in establishing an employees' fund. Decades of commitment to this cause by Philip Rosenthal, the Social Democratic industrialist, came to nothing; he had often and earnestly urged that the employees should have 'their say and their share'.

The implementation of 'more democracy' entailed major steps which were useful in giving women equal rights in law: they involved the divorce laws and regulations governing use of surnames, standardization of pensions, and measures intended to bring more women into politics. I myself had only one woman in the actual Government, but for the first time there was a woman junior minister in the Chancellery, and two women permanent under-secretaries in the civil service. In fact social pressure was not yet strong enough to bring more women forward. Signals may be sent out from above; change must come from below.

Social justice was at the top of the list of reforms, and was unattainable without educational reform. Educational reform was intended to mean equal opportunity, and was not necessarily linked to change in educational content; in the battle that raged around 'basic guidelines', suggestions that might have found broad agreement were lost. But there is no doubt that the educational reform we had set in motion at the beginning of the sixties, partly in alliance with FDP politicians, changed the face of German society. The number of children completing a course of higher education shot up, and the number of students, including the number of working-class students, tripled between 1965 and 1980. Our failure to correlate various reforming theories and purge them of their dross had consequences that were to give us problems over and beyond educational policy. The counter-movement was able to become so powerful only because a middle way of reform had not yet been found, and many of us could no longer relate quantity to quality.

The Federal Ministry for Education and Science, as yet undivided and still including the Ministry for Scientific Research, was headed by Professor Leussink and Klaus von Dohnanyi, and it was an influential department in the context of reform policy. An addition to the Basic Law gave the Federal Government some of the responsibility for educational planning. The *Länder* could not have provided all the necessary funding by themselves; educational expenses per head of the population were multiplying by five. The Federal Government thus also had some influence on content, which favoured reform – or not, depending on your political viewpoint, and that was not always or necessarily a party political viewpoint. I am still not happy to think that at the level of *Länder* competence the SPD allowed the omission of German as a compulsory subject from the *Abitur* curriculum, and the disappearance of History from the syllabus.

Quite a number of our party members, who would have liked to overturn the economic power structures but dared not because of resistance from powerful interests and because they would have overreached themselves, became all the keener on social change through the educational system. It was a substitute, so to speak: almost all the young deputies of 1969 who considered themselves left-wing made straight for the Bundestag Committee on Education and Science.

Educational reform was not fully achieved, and would not have been even if it could have been carried through by the Chancellery. But as the Federal *Länder* retained major powers, and not even minimum consistency between them could be contrived, the status of educational policy rapidly declined. However, we had shown the way, even if we could not ensure success. Things were different in the field of construction. That example may show how reform policies were brought to bear in many different spheres. I think with particular pride of the Town Planning Act of 1971. This made it possible to preserve the historical heritage and open up the way to the future for many of our cities.

My proposal at the Saarbrücken Party conference in the spring of 1970 for a costed approach to reform did not get very far. I was anxious that we should be clear about the price to be paid for reforming policies on the principle that you cannot make more than one use of a predetermined public part of the national product. Also, that it is a good thing to know what consequences will flow from which redistribution process or which tax burden. At a time of great economic uncertainty, it proved impossible to give financial guarantees for a medium-term programme. Younger critics, impelled by older ideas, exhorted us not to get bogged down in questions of 'practicability' but were ready enough to reach for outmoded dogmatism themselves. We were not successful in gauging our mandate accurately and publicly enough to take the wind out of the sails of the Opposition, which was constantly predicting the ruin of the state. Debit and credit were too far apart. We suffered considerable setbacks in the Landtag elections.

Was this uncertainty, and the argument between those who were taking stock and those who wanted to press forward more quickly, connected with the appearance on the horizon of new challenges and new viewpoints? Without knowing it, we were coming to the end of the time when we could afford to see the future as a simple extension of the past and its lines of development. The question of the quality of economic growth, and the suppressed suspicion that a modern industrial state like the Federal Republic of Germany functioned by laws of its own, were in the air even before the initial momentum of the reforming era had slowed down.

Altogether, more was expected of the new Government than it could perform. Nor was the Government free from the temptation to take on too much at once. Some of our comrades in arms thought they were serving the good cause by hailing every kind of technical adaptation as a reform, or by regarding lists of good intentions as a programme. We were not sufficiently wary of false prognoses. However, even without such flaws, we would have had to face vigorous opposition on our home policies.

How does the balance-sheet look now? To me, it looks quite good, like my memory of the reform years themselves. I am particularly glad to think of the commitment made by the intelligentsia to the triple endeavour of securing peace, a vigorous democracy and social regeneration. Günter Grass played a particularly outstanding part, at the head of a considerable number of writers and artists. He had already accompanied me to a number of functions during the 1961 election campaign. Later he set up his own electoral initiatives and probably brought us votes; he certainly brought colour into the business of politics. Town planners, theatre people, natural scientists and teachers put their expertise at our disposal and spoke in public for us. Grass himself, Heinrich Böll, Walter Jens and Max Frisch spoke at party meetings.

The image of the snail as symbol of progress is Grass's. It could not bring an audience to its feet, yet it was a very welcome companion on our reforming way. Over the years I have found I can make less and less of that snail: which way is it crawling? And do I know who may crush it? Progress is not inevitable, and setbacks as well as leaps forward are part of the historical process – not that snails can leap.

I was glad we succeeded in entering into frank dialogue with both Churches and in narrowing down the grey zones of tactical relations; however, I do not want to give the impression that I was the promoter of that dialogue. Rooted in the Protestant tradition, and resenting a Lutheranism that had stood by a totalitarian state, close to Evangelicals in Scandinavia and Berlin from whom I would not let my agnosticism separate me, I did not find it difficult to work on building up a partnership with the Churches and the religious communities. The idea that a political programme can serve as a substitute religion, however, was as alien to me as the suggestion that a political party as a whole can be Christian.

And the darker side of my memories? Like many other states, the Federal Republic was not spared the threat of various forms of terrorism. This dreadful threat did not make government any easier, and it certainly did not ease the way to reforms. Terrorist attacks organized from outside – like the one on the Israeli team at the Munich Olympics – were outrages. Aircraft hijackings – like the one undertaken to exert blackmail for the release of the surviving perpetrators of the Munich attack – were a new kind of challenge. Finding the requisite combination of flexibility and the ability to stand firm became harder and harder. I was brought to the brink of despair by the way in which several small extreme left-wing groups slid into a policy of destructive negativism; it was all the more depressing when intellectual justification was sought, and necessary distinctions were not made. I was also distressed, but not surprised, when such evil proceeded from the extreme Right.

The democratic state must act consistently and firmly; there is no alternative. But I resolved to withstand hysterical reactions and allow as little injury as possible to the constitutional state. Protecting the lives of citizens and the foundations of the community is a duty that cannot be evaded. None the less, it is important to discover the causes of aberrant tendencies. And democracy cannot reject people who have put anti-social aberrations behind them.

I have seen how planned attacks and abductions can change the lives of individuals and families, and experienced the alienation effect of being able to address large meetings only from behind bullet-proof glass. The security service dealing with the first generation of the so-called Red Army Faction told me my appeals had helped to remove the ground from under its feet: a ground made up of various diffuse sympathies. But what was the use of that, if it was always going to consolidate itself again?

Non Olet

Aligning our Eastern front was a watershed. Yet to a great extent our foreign policy was distinguished by its continuity, which was hardly surprising. I neither changed my convictions nor burned my files when I moved from the Foreign Ministry to the Schaumburg Palace. But the new Opposition in Bonn, inadequately prepared for that role, insisted on making foreign

Willy Brandt's mother

Willy Brandt's father

Childhood photographs, 1915–25

Barcelona, 1937

1945, photograph from
Norwegian military passport

Julius Leber before
the People's Court, 1944

Kurt Schumacher, Franz Neumann and Ernst Reuter, Berlin, 1948

Ernst Reuter with Kurt Schumacher in his Bonn apartment, 1952

The Governing Mayor at the Police Show in the Berlin Olympic stadium, 31 August 1958

Meeting outside the Schöneberg Rathaus on 16 August 1961, three days after the building of the Wall

With Kennedy and Federal Chancellor Adenauer driving
through Berlin

With Lyndon B. Johnson after John F. Kennedy's funeral in
Washington, 1963

Farewell visit to Berlin by
Chancellor Adenauer,
October 1963

Federal President Gustav
Heinemann with Willy Brandt
after his appointment as Federal
Chancellor in 1969

The Brandt Cabinet outside the Villa Hammerschmidt on 21 October 1969.
Front row: Gerhard Jahn, Käthe Strobel, Federal President Gustav Heinemann,
Federal Chancellor Willy Brandt, Walter Scheel, Karl Schiller, Georg Leber;
second row: Helmut Schmidt, Alex Möller, Erhard Eppler, Hans-Dietrich
Genscher, Walter Arendt; third row: Egon Franke, Lauritz Lauritzen, Hans
Leussink, Horst Ehmke, Josef Ertl

With Leonid Brezhnev after signing the Moscow Treaty in 1970

Constructive vote of no confidence, 1972. Rainer Barzel offering congratulations

DET NORSKE STORTINGS
NOBELKOMITÉ

HAR OVERENSSTEMMENDE MED
REGLENE I DET AV

ALFRED NOBEL

DEN 27. NOVEMBER 1895 OPPRETTEDE
TESTAMENTE TILDELT

WILLY BRANDT

NOBELS FREDSPRIS FOR 1971

OSLO, 10. DESEMBER 1971

Certificate for Nobel Peace Prize. Awarded to Willy Brandt in 1971

With Günter Guillaume

Handwritten letter of resignation
to the Federal President

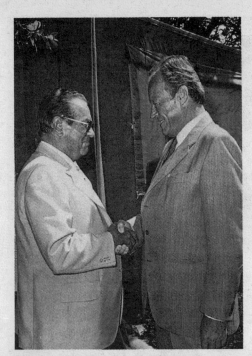

With Josip Broz Tito, 1975

With Helmut Schmidt, 1982

Meeting of the Socialist International in Madrid, 1980. Left to right:
Shimon Peres, Willy Brandt, Bruno Kreisky, King Juan Carlos of
Spain, Felipe Gonzalez, Queen Sofia, Joop den Uyl, Trygve Bratteli

With Indira Gandhi in New Delhi, summer 1984

With George Bush in Washington, 1985

With Deng Xiaoping in Peking, 1984

With Mikhail Gorbachev
at Bonn railway station,
1989

With Walter Momper
at the Brandenburg Gate,
10 November 1989

Mass demonstration in East Berlin, end of October 1989

The Wall falls. Potsdamer Platz, 12 November 1989

policy a battlefield in domestic policy. Every opposition is exposed to this temptation, and German Social Democracy too had succumbed to it in the first decade of the Federal Republic's existence. In this particular case, moreover, issues relating to the division of Germany and how it might be overcome were raised every time our relationship with the victorious powers in general and East–West relations in particular came up.

Discussion of the treaties became more acrimonious than I had expected. This was not just because the leadership of the Union and not a few of its adherents had got it firmly into their heads that they were the natural party of government; they also seemed to believe they had been granted the wisdom of Solomon in matters of foreign and German policy. From wrangling over the treaties arose the battle to bring down the Government.

Gerhard Schröder, my predecessor at the Foreign Ministry and now Chairman of the Foreign Affairs Committee of the Bundestag, did not conceal – even publicly – that this was the issue at stake. At the beginning of 1972 he wrote that opposition to the treaties was 'a necessary attitude in domestic policy'. Yet the previous year, when he visited Moscow on an exploratory mission, he had adopted a very moderate attitude, and gave me the impression in his report that he and a number of his party colleagues would not put any obstacles in our way over ratification. But he was not speaking for those Christian Democrats who, without the insignia of power, could not reconcile wishful thinking and reality. I was sorry that Gerhard Schröder too put supposed party interest first, against his better judgement.

At the end of October 1969, three days after my government took office, we revalued the Deutschmark upwards against the dollar; during the election campaign Karl Schiller had argued intelligently and cogently against Strauss on this subject, although his argument went above most people's heads. At the end of November we signed the non-proliferation treaty that was still pending. At the beginning of December I and Georges Pompidou, elected to succeed de Gaulle in June 1969, helped to ensure the success of the summit conference at The Hague: the European Community was to admit the United Kingdom and steer a course towards economic and currency union. None of this carried any weight when ratification of the Eastern treaties came up.

The Opposition had one vote more in the Bundesrat than those *Länder* which supported the Federal Government; accordingly, the *Länder* chamber opposed ratification. In the Bundestag the so-called First Reading of the Moscow and Warsaw treaties took place at the end of February 1972. In the debate, I said that it would be absurd to suppose 'that the leaders of the Western Alliance, with the President of the United States at their head, would pursue and support a policy which deliberately aimed to weaken that Western Alliance'. Today, I said, we could be among the pacemakers of a new policy; tomorrow, at best, we would be counted among the stragglers.

Our small governmental majority became shaky directly after that debate on ratification, although not because of any new arguments advanced on the subject. The situation had been changed by the great success achieved by the CDU directly after Easter 1972 in the Baden-Württemberg Landtag elections; the Social Democrats no longer had a share in the Stuttgart government. Subsequently, those around Rainer Barzel (who had replaced Kiesinger as CDU Chairman in 1971), in agreement with the Chairman of the CSU, Franz Josef Strauss, decided to aim for a constructive vote of no confidence: i.e., proposing Barzel for the office of Chancellor and pinning their hopes on luring several deputies and their votes away from the coalition.

A legitimate difference of opinion descended into a sordid attempt at manipulation. Money was involved in 1972, and not for the first time. Money had entered into it after the 1969 election, in line with the Latin tag that it does not smell: *non olet*. Accusations of a policy of surrender and the selling-out of German interests were used as justification.

Part of the campaign against my government was conducted

by means which were on the very edge of legality, or just over it. Civil servants were induced to reveal confidential, even secret documents to fuel the polemics. This sort of thing began the very month after the change of government in 1969. Drafts such as those for the treaty with the Soviet Union were traded on the open market – with the result that certain further compromises became practically impossible. The Foreign Ministry counted no fewer than fifty-four cases of the leaking of state secrets during the first eighteen months of my government, the work of those who insinuated that 'German interests were being sold out'.

I was angrier than seems appropriate, in retrospect, to find that civil servants who failed in their obligations in this way saw themselves as 'Resistance workers', adding fuel to a distasteful campaign. Investigation of the culprits was an empty formality and ended nowhere. Attempts were also made to get at American sources. Eager, indeed fanatical, envoys of the Opposition, determined spokesmen for the expellees' associations, and alleged upholders of the interests of the Fatherland set to work in Washington and other capitals; however, their occasional successes could be countered, unlike those poisonous darts shot by the press at home, including the politically oriented popular press.

The talented and highly successful publisher Axel Springer of Hamburg had been rather favourably inclined towards me and my party in the immediate post-war period. He did not like Adenauer; it was his firm belief that German unity was not safe in the Chancellor's hands. He felt very close to Berlin, and showed it when he settled in the city in both his business and his private life. Had there been any chance of it after the 1961 elections, he would not have been averse to accepting the Department of All-German Affairs in a Brandt Cabinet. He thought he could explain to the Russians their own interest in a solution of the German question. When he and Hans Zehrer, editor-in-chief of *Die Welt*, came back from a visit to Moscow early in 1958 – they had discussed it with me beforehand – he was very disappointed; he had been fobbed off with a pre-fabricated interview with Khrushchev.

Our friendly relations suffered when he urged me in the Schöneberg Rathaus to agree to a regional commercial television station; he saw West Berlin as a way of opening up the Federal Republic. It seemed to me unreasonable to take advantage of Berlin's special status in this way; moreover, my party had reservations about private television companies. The rift became wider over our different opinions of *Ostpolitik*. Once he realized that it would not be easy to bring the Soviet Union to a different way of thinking, Springer veered to outright opposition, which could not be reconciled with the *Ostpolitik* approach.

Organs of the press put pressure on public opinion; people with money put pressure on the Free Democrats. It was suggested to their leaders that they could not count on donations from industry if they went along with – and then stayed with – the Socialists. Even in the weeks before the formation of the Government in the autumn of 1969 there were rumours that those who changed sides would be 'looked after', and talk of attempts at enticement, consultancy deals and the promise of donations. An FDP colleague confirmed that 'the CDU/CSU made financial offers to individual deputies of the FDP'.

In fact, Barzel failed in the ballot on the 'constructive vote of no confidence' on 27 April 1972. He had counted on 250 votes, would have needed 249, and actually got 247.

A superficial view of the ballot might suggest that three FDP deputies had voted for Barzel, so at least two Union deputies must have voted against him. In fact it was more complicated than that, but it has never been possible to reconstruct the whole course of events. Dr Barzel wrote in his memoirs in 1978 that there were 'three votes from his own camp' missing. He did not know why two voting cards had been specially marked with pencil; nor did I, and I still do not. Barzel assured me that he had not induced anyone to change sides, either directly or indirectly. An experienced contemporary historian thought that the Opposition leader had been 'let down by his own side'. Herbert Wehner, who in 1972 was Chairman of the Parliamentary SPD, remarked briefly in 1980 that he knew of 'two people who really contrived the whole thing; I was one, and the other is no longer in Parliament'.

My own knowledge of any improper 'offers' was initially limited to the reports from FDP colleagues in the autumn of 1969; then to the admissions of Wilhelm Helms, an FDP deputy who voted with the Opposition; and at the very most to my suggesting to Dr Günther Müller, who had fallen out with the Munich Social Democrats, the prospect of a seat for Nuremberg that was going to be free. Nothing came of it, and he has settled well into the CSU.

More important was something that came to my ears in 1972. In April, not long before the unsuccessful attempt to topple me as Chancellor, two SPD deputies for the Palatinate – Dr Bardens of Ludwigshafen and Pastor Kaffka of Frankenthal – came to the Chancellery to describe the intrigues of a regional firm: there had recently been concrete negotiations over 'sales' at a country estate in Austria, and several FDP deputies had taken part. The instigator was named as Franz Josef Strauss, Chairman of the CSU. I do not know that that has ever been contradicted.

In the summer of 1973 a Württemberg CDU deputy, Julius Steiner, said he had received 50,000 marks from Karl Wienand, business manager of the Parliamentary SPD, for not voting for Barzel. He was not a particularly credible witness; he also said he had been an Eastern agent. His evidence, which did not stand up to examination, caused considerable uproar. People who had taken hardly any notice of well-substantiated reports of bribery 'on the right' were particularly loud in their protests. Even more surprising were those left-liberal sympathizers who could not wait to join in, acting as if they or I were somehow to blame.

A parliamentary investigatory committee found nothing. The insinuation that the then head of the Chancellery, Horst Ehmke, had misappropriated 50,000 marks from the Treasury was certainly false. However, the Government that had stood up for itself so well in the autumn of 1972 suffered. Inventions and unproven claims will easily help to poison the political climate.

Franz Josef Strauss, one of the great talents of the wartime generation, tolerated or had a hand in many dubious activities. His influence would have extended further if he had built in stronger safeguards. For years he kept stumbling over self-erected obstacles, including his own unbridled thirst for power; he thought that he would be able to snatch at the crown in a time of crisis. But the crisis did not come, and the crown was hung too high. He was trapped in the role of blusterer – efficient in national politics, ambitious in international politics. It did not go against the grain for me to seek him out and wish him well on his seventieth birthday in 1985. Strauss divided the public into friend and enemy as no one else did; he clasped the one to his breast and spurned the other. I was neither his friend nor his enemy.

We were almost the same age. He was not of upper-class origin either, but the influences that had shaped us were very different. We came to know each other, indeed to know each other well, when we were both among the younger members of the First Bundestag. Unlike me, Strauss exercised direct influence. He intended to have a say in the structuring of power in the new Federal Republic. The thirty-four-year-old General Secretary of the Bavarian CSU had thrown his weight into the scale when the idea of a grand coalition was rejected and Adenauer was given the job of forming a group to the right of Social Democracy to govern the country; it should be remembered that Kurt Schumacher, leader of the SPD in those early years, was also against a coalition. The young Bavarian deputy, full of self-confidence but good company none the less, advanced quickly; Adenauer took him into the Cabinet in 1955, and he became Defence Minister only a year later. He seemed to shake off his involvement in a number of dubious affairs quite easily.

I might well have wanted nothing to do with him. Before the 1961 Bundestag elections he afforded protection to those who tried to libel me – to put it mildly – with a flood of publications; he it was who instantly classified those whose political thinking differed from his as 'tools of Moscow', and was quick to ask meaningly: 'And what were you doing in those twelve years outside Germany?' However, I sought him out shortly after the election to suggest the idea of an all-party government, or at least a broad-based foreign policy. His own mind was always set on succeeding Adenauer, with Ludwig Erhard as the intermediate link. It did not work out; in 1962 he had to resign because of his impossible behaviour in the case of trumped-up treason charges against the magazine *Der Spiegel*. [In consequence of an article attacking his nuclear defence policy and allegedly revealing military secrets, he had ordered illegal raids on the magazine's offices and the arbitrary arrest of its proprietor and editorial staff.] I was impressed by the serious way he subsequently took up neglected areas of home policy, and I was not particularly bothered by his performance as a kind of German Gaullist in foreign politics; I never took it entirely seriously.

At the end of 1966 we found ourselves on the same Government bench in the Grand Coalition; two years before, I had had to promise my party that this very thing was out of the question. Strauss was a good Finance Minister, and he did not even try to make difficulties for me in foreign policy. His double-act with the Economics Minister Karl Schiller worked very well until they disagreed over the upward revaluation of the Deutschmark. He never could handle his failure to get a firm grip on the CDU. In 1980, when he was the Union parties' joint candidate for Chancellor, the result clearly did not come up to his expectations. Not only the situation but his own nature prevented him from becoming Federal Chancellor. However, there is no doubt that he played a major part in the modernization of Bavaria. His talent for demagogy really unfolded when, attacking Helmut Schmidt, he described conditions in Bonn as those of a pigsty, and advised his followers to make it all seem even worse. His threat to make the CSU a separate fourth party throughout the Federal Republic was unconvincing. Since he must have known that the CDU would then instantly set up in Bavaria, he was sharpening a bladeless knife.

A comment Strauss made in the last thing he wrote is the key to his political orientation. He said, of Helmut Schmidt's *Menschen und Mächte*, that he and Schmidt had both been through the war as lieutenants in the reserve, and their experiences at the Eastern Front had been a determining factor 'both for the firmness with which we represented German interests in negotiations with the Soviet leadership, and for our passionate support for peace in the world'. This led to bar-room philosophy of an elevated nature, such as his thesis that a Soviet urge for expansion was a constant. The opposition between East and West became an obsession, removed from awareness of historical change. As so often, Strauss had fallen far behind his own powers of discernment.

He was not choosy when it came to picking either the places he visited or the people he talked to. He praised both General Pinochet and President Botha. Not least, the Communist leaders exercised a magical power of attraction on him, in Bucharest, Tiranë, Beijing, or capitals closer to home. He was a welcome guest in China at the time of Mao, who met conservative politicians of the West in the hope of finding a major and potentially mighty ally against 'the Russians'. At the same time, Strauss was disappointed to be cold-shouldered by the Soviet leadership. He was still trying to get an invitation to Moscow at the end of the sixties. In the early seventies I defended him to the Soviet leaders against misconceptions and unjustified accusations. He met Brezhnev in Bonn. Finally, at the end of 1987, he did manage to get to the Kremlin, where Gorbachev met him. Ambassador Dobrynin, who was responsible at the time for the Soviet Communist Party's international relations, sought advice in Bonn. I could hardly have opposed the visit. When I met Gorbachev myself three months later, he asked me, 'Will you have a grand coalition?' I replied, 'Your friend Strauss seems to like the idea. I have doubts myself.'

Strauss could propose no alternative to our treaties policy, and did not impede it in any major way, apart from inducing the Free State of Bavaria to appeal to the Federal Constitutional Court over the Basic Treaty on relations with the GDR. That manoeuvre largely failed. To the alarm of some of his party friends, in his last years the Chairman of the CSU not only worked for an easier relationship with Erich Honecker but was helpful in getting bank credits for the GDR. One thing he never achieved was a meeting with Fidel Castro; he had even fixed on the Spanish head of government as someone to negotiate it. No, Strauss was certainly not a nonentity; he was more like a powerful engine with a weak brake. A strange mixture of ruler and rebel. A restless spirit ranging from extremes of prejudice to remarkable penetration. German politics would have been duller without him.

Two foreign engagements under the same star: a few days after Strauss's visit to Moscow in January 1988, Honecker was in Paris. Both, independently, thought they had had to wait too long. But for our *Ostpolitik* the former would never have been received in the Kremlin or the latter at the Élysée Palace. And both politicians, who learned to value each other, were aware of that. It had taken a long time, but things were moving after all.

The Sublime and the Ridiculous

On 28 April 1972, the day after the 'constructive vote of no confidence', the Chancellor's Budget failed to be carried; the voting was equal – 247 for, 247 against. That evening I asked the Opposition and Coalition leaders to the Chancellery bungalow to discuss how we should proceed now. It was a long evening. A series of similar meetings ensued within the next two weeks. We did not devote much time to the budget itself; the point at issue was not to delay agreement to the Eastern treaties. I pointed out, as I was bound to, that the international timetable for détente would not tolerate postponement. The Allies had made that clear: Nixon wanted our treaties ratified before his visit to Moscow. And Pompidou, I knew, had told Barzel that if the treaties were thrown out a serious situation would be created. We also wanted to come to an understanding on bringing forward the date for new elections.

To get the treaties moving, and at least induce the Opposition to abstain from voting against them, it was proposed that a resolution should be presented to the Bundestag, in conjunction with the Second Reading of the ratification bill, and if possible unanimously adopted. We offered Government help in formulating it, and this was accepted. We did yet more, letting the Opposition know that some of their suggestions had already been adopted during negotiations on the treaties.

Discussion on the evening of 28 April was not entirely objective, let alone harmonious. Gerhard Schröder, the former Interior, Foreign and Defence Minister, said not a word. Rainer Barzel thought fit to suggest that the Allies felt only a lukewarm interest in our policy; Strauss contributed little to the discussion, but I had the distinct impression that he would not make serious difficulties; it was in his interests at home to get the treaties off the agenda of German politics, although he hid the fact behind an apparent wish to attack them. A mild explosion threatened when Helmut Schmidt mentioned the collusion between the Opposition and certain indiscreet civil servants, and Strauss retaliated in the same vein, saying Ehmke had misused the Federal Intelligence Service. Not only was that unjustified, it could have provoked a well-substantiated and vigorous counterattack. The minutes of the meeting say merely: 'As the discussion threatened to become unpleasant, it was decided to adjourn for supper. There were sharp remarks now and then during the meal, but the atmosphere soon became easier.' Both sides then consulted separately. Finally, I summed up: the Opposition thought the Government was in danger. The Government itself did not share that view; it certainly had considerable difficulties, but it would stand or fall with the treaties, and if the vote went against it then it would go to the country.

Two days later, on 1 May, the Opposition leader Rainer Barzel visited me at my official residence, without publicity, to put an astonishing proposal to me: would I agree to be elected Federal President? The Union would vote for me. He could then become Federal Chancellor – with the votes of the SPD – of a broad-based government. President Heinemann would certainly let us persuade him of the advisability of his early resignation. Would that not be a fair way out and an opportunity to take national responsibility together? I could see the suggestion as neither a way out nor an opportunity for anything. I said that my party would not enter into such an arrangement, which would damage the credibility of all concerned.

May Day 1972 was an impressive occasion. In the morning I spoke to 100,000 people in Dortmund and marched with steelworkers in the Westfalenpark. The waves of debate were beating unusually high in the country. On the day that the vote of no confidence failed, countless messages of goodwill reached me. No other political subject aroused so much popular feeling. The general opinion was that something odd was going on in Bonn, and an attempt was being made to force the Chancellor out of office by reprehensible means. People were also asking whether it was right to carry on with a mandate when the political fronts changed. I could understand this objection, but I had fundamental reasons for not drawing the same conclusion as the critics.

Between Wednesday 3 May and Saturday 13 May inter-party discussions followed one another thick and fast. They all revolved around the content of a joint resolution, and what should be said to other governments: in particular, that a *modus vivendi* was no substitute for a peace treaty. The Opposition wanted to find out whether the Government of the Soviet Union would accept without protest a Bundestag resolution interpreting the treaties. The upshot of all this was the grotesque situation whereby the USSR Ambassador, Valentin Falin, sat in on inter-party parliamentary party meetings where he had no right to be, giving answers known to all in advance. Falin stuck to the view that the treaty of August 1970 was to be interpreted only in the light of its own content, and that the resolution, most of which had now been negotiated, contained nothing new. After a difficult discussion, he said he would accept the resolution but would not actually state that he was accepting it, because to do so would have further diplomatic significance. He would say that he was passing it on to his government. He also stated that he had not said there *would* be no objection, only that he did not *expect* there would be any objection. At the end of this peculiar procedure, the Opposition leader again emphasized that neither did he want the treaties to fail.

The all-party resolution secured the German 'right-wing' position, and was acknowledged in Moscow. Should not the Opposition, or large parts of it, have found it easy to accept the treaties now? It did not work out like that. Strauss and several right-wing CDU members wanted a flat 'No'. To keep the Union parliamentary parties together, their leaders agreed, after heated discussion, to abstain from voting on the treaties; the representatives of the expellees' associations, however, were to be allowed to vote. On 17 May 1972 the Moscow Treaty was ratified in the Bundestag by 248 to 10 votes with 238 abstentions. The Warsaw Treaty was ratified by 248 to 17 votes and 231 abstentions.

Six months after the November elections Rainer Barzel resigned. Karl Carstens, a state secretary of many years' standing and later President of the Federal Republic, became Chairman of the CDU Parliamentary Party. Helmut Kohl took over the chairmanship of the Party itself. Adaptation to the realities of foreign politics, however, was a protracted affair that went on for years.

For the time being the rearrangements necessary for a new coalition with the FDP were not made. Barzel indicated as early as 1972, with cautious reference to the FDP leadership, that ratification of the treaties would remove 'the clips holding the existing coalition in place'. Or he may have said 'fetters', rather than 'clips'. Not every leading Free Democrat of the time had also been a leading supporter of *Ostpolitik*. But it was to be another decade before a new coalition of parties was formed, and this may be ascribed to the rigidity of the Union. Only when it overcame its pro-*Ostpolitik* reputation was the FDP able to reorientate itself.

Longer hesitation would not only have made a shambles of foreign policy but would have had harmful effects on domestic policy as well. There was much disillusionment in any case and we were treading a very fine line, as witness the Extremists Decree of January 1972. It was important not to blur the lines of policy at home for the sake of a bitterly contested foreign policy; whether we liked it or not, we had to keep hammering home the fact that rapprochement with the East was not going to usher in Communism, until finally words became inadequate. The Extremists Decree cannot be understood without *Ostpolitik* and the struggle conducted around it.

The interior ministers of the *Länder* and their heads of government thought they should do something to counter the 'march through the institutions' announced by the radical student opposition. More notice, they decided, should be taken of the constitutional loyalty of members of the civil service. The principle was not new; rather, the issue concerned the application of the law already in force. On the initiative of Social Democratic Interior Senators of Hamburg and Berlin, the *Länder* leaders drew up a joint statement of 'Principles on the Membership of Extremist Organizations'. I supported it when the prime ministers met at the Chancellery on 28 January 1972. There was no question of anyone's dictating to anyone else, and I did not evade my share of responsibility.

The idea of the 'principles' of January 1972 was to consolidate the existing framework of the civil service law and to standardize the practices of examination and appointment. Nor did the decree embodying that aim contain anything new in content. What was new was the fact that standard inquiries were now made of the Office for the Protection of the Constitution, which caused considerable perplexity, more so in some *Länder* than in others. The prevailing climate in the Federal Republic meant that the decree was brought into operation almost exclusively against people of the Left, hardly ever against those of the Right.

The characteristic nature of the German concept of the civil service had a good deal to do with various misunderstandings over cases where people were banned from following their professions. It was not easy to show why teachers, post office officials and railwaymen should be subject to the same standards as those necessary for people employed in areas where security was a factor. In 1976 I had some difficulty in keeping François Mitterrand from providing a 'Committee for the Defence of Civil and Professional Rights in the Federal Republic of Germany' with even more ammunition than it already had.

My party's attitude and my own were not free from tactical considerations. In the Union camp, they were toying with ideas of an addition to the Basic Law, which we did not think sensible. We were also anxious to keep the CSU and CDU from appealing to the Federal Constitutional Court; they wanted the DKP either banned or declared the reincarnation of the already banned KPD. After the changes of government in Greece, Portugal and Spain, that would have made us the sole country in our part of the world which could no longer afford the luxury of a legal Communist Party.

I cannot state positively that anyone in the Government or the leadership of my party would have opposed such a ban. Nor did we see the subject as more important than others. Gustav Heinemann did not put his serious reservations to me until we were both out of office. I found much support for moves to stop prying and intimidation; such distrust, I thought, was not at all the way to deal with the critical young.

I was in favour of Social Democrats marking themselves off clearly from Communists, and refusing to enter into dubious 'action groups' with them. But it seemed to me a mistake to try conducting political arguments with the help of the police and the public prosecutors. I felt the same about the independent revolutionary groups which formed before, during and after the 1968 movement. My party opposed those who wanted to discipline people for formal membership of such groups or for standing as their candidates; we thought that people should be barred from the civil service only for their actual conduct, i.e. active opposition to the Constitution.

A Victory Runs Away

The nineteenth of November 1972 brought a tremendous electoral success for the Social Democratic–Liberal coalition, the Social Democratic Party and myself, in spite of all the squabbling about the early election date and the alarm resulting from terrorist activity. Over 91 per cent of voters went to the polls, giving the SPD 45.8 per cent of the vote. In fact it was over 49 per cent on the first ballot; we had won over three million more votes. The Free Democrats achieved their aim by getting 8.4 per cent, and did not need to worry about their parliamentary existence for some time yet. The Union parties dropped to 44.9 per cent, and for the first time in the history of the Federal Republic they were no longer the strongest parliamentary party. They remained a considerable Opposition.

The election had decided the argument about the treaties. But they were not the only object of dispute. Without a convincing economic and social policy even *Ostpolitik* would have been worth only half as much. The Opposition challenger had done the rest; Rainer Barzel did not attract voters. Who could have doubted that the Government would steer a course into politically calm waters that were secure for parliamentary life?

The Social Democrats had not become weaker under my leadership, but had risen from a good 32 per cent to nearly 46 per cent of the vote over four Bundestag elections; the number of party members had risen from 650,000 to a million. I knew that one should not set too much store by such figures. However, I had to acknowledge the fact that some people, even in our own ranks, resented decisive long-term success and found it hard to stomach. Perhaps I should say *particularly* in our own ranks. German Social Democracy has a tradition of the moral respectability of failure, and the flavour of success has a suspect aftertaste. When I resigned from the party leadership in 1987 I warned, with good reason, 'We should not resent those among us who are successful.' After the election victory I came under pressure not for losing but for winning, and because of the reasons why we won.

In the election I had said, and it became a slogan on the posters: 'Germans, we can be proud of our country.' That claim, as accurate as it was unusual, referred to the economic development of the Federal Republic and to the fact that we had become the internationally acknowledged promoters of a peace policy showing the way to the future. At the Dortmund party conference before the election, I had urged a new social and liberal middle way, pleading for tolerance and understanding. I did *not* recommend that my party members should be over-confident or allow order to fall into disarray.

Yet the difficulties we had overcome so laboriously in the election campaign, and the activities of certain able but temperamental prima donnas in the Cabinet, should have made me stop and think; Alex Möller had resigned as Minister of Finance, although there was no need for him to do so, and a year later Karl Schiller, our 'Superminister', left not only the Cabinet but also, temporarily, the party. Now the 'Left' went to work. There was a feeling that various experiments in governmental control should be made – as if the SPD had an overall majority by itself and did not still depend on a coalition partner with an eye to its own prestige and the posts it held; and there were other ways in which we had to avoid conflicting with our mandate. I warned against eccentric or self-destructive tendencies. In a letter written from hospital to the Social Democratic deputies and Cabinet members, I urged them not to overdraw our account.

I had gone into the University Hospital because I had been suffering from throat trouble for some time, and found public speaking increasingly difficult. I had promised my doctor to have an operation directly after the election. Professor Becker removed a tumour which he described as 'bordering on malignancy'. During this minor operation there was a technical mishap which meant that I nearly suffocated, while remaining conscious of what was happening. I was not allowed to talk, see visitors or smoke; I felt all these deprivations. I wrote down my ideas for the formation of the new Government, with results as undesirable as they were disagreeable.

Through the head of the Chancellery, I sent a long memo to the SPD Parliamentary Party leaders and for the information of my second deputy in the party chairmanship. Later the memo was said to have been mislaid in someone's bulging briefcase. I received no feedback from the talks held in my absence with our coalition partner.

The internal balance of the Government was upset by agreements made during my illness, and which I did not feel strong enough to correct. I had told Walter Scheel before the election that the Free Democrats would also be represented in economic policy in future, and the agreement was to be honoured all the more quickly after our election success. But I had never intended giving the Free Democrats either the Economics or Finance Ministry in addition to the classic ministries of Foreign and Interior Affairs, plus Agriculture. Combining the post of Minister of Economics and Minister of Finance was not a good idea in the long term; the job was bound to make excessively heavy demands on even the most gifted of superministers. When Helmut Schmidt agreed with the Free Democrats on the distribution of these departments he was assuming that Hans-

Dietrich Genscher would take over at Economics: I would have agreed to that, provided that the Interior Ministry had a Social Democratic head and that the FDP was given another, fourth department instead.

It turned out that the FDP wanted to head the Economics Ministry and took it for granted that it would also retain the Ministry of the Interior. In mid December I told my parliamentary party that I had agreed to give our Free Democrat colleagues another ministry, but not one of the 'classic' departments. Beyond this actual incident, giving me advance notice of a certain loss of authority, the experience taught me that there should be no question of 'inheriting' certain ministries in a coalition government extending over several terms of office.

My second election as Chancellor, in the middle of December 1972, went smoothly. I was elected by 269 votes to 233, with one spoilt paper. It was assumed that two coalition deputies had not voted for me – or perhaps a few more if one or two of the Opposition had voted for me, which was not impossible. But in view of the obvious ratio of strength in the Bundestag it was not a cause for concern.

My statement of Government policy in January 1973 struck some new notes, but could not overcome the malaise that had become perceptible in December. Instead, I was forced to realize that my remarkably harmonious co-operation with Walter Scheel was coming to an end.

That summer the FDP Chairman and Foreign Minister wondered aloud whether the common ground of our coalition was becoming exhausted, and if so how. During 1973 it also became clear that loyal SPD members whose support I valued were distancing themselves. One complained of 'debilitating self-satisfaction' in the Government. Another said that when he looked for something to hold on to, he 'all too often found empty air'. Helmut Schmidt complained that domestic policy was being neglected, and repeated his fears that the SPD would become a 'Nenni-style party'. I found it hard to understand his belief, expressed both verbally and in a letter, that the SPD was turning itself into the kind of party led by Pietro Nenni. Quite apart from anything else, there could be no comparison between the situation in the Federal Republic and in Italy.

Schmidt, later to be Chancellor, sometimes suffered from thyroid trouble. He had taken over the Ministry of Defence without great enthusiasm in 1969 and then headed it brilliantly. The resignation of Alex Möller made him anxious not to lose any of his department's budget. His criticism of Karl Schiller had hastened the latter's alienation from the rest of the Cabinet. His warning against 'over-enthusiasm for reform' was not especially helpful, and he was anything but lacking in self-confidence. Perhaps he feared that the chance for responsibility at the top might pass him by.

An eminent contemporary historian has summed up the relationship of several Cabinet members to each other and to the Chancellor by saying they would rather have worked 'against one another than for him'. There is much truth in that. Strong personalities are one thing, consideration for colleagues another. Team spirit is more easily found among mediocrities.

It was not so different with my closest colleagues, who were supposed to stand by me and support me in my second period of office. They had plenty of knowledge and experience, but not enough to make them a working unit. There was a good deal of friction, and it became worse. I would agree with those critics who say, if sometimes rather bluntly, that politics on the personal level is not among my strongest points.

However, the oft-repeated criticism that I gave home policy a back seat was neither just nor true. On the other hand, I found out how badly we lacked support when it came to coping with the oil crisis at the end of 1973. The price rises forced on us from outside were excessive, the measures taken by the EEC, independently and together with the Americans, were inadequate. The world had been in a state of economic turbulence for some years, particularly since Washington's monetary decisions of the summer of 1971, with growth stagnating, and unemployment and price-levels rising. How could we make it clear that the causes lay outside our own frontiers? Competition for a market share became fiercer. There were wildcat strikes, something unusual in the Federal Republic.

The oil crisis that affected the economy had grown out of the political conflict in the Middle East set off by the Yom Kippur War. I was accused of coolness towards Israel. That was far from the truth, but it affected my position as head of government.

At home, four currents intersected and met, swelling to a single broad stream that swept away the fragile structures damming it. A law to safeguard energy supplies was hastily passed by the legislative bodies, although there was no suggestion of looking for alternative sources of energy. The experimental ban on Sunday motoring was intended to emphasize the need to conserve energy, and was accepted with quite good grace, but that was all. The proposal to introduce a general speed limit came up against resolute opposition from our Free Democratic colleagues. The majority of those who usually swore by all things American found wide public agreement when they demanded 'freedom on the roads for free citizens'.

At boardroom level the mood was melancholy, with no talk of getting something done or rolling up our sleeves. A spokesman for the Ruhr industries seriously tried to tell us that the situation had never before looked so gloomy during all his forty years in the coal and steel industries. I had to ask him to think back soberly over those years, including as they did the world economic crisis, dictatorship and war.

A small group of specialist technical staff made considerable difficulties; the air-traffic controllers backed their demands for higher pay and better working conditions with a month-long work-to-rule. They aroused the wrath of air passengers and showed up the Government as incapable of acting. There was more than a little justice in their demands, and the Government would have shown to advantage by exercising a little more flexibility. But the conflicting interests could not be reconciled: that was the abiding impression, and it undermined authority.

Finally, I clashed with trade union leaders, particularly Kluncker, leader of the Public Utilities and Transport Workers' Union, representing those employed in the public services. They adhered to their inflated demands of the autumn of 1973, disregarding the new economic situation when wage negotiations began early in the New Year: they wanted a 15-per-cent wage rise and more holiday pay. Obviously no public authority employer can simply do what the unions demand. Obviously again, there is a special tension between a Social Democrat public employer and the unions. But now there was far more than just a tense relationship involved. I was convinced – and I had expert opinion on my side – that a wage rise in double figures would have a bad effect. Schmidt, as Minister of Finance, agreed, but kept rather in the background and went off to a conference in Washington. Federal President Heinemann advised standing firm; he said I should not hesitate to threaten to resign. He was right, for even more than other political parties in power, Social Democrats have to show that they know how to manage the taxpayers' money.

However, the idea of standing firm went overboard when on 11 February it was announced and became generally known that though the Federal Government might have overall responsibility it did not in fact make the decisions. The authorities in the *Länder* and in local government felt unable to withstand the pressure. The Mayor of Frankfurt urged me, on behalf of himself and his colleagues, to refrain from Federal intervention; he managed to reach me by telephone during a Cabinet meeting, something which had never happened before. The idea of unemptied dustbins alarmed the city fathers even more than the prospect of public transport grinding to a halt. We were asked to agree to an 11-per-cent pay rise, with a few extras, and we did. I was well aware of the loss of face this entailed, and it turned out even worse than expected. There was no saying what effect the announcement of my resignation would have had. Our relationship with faithful adherents and leading figures in the trade unions would have been impaired, but it was impaired anyway. Economic insight, political responsibility and personal self-respect should have made me announce that I would resign.

Early in March 1974 the SPD put up a poor showing in the Hamburg City Assembly elections. Its share of the vote sank from over 55 to a bare 45 per cent; we also suffered losses in Schleswig-Holstein and Hesse. No one yet realized what great swings there would be in the behaviour of the electorate in the big cities, so the reaction was dramatic. Leading Hamburg politicians managed to ignore any local failings and laid all the blame on Bonn. In the party committee, and in public, the Finance Minister, Schmidt, who was also a Hamburg deputy, inveighed against unreliability, weak leadership and discord. It was true that the Young Socialists were acting as if they were a separate party within or indeed outside the Social Democratic Party. There were considerable contradictions in what they stood for, and the noise they made was in inverse proportion to their influence. Why, then, did I not oppose them more strongly? First, because I remembered my own youth and knew that discontent is not the worst thing in the world. And second, I could not see that it would be a good thing for administrative routine to go forever unchallenged in my party, even if the challenge took uncomfortable forms.

In sum, the process of erosion continued. On my sixtieth birthday in December 1973, in spite of all the kind things said to me, much was said and written of the 'cracks in the monument'. Journals which had shown me much goodwill were becoming cooler than I liked. The air I breathed had grown thin. Foreign contacts seemed to be suffering. When I was in Paris in April 1974 for the funeral of Georges Pompidou, I did not find anyone very interested in talks. Was there anything in the theories of those who thought they could tell simply from my appearance that I no longer relished so-called power, or was actually rejecting it? I cannot give a definite 'No'.

I do contradict the superficial theory which holds that my time as head of government would have been up anyway, and that the incident of the spy behind the scenes merely dealt the final blow. That is a simple but mistaken view. I believe I could have found the strength to overcome the difficulties that followed our electoral triumph and begin a new chapter in both domestic and foreign policy. And attitudes and opinions are very quick to change ...

5

Some Endings

The Spy Affair...

On Wednesday, 24 April 1974, I arrived back at noon on an official plane from Cairo, where I had been holding talks with Sadat; before that, I had been talking to Boumedienne in Algeria.

Genscher, the Minister of the Interior, and Grabert, the head of the Chancellery, were waiting for me at Cologne–Bonn airport. Even from a distance I could see they had something of significance to tell me. Herr Guillaume, one of my advisers, had been arrested at his apartment that morning on strong suspicion of espionage. His wife had also been arrested. Günter Guillaume had revealed that he was 'a citizen and an officer of the GDR', making life rather easier for those who had to convict him by this confession, since the material prepared for use in court by the investigators left something to be desired.

The news was a great blow, although I cannot say it knocked me sideways. I knew that for nearly a year there had been a vague – as I thought – suspicion of the man who arranged my contacts with the party and the trade unions, fixed my engagements and accompanied me on visits to the provinces. I had not taken the suspicion seriously, and – not for the first time – found I had overestimated my knowledge of human nature. Nor had I thought it probable that the authorities of the other German state would have planted an agent disguised as a conservative Social Democrat on me when I was endeavouring to ease inter-state relations in the face of great resistance. There were certain peculiar features that encouraged my trustfulness: Guillaume was not someone who actually took part in political discussions, only a reliable aide; not a partner in serious conversation but a good, methodical worker. As I had told the chief of the service involved, I did not especially like his company near me or for very long.

I did not know or even guess that his unmasking meant the end of my chancellorship. Of course I had to expect to face critical questioning – from the press, from the Opposition. But I thought I could deal with that. Even now, fifteen years later, I cannot nod my head and agree with those who tried to salve their consciences by saying I would not have stayed on long as head of government anyway. This version of events does not become any more accurate simply because it is the one that has been adopted by interested persons of more than one party in more than one German state.

Common sense should have told me to concentrate my attention on this critical espionage case when I got back from North Africa; I should have had all the cards put on the table and cancelled all except my most urgent engagements. Instead, everything went its usual way. On the day of my return I want to the Adenauer House to congratulate Kiesinger on his seventieth birthday. Before and after that I worked at my desk on a coalition discussion on land law. On the Thursday I went to open the Hanover Fair. On Friday morning I attended the Bundestag for the *Aktuelle Stunde* [Topical Session] on 'the case', and then made a prepared contribution to a debate on the reform of Article 218 of the Basic Law. In the afternoon, there was a meeting with Government members of my party, to deal with an intended Cabinet reshuffle among other things. In the evening I went to the Swedish Embassy, and met a friend from my Stockholm days, the writer Eyvind Johnson, who was awarded the Nobel Prize for Literature that year. At the weekend I prepared May Day speeches to be delivered in Hamburg and at various other places afterwards.

The fact that I spoke without preparation during the *Aktuelle Stunde* does not support the view that I felt I was under dangerous pressure. My giving an incorrect reply on an important point and failing to set myself right immediately shows not only how memory can let you down, but how difficult it can be not to have proper administrative back-up. I began by deploring the fact that there are times when one thinks, 'Am I to be spared nothing?' I added that I was not responsible for security checks on those who worked for me – no Federal Chancellor was. Also, and this was factually correct, but the effect was unfortunate, that I had entirely forgotten about Guillaume's presence during my vacation the previous summer. I had not given Guillaume any secret documents to deal with; that was not part of his duties. Finally, two more sentences in my brief statement were mixed up to misleading effect. In one I spoke of the antagonism of the East German state, in another of disillusionment with human nature. It was soon being said that I had admitted to harbouring illusions about the East. In fact I was merely horrified by the now obvious extent of hypocrisy and abuse of confidence.

I had simply put out of my mind, and no one drew my attention to it directly, the fact that in July 1973, when Guillaume was with me in Norway on behalf of the Chancellery office, several confidential documents, some of them in cipher, had passed through his hands. He collected material from the nearby telex office set up by Federal German Intelligence and took back papers that had been worked on. He had nothing to do with any classified material at the Bonn office, although in 1970 the Office for the Protection of the Constitution, after screening him twice, had said there was no reason why he should not be authorized to deal with coded material 'up to and including Very Secret'. After examination of the documents in the records office, the head of the Chancellery confirmed a few days later that only two confidential documents had passed through Guillaume's hands there, and they could be described as of trifling importance.

The documents involved in Norway seem to have been four telexes marked 'confidential' and twelve marked 'secret', containing accounts of talks held in Washington by the Foreign Minister and the Defence Minister. It was pure fiction to speak of a highly confidential letter to me from President Nixon. I could not say then what I say now: I thought the only serious aspect of the affair was the principle involved, and it was not otherwise of any vast importance. An early remark to the effect that the content of those documents had in any case soon become public knowledge would have looked as if I wanted to make light of the leak, and that would not have been objectively or subjectively justified.

The significance of the material sent me from Washington was greatly exaggerated by the media, who were not in possession of the relevant facts. The documents chiefly concerned the ministers' irritation with Pompidou's Foreign Minister Michel Jobert, who also visited Washington at the end of June and proved intransigent over a joint American–European statement. That was no secret. A careful study of the press could also have provided information about the relative strength of NATO and the Warsaw Pact.

In their subsequent publications Guillaume and his masters – or the other way around – suggested that they had been very successful, with far-reaching consequences for 'the Socialist state community' – and of course for peace, too: 'I wanted to act as a political pioneer in helping to activate our peace policy,' said Guillaume. 'I was never given any other task...' Self-adulation and boastfulness are characteristics of the profession.

In fact Guillaume's information seemed to have derived essentially from Social Democratic Party gossip. But I did not feel like putting forward qualifying arguments which might have made it seem that I was trying to make light of the affair. Moreover, reactions ranging from the agitated to the hysterical were soon aroused, for no apparent reason other than sensationalism. It was only to be expected that the parliamentary Opposition would not remain passive, and it could hardly be surprising that latent prejudice surfaced in many areas. The brazen insouciance with which certain bureaucrats working in security sought to divert attention from their own omissions was alarming. They were more concerned for an ill-informed public's hunger for sensation than for mistakes and failures in their own professional fields.

If there were serious grounds for suspicion, the agent should not have been allowed to stay in immediate contact with me; he should have been moved to some other position where he could be kept under observation, or even promoted. Instead of protecting the Chancellor, those concerned made him an '*agent provocateur* of his own country's secret service'. The French commentator who made that comment described my acceptance of advice to leave Guillaume where he was as 'a sign of gullibility'; the advice had been given me by the minister ultimately responsible. I have not given credence to the much more serious suspicion, directed against the upper echelon of the Office for the Protection of the Constitution, that I had been lured into a trap.

However, it is a fact that Guillaume was neither picked up at one of his assignations in the Federal Republic, nor kept under observation at all in the summer of 1973 in Norway, or the autumn of that year in the south of France. It is also a fact that officials of the investigatory authority, when Guillaume refused to explain himself after his arrest, prepared an alternative theatre of war: my private life was dragged into it and caricatured. Over-zealous champions of security, including political opponents and some very strange guardians of virtue, produced a curious piece of patchwork which took on a life of its own, and in the face of which I felt bewildered and powerless.

On the afternoon of that 26 April of the *Aktuelle Stunde* in the Bundestag, Helmut Schmidt and I joked, after meeting our Cabinet colleagues, that the investigators would be looking into Guillaume's relationships with the office secretaries. We did not know what was yet to come. However, I suspected, and said, that we might be dealing with a 'natural phenomenon'. It seems that I was already no longer sure that I could weather the storm. In a conversation one night a little later I expressed the fear that I might be set at a disadvantage in imminent and important talks with the East – the Moscow leadership had put out feelers after a meeting with Honecker.

Everyday concerns of my personal health also blurred the picture; on the Friday evening, when I came back from the Swedish Embassy, I had to take to my bed with a stomach upset picked up in Egypt. After the weekend I went to the dentist to have two molars removed. When the whole thing was over Klaus Harpprecht wondered how it would have worked out if I had not had toothache and the weather had been sunny.

Still rather groggy, and after a Cabinet meeting – my last – I flew to a meeting in Saarbrücken on 30 April, and on to Hamburg that evening. Meanwhile, rumours were rife. I was told that Guillaume had said it was not part of his job to report on my private life. The press published prurient hints, with obvious intent. Before I flew to Saarbrücken Gerhard Jahn, the Minister of Justice, anxiously called on me for a short talk; he had heard hints from the Federal Prosecutor's Office that Guillaume might have 'provided me with girls'. I told Jahn this was ridiculous, and I wanted him to tell the person responsible that I was not going to trouble my head over such rumours. Later, I wished I had pounded the table with my fist and demanded an end to such nonsense at once. But would it have been any use?

On 1 May, breakfasting in the Hotel Atlantic, I took a call from Genscher, the Minister of the Interior. A colleague of his was on his way with a document, the contents of which he advised me to consider at once. After my speech, I withdrew to a room in the trade union building and read a note – handed to me in a sealed envelope, and which I returned – from the head of the Federal Criminal Investigation Office. It said that interrogation had produced details concerning intimate acquaintances, who were named, during my 'political travels', and that some of these actual or assumed 'acquaintances' were on file.

What, then, had gone on record? It was sheer fantasy. First a muddled mixture of events, part observed, part imputed; second, remarks about a dear friend, a woman whom I had been meeting for years without the slightest hint of secrecy, and who had done nothing at all to deserve the attentions of the security police. A 'relationship' with a close friend's wife was insinuated, without the slightest foundation. An interview given one evening in Copenhagen – Guillaume had not been in Copenhagen – was made to look like an affair. A Scandinavian woman journalist was still complaining years later that something she had let slip was being repeated. A woman journalist who was alleged to have left a necklace behind wrote to me later that at the time she 'never wrote about the days of intolerable questioning by the police; they were after you more than after the spy'. Nor would any of the rest of it have laid me open to any accusation of disreputable behaviour, if everything had been dealt with in a straightforward manner. I heard that in Cabinet circles in Paris all the incident did was arouse mirth.

I must admit that I was rather shaken by what I read in Hamburg. The Minister of the Interior advised me, over the phone, to call the Prosecutor-General – Siegfried Buback, murdered by terrorists a few years later, who had just been appointed to that post – and help him 'to get things sorted out'. I thought this was going too far, and pointed out that I had no intention of saying anything about such a document; I could not see that anything criminal was insinuated, and Guillaume had no knowledge that could hurt me. I called the Minister of Justice and suggested that the three of us should meet next Monday, or if necessary at the weekend. I did not think this aspect of the affair especially important. Or perhaps I could not bring myself to act energetically on my own behalf.

I spent the afternoon and evening of 1 May in agreeable company on Heligoland. Here, the security man who had been assigned to me ever since I was Foreign Minister told me he had been summoned back to Bonn for further questioning. A good week later, when I had resigned, he wrote to me to say that in the course of the interrogation he had been faced with the prospect of coercive detention and he considered laying a complaint. He and his colleagues, he said, had 'been forced to make statements the point of which we did not understand until today'. On the evening of the day I hauled down the flag, the same security officer told me, with tears in his eyes, that his impression was that damaging material to be used against me had been put together 'in advance'.

A few weeks earlier, at the Lower Saxony Police College, I had thanked 'those gentlemen of the Bonn Security Division who have done much difficult work over the years'. Some weeks later, when I was no longer in office, the Chief of the Federal Criminal Investigation Office intimated to me that he had not foreseen what would happen; there had been a great deal of talk. There was also talk that I entertained the idea of suicide: a gross exaggeration of the fact that I was very depressed.

The second of May was the day when the advance parties of the staff of the Permanent Missions in the two German states took up their posts. On that day the Federal Navy vessel *Köln* brought me back from Heligoland to the mainland; I had various engagements to fulfil between Wilhelmshaven and Nordhorn. I found firm backing everywhere when I said I was not going to let a minor irritation divert me from what was a correct, because necessary, policy. Next day the normal work of the Chancellery took its course. Helmut Schmidt told me about difficulties he expected to encounter in drafting the new budget and in tax reform; in private I told him not to be surprised if he found himself Chancellor in the near future. I saw the President of the Federal Audit Office, and signed the law on financial adjustment between the Federation and the *Länder*. My last foreign visitor was Mario Soares, about to return from exile to Lisbon; the Portuguese 'Revolution of Flowers' had begun.

The same day the heads of the two security services, who had not managed to get together during the observation period, took the fate of their country in their hands. The able Chief of the Wiesbaden Criminal Investigation Office sought out Günther Nollau, the supposedly able President of the Office for the Protection of the Constitution in Bonn, and gave him his report; it contained all the gossip that had been put together during the interrogations of the previous few days. Nollau wrote that if Guillaume mentioned certain 'painful details' at his trial the Federal Republic and its government would look ridiculous; but if he said nothing, the GDR Government would have 'a means of humiliating the Brandt Cabinet and the SPD'. According to a later account, Nollau answered the vital question put by the head of the Security Division in the negative. That question was: 'Are the private lives of the people we protect any of our business?'

According to Nollau's diary for 3 May 1974, he and his colleagues had come to the conclusion that 'someone must urge the Chancellor to step down'. It would have to be someone of political and moral authority; he would tell Herbert Wehner, Chairman of the Parliamentary Party. So he did. It was said that Wehner had put me under pressure to resign, on the grounds that I was vulnerable to blackmail.

It was not like that. We met in Münstereifel on 4 May, because I had invited trade union leaders there over the weekend to discuss questions of economic policy. In conversation with Wehner, when I mentioned the news stories and rumours of the last few days, he spoke of a 'particularly painful item of news' he would have had to break to me if I had not broached the subject myself. I was not sure what he meant; he dropped vague hints about a long report, saying he had not noted all the details. Two days later, during coalition talks in Bonn, he repeated that he had 'forgotten names and details on purpose', and then came out with a woman's name that was very much on the wrong track. Whatever way I decided, he said, he would go along with my decision; later he said he had expressed 'unreserved loyalty in every conceivable development'. The next day, still in Münstereifel, Helmut Schmidt argued vigorously against the decision I had now taken to resign. Two close colleagues had already tried to dissuade me. All concerned said firmly that I must certainly stay on as Party Chairman.

On the Sunday evening, when I was back in Bonn, I wrote to the Federal President offering my resignation; I did not revise my letter on Monday. I showed it to Walter Scheel, who thought we could still sit it out. Egon Bahr suggested I should ascertain the strength of my support.

On 6 May there was a swift succession of meetings and discussions. In the evening the head of the Chancellery took my letter to Gustav Heinemann, who was in Hamburg. My FDP colleagues were still advising me not to resign. Earlier, one last visitor, Prosecutor-General Buback, had been to see me with the Minister of Justice. I expressed my astonishment at the interest the investigatory authorities had shown in my private life. The whole thing was obviously a pack of nonsense, I said. Guillaume had no information about me which affected the interests of the state. Buback said the ascertainment of private details had been advisable; it was necessary to find out whether Guillaume's breach of confidence, or treachery, had extended to that area too. He added that he would have the interrogation of the security officers brought to an end. At the end of May the Minister of Justice – Hans-Jochen Vogel now held that post – told me that no construction suggesting the leaking of secrets would be put on 'that area' any longer; he had asked the Prosecutor-General to proceed accordingly. Years later a television journalist planning a film on the Guillaume case came upon a document which ought to have gone into the shredder long before.

In my letter to the Federal President I gave as the reason for my resignation 'negligence in connection with the affair of the agent Guillaume' for which I took political responsibility. In the letter to Scheel, who as Vice-Chancellor had now taken over, I added before 'responsibility' the words 'and of course also personal' in brackets. I did not mean the idea of negligence to be understood in a legal sense; I merely thought anyone who had accepted incorrect advice had himself acted negligently. I believed one should take the consequences, and told the SPD Parliamentary Party of the Bundestag, on the morning of 7 May, that I was resigning my office on account of 'my practical experience of that office, my understanding of the unwritten rules of democracy, and to protect my personal and political integrity' – in that order. However, I was not unaware that Federal Minister Ehmke, and Grabert as head of the Chancellery, had offered to resign their own offices if I thought it right. The question of my personal responsibility troubled me more than my close colleagues thought was justified, and indeed in retrospect more than I myself think was justified.

There was no lack of expressions of sympathy and bewilderment. I was exhausted, and wondered if I would be able to get over the campaign in the press. Over and beyond my own misfortune, would people realize how easily a constitutional organ could be dragged into what were almost conspiratorial activities, with intriguing security agents looking through keyholes and setting off hysterical reactions? I may add that colleagues in other countries told me they could not understand such provocation and such a reaction.

Although the Government was not going to anticipate the criminal proceedings, it set up a committee and requested an expert opinion. Theodor Eschenburg, chairman of the committee, said that according to the Basic Law the Chancellor bore the principal political responsibility; however, his resignation – probably occasioned rather than entailed by the affair – had not been necessary. Resignation 'because of this incident which arose from blunders and organizational failures not of the first importance' had been beyond the horizon of expectation of public opinion and the people.

So did I have to resign? No, it was not imperative, even though the step appeared to me inevitable at the time. I took political responsibility seriously, and perhaps too literally. It is a fact that I took much more upon myself than I really had to answer for. Difficulties in and with the Government had increased since the beginning of 1973, weakening my position and no doubt also my ability to stand firm. It is likely that I would have reacted more vigorously in different circumstances. In any case, the situation called for a Chancellor who could devote himself wholly to his task. I cannot agree, as Günter Grass suggested in *The Flounder*, that I felt a revulsion from power. But I will admit that the intrigues affected me, and it would have been strange if the distress occasioned to my family had not troubled me. Egon Bahr said it had been pointless to try dissuading me, for either I had made my mind up firmly in advance, or I would not have had the strength for the fight. Both those propositions are correct, and I will add that in the physical and mental condition of my later years I would *not* have resigned; instead, I would have cleared up the whole affair as far as possible.

... And the Silence

Helmut Schmidt, five years my junior, had become my rival within the Party, but his attitude in the days before and after my resignation was irreproachable. He thought he had 'behaved badly' at Münstereifel, had been 'rather too heated', and owed me an apology. In fact he had said it was over-reaction for a head of government to resign over 'trifling' matters, and had urged me to reconsider my decision. At all events, he said, I must stay on as Party Chairman. 'You can hold the party together; I can't.'

When it came to the point of my resignation on 6 May, I gave him some friendly advice in the Schaumburg Palace, into which he would soon be moving – for the time being anyway, until the new Chancellery was ready. I said he should not speak as if he had taken over a failing firm. His reaction to that was not long in coming. Three days later, in his address to our party council, he said that the firm of the Federal Republic of Germany was nowhere near going into the red; we were 'a perfectly healthy business, one of the healthiest in the entire world economy'. And indeed, government borrowing in 1973 was in the region of 57 million Deutschmarks – a figure that had risen to 341 million in 1983 and almost 500 million in 1989.

It would be stretching the truth to say that Schmidt had made life easy for me when he was a Cabinet member. Alex Möller, the Minister of Finance, had resigned in May of 1971 because of his disagreements with Schmidt as Defence Minister. Karl Schiller, Minister of Economics and Finance, had also resigned in the early summer of 1972 because his running argument with Schmidt was taking grotesque forms. When I designated Schmidt my successor and the new Superminister, I was unofficially making him Number Two in the Social Democratic Cabinet team. It was understood as it was meant – a preemptive decision on the eventual succession. Even though our great election victory intervened, so that it might have been possible to reshuffle the cards, at that juncture it would have been senseless not to stand by the logic of the situation. I therefore nominated my successor, and was glad that Helmut Schmidt was unanimously approved by the relevant party committees.

The differences of opinion between us had been largely caused by differences of temperament; if we had taken them too seriously it would have done excessive and unnecessary damage to our collaboration. We understood ourselves and each other to be German patriots with a sense of European responsibility, and never failed to respect one another, even when our opinions differed quite widely. We always felt that we could achieve much together – for our country and for our party. We had devoted ourselves to German Social Democracy, coming to it from very different directions. We remained bound to it in our different ways, but with the same wholehearted commitment.

Schmidt had had no part in the Guillaume affair. However, he was not spared discussing the matter with Honecker a year later. Their meeting in the summer of 1975, at the European Conference in Helsinki, did nothing to clear up the affair. For the rest, the authorities in both German states had to have a common interest in the further development of practical co-operation. Subsequently, East Berlin repeatedly asked the Federal Government for an early release of the convicted spy. Guillaume was eventually deported in 1981.

My own help was sought, several times, for the possible use of Guillaume as a counter in an exchange of prisoners – first by the head of the Chancellery in May 1976, and then, on several occasions, by the head of the GDR's Permanent Mission in Bonn. I always took the line that I had no personal grudge to settle, but I could not be expected to take the initiative in this matter; I would not stand in the way of the Federal Government's doing what it thought objectively advisable and legally permissible. I did not change that attitude when reports appeared in the press larded with unpleasant aspersions, as they did from time to time. There was no lack of aspersions anyway. Defectors told the German and Allied secret services nonsensical tales of secret visits I was supposed to have made to East Berlin and Moscow, first as Mayor, then as Federal Chancellor. The employees of one large publishing firm showed off to their colleagues with material implying that I had discussed secession from NATO with Brezhnev; accusations of treason were ready and waiting in case I 'stuck my neck out too far'.

Once the spy had been unmasked and I had resigned, the public took an understandable interest in knowing how he got into the Chancellery as an assistant adviser in January 1970. Had it been just a question of a routine process? In fact routine was not involved, but the internal arrangements of the Social Democratic Party certainly were. Herbert Ehrenberg, head of the Department of Economics and Social Policy in the Chancellery before becoming State Secretary and Federal Minister, had taken Guillaume on as an assistant adviser on 'links with the trade unions and other associations'. Ehrenberg thought him a reliable person rather on the right of the party. In the

1969 campaign, he had been Federal Minister Georg Leber's successful constituency agent; Leber recommended him, and so did his State Secretary Holger Börner, later Federal organizational manager and Prime Minister of Hesse. Most of those involved, however, subsequently suffered lapses of memory about the extent to which they had backed him. Personally, I did not find Guillaume particularly likeable, even when he performed his organizational duties satisfactorily. I had thought of getting him moved elsewhere in the autumn of 1972, not because I had any suspicion of him but because I thought his views were limited. His mixture of servility and joviality got on my nerves, but I did not make a fuss about that. It was more important that he managed my engagements diary well and reliably.

He moved into close contact with me after the summer break of 1972. The former Essen Party Secretary Peter Reuschenbach, later Mayor of Essen, was standing for the Bundestag and was very keen to have Guillaume first deputize for him and then take his place. Guillaume's outwardly correct behaviour and succinct answers attracted attention. When a new party chairman was to be elected in Frankfurt and I wanted to know what to make of him, the answer came back, quick as a flash and perfectly cool: 'I can tell you one thing, he's a Communist.'

The Guillaumes had come to Frankfurt by way of West Berlin, allegedly as refugees. The next year he joined the SPD, and in 1964 he became organizational manager of the subdistrict and in 1968 of the party in the City Assembly, to which he was elected the same year. Its chairman, Gerhard Weck, was a refugee from Saxony who had been imprisoned by 'State Security' for most of the Nazi period and for some years afterwards. He became Guillaume's patron; death preserved him from bitter disillusionment. Frau Guillaume had a job in the Wiesbaden State Chancellery.

As a witty Frenchman once said of an execution, the details are of no importance. In the present case, however, they may be of interest. For instance, the Bundestag investigatory committee discovered that Guillaume's screening had been slipshod. More than one authority had noted suspicions but never followed them up; they dated back to the years 1954 and 1955, before he moved to the Federal Republic. The head of Federal Intelligence, General Wessel, had recommended a thorough examination of his background, and suggested giving him different work. That advice was not taken.

I learned later that Horst Ehmke, as head of the department concerned, conducted an intensive interrogation, and after two interviews the Office for the Protection of the Constitution certified him safe to be entrusted with coded documents 'up to and including Very Secret'. I did not know that at the end of 1969 Egon Bahr, deputizing for Ehmke, had indicated a possible security risk and put it on file. In 1973, as I was still sticking to the advice I had received to say nothing to anyone if possible, I said not a word to either Bahr or Ehmke, who would have made me more aware of the problem.

At some time in 1970 or 1971 someone, probably Ehmke, noticed that there had been questions about the career of Guillaume, who came from 'over there'. Remembering many cases I had encountered in Berlin, I thought it was the same old story: there were suspicions of refugees from the GDR, most of them unfounded. When Reuschenbach left in 1972 and Guillaume became available, I asked, in passing, if there hadn't been something that needed another look taken at it. The response from my office was that everything was in order; groundless aspersions were always being cast against people from the GDR, and after all, the man had done good work in Frankfurt.

The Bundestag investigatory committee looked closely and critically at the curious conduct of the President of the Office for the Protection of the Constitution between May 1973 and April 1974. It concluded that the information given by the Office to the Interior Ministry was inadequate, and that slackness and negligence were characteristic of Nollau's office. The committee spokesman Gerster, of the CDU, spoke of a serious, indeed gross, dereliction of duty; Nollau had shown himself unfit to be head of the Office. This was a harsh verdict, but it had support, and not just from the party political viewpoint. A number of employees of the Office had written to me the day after my resignation, saying: 'You are not responsible. Other people are. We send you our admiration and our thanks.'

I had many decades of parliamentary experience behind me, and I needed no telling that investigatory committees seldom succeed in establishing the truth. Either the motives of the parties and their representatives are diametrically opposed, or they coincide. In this case it was in the interests of all sides to spare the Minister of the Interior: the party to which I and, even more important, the new Chancellor belonged did not want to injure Genscher, our coalition partner, and the CDU/CSU, now led by Helmut Kohl, with Strauss at his side, did not want to alienate him as their future colleague in government.

What had been the previous history of the affair? On 29 May 1973 the Interior Minister came to see me after a coalition meeting: did I have a man with a French-sounding name working closely with me? I mentioned Guillaume and his job, and asked why. He said Nollau had been to see him, and asked him to agree to having the man kept under observation. There were matters from the fifties that were not clear, and radio conversations far back in the past which might be grounds for suspicion. They wanted G. kept on in his present post. I naturally agreed to his being kept under observation, and asked if the recommendation to leave him where he was applied to my forthcoming vacation. As neither of my personal advisers was available, for good private reasons, G. had been assigned to go to Norway with me in July; he was to be allowed to take his wife and son.

Next day, on 30 May, the Interior Minister came to see me again and said, after what I supposed was contact with Nollau, that the holiday arrangements should not be changed either. Later, Genscher said it was more of a misgiving than a suspicion that they entertained at the time. I did not take the warning too seriously myself; after all, I thought, there are special services to deal with such matters. The heads of those bodies, however, were acting as if they were writing the script for a third-rate spy film.

Nollau, as he admitted, had been very much against 'informing the Chancellor at this point in time'. Afterwards, he even made use in argument of the fact that I had spoken in confidence to the head of the Chancellor's office on 29 or 30 May, and the head of the Chancellery on 4 June when he was back from holiday. He himself thought it advisable to discuss the matter with persons outside the Government.

I put those two officials in the picture on my own responsibility, thereby making more than one additional mistake. I should have asked Nollau or Genscher to discuss all questions arising from their suspicions with the head of the Chancellery and – of course – to bring the Chancellery security officers into the affair. One way or another, the question of the handling of confidential or secret telecommunications during my vacation should have been discussed. That is, unless the service keeping Guillaume under observation had its own reasons for wishing to preserve the status quo. That was not my business, and I could not know that it was all going to be twisted into a rope for my own neck.

I was asked not to change Guillaume's employment in any way. However, Nollau and his colleagues did not know what his employment in the Chancellery actually was. As the investigatory committee found, they did not even know that Guillaume and his family had moved from Frankfurt to Bonn. According to Nollau, they were still assuming at the end of May 1973 that G. worked in the economics department. 'The Chancellery did not tell us he had been promoted to the head of government's office.' It would have taken no undercover work, merely a telephone call, to discover that an internal directive dated 30 November 1972 had appointed G. to the Federal Chancellor's office to carry out the tasks previously performed by Reuschenbach. The President of the Office for the Protection of the Constitution and the Interior Minister were assuming that an adviser with G.'s terms of reference – and with authorized access to secret files – would not be concerned in any way with 'affairs of the government', not even if he was the only adviser accompanying the Chancellor on vacation.

And so to Norway. Nollau – according to his statements to the investigatory committee and his later publications – said that he had discovered I had gone on holiday only at the beginning of July, from the newspapers; there had been no communication from the Chancellery. He decided – whether as a matter of bureaucratic routine, or for some other reason – to suspend observation; it was unlikely 'that Guillaume would meet a courier of the GDR secret service in the solitude of the Norwegian mountains'. He drew his own imaginary picture of the area around Hamar, unimpeded by any actual knowledge of the place. The Office for the Protection of the Constitution had the opportunity and indeed the duty to ascertain the details of these simple facts and G.'s employment. Once I had agreed to having him kept under observation, the appropriate inquiries would have to be made through the Chancellery, its head, the head of the Chancellor's office or the security officers. What made Nollau claim to have heard of my visit to Norway only after it had begun? After all, on 30 May the Interior Minister had advised me to change none of my holiday arrangements, and Grabert, head of the Chancellery, had asked Genscher about it again on 5 June. Had control over the operation been lost? Was there an attempt to cover up inefficiency? Or what?

And why did the Office content itself with vague information from the Interior Minister that G. was 'not concerned with governmental affairs'? What grounds were there for concluding that his employment would be confined solely to 'party matters', even during my Norwegian vacation? It was obvious that the adviser accompanying the Chancellor would have to be the link between him, the Chancellery and the party in all governmental affairs. Had I not expressly asked whether the advice to carry on as usual applied to this point too? If Nollau's people were not clear about that, they should have made inquiries. It may be that keeping Guillaume under observation was too much for them, in which case they were more than ever bound to use their discretion in getting in touch with the Chancellery and taking another look at the general recommendation to carry on as usual. Nollau's office was bogged down in inactivity and wrapped itself in silence.

However, I assumed observation was continuing in Norway. And if the Office for the Protection of the Constitution did not want to approach the Security Division for assistance through one of its officials, what would have been more natural than to bring Federal Intelligence into it? Its employees used a telex office very close to the one we used. The investigatory committee concluded that the telex operators working for Intelligence could have been asked to undertake courier service (to and from my house) as well as coding and decoding.

After that I heard no more of the matter. Now and then I made inquiries of State Secretary Grabert, who regularly replied that there was nothing new in the offing. This silence lasted until 1 March 1974, when Genscher came to see me, with Nollau, and said suspicions had reached a point where it seemed advisable to hand the matter over to the Public Prosecutor's Office. I agreed; I still feel sceptical about this move, especially because of a mistake made by Nollau; he said that one of the (old) radio messages they had decoded mentioned Guillaume's two children. I said that as far as I knew he had only one, a son. Congratulations had indeed been offered in a radio message to 'the second man'; the reference was to the birth of his son – back in the fifties! Early in April 1974 G. apparently paid a brief visit to the south of France. Nollau said he had asked his French colleagues to keep him under observation. One version goes that nothing worth observing happened. The other says Guillaume noticed he was being watched. According to Nollau, the head of French counter-espionage first learned of the Guillaume case 'when I told him about his forthcoming visit to France in April 1974'. However, a well-informed French journalist has said that the French secret service – 'strangely enough' – knew more about G. than its German counterpart.

It seems entirely to have escaped the notice of Nollau's office that G. had accompanied me to the south of France in October 1973. The French secret service – always supposing it knew about this at all, since Bonn had told it nothing – had lost track of him. I was spending a few restful days on the Côte d'Azur, in the pleasant company of Renate and Klaus Harpprecht; the publisher Claude Gallimard had lent me his house. It was the business of the deputy head of the Chancellor's office to pick the staff to accompany me. G. had applied, successfully, to join them. In his book vindicating himself he describes himself as my 'travel courier'. In fact he took some leave due to him, travelled alone, and claimed his travelling expenses from the Party Treasurer. The German secret service proceeded on the principle that though everything was not to be left just as it was, there should be as little alteration as possible. Its head did not even know that Guillaume had travelled to La Croix-Valmer at the same time as I was there.

G.'s book, published in 1988, says that during this October vacation of 1973 he visited the Picasso Museum in Vallauris and met a 'highly placed man' from his own secret service. This man told him to get out while the going was good. What he does not say, and what the head of German counter-espionage obviously did not know, was that G. had booked a room at the Rotonde where some security agents were also staying. One evening there was some drinking, and when Guillaume fell asleep on his bed a notebook fell out of his pocket. A security man carefully put it back in his pocket again. He blinked and apparently babbled, hard as this is to believe, 'You won't get me, you pigs.' No one reported this at the time, as far as I know, and I was told about it only considerably later.

When Nollau spoke to me on 1 March 1974 in Genscher's presence, mentioning certain tangible clues, he added that the arrest would be in two or three weeks' time. At the end of those three weeks the head of my office and I were walking in the

Chancellery gardens, and one of us remarked, 'Nothing's happened; perhaps there was nothing in it after all.' The 'perhaps' was in the sense of 'let's hope', but who was going to believe that after Guillaume's arrest, particularly in the face of the popular agitation then prevailing?

Who was pursuing what interests? Nollau wanted to distract attention from his inefficiency, and was disappointed not to get more recognition of his 'success'. Genscher, who as Minister of the Interior was ultimately responsible for the Office for the Protection of the Constitution, was principally anxious to come out of the affair unscathed. I had no wish to make work more difficult for my party and the Government. Helmut Schmidt was concentrating on his own task, but he made sure that Nollau took retirement shortly afterwards, whereupon the Interior Ministry gave him leave to write what he liked. Wehner and others suggested, more or less confidentially, that my resignation would have been only a matter of time even without the Guillaume affair. The East Berlin version, filtered through Moscow, was that I had really resigned because of opposition within the party and conflicts with the unions.

At whose door should responsibility for the handling of the Guillaume affair actually be laid? I do not doubt that politically and personally motivated malice entered into it where some of the participants were concerned. But that was possible only because indolence and inefficiency had united, with serious consequences, in a large area of internal security.

In December 1975 the Supreme *Land* Court of Düsseldorf sentenced G. to thirteen years' imprisonment. He served seven of them. In the same year, 1975, the Federal Prosecutor's Office instituted preliminary inquiries against me in connection with the 'conveying, through Guillaume, of knowledge that should have been secret'. Similar inquiries were instituted against Genscher, Grabert, the head of the Chancellor's office Wilke, and Nollau. As no criminal offence was concerned, no preliminary proceedings were instituted.

During the Düsseldorf trial the judge raised the question of whether I would say – in camera – what Brezhnev had said to me about the Guillaume case. I said, truthfully, that I could add nothing that would be of any use. When I saw Brezhnev in Moscow in the summer of 1975, he had to think about it before bringing out a few sentences: he was sorry, but his side had nothing to do with it, and he too had suffered disillusionments. Those close to him said he had been 'furiously angry' when he was told in the spring of 1974. I did not feel obliged to take this remark at face value.

Ten years later – the first time I had set foot on East German soil since my visit to Erfurt – I met Erich Honecker. Our talks were on current affairs, but I was prepared for comment on my own. Sure enough, the Chairman of the Council of State paused, looked solemn and took a deep breath, while I smiled inwardly. He too, he said, had first heard the story from the newspapers. He would like to add 'just a word': he had been Chairman of the Defence Council at the time, and when it happened he had blamed 'our people' very much. Moreover, no NATO document had ever been through his hands, and if he had known about the affair he would have said 'Throw the man out!' Whatever one might think of that, the upshot of the confusion was that an intermediary, on Honecker's express instruction or perhaps just at his instigation, had sought to specify that: 'It wasn't us, it was the Russians.' Such comments had found their way to Moscow, arousing considerable annoyance there.

When G.'s memoirs – cleaned up, glamorized, and given the blessing of Markus Wolf, the retired head of the Department of Information in the State Security Ministry – were brought out at the end of 1988 by the GDR's military publishing firm, and extracts appeared in the Federal Republic, speculation was rife. An intrigue against Honecker? Who was trying to show that his hands were clean, and at whose expense, a decade and a half later? And why? It was not unlikely that Mischa Wolf, Guillaume's former boss, was trying to offload responsibility on to Honecker. I let the GDR leadership know that I was somewhat displeased, and there was a prompt reaction. The

Chairman of the Council of State was sorry – the GDR leadership was itself displeased – and told me that those responsible had been told to pull in the few copies of the book distributed and pulp the whole edition. He did one more thing: he sent me a copy – apparently his personal property.

Holding Together

The period just after my resignation was not an easy one; I could hardly have expected that it would be. I had a heavy burden to bear, but anyone who is not prepared to shoulder such a burden had better not go into politics. The pressure of decision-making was taken off me, but I had hardly any more time than before. I lived under rather less stress, although at first there were some qualms, and questions which were easier to ask than to answer.

A few personal friends, and some leading churchmen, helped me to make the transition reasonably well, and without bitterness. There was no point in making a fuss; I did not and do not care for that sort of exhibitionism. But I was glad to have a pleasant conversation in Berlin a few days after my resignation with Bishop Scharf, who had some understanding things to say. He and I had known each other for years, and I had had the encouraging advice of the German Evangelical Church in Bonn, and in Berlin before that. The Protestant Church had handled the old alliance of throne and altar well, and survived confrontation with brutal dictatorship; German Social Democracy now appeared the predominantly Evangelical party – in its upper echelons, to an almost exaggerated degree. I could have no objection to that; my background in a Hanseatic port and my contacts with Scandinavian Lutheranism had imbued me with Protestant habits of thought, but armed me against any kind of missionary zeal. I had no time for the extension of Church influence by other means, nor do I now.

Easing the relationship with Catholicism was much more difficult, but it had to be done for the sake of democracy, including party democracy. Over the years a series of contacts were made for discussion, not always formally. Cardinal Döpfner had told me, when we were both in Berlin, that there were indications of a bridge between his Church and my party, but it had yet to become viable. When we met again in Munich our experiences on both sides had brought us much closer; he described his turbulent young priests, and added, 'Not so very different from you and your Young Socialists!' After my resignation the Cardinal – speaking for his brother bishops as well as himself – expressed his 'sympathy for the human disillusionment' I had suffered. That went too far for some people, and it was disclosed that the letter had not actually been discussed in advance with the other bishops.

I could give more time to the party now. I went to regional conferences, did what I could to hold together mutually repellent forces, and tried to suggest new departures. Last but not least, I was anxious that the Federal Chancellor should not have to watch his back. Nothing was further from my mind than to compete with my successor. Either you are a head of government, I knew, or you are not. Building up a rival position would have gone against my nature and all I had learnt. I also knew the importance of the link with one's party, and that it is particularly worth listening to what the party is saying if what you hear is surprising rather than convincing. I knew that the party should not let its attentions stray very far from the realities, but that I could hardly give orders.

Helmut Schmidt continued to be one of my two deputies as SPD Chairman until 1982. From 1973 to 1975 the other deputy was the successful Prime Minister of North Rhine-Westphalia, Heinz Kühn, and from then until 1979 the experienced Mayor of Bremen, my friend Hans Koschnick; during those years, then, three men from Hanseatic cities were at the head of the German

Social Democrats. The distinction between being head of government and leader of the party is not part of the Anglo-Saxon or the Scandinavian tradition. I myself had retained the chairmanship of the party when I entered the Government and when I became Federal Chancellor; in Berlin, I had agreed to uniting both functions in myself to help avoid friction. However, I never felt there was a single generally valid prescription for this formal question. It all depends on the situation and the people involved. What is advisable today can be inappropriate tomorrow.

In the present case Helmut Schmidt had explicitly asked me not to give up the party chairmanship. Subsequently he told me and other people too that it was helpful for him not to have to devote a great deal of attention to the party and its 'kindergarten' as well as to the chancellorship. Over the years occasional differences of opinion were bound to come up; they arose from our different areas of responsibility. When his chancellorship came to an end in the autumn of 1982 Helmut Schmidt seemed to think for a while that this could have been avoided if he had been Party Chairman. He wrote to me then, with welcome frankness and no personal ill feeling at all, saying that in retrospect he thought it was a mistake not to have taken on the party chairmanship himself, or to have been a contender for it.

I answered equally frankly: 'You yourself must really know that you would not have stayed in office any longer without me; in fact you might well not have held office as long or perhaps as successfully.' Drawing up the balance-sheet, I added 'that I have endeavoured to hold our party together – which is the duty of the Chairman in view of the real dangers of drifting apart. At the same time I have worked to ensure that the Chancellor received proper support'. That also applied, I said, in situations which had demanded a good deal of me and sometimes went to the limits of my self-respect. I had contributed, I said, 'to the majority acceptance at party conferences of certain difficult items that you, as head of government, thought essential'. I also cited our relations with our coalition partner.

Helmut Schmidt was particularly disinclined to agree with me over what he felt was 'Young Socialist arrogance', 'quasi-theological pontification in foreign and security policy' and 'economic nonsense' – and in part he was right. He also included in this list 'an opportunistic attitude towards the current, third manifestation of a middle-class German youth movement, distinguished by an idealistic and unrealistic romanticism'. This was indeed a serious point, though it did not answer the question of whether the emergent Green Party would really become very big very soon and lure a great many young people away from Social Democracy.

His opinion on this matter arose from fears that the left of the party – or what was regarded as its left – might try, opportunistically, to 'steal a march on the Greens'. Mine was that we should take the fear of nuclear energy seriously, and investigate the uneasiness aroused by socially and ecologically unbridled growth. I wanted at least to try to understand a generation that had grown up believing anything went, and then discovered what an erroneous article of faith that was. There was no reason why the 'rising tide of indignation' in the environmental and peace movements should necessarily flow into a party of its own. I wanted as many as possible of these restless, idealistic young people to find their home in Social Democracy, and thereby prevent the development of separate parliamentary representation for them, although perhaps the attempt was doomed. I certainly wanted to see them honing their sense of reality inside the SPD rather than outside it. But on how to meet the younger generation and answer their new questions, Helmut Schmidt and I had to agree to disagree.

It was indisputable, said a cautious commentator later, 'that Brandt allowed neither himself nor his followers to fail in proper political loyalty to his successor', adding that more than once this loyalty had taken me to the limit of 'what he really thought he could expect of himself and his party'. Another commentator wrote: 'Under no other Chairman would the SPD have followed

Government policy so far without rebelling or falling apart.'
Hans-Dietrich Genscher, still Chairman of the FDP, confirmed
from his own viewpoint that I had acted very correctly in
avoiding any poaching on my successor's preserves in the office
of Chancellor where Government business was concerned,
although 'some people interpreted that as lack of support for
Helmut Schmidt'.

Having had a large apparatus at my disposal for many years,
I now had to learn to handle the party chairmanship, which
was linked 'only' with the parliamentary mandate. From an
official residence, I moved to a home without the factotums
who attend the Chancellor, and set up in an office which I had
used only as a supplementary one before. The information
available to a head of government no longer automatically
appeared on my desk. But I had little cause for complaint. I was
informed of Government business through meetings which were
frequent rather than occasional. The Chancellor also kept me
up to date with important developments in foreign policy, and
I could obtain information from the Foreign Ministry whenever
I asked for it. The absence of secret reports did not bother
me; I had learned that the careful reading of certain foreign
newspapers in addition to the national press produces more
information than most of the documents officially stamped
'Secret'. Scientific institutes, too, publish a good deal more
information than most politicians are aware of.

My attention and a considerable part of my work continued
to be devoted to European affairs. One result was that in 1979,
when the first direct elections were held, I took my seat in the
European Parliament as my party's leading member. I had
entered the Parliament with the idea of first enlarging its competence, and then determining its constitution by national elections. The heads of government acting as a ministerial council
decided otherwise, and did not even pick on a single location
for the Parliament; it moved between three cities – Strasbourg,
Luxembourg and Brussels – and allowed itself a good deal of
idling in neutral gear. As a permanent proposition, it did not

make much sense for me to sit in both the Bonn and the Strasbourg parliaments, and in 1982 I resigned my seat in the European Parliament. From a distance, I have been glad to see my colleagues there managing to gain ground, if slowly.

Of course – how could it be otherwise? – East–West relations remained especially important to me. Few people yet guessed how soon they would be back at the centre of interest. Under Gerald Ford, who had taken over from Nixon and was well liked for his affability, the word détente dropped out of the vocabulary, in the name of alleged realism. Bonn went along with the *Zeitgeist*, announcing a 'realistic' policy of détente – as if there were an unrealistic one to be replaced. I felt as little offended by this as by later accusations of the visionary euphoria that was supposed to have attended our *Ostpolitik*. Short-winded competitors are easily overtaken.

When Federal President Richard von Weizsäcker invited some of my companions in public life to a dinner for my seventy-fifth birthday, many people were surprised by a remark made by François Mitterrand; he said that in the seventies we had talked much more about the Western European community and its union than about prospects for Europe as a whole. It is hardly surprising that we had been especially concerned about the dictatorships of our Southern European neighbours. Those southern countries soon set about shaking off dictatorship.

In Greece, I had been able to assist some victims of persecution – including families of people in prison, through the agency of our Embassy. I was given more credit than was due to me for this assistance when I visited the country in the spring of 1975; six years earlier, when I stopped off in Athens on my way back from Turkey, I had made a point of staying on board my plane. I applied strict criteria in the West and where governments wished to be considered part of the West. I never managed to form very close links with Andreas Papandreou, who was soon to become a leading figure in Greece. He had difficulty in coming to terms with European Social Democracy, and I had to respect the fact that he did not really want to do so.

Spain was a different matter. From the first, I felt a liking for the young lawyer Felipe Gonzalez, who had taken over the leadership of the PSOE [Partido Socialista Obrero de Espagñol, Spanish Socialist Party], with its wealth of tradition, at a conference (in France) in 1974; it has been fascinating to see Spain find its way into the modern world under his prudent and courageous leadership. In the autumn of 1974 he visited Lisbon 'illegally' to talk to me. When he was prosecuted for subversive activities I asked Gerhard Jahn, the former Minister of Justice, to attend the trial as an observer; it was stopped and later suspended. The next year Felipe was denied a visa to travel to Mannheim for the SPD party congress. It may be wondered, then, how he got there, even if he arrived a day late. I had called our very active Ambassador in Madrid, and asked him to get in touch at once with Juan Carlos, who was then being trained for the functions of head of state – Franco was still alive at the time. As a result Juan Carlos told the general acting as Minister of the Interior to issue the visa at once. I have met the King from time to time, and on a particularly critical occasion he telephoned me. King Juan Carlos has turned out to be a piece of great good fortune for Spanish democracy.

The complaint has sometimes been raised that parties and institutions of the Federal Republic gave only moderate assistance to related groups on the Iberian peninsula. That criticism has always annoyed me. I have always felt that sending material aid too was desirable and praiseworthy. I am still proud to think that under my leadership, the SPD sent more than fine words to help Spanish democracy to its feet. And until long after the Second World War the twentieth century has not been noted for any excess of European solidarity.

The enemy of the Portuguese dictatorship, Mario Soares, refounded his party in the spring of 1973 in Münstereifel. It played an important part when the young officers who were behind the coup of 1974 could not come to terms with the forces of political democracy. In the autumn of that year I was in Lisbon, and saw the withering of the carnations that had symbolized the Revolution of Flowers; the Communist Party leaders were on the point of seizing power and ousting democracy, so recently acquired.

I thought developments in Portugal very alarming – because of pressing appeals to me from like-minded friends and because of my own experience and understanding of the subject. The situation could pose a threat to the necessary changes in Spain and even cause an international crisis. I felt there might have been some miscalculation on the Soviet side, particularly as the Americans were sending out very dubious signals. Secretary of State Kissinger feared an alliance between Socialist revolutionary officers and apparently moderate Communists, and concluded that Italy and other countries might fall prey to illusions, with menacing consequences. He saw an approaching danger of the whole of Southern Europe's becoming 'Marxist'. When I was in Washington in March 1975, he accompanied me to President Ford. I spoke of my anxiety and asked for helpful frankness. At the same time I asked the presidents of Mexico and Venezuela to intervene with the Soviet Union to clear matters up. They were very happy to do so, and at once; the prospects for Spain were of particular importance to them.

Early in the summer of 1975 I went to Moscow myself and warned Brezhnev how fateful a misjudgement of the Southern European situation could be. I gave him a letter from Mario Soares and tried to explain what a strain the Soviet leadership would be putting on East–West relations if it thought it could get a footing on the west coast of the Iberian peninsula. In this case, it was easier to make the Russians think again than to move the President's adviser in Washington from his *idée fixe*. In the summer of that year, around the time of the Helsinki conference, Bruno Kreisky told me how, in Kissinger's circle, the word was that all efforts on behalf of Portuguese democracy were useless and that Soares must be considered a kind of Kerensky. At a conference in Stockholm between friendly heads of government and party leaders, I suggested a committee to defend democracy in Portugal, and undertook to be its chairman. Without such international backing the attempted *putsch* in Lisbon in November 1975 would not have fizzled out so easily.

I was not especially enthusiastic when I was made President of the Socialist International – I was still Federal Chancellor at the time. That loose association of Social Democratic parties, which dated back to a congress in Paris in 1889, had been refounded in Frankfurt in 1951. The impression I had gained of it from various conferences was not particularly favourable, and I doubted that much could be done within its traditional framework. For a long time I was in favour of the SPD's concentrating on the important areas of European co-operation, and making contact, free of ideological blinkers, with politically related groups in other parts of the world. The extensive and impressive international participation in our Mannheim party conference was the result of that effort. The next year, in May 1976, I helped to organize a conference in Caracas, where European Social Democrats talked to a very diverse gathering of representatives of democratic parties from Latin America and the Caribbean.

Meanwhile, Bruno Kreisky and Olof Palme had persuaded me not to refuse the presidency of the Socialist International; they said I might be able to reinvigorate the 'traditional club' and overcome Eurocentrism. We met now and then in a friendly atmosphere to discuss world events, without the pressures of a time-limit or an agenda. The three of us had published a little book of letters and records of our conversations in 1975, writing about past experiences and outlining probable developments; the need for international co-operation that really deserved the name was one of the conclusions we reached. All three of us led large and influential parties, and we were friends who could discuss anything, and had power to make things happen. I was eventually elected President of the Socialist International at a congress in Geneva in the autumn of 1976.

I had met Robert McNamara when he was Kennedy's Secretary of Defense. He became head of the World Bank in the autumn of 1968. At the end of 1976 he sent a messenger to ask me if I would be ready to assemble and chair an independent international commission to produce new ideas on development policies and make some concrete recommendations. I was chary at first, because I did not want to disturb other initiatives, and it took me many preliminary talks to find out what could be done and what could not. I have never been sorry that I finally agreed. The subject was an important one. However, the result reflected little more than superficial interest. The Independent Commission on International Development Issues was set up in December 1977 at Schloss Gymnich, with the friendly approval of the Federal President and the Chancellor. After two years and many discussions, not all of them fruitful, our report was published at the end of 1979. Both tasks, the International and the Commission, meant a great deal of travelling; in the autumn of 1978 I came back from a congress in Vancouver, Canada, with a protracted cardiac infarct. My life ran in more ordered tracks thereafter.

In domestic politics, the situation – leaving the effects of terrorism out of account – was marked by stability; the immediate problems facing the Federal Government arose from difficulties in the world economy. People in most other countries, including European nations, would happily have changed places with the West Germans. The Social Democratic–Liberal Government and the Social Democrats who were the larger partner in it did not do badly. In the Bundestag elections of 1976 the SPD lost over a million votes by comparison with 1972, while the CDU/CSU, with Helmut Kohl as their candidate for Chancellor for the first time, had their second-best result after Adenauer's triumph. In 1980, Franz Josef Strauss tried to put obstacles in Kohl's way and make his own mark; he polarized public opinion and thus did the FDP some good. The Social Democrats improved their standing by a few decimal points, rising from 42.6 to 42.9 per cent of the vote.

Both election campaigns – although not those campaigns alone, and not only in Germany – were disappointing because the points at issue were over-simplified. Much energy was expended in quarrelling over 'Freedom versus Socialism', giving the impression that the Federal Republic was seriously threatened by the spectre of anti-Americanism. In the heat of battle, and because I had put so much into it myself, I went too far at the Mannheim party congress of 1975, when I said of the Union that in their present state they were not fit to govern and would be 'a security risk to our country'. It was said, rightly, that I should not have employed a term from defence policy; but I was attacking irresponsibility, demagogy, and blatant egotism. And I did not hesitate to say that the changes in the world posed more problems than we were able to answer. However, I will admit that I too have found it easier to go in search of new issues than to persevere in the search for solutions.

The proposition that modern industrial societies cannot be governed, which often aroused a lively response, showed how shaky the ground under our feet had become. It was inevitably difficult for Social Democracy to adjust to change; the new shape being given to the social structure as a result of technological revolution was not obvious at first glance or even at second. At the end of the seventies and the beginning of the eighties, there were moments when I myself doubted if it was right for the outer fringes of the party to remain part of it. Where the traditional bearings are gone, disorientation is bound to set in; but predictions of imminent splits were not fulfilled. I was less concerned than it may have seemed by accusations that I had been too philosophical and too forbearing. The only alternative would have meant early loss of governmental responsibility, and a considerable blow to German democracy. There was a price to be paid for my efforts – both intellectual and emotional – to hold the party together. But you can never have everything at once.

All's Well That Ends Well

In retrospect, the dispute about medium-range nuclear missiles in Europe looks grotesque. Yet there is a moral in it: popular simplification on both sides makes complicated matters even more complicated. The dispute – not just an international one – laid a considerable burden on Helmut Schmidt and his government. The attitude of the Allies was not clear. At home, a considerable part of the general public felt too much was asked of them, and the peace movement gained many recruits. There were heated discussions within the party.

The Soviet Union had reached a dangerous stage of over-armament in a major area with the installation of their triple-headed 5,000-kilometre-range missiles, known in the West as SS20s; few would have disputed that. Some people were quicker than others to point out that the Americans were not defence-less. The appropriate Western reaction, and whether the problem would be settled by a parallel increase in armaments (on German soil in particular), were subjects of debate in both the governing parties, but the strongest reservations were found outside the political parties. In the early eighties the Federal Republic saw the largest rallies of the post-war period assemble to demonstrate against the arms race. I thought that young Germans had gone out on the streets in great numbers for worse causes than peace, and said so. They were accused of naïvety because they found it difficult to follow the arguments of conventional military-political logic. Their commitment was not predominantly fuelled by pacifist principles, and certainly not by the influence of Eastern propaganda. The movement coincided with government by a coalition which hardly anyone believed would survive the next election.

In the autumn of 1981 I tried – in a conversation with Secretary of State Haig at the State Department, and on other occasions – to convince the American government that it was a mistake 'to regard the peace movement as anti-American, neutralistic, or against its own government'. I had already warned Brezhnev against the error of evaluating protest by a large number of people, mainly young, as something in the nature of a pro-Communist movement.

The break-up of the Schmidt–Genscher Government in the autumn of 1982 was not the result of the Chancellor's own party failing him in the dispute about the missiles. It was the leaders of the Free Democrats who thought that next time round the Social Democratic–Liberal majority would be lost, and with it their participation in an SPD-led government would be gone. Agreement on the Federal budget and measures to halt the rise in unemployment had been extremely difficult to achieve. Coalition talks became farcical games of hide-and-seek. Strauss and his henchmen, who had a vested interest in cultivating or sometimes inventing differences of opinion between Schmidt and his party, left it in no doubt that the Social Democratic–Liberal coalition would fall on its economic and social policy in 1982.

Even more misleading than the hotch-potch of political incidents at home was the assumption that Western armament brought a new leadership to the fore in the Soviet Union. It certainly needed one, for several reasons. But no one can seriously suppose that Mikhail Gorbachev's emergence at the top early in 1985 was the result of a NATO decision taken in December 1979. When the new General Secretary took office the Soviet Union had over 350 SS20s (that is the general estimate), two-thirds of them pointing towards Europe, and more of a nuisance to Gorbachev than a guarantee of security from the start. He therefore argued for the resumption of the negotiations that had previously been broken off. In President Reagan he found a partner flexible enough to change course himself and break new ground in security policy. The reduction in the number of land-based medium-range missiles stationed in Europe was so highly valued because it went beyond all expectations. The agreement had little to do with any decisions taken by the Bonn Government or by NATO in Brussels.

Helmut Schmidt was right to be anxious about potentially offensive Soviet weapons in general and the new rockets in particular. He wanted negotiations to provide the highest possible stability and the lowest possible level of arms. It troubled and wounded him to find that his fears were not taken seriously in Washington when Jimmy Carter succeeded Gerald Ford in the White House. Carter's security adviser 'Zbig' Brzezinski and the self-confident Chancellor in Bonn did not get on well, and did not bother to disguise the fact. Hardly anyone, even those who professed it was their aim, thought that the threat would be removed entirely. Schmidt and I both spoke of it, independently of each other. So did some of his and my British friends. So did François Mitterrand before he became President: 'No SS20s and no Pershing 2s.' The great communicator in the USA made an historical breakthrough when he trusted his instinct and his wife's advice more than the experts with their batteries of facts and prejudices.

However, I did have considerable reservations, feeling that a German head of government in our times would be overreaching himself if he thought he could take the lead in a strategic East–West issue. One might well imagine that German guidance would be far from welcome, particularly in an area which the Great Powers – including the purely nominal ones – wanted to keep closed against intruders. Looking at it from another angle, if the worst came to the worst American nuclear weapons could be fired from the Federal Republic and reach the Soviet Union within a few minutes. There was a politically emotional dimension to the technical qualities of the new weapons, and one which was bound to dramatize the operation from the Russian viewpoint: Moscow felt the Pershing 2 a considerably greater threat than the device it was to replace. So did many Germans, remembering the last war.

Some of us had other questions: what would happen if the philosophy of the balance of power were more widely dispersed regionally – and watered down? What did the Euro-strategic balance that was being discussed actually entail? Was it not advisable to put up reluctant opposition to those circles in the USA that aimed to decrease the risk of world-wide confrontation, and America's own destruction, by making it possible to wage nuclear war in Europe if such a war could not be avoided? On the other hand, was not the danger of political blackmail by means of the new weapons greatly exaggerated? We had survived the crises in and around Berlin because our political will was stronger than the material forces ranged against us.

This was the salient point: some thought the role of weapons and associated lines of thinking more important than did others. And some, particularly in military matters, appeared convinced of their cause while others did not conceal serious doubts. I did not regard conventional geopolitical ideas in general and the certainty of a continuing Soviet urge for expansion in particular as immutable factors. The invasion of Afghanistan by the Red Army in December 1979, when NATO had taken its 'dual-track' decision [see p. 326], seemed to prove the pessimists right. Of course, the decision to move south had not initially sprung from the East–West conflict, but it was a serious matter and bound to cause concern.

No, I had no time for geopolitical simplification. Even as Chancellor, and yet more so later, I could not see that the logic of deterrence and the spiralling balance of power was as logical as all that. The arms race would not come to a halt, and the danger of a major disaster would become increasingly likely, while enormous resources would have been squandered. What was the logic of that?

The Americans and Russians had excluded the so-called Euro-strategic arms system – those of the two World Powers and the nuclear forces of the French and British – from consideration when they signed SALT 1, the Strategic Arms Limitation Treaty; 'strategic' in this context always referred to intercontinental weapons of destruction. The question of the missiles thus excluded came up again when President Ford and Secretary of State Kissinger met Brezhnev and Gromyko in Vladivostok at the end of 1974 and worked out the basic features of a SALT 2 agreement. When Ford came to Bonn in July 1975 he told Chancellor Schmidt that in distant Siberia they had reached extensive agreement, except about the future of the Euro-strategic weapons systems. However, the President promised his German ally to make a serious effort to include Soviet medium-range weapons in the SALT 2 talks. The Chancellor had already told Brezhnev in the autumn of 1974 that he was anxious about the concept and proliferation of SS20 missiles. The General Secretary's answer had been to point to the superiority of the American air forces.

After the SALT 2 breakthrough, Helmut Schmidt had something else to consider: the former American superiority in intercontinental weapons, which had compensated for the deficit in Euro-strategic missiles, no longer existed. Moreover, the Chancellor had not expected that Ford's successor Carter, elected at the end of 1976, and his security adviser would pay so little attention to German warnings and arguments. Carter did not recognize a qualitatively new danger; he thought it militarily superfluous and detrimental to American interests to step up armaments in response to the SS20s, and he feared negative effects on the process of strategic arms control. Nor did his hint that missiles programmed to hit German sites could be diverted to countries outside Europe impress the Chancellor. Professor Brzezinski told him, at least twice, that he was concerning himself with matters which were not the business of the head of government of a non-nuclear country. Washington ironists drew a comparison with Senator John F. Kennedy who, when he was running for President, found a gap in the American missiles system which later turned out to be non-existent. But whatever the ironists might say, it could not be satisfactory to anyone truly concerned for security in Europe to know that there was a grey zone in the Soviet and American arsenal which was not discussed in the context of either the SALT talks or

MBFR, the Mutual and Balanced Force Reductions discussed in Vienna.

Secretary of State Cyrus Vance, a member of the East Coast establishment and well disposed to German friends of America, said some years later that Washington had hoped to discuss matters without a lot of publicity and prepare a study of the nuclear requirements of NATO beyond the seventies; after the 'Schmidt speech' that was no longer possible. He meant Schmidt's speech in London in October 1977, the subject of which was the lack of parity in the tactical nuclear and conventional sectors.

It was another year before Carter instigated Four-Power talks of a unique kind. Early in January 1979 he met the French President, the British Prime Minister and the German Chancellor in Guadeloupe. After Washington had decided on 'modernization' in the summer of 1978, and motivated the industry involved, the President of the USA came to accept considerations he had never entertained before. He said that the USA was ready to deploy weapons to close the gap. Callaghan advised offering to negotiate with the Soviet Union first. Giscard d'Estaing suggested letting the Russians know that American missiles would be deployed if negotiations did not produce a result in a given time. This proposal was adopted.

The German Chancellor insisted, for good reasons, that before any missiles were stationed there must be a joint decision by NATO, and that the weapons must be under the sole control of the United States; on no account must they be exclusively deployed in the Federal Republic.

The Council of NATO made its decision in mid-November 1979 in Brussels. The model of the Four-Power Guadeloupe conference was not imitated. The contradictions between technical possibilities and political intentions did not redound to Washington's credit, and there was rather too much noise from those who were less concerned with a counterweight to the SS20s than with a wish to have additional options on German soil. In spite of Guadeloupe Carter had not brought up the question of the SS20s when he went to Vienna to sign SALT 2 in June 1979, six months after the Four-Power meeting. It was thought in the Chancellery that Carter's discussions with Brezhnev amounted to no more than a comment exchanged in the lift.

In December 1979, then, came NATO's dual-track decision: 108 Pershing 2s and 464 cruise missiles to be deployed in Europe, the new Pershings, which were regarded as particularly advanced, being deployed exclusively in the Federal Republic of Germany – unless the negotiations offered to the Soviet Union produced results within four years. There were soon suggestions, not least on the German side, that if the missiles were deployed in Europe then it would be preferable to have them sea-based, but this option was rejected as being too expensive and lacking in precision.

Many small indiscretions showed the world that those in power in Bonn and Washington at this time did not get on well together. Even later the ex-President accused the ex-Chancellor of fabricating the missiles controversy; he described a discussion in Venice in June 1980 as the least satisfactory he had ever had with a foreign leader.

Helmut Schmidt was not dissatisfied with the dual-track decision in favour of negotiations and if necessary of the step-ping-up of armaments. He had no difficulty accepting his party's decision in December 1979 on a stipulation to resolve this issue: no deployment of missiles if negotiations allowed an expectation of progress. He was reckoning that the eighties would see 'sabre-rattling with medium-range missiles', and was troubled by the prospect that in the natural course of things 'Brezhnev and his team' would no longer be in office. For all their other differences, he thought the General Secretary in Moscow understood him better than did the occupant of the White House. However, nothing binding came of Brezhnev's visit to the Federal Republic in 1978, when I myself met him in Bonn and at the Schmidts' in Hamburg: it was 'important that no one should strive for military superiority' and there should be an endeavour 'to achieve approximate equilibrium and parity'. Both sides had been looking at the map.

Helmut Schmidt visited Moscow six months after the dual-track decision. The Soviet leadership revised its over-hasty decision to give a flat refusal to negotiations. The Soviets now agreed to sit at the same table as the Americans. I had advised this even before the NATO decision, and wrote to Brezhnev in the middle of December 1979 with the explicit consent of the Federal Chancellor. I did not conceal my fear of a new turn of the armaments screw, and urged that good use should be made of the three or four years the Western Alliance had allowed for negotiations. My impression was that these things were decided by the general staff in Moscow. The information that sometimes reached me from the Central Committee suggested that the Soviets would not be drawn into another confrontation, and would not help to destroy détente. Whatever was to be thought of such communications, the interests behind them seemed to me worth noting.

Moscow and Washington had been talking to each other again since late 1980. Before the summer break of 1981, when I visited the Soviet Union after an absence of six years and had a heartening discussion at the World Economics Institute of the Academy of Sciences, I found Brezhnev in a very poor state. He had trouble even in reading aloud, both in negotiation and at table. At meals he simply toyed with a starter. He was quite lively again when he came to fetch me from the guest house on the Lenin Hills and take me to the airport. Earlier, over a stiff drink such as the doctors had long ago forbidden him, we had discussed the missiles again: what did 'zero' really mean to me? Where could he fall in with the Americans on the road to that goal? Did I think there was any chance of coming to an understanding with the new President? Boris Ponomaryov, who had been involved in the Soviet Communist Party's international work ever since Stalin's time, put in a good word for Reagan: he had visited him in Sacramento when he was still Governor of California, at the head of a delegation of the Supreme

Soviet, and they had gleaned a favourable impression of his frankness and lack of pretension.

Brezhnev's after-dinner speech of 30 June said that the USSR was ready 'to halt the deployment of our medium-range missiles in the European part of our country the day negotiations on the matter begin', and on condition the USA would act in the same way. My answer was to confirm that we were in favour of negotiations with the aim of rendering further armaments superfluous and making it possible to reduce existing arms.

Before I left for the Soviet Union at the beginning of May 1981, I had received an undated document from the Central Committee speaking of a shadow that would be cast over 'Soviet and West German relations' by missiles that could reach Soviet territory and 'provoke a war against the Soviet Union'. The reply I gave the Kremlin was that it was understandable for the Soviet Union to feel threatened by the new weapons. But we ourselves felt endangered by the SS20s. The threats on both sides must be reduced through negotiations very soon.

For a long time it looked as if nothing would come of the American–Soviet negotiations that finally began in Geneva in November 1981. The Soviets were hard to shift; the Americans scarcely advanced beyond propaganda. It was widely assumed that Reagan had mentioned the zero option in the secure expectation that the Soviets would not accept it. At the beginning of March 1982 I heard from Brezhnev that the Soviet Union was against the zero option; I replied in the middle of the month saying why I thought the American proposal might bring progress into the negotiations.

In July 1982 the leaders of the delegations took their famous 'walk in the woods', set their sights on compromise – and were called off by their respective headquarters; the German Chancellor was not even properly informed, let alone consulted, which was bound to irritate him. Geneva was doomed to failure so far as the subject of these negotiations was concerned. Brezhnev's successor Andropov, a very sick man, came on the scene too late when he tried to get things moving in the autumn of 1982; his proposal aimed at 'equilibrium' in relation to the British and French potentials. It had to be realized that he could not yet permit himself and his military men to go further. In September 1983, Andropov wrote to me about the counter-measures which would be taken if the Federal Republic 'becomes a bridgehead for the stationing of American first-strike rockets'. I replied in a letter dated 22 September 1983, and felt bound to remind him – saying 'You make the first move!' – that the Soviet Union should do what it could: 'Nothing could hold out better prospects of success in this endeavour, and of the prevention of the stationing of more American missiles, than such a dramatic step on the part of the Soviet Union, a step which can be taken unilaterally even if American missiles are still deployed. This is a contribution the Soviet Union and no one else can make. I know how hard it must seem, but it would safeguard the security interests of your country.' I added that our expressing an opinion on these issues vis-à-vis Moscow as well as Washington was 'something that would certainly not be possible but for the relations developed on the basis of the Moscow Treaty'.

Arms were deployed in accordance with the decision of the Western Alliance. The stationing of Pershing 2 missiles began on 22 November 1983, and the next day the Soviets left the negotiating table in Geneva. Resolutions, protests and sit-ins fizzled out, and the West had to stand by and watch the Soviet Union stationing short-range 'tactical' nuclear weapons near their borders again: in a given eventuality they were to take out the missile bases in the Federal Republic.

Not until the beginning of 1985 did the foreign ministers of the nuclear World Powers pick up the threads of discussion and raise the delicate subject once more. In April, just after he had taken over the leadership, Gorbachev announced a halt to the deployment of weapons. In autumn 1986 he and Reagan only just missed achieving a breakthrough at the Reykjavik summit, which was seen as sensational. An agreement seemed to be only a question of time, not of principle. At the end of 1987 the INF agreement was signed in Washington.

In discussions with far-sighted friends in Washington, among others, I had always dwelt on the simple truth that there must be talking if the instruments of destruction are not to take on an independent life of their own. I could not expect to be regarded as a hardliner, but where the rumour came from that I opposed Helmut Schmidt over the missiles I still do not know. If anyone had said Strauss I would have been ready to believe it, since he admitted freely that he thought the section of the dual-track decision referring to negotiations a monstrosity.

Looking back, Helmut Schmidt has said he thought there were some Social Democrats who applied a double standard to the World Powers, and had represented the Federal Republic as a mere bridgehead for preserving American interests in Europe. I did not feel hurt by that, or by something Giscard d'Estaing claimed to have heard from his friend Helmut when they were discussing the neutron bomb in 1977. 'Willy Brandt brought everything into play against me, as usual.'

This is the distorted variant of that version of events which says the Social Democrats let their own Chancellor down. False versions become no better, however, when they appear in new editions. And the former French President must have known that a Social Democrat would not have remained head of government for a fortnight if I, as Party Chairman, had thought he was unsuitable. In fact Helmut Schmidt and I were not in confrontation but on the same side at the two crucial party conferences concerned, in Berlin in December 1979 and in Munich in March 1982. The Chancellor would have lost his majority, particularly with regard to foreign security policy, if I had not helped to ensure that he got it. We certainly did not agree on every detail of the situation, and we certainly did not emphasize the same aspects. But in Berlin in 1979 Helmut Schmidt not only campaigned for the dual-track decision, which was due to be settled in Brussels that month, he also paid tribute to the important results to date of détente policy. I was also able to point out that the initiative of the Federal German Chancellor meant that the Brussels decision contained a section on negotiation as well as a section on defence. Whatever kind of difficult interim decisions became inevitable, I argued, the basic decision to decrease tension would not be affected. Neither of us wanted a return to the illusions of supposed strength or the sterile uncertainties of the Cold War. Humanity was in danger of arming itself to death; it was therefore vitally important to achieve military balance on as low a level as possible.

There was no reason for anyone, least of all myself, to feel great enthusiasm. On the other hand I knew it would have been foolish for the party to try interfering in the Western Alliance's negotiating machinery or take over functions that were properly those of the Government. However, it seemed to me appropriate to formulate expectations that might be called conditions. Even in retrospect, I think we had a right to insist on the ratification of SALT 2, so that a first interim agreement could be made at the MBFR talks in Vienna, and good progress could be made in the Geneva negotiations.

In Munich in April 1982 I found the party conference ready to agree to do everything humanly possible to conclude the Geneva talks successfully. My appeal included advice to abstain from anything that could endanger such success. Now was not the moment, I said, to bring the dual-track decision up again and give the Soviet side an excuse to withdraw from serious discussion: 'If there are no negotiations, we have lost.'

Intending to make this quite clear I wrote in the draft of my Munich speech: 'No one has our agreement to the stationing of missiles on German soil in his pocket. I will also say explicitly, no one has *my* agreement.' On such occasions Helmut Schmidt and I used to exchange our texts, and he wrote on the margin of my draft, 'I would like to discuss this with you, please.' As a result I omitted both remarks; the Chancellor thought they would present him with unnecessary difficulties. We carried the motion with a big majority.

After the change of Chancellor in October 1982, however, a

legend arose in the FDP and elsewhere to the effect that the Social Democrats, in league with other ill-intentioned persons of a leftist persuasion, had denied Helmut Schmidt another term because of the dual-track decision. This misconception dominated the elections to the Bundestag in early 1983. We stuck to our thesis that Soviet missiles should be decreased to the point where American missiles did not need to be deployed; we did not want to be threatened by rockets directed at us from the east by others, nor did we want others to be threatened by missiles from our soil. The party drew its conclusions after the election. It condemned over-hasty arming, and urged serious negotiations in the spirit of the dual-track decision.

I was one of the great majority of party delegates meeting in Cologne who voted against the deployment of Pershing 2 and cruise missiles, against a background of shadow-boxing in Geneva. I believed there was a shorter way to achieving arms reduction and control. My advice was: 'We must take the other side at its word and stop putting new obstacles in our own path.' Shortly before this, in the Hofgarten in Bonn, I had addressed a protest meeting of the peace movement, failing to win the approval of that part of my audience which wanted to hear nothing but attacks on the Western Powers, NATO and the Bundeswehr. They had come to the wrong address, and the catcalls of a vociferous minority were not going to bother me.

At that large gathering in Bonn I said: 'The Bundeswehr, as the army of a democratic state, had the task of helping to ensure peace. Its members, like the rest of us, have a vital interest in seeing that what we all want to secure is not given up to annihilation.' My main concern was for the idea certain powerful people had 'taken into their thick heads, that the deployment of Pershing 2s is more important than the removal of SS20s'. We not only should but must say no to that.

Andropov wrote to me on 30 November 1983 saying that his side now felt 'bound to take steps to neutralize the danger of war'. Konstantin Chernenko, Gorbachev's immediate and short-term predecessor, was putting it thus at the end of March

1984: 'It is important to restore an atmosphere of international trust.' Signs multiplied that there was consideration of a new phase of détente. But few yet guessed that a few years later both nuclear superpowers would be undertaking to remove and destroy the medium-range missiles in Europe.

A Cheerful Goodbye

In the summer of 1986 I announced, in passing, that I would be standing for the party chairmanship for the last time at the Nuremberg party conference. I had held the office for nearly a quarter of a century. During that time my party had become considerably stronger, and its weight in German politics had increased. It had been in government in Bonn for over sixteen years, and now found itself facing new challenges. I did not feel like retiring from an active working life, but I was less at ease now with the routine and the undemanding intellectual level of party political activity. A man who has no more personal ambition, and has seen it all, loses interest in struggling against the usual run of officiousness, and as one grows older certain things seem less important than they once did. I would not say that that implies a deficient sense of duty. No one has a duty to make himself miserable and pretend he is enjoying things that have become mere habit.

I might have known it is a mistake to announce one's retirement two years in advance. There is truth in the maxim that tells us not to talk about such things, but just do them. A man who divests himself of power risks losing his skin before he can spare it. Not only does the succession become an object of endless discussion, but people seize the chance to settle old scores, or offload blame on to someone about to retire.

The Bundestag elections of January 1987 were unsatisfactory

for both large parties. Helmut Kohl swallowed his chagrin, for he could continue in government. The SPD had 37 per cent of the vote, even less than the disappointing results of the previous election. Failure weighed all the more heavily because our declared electoral aim had been an absolute majority. And disappointment faded no faster because neither the media nor our own supporters had thought that aim was really within reach. It is thought wrong for parties to seem over-optimistic, but all the same a popular party is doing itself no favours if it seems to think it can evade the laws of electoral behaviour, or incurs suspicion of setting itself a maximalist aim so as to avoid thinking about either possible coalition partners or political content. After all, the idea of absolute majorities – particularly at national level – is not always viewed sympathetically; many voters fear that such a majority could lead to over-confidence.

Apropos of political content: the party's hope for an absolute majority went hand in hand with an appeal to 'the Centre'. It is a truism that if you want to win votes you cannot orientate yourself by fringes or even minorities. But is the majority actually to be found in the centre? You may as well ask how many angels can dance on the point of a pin. Out of a desire for unity, or innocuity, or both, it is easily forgotten that the electorate must know or must at least suspect what you stand for and what you oppose.

Johannes Rau, Prime Minister of North Rhine-Westphalia, the biggest of the Federal *Länder*, had been asked by the whole party leadership to stand as our candidate for Chancellor; I had explicitly encouraged him. He had an absolute majority in his home province, just as Oskar Lafontaine did in the Saarland; Lafontaine was its new Prime Minister and his star was just rising. Both had managed to keep the Green Party out of the Landtag of their respective *Länder*, against different backgrounds of events, in the spring elections of 1985. But what was possible in Düsseldorf and Saarbrücken might not be possible in Bonn. There might be dispute in some party circles about the propositions – first, that the Greens could not be kept out of

Parliament at Federal level, and second, that they were not to be taken seriously as coalition partners in their present state – but not in the leadership. However, only a few days after the election we agreed to not exchange recriminations among ourselves, but cross swords with our proper adversaries, our political opponents. It proved true that concord is reached when you and others have enough in common, and at least some of your own requirements can be realized. Argument within the party was increasingly eased through the agency of the town halls: up and down the country decisions on who should become or remain mayor, and with whom they could work reasonably well in a common political cause, were made from very practical viewpoints.

Some experts who thought they knew more than others about elections did not like to admit that they had been banking on a fragile majority strategy. But as always, if you are not sure of yourself, you will not be much in demand. It seemed sensible, therefore, to let a party leadership that would in any case soon have to be replaced pay for the disappointment. Perhaps unnecessarily but not wrongly, I had told a reporter on a major weekly in the late summer of 1986 that 43 per cent would be a good result, especially as the point of departure for a campaign which had not yet begun. And it surely would have been a great success, compared with the 37 per cent we actually got. I will admit that anyone who had believed firmly in an absolute majority, for whatever reason, was bound to see doubts expressed about his prophetic powers; at the same time, however, some strategists seized, at the middle level, on the chance of a scapegoat in the quite likely event of our absolute majority turning out to be a castle in the air. When it did indeed turn out that way, it proved the truth of the old proverb that victory has many fathers but defeat is an orphan.

Discussion of the form and content of the election campaign, and argument over the interpretation of its result, had not yet died away when a personal decision showed me that the basis of trust in the upper levels of the party had been shaken. The post of spokesman for the Party Committee fell vacant. In the inner circle of the party leadership there was no doubt that a woman should be appointed.

I had firmly supported the idea, and even exerted a certain amount of pressure to get to grips with the problem of the rather small proportion of women holding Party offices and parliamentary seats. The SPD, which had introduced votes for women after the First World War, had taken its time over introducing equal rights, even in its own ranks. When more general urging proved fruitless I used some leverage, and at the party conference in Berlin in 1979 I managed to get the number of members of the Party Committee increased, for otherwise there would have been no significant female representation at that particular level of the leadership. Previously, in the first direct elections to the European Parliament, I had made my candidature as leader conditional on a number of women getting safe seats. When I supported proposals going a good deal further in 1986, I was amused by the fury of male colleagues. A few years later that had entirely evaporated. At the Hamburg party conference in 1977 less than 10 per cent of the delegates were women; at Münster in 1988, women accounted for more than a third of the total. There was hardly any need for the quota ruling in favour of women. In the spring of 1987, in any case, it seemed to me important to appoint a woman to the spokesman's position, and a pleasing appearance should not count against her.

I met with no opposition when I said that the future holder of the post did not absolutely have to be a party member; indeed, I thought it possible that an intelligent person not afflicted with bureaucratic myopia might actually find that he or she had a special ability to put over our home and foreign policies to the public at large. Whoever occupied the position was not going to be working inside the party, but presenting it to the outside world. Within the small circle in which we discussed the matter, it was not even seen, or at least not mentioned, as an objection that my candidate's parents were not German; she was a German-born Greek who had been educated in Bonn and later gained her doctorate there. When my proposal was made public, there was a storm of protest in some sections of the party, especially violent in the ranks of the parliamentary deputies. To some extent, I could understand uneasiness about the fact that she was not particularly closely connected with the party, but a bad, frowsty smell surfaced here and there where the honest smell of the stables would have been preferable. I could not understand why Social Democratic women, so keen on equal rights in general, showed so little interest or even indignation in a concrete instance. I thought the argument that she lacked experience in journalism a mere pretext; it was put forward from a quarter where they knew how to raise a journalistic furore without bothering much about the political complexion of their opponent. It was obvious that some people saw and made use of a chance to put a spoke in my wheel, so that could easily be shrugged off. But it hurt me to find letters on my desk attacking foreigners – even from within the party itself and its close vicinity. Not all of them were thought fit for me to see.

If I had insisted I could have forced my proposal through. But I did not, and Peter Glotz, the astute organizational manager of the Federal Party, advised me to give way. He retired at the same time as I did.

I could not help seeing that trust had worn very thin, and I would not close my eyes to it. On 23 March I told the Party Committee I was thinking of retiring, asking Dr Hans-Jochen Vogel, Chairman of the Bundestag Parliamentary Party, to take over from me with Oskar Lafontaine and Johannes Rau as his deputies. No one was surprised. I felt confirmed in my decision by a long conversation I had had with younger party leaders the previous weekend.

I told the Committee I felt I ought to retire if I met with such a lack of understanding over a matter which was not even of vital importance. A good deal of what I had read and heard about the incident had horrified me; I thought we were beyond that sort of thing. I added: 'When a prop which has remained in place for a long time will no longer hold, when a personal issue becomes a major affair of state, and I see an influential minority of elected representatives falling out of line, then I think, at my age, that it is time to turn the page.'

There are worse things than making way for someone else, particularly when you know that there is a younger leadership group standing ready to move up, and when you have been able to breathe new life into a programme. Heinrich Albertz, first my deputy and then my successor in Berlin, wrote cogently (and said that it was also true of leadership in the Church) that the man at the top never has a very easy time; he depends on others and they depend on him. 'There is always someone sawing away at his chair, usually several people; it is difficult for people to deal with one another candidly.' To which one might add that if people are sawing away at your chair, you can try persuading or forcing them to stop, and when you can no longer manage it, and you no longer feel like persuading or forcing them, you should leave. Heinrich Albertz's letter led me to acknowledge that by stages I had been enjoying politics less and less, probably since the moment when the Social Democrats lost government office. Keeping the party up to the task of government was a great challenge, and when that challenge was gone the excitement and pleasure faded. It took me some time, a time of transition, to be sure of what I suspected: that younger forces were needed to lead the party out of the inevitable phase of self-discovery and back to power. That was all the more important because the party political landscape was in upheaval and youthful candour and flexibility were needed.

In those years when the Greens became independent and made life difficult for the SPD and its Chairman, I never doubted that it could only be a question of time before something similar or even more unwelcome happened to the other big popular party. Nowhere was it written, certainly not in the Basic Law, that the Federal Republic must live for ever with a two-and-a-half party system. I could see no threat to democracy in the loosening of that system, but I did in the hysterical reaction to it. No democracy can exist without self-assurance. It is still my fear that it might not be as firmly established in the Federal Republic as we had believed for four decades.

I offered my formal resignation at an extraordinary party conference held in the middle of June 1987, in the Beethoven-halle in Bonn. The assembled company was generous with its bouquets, both real and metaphorical. My farewell speech had a very friendly reception from the people in the hall and from a wider audience outside it. I was made Honorary Chairman, and promised myself even more than others to make very cautious use of that privilege. I looked back not in anger but in gratitude for the many happy years I had enjoyed, and I looked to the future with a light heart and my spirits high. I found it easy to say goodbye.

I was not going to lapse into idleness, which I would not have enjoyed. I was heartened by the many tokens of affection and the requests for advice that I received, from far beyond the ranks of party members. There were plenty of invitations, major and minor, from near and far, issued in the mistaken assumption that I would need something to fill my time. The ability to choose between them without having to consider too many other factors was a new sensation to me. I will admit to being glad when contemporaries both known and unknown sent me reading-matter I could not have found for myself: reminiscences of the years of Nazi terror, of exile, of the Resistance in Berlin, of grim confrontations with Communists. And why not also admit that I was touched when I received letters or notes – handed to me in a market-place, a pub, a plane – in which ordinary people, not least among them East Germans and new German citizens of various nationalities, said they understood me and would not forget me? There can hardly be a better present than to be told: 'Thank you for all you have done for us.'

6

The Principle of the Future

North–South Passages

At the beginning of 1980 the report for which I was responsible was published in more than twenty languages: *North–South: A Programme for Survival*. Its aim was to breathe new life into the flagging discussion of North–South issues. To a certain extent it succeeded, although the political action needed was slow in coming.

It was well worth the trouble, and not just because meeting people from other parts of the world and learning about their ways of thinking and reacting was a great gain. The experience helped me to understand the great social question of the late twentieth century. Whether and how humanity survives depends on the answer.

Our actions are generally determined by necessity, sometimes by chance. It was natural for me to remain concerned with the issues of peace and European union. The North–South Commission was not a substitute, but something I did in addition. After all, the subject had not been a closed book to me before I took on the chairmanship of the Commission. I had begun to perceive the existence of a new dimension when I was talking and writing about post-war policy while in Scandinavian exile. In 1962 at Harvard, I suggested that East–West problems would overlap with North–South problems. Barely a decade later, when I was awarded the Nobel Peace

Prize, I said that a poisoned, hungry humanity would not be content with our kind of peace. That same year, at Yale, I added that humanity must develop the power and ability to withstand self-destruction. In New York, when we had joined the United Nations in 1973, I said that where hunger ruled there was no lasting peace, and if we wanted to banish war we must also banish famine.

For many years, I had been distressed by the extreme poverty which was a particularly glaring phenomenon of such regions as Africa south of the Sahara, the Indian subcontinent and the outlying barrios of Latin-American cities.

There is no shame in admitting that the problem was not to the fore of my mind during my years of governmental responsibility. In foreign policy I had to concentrate on immediate and urgent concerns or I could not have achieved anything in the field of *Ostpolitik*. However, North–South policies were becoming increasingly important through the work of such men as Erhard Eppler.

There was some confusion over the new terminology involved. Why 'Third World'? It did not simplify matters much to explain that the term was coined by a French writer on analogy with the 'Third Estate'. And what exactly was meant by 'South'? In the summer of 1978 an ex-President of the Swiss Confederation asked what brought me to Geneva so often. I told him the secretariat of my North–South Commission was based there. 'Ah, yes,' he replied understandingly, 'the Italians as usual ...'

The then President of the World Bank, Robert McNamara, was concerned with new ideas for developmental policy. I wanted to take things further and see questions asked that did not relate solely to solidarity with the poor, whether that solidarity was motivated by charity, a sense of justice, or anything else. I thought it was in our own interests to help overcome poverty in other parts of the world. There was no need for a specific explanation that compromise between North and South also affected peace.

In fact the initiators of the Commission, its members and its collaborators hoped that East–West experiences would be useful in the formation of a new North–South policy. Had we not learnt how co-operation can build up trust and change the whole character of a conflict? The Commission, meeting in Bonn in December 1977, hoped to show the governments of the industrial and the developing countries that they must go to meet each other, in the interests of both or indeed of all sides. No one supposed that the overlapping of interests meant that they coincided. Real insight was one thing, the erroneous belief that action would more or less inevitably follow it was something else. However, I did not allow myself to be deterred by the suggestion that we were trying to divert and placate opinion.

I would have thought it dishonest to pretend that differences of opinion did not exist, and foolish to ignore real conflicts of interest. Our working hypothesis was that in the medium term many interests would intersect in North and South, and that a faster tempo of development in the South would also benefit the people of the North. The developing countries themselves, I argued, could not be indifferent to the economic welfare of the industrial countries, or the prospects for a reasonable transfer of resources would be poor. I thought all this was obvious enough.

Apropos of resources: when I told McNamara I was willing to head the Commission I made one condition, which was accepted at once: it was to be independent of the World Bank. This was in notable contrast to the group chaired by the Canadian Nobel Prize winner Lester Pearson, which had reported in 1969, and which contained only two representatives of developing countries. The funds that we needed for our meetings and in particular for our secretariat were donated by several governments, notably The Netherlands.

It was not easy to assemble the twenty-one members of the Commission, three of them ex officio. It was especially difficult to reassure our colleagues from the developing countries who feared they might not get a proper say in our discussions. In fact nothing was ever put to a vote; instead, we adopted the consensus that I usually tried to find whenever I chaired any committee. But it was not only the opposition between North and South that made it difficult to come to a consensus; the political standpoints of our members were equally important. The Commission included the former Prime Minister of the United Kingdom, Edward Heath, a Conservative, as well as the Social Democrat Olof Palme, who was always looking for policies that would create employment; an experienced Canadian trade union leader as well as a banker who had been Trade Minister in the Nixon administration; Eduardo Frei, the Christian Democrat ex-President of Chile, whose ideas differed from those of 'Radicals' from Algeria and Tanzania. Prominent among the Third World members were L. K. Iha, Governor and former President of the Indian Central Bank, and Sir Shridat Ramphal, the Guyanese Secretary-General of the Commonwealth. Our ranks also contained a woman publisher from Washington and a woman banker from Kuala Lumpur. Pierre Mendès-France was able to take part only in our first working meeting because of his serious state of health; he was replaced by Edgard Pisani, whom I had known since he was Minister of Agriculture under de Gaulle.

As for members from Communist-ruled states, the time was not yet ripe for that. However, working discussions were held in Beijing and Moscow, and I myself made sure that the Eastern European governments, including the Government of the GDR, were kept informed of our progress. 'The East' was represented on subsequent commissions on disarmament, under the chairmanship of Olof Palme, and on the environment, under the chairmanship of Gro Harlem Brundtland.

International reaction to the Brandt Report and its recommendations was considerable, but little practical action was taken by any governments. Of European nations, Britain and The Netherlands showed a lively interest in our findings published in 1980; however, the German and French governments paid us no more than lip-service. The world summit conference on the economy in Venice noted our recommendations and promised, without pausing for much thought, to follow them up in detail. But Washington was paralysed by the hostage-taking in Teheran, and used the Soviet invasion of Afghanistan as a reason to discontinue détente with Moscow. Tribute was paid to the Report in more than three dozen speeches at the United Nations General Assembly, mainly by delegates of the 'have-not' countries, who thought they would now at last get more co-operation. Our proposals received a great deal of attention but little favourable response from the International Monetary Fund and the World Bank.

No one can expect independent commissions, even under more favourable circumstances than those of the time, to make an immediate difference to the conduct of governments. They are more likely to help in forming opinions and in encouraging forces that may be able to influence government actions in the next round, or the next round but one. This was what happened to the Palme Report of 1982, which established the concept of collective security, and the Norwegian Prime Minister's report of 1987, mandated by the UN General Assembly, which appeared under the title of *Our Common Future*; it ranged wide, bringing together problems of the environment and of development. Meanwhile, a South–South Commission, under the chairmanship of Julius Nyerere, sought to inject new factors into the international debate from the viewpoint of the developing countries.

The Brandt Report's influence on the international debate derived not so much from the formulation of its separate proposals as from its new perspective. We said that our concern was not solely with development aid from the industrial countries, important as that was, but with conditions for common survival; not with praiseworthy acts of charity, but with structural changes to enable the developing countries to stand on their own feet in the future. In the process, many misconceptions in the Third World would have to be swept aside. The Commission did not identify itself with maximalist, comprehensive demands for a 'new world economy', ideas such as those considered by the United Nations in 1974–5 – as if the resolutions passed in its glass palace in New York could have revolutionary consequences world-wide.

There was an extremely dangerous time-bomb to be defused: no more, no less. The extreme contrast between North and South had to be alleviated by equitably negotiated measures. Consequently, my colleagues and I recommended a combination of minor steps, such as a somewhat improved flow of funds, and basic reforms such as international levies intended for specific purposes. Everything suggested that the requisite change would not take place dramatically. My reforming credo ran: look to the far horizon, but keep your immediate aims close enough to be approachable.

Along with the main report, we included a programme for immediate action to be taken in 1980–85, which was meant neither to be a substitute for longer-term changes nor to conflict with them. We felt that immediate measures were required in the energy and food sectors if the world economy was not to suffer severely.

A certain opportunity seemed to appear on the horizon when a North–South summit was planned for the autumn of 1981, in line with our suggestion, but it did not lead very far. I had been greatly in favour of occasional high-level meetings for serious discussion, with a small group of heads of state or government sounding out possible compromises; no state should be allowed a say in the decisions of any other. I was extremely sceptical about mammoth conferences, or anyway more sceptical than many of my colleagues, who expected great things of the United Nations. I thought that states which were in a similar position should get together and make their joint interests felt. However, we agreed that a summit of moderate size, including heads of government from both North and South – and also, we hoped, with the participation of the East and China – could further international decision-making. We thought that the number of participants should be small enough to make genuine progress possible, but large enough to be representative and for its statements to carry weight.

After laborious preliminary discussions, a first meeting took place in Cancun, Mexico, in October 1981, between delegates from twenty-two countries. Bruno Kreisky had agreed to chair it with the President of Mexico. Against other people's advice and expectations Ronald Reagan, the newly elected President of the USA, also decided to take part. The Soviets did not attend, although as I had assured myself in Moscow in the summer of 1981, they had considered the invitation seriously. The Chinese were represented by their President, although he contributed very little. Participants from the industrialized countries were the Federal Republic of Germany, France, the United Kingdom, Japan, Canada, Austria, Sweden and the USA; from the developing countries, Algeria, Bangladesh, Brazil, China, the Ivory Coast, Guyana, India, Yugoslavia, Mexico, Nigeria, the Philippines, Saudi Arabia, Tanzania and Venezuela; finally, the United Nations Secretary-General also attended. European representation suffered considerably from the fact that neither the German nor the Austrian Chancellor could come to Cancun for health reasons. I myself did not accept the invitation issued to me personally by the Mexicans because of misgivings concerning protocol expressed by some of the non-aligned countries, including Algeria and Yugoslavia.

After the summit, President Reagan thanked me for the contribution my report had made. He emphasized the importance of development aid for many countries, while at the same time he thought that private investment should be given more weight; efforts were being made by the International Monetary Fund and the World Bank to use the available funds more effectively. All this sounded good, but it ignored a basic problem: in the poorest countries, the choice between private investment and public aid simply did not and does not exist. As in the dogmatic conflict between free markets and planned economies, the financial dispute is in danger of focusing on false alternatives.

More private or more public finance? More multilateral or more bilateral co-operation? Both are needed.

The recommendations of the Commission were not conspicuous for radicalism, particularly not in matters of money and finance. None the less they were found irksome, which was in their nature: we proposed new special drawing rights on the international institutions in Washington, and requested preferential treatment for Third World countries in the distribution of funds; only thus, we said, could long-term economic and social development be secured.

We said that the International Monetary Fund, a focus of controversy at the time because of its harsh lending terms, should avoid 'inappropriate or excessive regulation' of the economies of developing countries, and 'should not impose highly deflationary measures as standard adjustment policy'. We also asked the IMF and the World Bank for greater involvement of the developing countries in management and decision-making. These proposals were reiterated and given specific form in a supplementary report that appeared at the beginning of 1983. We again urged an increase in the capital of the World Bank – which happened, to a modest extent – and the raising of the gearing ratio between capital and the volume of lending from 1:1 to 1:2.

This second report – *Common Crisis: North–South: Co-operation for World Recovery* – was written under the influence of the debt crisis that first affected Mexico, in 1982, and spread to almost every country in the Latin-American subcontinent over the years that followed, also casting its shadow over development in other parts of the world. Hardly surprisingly, it was difficult for democracy to assert itself and even more difficult for it to make any headway amidst exorbitant debt-servicing payments. Whose fault was the debt crisis? There is no denying the fact that financially powerful circles in the countries affected omitted to shoulder a minimum of national responsibility, and in more than one case the extent of the private flight of capital was and still is in equilibrium with state indebtedness.

There is no reason why we should close our eyes to defects in developing countries, or fail to point out conduct that should be changed. Remonstrations of this kind, of course, are useful only if they are neither hypocritical nor arrogant. Waste and corruption, oppression and violence are to be found in many parts of the world: a situation which will long continue. For that very reason, we should not postpone efforts towards improvement in international relations until these and other evils have been eliminated. In the introduction to my Commission's report, I wrote: 'We in the South *and* the North should frankly discuss abuses of power by elites, the flare-up of fanaticism, the misery of millions of refugees, or other violations of human rights that harm the cause of justice and solidarity, at home and abroad.'

The Brandt Report was not solely concerned with financial issues, and was certainly not based on 'outright Keynesianism', as alleged by critics. But of course we could not pretend that money played no part. In both reports, therefore, we endorsed our support for the so-called 0.7 per cent aim: in accordance with the resolution of the UN General Assembly of October 1970, from which only the USA abstained, the industrial countries were to make at least 0.7 per cent of their gross national product available for public development aid; the Scandinavians and the Dutch achieved this, but approximate rates at best were obtained elsewhere. Our recommendations were if anything too detailed, but they were highly relevant. We described ways of making public funds available for long-term financial transfers; how an international system of progressive taxation might be set up, with the Eastern European states and the developing countries (except for the very poorest) participating; how funds could be 'automatically' raised by modest international levies, whether on the manufacture or export of weapons, or on the common property of all mankind, particularly the resources of the seas.

The incoming funds, we suggested, should go into a new institution with fully international membership, a World

Development Fund, which would channel them. The proposal did not aim to replace the Bretton Woods institutions of the IMF and the World Bank; the WDF was to complement them, channelling credit into specified programmes – policy lending – but certainly not decreasing the flow of credit from commercial banks and other private sources. We believed that many kinds of financing were required to exploit energy sources as well as mineral resources in the developing countries. The proposed Energy Agency, supported by the World Bank, was the one new organization we thought should be set up immediately.

The industrial nations were and still are interested in safeguarding oil supplies. The developing countries had always upset the imponderables of raw materials markets as a whole. The Commission thought they should also be more involved in manufacturing, marketing and distribution. As for the stabilization of raw materials prices, UNCTAD, the United Nations Committee for Trade and Development, had been working since 1973 on an 'integrated' programme to be financed from a common fund. We supported its efforts to obtain international agreement and argued that any country with an interest in calculable and secure supplies of raw materials could not oppose price stability, if only because of the investment necessary to exploit mineral resources. What do people gain if they have to pay for an imported tractor or a 'hard' dollar with ever more coffee or copper? We were aware that agreement on raw materials and the stabilizing of profits were not universal panaceas, but they were a step on the way to making the developing countries equal trading partners. Consequently we opposed protectionist tendencies in the North and argued for keeping the markets of industrial countries open to the South. Only then would the developing countries themselves be able to buy and to afford credit.

Then there were the multinational companies that play a central part in international trade and in North–South relations in general. We wanted effective laws and international guidelines for conduct that would prevent their business practices from inhibiting competition, and at the same time influence technology transfer favourably and at reasonable cost. Against this background we confirmed that a country had a right to dispose of its own natural resources, but we believed there should be appropriate and effective compensation in the case of nationalization; similar principles should be introduced into national legislation, and international arbitration mechanisms should be increasingly applied.

Were we simply talking to the air? Had we miscalculated the chances of having our proposals put into practice, or had we failed to take adequate account of certain factors such as population explosion? However that may be, North–South relations did not improve, they actually deteriorated in the eighties. Our thesis of growing mutual dependency did not hold good. Statistically speaking, the mutual economic involvement of industrial and developing countries has not increased; on the contrary, the two sides have moved even further apart, and it appears that fewer and fewer countries are really 'developing' at all.

While considerable progress was made in some parts of the world, particularly South-East Asia, others have endured appalling shortages and setbacks, in agriculture and industrialization alike. Urgent reforms in the health and education sectors fell by the wayside because the financial bottlenecks became even narrower. In many countries, particularly African countries, the standard of living of large sections of the population has fallen drastically, among people who were far from prosperous even before the crisis.

It was typical of the eighties that all efforts for a constructive North–South dialogue failed or petered out. So-called global negotiations under the auspices of the United Nations came to nothing. The North–South summit in Cancun, mentioned above, led nowhere. Only a few outstanding Third World countries were in a position to win concessions from bilateral negotiations. The great majority of developing countries had to accept their powerlessness to influence the rules of the international game, and the fact that so far as they were concerned those rules were getting stricter. New barriers were erected around the markets of the industrialized world; protectionism was on the increase, profits from raw materials on the decrease – because of product substitution and cuts in consumption – and the quality standards for industrial goods could be met only by very advanced countries.

At the end of the eighties at least 800 million people were living in absolute poverty. In most African countries, real income was no higher than it had been two decades before. Millions of people have died of starvation and malnutrition in Africa and in other parts of the world.

Latin America, once regarded as an up-and-coming continent, became caught in the toils of a severe development crisis. The gloomy prospects for Africa and large parts of Latin America, as well as the Caribbean islands, are made no brighter by the display of colourful Asiatic 'prescriptions for success'. The impressive rise of several Asiatic states cannot be too highly rated, but even within their own vast continent its impact has been localized, and it put Latin-American poverty in an even worse light. 'No democracy without bread' is a truism everywhere. But in Buenos Aires President Alfonsin told me frankly: 'You come with flowers today; let us hope you will not be back soon to lay wreaths on the grave of Argentine democracy.' A few days later, in Cartagena, the President of Colombia said: 'Hunger, unemployment and illiteracy are the agents of subversion.' The Peruvian head of state said, of the burden of debt: 'We are having an operation without anaesthetic; they want us to feel the pain.' Two years later, when I was in Peru again, armed fighting had made its way into the streets of Lima. Thirty months later, at the beginning of 1989, when Carlos Andres Perez had just been sworn in again as President after a legally prescribed interval, the conditions imposed by creditors led to price rises and set off violent rioting in Venezuela.

The bitter lesson of the eighties is that anyone who misses a chance of practical co-operation and allows free play anywhere in the world to avoidable oppositions – East against West, North against South – is conspicuously failing to meet the needs of our time. Isolated discussion of partial aspects – debt or raw materials, food or the birth-rate, soil exhaustion or deforestation – lead nowhere on their own. Everything still turns on mutual dependence and the global view.

I have striven to promote public awareness of the connections between famine and war, armament and retrogression – and not only in the context of the work of the Commission. History has taught us how wars bring famine in their wake. It is less well known that mass poverty can end in chaos. Where hunger reigns, peace cannot live. Those who would ban war must also abolish mass poverty. People with enough to eat are not necessarily free, but the starving are *never* free.

In January 1984 Olof Palme's commission on disarmament and mine on North–South relations held a joint session in Rome. They spelt out the close connection between security and development: in view of economic pressure and social crisis, we said, the political instability of Third World countries could well increase and bring other forces into play. National security could no longer be maintained by military power alone. 'Security must be based on recognition of common interests and respect for common institutions.'

As Foreign Minister I had spoken of the emergence of common interests even beyond the European area, as Federal Chancellor I had urged a balance of security – instead of merely a balance of terror – and conciliation of interests. The outlook is not unremittingly gloomy, for since then there has been acceptance of a growing list of interests common to all nations, overriding state systems; it ranges from securing world peace and overcoming world hunger to control of the population explosion, the guaranteeing of energy supplies, and conservation of the natural environment. To speak of a new awareness of the world no longer has the ring of exaggeration. However, we must be careful not to assume that what are, objectively speaking, common interests will automatically lead to similar perceptions and the drawing of similar conclusions.

In the early summer of 1981 I spoke to Soviet scientists – more receptive to new ideas than was then usual at the top of the Communist Party – explaining why it was high time to face challenges independent of and overriding state systems. The topic proved as worthwhile in Budapest as it was in Ottawa and even East Berlin. I discovered, or was confirmed in my belief, that only a crisis can bring a change of awareness and liberate forces for action, though not always for the better.

If there was little recognition as yet of what institutional provisions would be necessary, neither the East nor the West opposed the view that we are becoming a mutually dependent world society. For that very reason, it is depressing that the eighties should have been lost years when bilateral negotiations led to hardly any progress in the field of multilateral co-operation, and impeded the regional co-ordination so urgently needed.

In 1988, honouring an old agreement with Indira Gandhi, I suggested a 'Cancun 2' summit, wherever such a meeting might actually take place and with whatever participants; 'Sonny' Ramphal and I sounded out Bush, Gorbachev and other world leaders. A new kind of North–South summit seemed desirable not to make decisions, but to initiate or accelerate important negotiations in other quarters. There is no doubt now that the USSR is prepared to take its share of responsibility; the Kremlin no longer sees North–South relations as simply a West–South affair.

There is a North–South policy on the European and international agenda that will not peter out so easily. In many quarters, debate on development policy falls back on the recommendations published by my Commission in 1980 and supplemented by its additional report at the beginning of 1983.

Has our work for North–South relations been worth while? Even if it had only meant adding a couple of slim volumes to the library of works on development policy, I would say that worse things have happened in the history of mankind, and answer 'Yes'. Incidentally, it is simpler to write a book alone than with two dozen other people, but that is the occupational hazard of drawing up a work setting out a programme, in which many people rightly wish their views to be reflected.

The threats that override state systems are now being understood. In all probability the dangers affecting the lives of millions of people and the existence of humanity as a whole will not be speedily eliminated. However, we are beginning to perceive opportunities for improvements in human welfare that would have been regarded as Utopian or crazy a few years ago. Science cannot create Paradise, of course, even in the future, but from the viewpoint of technology and organization it has begun to look as if even an expanding world population could be fed. That would be of little use, however, if climatic changes invalidate all conventional calculations.

None the less, the willingness of many states, including the World Powers, to co-operate in practical ways has increased and allows room for hope. The aberrations of the Cold War blocked opportunities. But many major if not irreversible changes are now perceptible in the policies of the Great Powers. However, without energetic commitment on all levels, from local to international, nothing will change the appalling fact that hundreds of millions of our fellow human beings are suffering in a world where not everyone can be rich, but everyone could have enough to eat.

Paradise Flawed

No sooner was the war over than a willingness to give humanitarian assistance was evident even in countries that had suffered greatly themselves, particularly the United States. Thousands of families and associations, church communities and institutions, trade unions and businesses contributed aid. Many individual refugees were given a chance of survival. Of course American self-interest played a part in the working-out at governmental level of the Marshall Plan for European reconstruction, the 'enemy states' not being excluded, but all experience shows that such factors are not to be deplored.

The Peace Corps, founded at the beginning of Kennedy's presidency, and many private organizations had shown more than token sympathy for the poor and underprivileged of this world. Development aid from the richest country in the world was important too, even if it fell short of the internationally agreed percentage of the gross national product – much further short, in fact, than European contributions. In the eighties, against the background of the debt crisis, more funds flowed back into the USA than it made available again. The American tendency to ignore the United Nations, keep out of committees on 'multilateral' co-operation and concentrate on its own arrangements also showed Washington in an unattractive light. If confidence in one's own strength grows, and partners in other parts of the world prove disappointing, there are bound to be reactions that are hard to counteract. For a long time, there was a degree of uncertainty in the areas of arms reduction and arms control that was of no benefit to the world. Change set in when Ronald Reagan found a partner in Mikhail Gorbachev who urged a new approach.

When George Bush took office he found that major steps towards the halting of the arms race had already been taken. Goodwill on both sides now marked relations between the nuclear World Powers, and some regional conflicts were being defused. One of the pleasant surprises of the late eighties was the fact that the conservative populist from California, of all people, in his second period of office, felt sure enough of his instincts to pick up the ball thrown to him by an unorthodox Communist Party General Secretary. When détente looked as if it might be failing, it was revived by the first disarmament agreement that really deserved the name.

While I had known all the Presidents since Franklin D. Roosevelt – although in the case of Truman only when he was no longer in office – and had had useful conversations with them, Reagan let his advisers persuade him against keeping an appointment for a serious talk with me; I took no offence, and it did not diminish my respect for a President who had begun by wanting to conquer 'the evil Empire' and then joined with his Russian opposite number to secure peace. His adherence to old prejudices in other areas was a different matter.

The official Washington of those years would have nothing to do with forward-looking North–South proposals. I spoke my mind about US operations against certain 'forces' in Central America and the Caribbean, and earned myself a black mark. In 1981, when I had business in New York, Alexander Haig invited me to the State Department. Our main theme was Nicaragua. Four years later, in a very pleasant and down-to-earth conversation with Vice-President George Bush, the main theme was still Nicaragua. While I was regarded, correctly, as an old friend of the United States by the Senate in Washington and important sections of the community, ideologists of the extreme right and over-eager gunslingers had me on their black list. This did not prevent Secretary of State George Shultz from giving me information, nor did it impress Paul Nitze, who briefed me whenever possible on the tricky negotiations in Geneva. With members of Congress the climate of discussion was warm – when the subject was German–American affairs, and in particular discussion of the East–West relationship and its military component.

From time to time I tried to counteract misconceptions in Moscow. In February 1980, I wrote to General Secretary Brezhnev, trying to persuade him to end the Afghan adventure, and advising him to sweep aside other obstacles on the way to détente. This was the time when the humiliating affair of the hostages in Teheran coincided with American indignation over the Kabul coup. I said, in particular, that President Carter had told me he was waiting for an opportunity to resume talks and continue the process of détente; when I asked whether he wanted to make things hard or easy for the Soviet Union, he said easy. He wanted to improve relations with the Soviet Union, he said, not to embarrass or offend it. I would not interpret anything too positively myself, I said, but thought it was worth thinking about this answer.

Both sides were informed of the results of a conference held at the beginning of February 1980 in Vienna, at the invitation of Bruno Kreisky and under my chairmanship, with the chairmen of twenty-eight Social Democratic parties participating. I outlined the factors aggravating the international situation: besides the incidents in Afghanistan and Iran, non-ratification of the SALT 2 treaty and the burden of the medium-range nuclear arsenal threatened to settle on détente and crush the remaining life out of it. 'We expressed criticism and raised our voices in warning where we thought it requisite,' I wrote, adding, 'But we also, and most importantly, expressed our deep anxiety lest the achievements of détente should be endangered, since we feared that a return to the Cold War would bring the world to the brink of catastrophe. We have seen ourselves confirmed in our belief that there is no reasonable alternative to détente.'

I have visited the United States many times, I have always felt at ease there, and I have always come back with new ideas. As Mayor of Berlin I was particularly dependent on American support. During my period of responsibility in Bonn I set great store on friendship with the USA, and not, or not only, because we in the Federal Republic of Germany had so much to thank the Americans for. When Richard Nixon received me as Federal Chancellor in the colourful setting of the White House garden early in 1970, I could say without a shadow of doubt that I acknowledged our close partnership on behalf of my fellow citizens and by their wish. I was all the more distressed when an unattractive fashion for anti-Americanism set in later, and was used as a weapon in Federal German party disputes. Attitudes that may have had some justification in Adenauer's time, and at least were kept within suitable dimensions – though they were uncalled-for even then – amounted to sheer spite when rehashed by people of a later generation.

The twentieth century will go down in history as the century of America. Even those who, like me, might have wished the United States to show a higher degree of constructive leadership must come to that conclusion. The United States decided the outcome of two world wars, even more emphatically in the second than in the first, and without withdrawing into isolationism again. The economic aid which benefited us as well as many others was not the product of altruism alone, but it was wise, and it worked wonders. We in Germany – or more precisely in those western zones which became the Federal Republic – were assiduously wooed and found the task of reconstruction eased, while critical confrontation with the past was correspondingly made more difficult. We had to bear part of the burden of the Cold War and adjust to new power relationships; worse could have happened. We had to make the best of the given situation. It would have been fatal to do anything else.

Our relationship with the rest of the world, including the United States, soon changed. We were standing on our own feet again, working out our own interests. In 1958, on the occasion of my first visit to the USA as Mayor of Berlin, I was still in the role of someone waiting on the victorious power. At the Waldorf-Astoria the press asked me what I felt about George Kennan's suggestion of the disengagement of armed forces in Europe; I said nothing. Only a decade later, as Foreign Minister,

I did not hesitate to support the concept of détente even in the United States, arguing for it against hardliners and hysterics of all kinds. Ten years later again there was some discord in the Atlantic Alliance because we in Bonn trusted our own – dissident – judgement of what was good for Western security. Times changed, but not the foundations of the relationship. However serious our differences might sometimes be, American assistance at the birth of the Federal Republic had made too deep a mark for our ties to be broken.

It is a long time since the United States was a land of unlimited opportunity, but its vitality and flexibility have never been extinguished. I have never felt there was just *one* America: dire poverty coexists with the impressive vigour of its economy, technology and army; dark reaction with astonishing progress. And alongside the influence of the East Coast and its still predominantly white Protestant establishment, there is the rise of the West and the South, with the emergence of tremendous energies as yet barely tapped. This was the America in which the descendants of African slaves broke through the barriers erected around them and began making their influence felt. An America in which money could never stifle the alert mind, and compassion could not be overcome by greed for gain. That other America, the America of civil rights and the social movements, was ever-present.

America also meant the talented and long undervalued Canadians to the north, and the numerous Latin Americans in the southern part of the double continent, restlessly pressing forward. Of course not a few of our American friends wondered whether their great country would be able to adapt fast enough to deal with the new problems that might drive the world to the edge of the abyss. I knew that it could not be done without America.

Fifty years ago, I had described what the United States meant to me as a German exile in Scandinavia, and my expectations of its post-war role; America had become a symbol of freedom and democracy to me long before I entered the testing-ground of Berlin. I set foot on American soil for the first time in 1954, when I visited New York and Washington, New Orleans and Chicago, Texas and California. Together with three friends and colleagues, Carlo Schmid, Fritz Erler and Günter Klein, I had accepted an invitation from the American Government; it was making an investment in giving people who had or were likely to have responsibility in Europe a chance to form their own idea of its mighty land, with all the variety of its different regions and the wide range of opinions among its people – in fact a chance of seeing far more than the view from any office could provide.

I will readily admit that commonplaces were what struck me most on that first visit. Seeing that America was a whole continent, something one realized even more from the air than when travelling by rail or road; understanding that its resources were not even all tapped yet, let alone exhausted; meeting many people who were mostly friendly and ready to help, not concealing an inquisitive naïvety. One soon realized that while the Old World had its charm and its value, European arrogance was out of place. The average American – quite likely to ask, 'Who's Kaiser in Germany now?' – does not know much about our part of the world. Do we Europeans know much more about the USA?

The knowledge of America I had gleaned from books was not extensive. It took me many visits to realize how little its political structures could be assessed by European standards. I have been deeply impressed, and always fascinated anew, by the change in relations between black Americans and the white-skinned majority of their fellow countrymen, culminating in equal civil rights. Another impressive, indeed moving lesson was the way in which the Americans faced the Vietnam War and tried to work through that painful experience.

I found it easiest to understand that not only the party political landscape but the concept of the parties themselves is rooted in its own tradition in America. Social and political bridges can be built between a European Social Democrat and an American Democrat; however, as soon as international questions came up, I was struck by the way I felt close to a liberal Republican but very distant from a conservative Democrat, particularly one from the Southern states. The two great parties have founded a specific North American tradition; they are broad-based alliances that cannot be compared to anything European.

Europeans, particularly German and Scandinavian Social Democrats who emigrated to America, left a number of footprints behind them, not only in the Middle West. Those footprints were never entirely obliterated, but the inheritance brought across the Atlantic by those emigrants could not be transplanted; on the American shore there was too much mobility in society. 'Alternative' America is alive and well in a number of groups and movements, some concerned with civil rights and the interests of the underprivileged, others rallying to the banner of progress in universities and churches. Although the churchgoing of many Americans Sunday after Sunday may seem to be just for show, the sense of human responsibility articulated in church communities is very encouraging. My first meeting with American Social Democrats was in a New York church.

The trade unions have exerted much influence over a wide area, particularly in the years after the Second World War, in foreign as well as in home policy, and have worked for the restoration and establishment of democratic structures, not least in Germany. Jewish organizations, and not only in New York and the trade unions, have shown concern for German opponents of the Nazi regime and for the democratic new beginning after the war in a manner that can only shame the rest of us; their work has still not been properly recognized. Curiously enough, German Americans have provided hardly any of this aid. When they have made any political statements at all, they have not been of a progressive nature. Ernst Reuter – in the middle of the Berlin blockade in March 1949 – said on his return from the USA: 'Brandt, if you want to meet Nazis today you will have to go to Chicago.' He did not mean Nazis in the literal sense, but the nationalistic German type that found even Bismarck too progressive.

In 1961, when I had paid my first visit to John F. Kennedy at the White House, he said goodbye with good wishes for my evening gathering, calling the Americans for Democratic Action, whom I was to meet, 'my liberal friends'. Martin Luther King spoke on that occasion, telling us of his dream of an America that had overcome racial segregation; he soon took up my invitation to Berlin. However, the leading personality present was Hubert Humphrey, the open-minded and eloquent senator from Minnesota, former Mayor of Minneapolis, rooted in the traditions of his region's party of farmers and workers. We had met on several occasions, including a visit of his to Berlin in 1959, after which he had a long talk with Khrushchev. With Walter Reuther, the strongly progressive trade union leader of Swabian descent, I had met Humphrey at several of the summer gatherings held in Harpsund by Tage Erlander, the post-war Prime Minister of Sweden and Olof Palme's predecessor.

In 1960 Hubert ran for the Democratic presidential nomination, although materially speaking he was up against hopeless odds. After Kennedy's assassination Johnson made him Vice-President. On the evening of the funeral a group of us, all good friends, met in the Swedish Embassy and allowed ourselves to be infected by the optimistic view that the gap would soon be filled and that everything would go on as before. That was not to be. Hubert Humphrey would have been elected President of the USA in 1968 instead of Richard Nixon – the figures were 42.7 to 43.4 – if the election campaign had lasted a few days longer and, above all, if he had not scrupulously observed official loyalty, but had distanced himself from the course adopted by President Johnson over Vietnam. In 1977 Hubert Humphrey died of the cancer from which he was already suffering when we last met – with Kissinger and other guests – for a dinner at the German Embassy. He made a speech of friendship which I never had the chance to repay.

The tragedy of Vietnam, which shook both America's credibility and its internal stability, arousing vociferous protest among the younger generation at home and in many other parts of the world, had begun under President Kennedy. It was a long time before I realized what the consequences would be, and then I tried to dismiss them from my mind. There is reason to suppose, as I was later able to conclude from confidential remarks made by his colleagues, that the young President would not have let the débâcle turn to catastrophe, and that he had decided to withdraw. Charles de Gaulle, remembering France's bitter experiences, had warned him in Paris in 1961 that once a nation had awoken and its social and revolutionary energies were unfolding, no power on earth could force another's will on it. 'You will sink deeper into a military and political morass with every step you take.'

Lyndon B. Johnson, who regarded Chinese 'world Communism' as even more of a challenge than the Soviet variety, wanted nothing but victory. The number of American soldiers stationed in Indo-China shot up after he took office; it was 14,000 when he became President, quarter of a million by the end of 1966, half a million by the middle of 1968. For all the political experience he had behind him, the Texan could not cope. When I visited him with Fritz Erler in the spring of 1965 he could hardly take his eyes off the press agency reports coming in, but spoke disjointedly of helicopters, Vietcong casualties and liberated villages. On another occasion he mingled statistics of this kind with Gallup Poll figures purporting to show that Robert Kennedy lagged far behind him in popularity. In February 1966 I attended a gathering in New York when he presented his policy as the only one possible; but many thousands of Americans were loudly proclaiming a different view in the surrounding streets. Bobby Kennedy was still demonstrating loyalty to Johnson that evening. Had he become President himself, he would have found the strength to put an end to the debilitating and demoralizing war. Like Martin Luther King, he was assassinated in the spring of 1968.

I have never believed in the domino theory – that if Saigon falls today, all Asia will fall tomorrow and Europe the day after. Nor did I believe that Berlin was being defended in Vietnam. But I was not indifferent to seeing the United States described in another part of the world as a 'paper tiger', as Mao put it. I thought it was certainly not for us Germans to put ourselves forward as lecturers in international politics and certainly not as moral judges; nor did I feel it advisable to interfere with the American Government in an area it said was vital. Consequently I swallowed my grave doubts and held my tongue where it might have been better to make my opposition explicit on the one hand, and on the other make open display of my suppressed sympathies. It was much the same in the case of Algeria. Not only the Right but even the democratic Left in Paris reacted violently if Germans expressed any sympathy for the supporters of self-determination. It is one thing to put opposition to colonialism on your programme, another to show that you mean it.

The rebellious young people at home, in many other parts of Europe, and earlier in America who felt called to protest against Vietnam saw no sign of the fact that I had more understanding for their sentiments than for their way of expressing them. It was some time, too, before the committee of my party cautiously formulated its concerned criticism. When I wrote to my colleague the Secretary of State in Washington I received an answer showing little understanding of our points. It is one thing not to let down friends, even powerful friends, who are having serious problems, and another to decline to show solidarity with them when they pursue mistaken policies. In the spring of 1967 I assembled our ambassadors to Asia in Tokyo, and there was no doubt about it: we could not identify ourselves with the war in Vietnam. We put it on record that Federal German policy should be to use its limited opportunities to work for a peaceful solution, in particular by putting economic co-operation at the service of consolidation. Prominent Japanese with whom I discussed the subject expressed themselves in similar terms.

I did not guess that the American bloodletting in Vietnam would go on for years. When I met Nixon in Florida late in 1971, he told me he was sure they were over the hill: South Vietnam now had one of the best armies in Asia, and it would prevail, while North Vietnam had no strength left to take the offensive against the South, and the number of American dead had fallen to a minimum. The latest bombing missions to North Vietnam had been preventive measures, he said, and too much should not be made of them. He added, with some irritation, that advice from third parties was not wanted.

Before the cease-fire was concluded in January 1973 – by Henry Kissinger in Paris – Nixon had reduced the number of American soldiers stationed in Vietnam to 50,000. The actual end of the war, two years later, was not at all as it had been envisaged. South Vietnam crumbled, both militarily and politically. It was a traumatic experience for a World Power that had lost a regional war, suffering many casualties, and could not understand why it had ever begun it. The relentless and painful self-examination indulged in by the Americans was never something that I saw as an expression of weakness. My assumption that it was actually a sign of strength proved correct.

The domino theory looked like coming to life again when the big guns were brought to bear against revolutionary movements of modest extent in the Americans' own hemisphere. I believe now more than ever that Fidel Castro did not intend a break with the USA; the White House did not pay enough attention to the reports coming out of Havana. In Vienna in the summer of 1961 Khrushchev tried to persuade Kennedy that Castro was not a Communist, but that economic sanctions might make him one. Although Central America, with the exception of Mexico, was not vitally important to the security of the United States, it reacted to the revolution in Nicaragua and the underground struggle in El Salvador as if there was imminent great danger; some leading European politicians also let themselves be persuaded that Soviet influence was a real threat. At the same time people around President Reagan were talking in a way that worked against peaceful solutions. Again, I can say this from my own experience: in the autumn of 1984 an agreement on Nicaragua was almost made on the sidelines of a conference in Rio de Janeiro. The Sandinista commander Bayardo Arce had consented to it, and the way seemed clear to elections in which the non-military resistance would take part. Arturo Cruz, the leader of that opposition, was also on the point of agreeing, but was prevented by his American advisers. The Venezuelan ex-President Carlos Andres Perez, who became President of his country for the second time early in 1989, and the German 'trouble-shooter' Hans-Jürgen Wischnewski, who had both worked very hard for the agreement, were not alone in their disappointment and anger.

Doubts in America about the nation's own role as a World Power went deep. Even deeper went the struggle to overcome racism. This was a subject close to my heart, partly because Professor Gunnar Myrdal, my good friend of the war years in Sweden, had just finished his great work *The American Dilemma*, commissioned by the Carnegie Foundation. On my first visit to the USA I encountered examples of blatant racism. In New York I visited the leader of the sleeping-car attendants' union, a member of the small Socialist Party. His post was about as high as a black American could go in public life; the job of sleeping-car attendant was reserved for 'Negroes'. In the South I visited a black high school – such schools did exist, but were totally segregated. I saw public transport where coloured and white people had to sit separately, and restaurants, hotels and other institutions which made it discreetly but unmistakably clear whose custom they did not want. And there were still clubs that Jews had to avoid.

This was in 1954. Less than a decade later black America, accompanied by courageous civil rights campaigners from the ranks of the white majority, was showing courage and power. It was refusing to accept discrimination any longer. An open-minded administration in Washington agreed. Robert Kennedy, the Attorney-General, sent in troops to ensure that black chil-

dren had transport and access to desegregated schools. He kept
the helmet of an injured National Guardsman on his desk. I
was able to discard my earlier conjecture that some of the
mainly black Southern states would end up leaving the Union.
Just a generation later black mayors were governing some of
the big cities. We had witnessed a great, glorious, and not
particularly bloody revolution.

A new figure on the political scene was Jesse Jackson, who
had been one of Martin Luther King's circle as a young man,
and seemed to have inherited King's charisma. It was too soon
for him to win a presidential nomination, but in the 1988
election campaign he played a part that no one could ignore. I
knew him from meetings in Germany and thought highly of
him. During the 1988 campaign in the USA I saw how much
more he had become than just a spokesman for the black
minority. His programme did not neglect the ambitions of those
who wanted more progress along the road to full equality, but
it went deep into important areas of new social responsibility,
and will continue to make itself felt.

There has been talk of the 'rainbow coalition', including
reference to progressive 'Latin-Americanization'. Emigrants
from South America and the Caribbean are changing the face
of the United States. Spanish has become an everyday language
in New York as well as in the South and the West (where there
is also a large Asiatic ethnic group). A European with my
background, remembering the excesses of a murderous racism,
can only applaud this modern revolution. Once again, America
had done better than we did.

It would have been surprising if the missionary zeal woven
into the fabric of life in the United States, and cultivated there
in many ways, had not had some startling political effects; it is
hard to follow America down many of the roads it took and
still takes because of this same inclination to improve the world.
It would also have been surprising if so rich and powerful a
state was not afflicted by a certain arrogance of power.

American missionary spirit is seen in the long-standing

tendency to divide the world into good and bad, equating Communism, or what is taken for Communism, with immutable evil, interpreting the idea of a free world in a characteristically American manner, and promoting the American way of life even in inappropriate areas. This tendency to simplify has led to many mistakes and misconceptions. Pétain's followers, Franco and Salazar, the Greek colonels, all had to be regarded as honourable representatives of Western values. Directly after the war, the American secret services even recruited some Gestapo men because it was thought they would be useful in the battle against the new arch-enemy. President Marcos was able to proclaim himself a beacon of democracy, Central American tyrants were supported all the more enthusiastically if they also put their killer squads at the service of foreign investment interests. Protesting Third World politicians were condemned out of hand as dangerous revolutionary opponents. And so on and so forth.

The honourable tradition of human rights was also inclined to fall into the hands of double-dealing or opportunist zealots; empty symbolism replaced realistic effort. But more important was the fact that America's original moral drive was not lost from sight, and unsparing critics spoke up again and again in America itself. The motive forces of a great nation that still has much to give its citizens and the world keep breaking through again.

Stalin's Second Death

Events within the Soviet Union and their effects have had a great influence on my political life; in my youth they brought me first high hopes, then bitter disillusionment. Stalinist crimes – euphemistically described as 'excesses' – were pushed into the background by my respect for the suffering and achievement of the Soviet people. In Berlin I had to resist a bid for power greater than anything that had united the partners in the coalition against Hitler. An understanding of the new facts of international politics which was not solely acquired behind a desk in Bonn made me a Chancellor who hoped to combine reconciliation with our Western neighbours and optimum relations with our Eastern neighbours. That could not be done without the Soviet Union, and certainly not in the face of its opposition. Nor could one wait for Soviet leaders whom one might like better than other Soviet leaders.

I knew nothing of a prominent Party Secretary called Gorbachev during Brezhnev's latter days. Then I learned, almost incidentally, that his career had been encouraged by Andropov, the former secret service chief now urging renewal, whose own health was very poor when he took over the office of General Secretary. Gorbachev invited me to visit him in the spring of 1985, a few weeks after his election in Moscow; half a dozen interested and experienced party friends went with me. At our next meeting in 1988 I was no longer Chairman of the SPD, but we still had plenty that we could usefully discuss.

On 5 April 1988 Gorbachev welcomed me in the Catherine Hall of the Great Palace in the Kremlin, the place where I had signed the German–Soviet treaty with Kosygin. Besides Egon Bahr, an expert on security issues, I was accompanied by the former Dutch Minister of Overseas Development Jan Pronk, a man of considerable international standing. When I introduced him, the General Secretary said this brought us to one of his favourite subjects: 'Second only to nuclear danger is the threat of social explosions in the Third World.'

Gorbachev's intelligent advisers soon numbered development issues, along with threats to peace and environmental damage, among those tasks for humanity which they ranked above contentious issues. One of the reforming professors asked what use the class struggle would be if humanity was lost. Moreover, it was now recognized that history was open-ended. Would anyone still have cared to support the thesis that the system in the Soviet Union, unlike that in right-wing dictatorships, was immutable?

In his book *Perestroika: New Thinking for Our Country and the World*, published in 1987, Gorbachev explicitly referred to the report of my commission. 'We have adopted many ideas developed by Social Democrats and the Socialist International, and worked out by the Brandt and Palme commissions.' Now, in conversation, he said my experiences were relevant; could we on our side not emphasize those points where opinions converged?

One may object that this was a tactical ploy, and wonder whether there were really no factors of major significance for survival still at issue. I had urged the advisability of discussing these very points at the Institute for the World Economy and International Relations in the summer of 1981: whether or not the human race had a common future ahead of it; the fact that we had not only to tame the means of mass destruction but to defuse the time-bombs of starvation and avert the threat to the natural environment. In fact many new ideas had already been dawning towards the end of the Brezhnev era, and not all the condemnations of him are entirely justified; it was he who said that the danger of war must be fought 'hand in hand with the USA'.

I cannot claim I had the chance to come to know the Soviet Union anywhere near as well as the USA. Apart from several visits to the capital, I have seen nothing but a little of Leningrad and the Crimea, and on the other side of the Urals only Novosibirsk and southern Uzbekistan. (I had worn a national costume there and *Der Spiegel* used the picture for their title page; Kreisky telephoned me to ask, 'What on earth were you doing dressed up as a Bohemian cook the other day?')

When I first visited Mikhail Sergeyevich Gorbachev in May 1985, he had been just two months in office. Since then, all and sundry have felt impelled to comment – on his ability or the threat he posed, his charm or his cunning. The prize for the least well-informed and useful estimate of the man must go to a certain German head of government. To assume that the new leadership had come to power as a result of a hard line taken by the West was particularly foolish, and so was the wish that it might not succeed in implementing a modern programme of *glasnost* and *perestroika*, because if it did it would be even more dangerous. Once again, ideas of further armament were abroad. It was to Reagan's historical credit that he did not adopt them as his own.

Even during that first meeting in 1985 I found Gorbachev a remarkably competent interlocutor, aware of problems, resolute, and at the same time easy in manner. The eternal debate about the role of personality in history took on a new and particularly striking aspect. The well-informed did not doubt that his arguments reflected much of what he and his wife had been thinking over the years. But even experts on the Soviet scene did not guess what a major turning-point he would represent both at home and abroad.

The new Soviet course in foreign policy was marked by a serious willingness to negotiate, and extended to the limitation of both nuclear and conventional arms. The aim of expansion outside Europe was renounced, as well as the Brezhnev doctrine which found such terrible expression in Prague in 1968 and had cast such a shadow over Eastern Europe. The other and equally pleasing side of the coin was Soviet readiness to help settle regional conflicts in other parts of the world: in the Gulf, South Africa, Kampuchea and Central America. In a private conversation during my visit to the Kremlin in May 1985 I asked

Gorbachev if he really intended to pull out of Afghanistan soon. 'Yes, if the Americans will let us,' he said.

He never read from prepared texts; he would go through the papers prepared for him and make some notes. He could listen, and change the subject. Gromyko, in his time, never joined in conversation of his own accord, and would only open his mouth when someone asked a question. To him, military security always came first in all matters of foreign policy, and was understood to be fundamental. This meant that there could be no real improvement in relations with the Americans. The Soviet version of the situation was that they had reached rock bottom in relations with the USA. However, military confrontation made trade as well as dialogue more difficult. The head of the International Department of the Central Committee of the Soviet Communist Party himself, Boris Ponomaryov – he had been there since the days of the Comintern – indicated that there were better times ahead: the General Secretary might not want to say so yet, but if the leaders of the two Superpowers met and stated that they did not want a third world war, it would give a significant signal. In November 1986, at the Two-Power summit in Reykjavik, it was indeed established that a nuclear war could not be won and must not be fought.

Only six months before, Gorbachev had said that the Soviet Union had 'no confidence in this administration'. Negotiations were resumed in Geneva in January 1985, but there was no sign of any positive result; on the contrary, forebodings were confirmed. 'The world is not just the USA, so we agreed to new negotiations. But no one should have expected us to perform a political striptease. We are in favour of serious policies, not playing games.' When I heard this comment, preparations for a meeting with Reagan were in progress, and it took place in Geneva in November 1985.

I had asked if the Soviet Union would not be well advised to decide on the bold step of unilateral arms limitation. Gorbachev said that in a tense situation unilateral measures were not a bold but a thoughtless step which would endanger world peace.

He referred to Andropov, who had said the Soviet Union was not naïve and could not take unilateral steps. Later this attitude too was critically examined, and the Soviets admitted they had neglected opportunities to reduce tension, thereby engaging excessively and unnecessarily in the arms race and putting a strain on their own economy. Gorbachev let his own thinking carry him forward, and was soon giving it as his opinion that relations between states should be 'de-ideologized'.

In his speeches and publications, the new Soviet leader clearly carried on from those lines of argument that Palme and I had worked out with our commissions, and which we had developed at the same time, or indeed ahead of him, together with our friends from all over the world. Most important among them were the reduction of confrontation, sensible limitation of military equipment, and the freeing of resources to save endangered lives and serve productive ends.

There was little talk of the 'common European home' in Moscow in 1985, or not yet. Gorbachev was still occupied with polemics. 'The American administration wants to overcome the division of Europe. What does that mean? If it means co-operating to bridge the military blocs, we are in favour of it. If it means swallowing up Eastern Europe and doing away with the socialist order, we are against it and will not allow it. Such plans could even lead to war.'

Is Gorbachev well disposed to Germany? I have been inclined to think so since my first meeting with him in 1985. The tradition in which he stands has taken on new life in his time. In conversation with me in 1985, at least, Gorbachev said: 'Our attitude to the German people is clear. We honour their contribution to culture and civilization, their literature and their technical achievements. The Soviet Union recognized that even when the Fascists were just outside Moscow. We did not confuse the German people with Fascism.' In fact the anti-German card had already been removed from the pack – which was by no means necessarily to be expected – over the Moscow Treaty. With it, one of the cohesive factors in the Eastern bloc had ceased to operate. Meanwhile, to awaken old resentments or even to stir them up, particularly in Paris, remained a temptation for leading Soviet politicians, one they could not always resist.

At the 1988 meeting I asked for further explanation of *perestroika* and the ideas connected with it. Gorbachev preceded his answer with an admission as surprising as it was frank: it was difficult, he said, to give actual content to the call for 'more democracy, more socialism'. The administrative system of the past had not worked well; it had turned against the people and the workers. Latent possibilities in society had to be liberated and traditional stereotypes thrown overboard. This sounded more plausible than the defiant statement: 'There will be no solutions outside socialism, no change in our intellectual position. We were born in socialism, we live in it, we have known nothing else.' Socialism – which he also suggested gave personal and political freedom apart from basic prerequisites – was to be freed, he said, from all that had distorted it. After Stalin's death Khrushchev had attempted much, but 'he often went only half-way'. There had been no real progress under Brezhnev, so the Soviet Union now needed democratization brought about by 'the participation of the entire population'. The central point of *perestroika* was 'to restructure our thinking', which as everyone knows is easier said than done.

He conceded, and this was not just Stalin's second death but more too, that socialism could not function without democracy. He did not mean that the new leadership would accustom itself to the idea of more than one party; instead, democracy was to be realized within the framework of *the* party which had to exercise the power of social organization. He promised his countrymen, and was trying to explain to the functionaries, that no more restrictions must be placed on scientific research. Questions of theory could not and must not be solved by political decree. 'We must have free competition of minds.'

The Russian leader was conspicuously unforthcoming about various developments within the bloc. He left little room for illusions. He would not explicitly confirm that more room was to be allowed to pluralism in fringe areas – pluralism that might even question the party's monopoly. However, he made it clear that he felt his own country was treading a strenuous path anyway, and it was not in his interest to have the Eastern bloc make it more difficult. Later he said: 'They can find their own way; we are keeping out of it.' I did not get the impression that he was at all clear yet about the dynamics that would loosen the constraints. History cannot be channelled as we please, but how would they have known that in Moscow?

Who stood behind Mikhail Sergeyevich Gorbachev, and who was against him? Even three or four years after he took office the constellation had scarcely altered. He was supported mainly by intellectuals, scientists and artists, younger people in the party apparatus and those who wanted reform, and the state administration. The great mass of the 'workers' was waiting to see, or was cautious in its opinions, particularly as the supply of goods was felt to be getting worse rather than better, and the campaign against alcohol abuse, though objectively necessary, seemed unhelpful. The army leadership were in earnest when they demonstrated loyalty; they were pursuing their own interests in economic renewal. Only a few weeks before his death Brezhnev had summoned leaders of the armed forces and told them that rising military expenses conflicted with the realities of the economic situation. It was not clear to an observer whether the KGB, the body responsible for state security, had transferred its allegiance to its former chief Andropov or was distancing itself from him. And who outside the Soviet Union could know what problems there were inside it?

As he wanted and indeed had to throw so much overboard, Gorbachev was particularly anxious to find a solid rock to which he could moor his boat. The natural candidate was Lenin, standard-bearer of the Russian Bolsheviks and founding father of the Soviet Union. Gorbachev was carrying on from the 'old man' Vladimir Ilyich, his New Economic Policy that was to have taken over from wartime Communism, and his warnings against Stalin, which had long been suppressed. Not surprisingly,

Lenin had to be held responsible for many commonplaces: that a distinction must be made between general and concrete issues; that the correct policy is the policy of principle; that you became a Communist only by accepting all the wealth of the past; that you must study your opponents because that makes the weaknesses of your own position clearer.

Intelligent people, of whom there is no lack in the Soviet Union, will not find it easy to see why new thinking and questioning should be anchored to that rock. Even Lenin's life and thought cannot always be taboo, immune from critical assessment. Wherever a democratic opening is made, the old mechanisms of control break down, and in the Soviet Union itself the original attempt to limit *perestroika* to reviving the economy on the one hand and dismantling blatant dictatorship on the other failed. While the internal dynamics of the democratization process were still hard to evaluate, the poor supply of goods posed major problems.

It was hard to understand how Soviet agriculture could still be in such a pitiful state, seventy years after the end of tsarist rule, with 30 per cent or more of harvest yield lost before it ever reached the consumers. It was hard to see how it could take so long for views to change. No modern economy can dispense with proper accounting, vigorous market impulses, or profitability. Gorbachev spoke fervently of the difficult task of taking some of the eighteen million state employees out of the bureaucracy and directing them into productive activities. He did not conceal the discontent and indignation spreading in the ranks of that bureaucracy. It was not clear to me how or indeed whether this resistance could be overcome. But I did not doubt for a moment that one should wish the reforms and the reformer every possible success.

I was deeply moved to hear in April 1988, very soon after my arrival in the Soviet Union, of the rehabilitation of Karl Radek, the Polish Communist of partly German origins, who had escaped the death sentence in one of the Stalinist trials only to perish in a gulag.

I was also moved to hear that 6,000 books that had been kept under lock and key were now once again available to historians. Not least for the sake of their families, I welcomed the official rehabilitation of victims of terror and the relentless revelation of what German and other exiles had suffered under Stalin's regime. But I could not go along with that zeal to discover the truth that took the form of discovering whether a man like the Old Bolshevik Nikolai Bukharin, apostrophized by Lenin as the 'darling of the Party', had erred less in one particular year than in another. Why not leave all that to the historians? Why go up another blind alley? If the Communist Party is to go on deciding what history approves and what it rejects, the way to democracy is still a long one. In 1987, and going much further than Khrushchev, Gorbachev had recorded those 'real crimes' of which thousands of Soviet citizens had been the victims. The guilt of Stalin and his henchmen was great and unforgivable, he had said – 'That, comrades, is the bitter truth.' The bitter truth is not usually the kind that people like to hear. But the new Moscow leadership cannot be too highly praised for what it has done for morale in the Soviet Union and in the countries allied to it.

A private conversation during my visit in May 1985 impressed itself on my mind because of the frankness with which Gorbachev replied to questions of the sort we have become accustomed to calling 'humanitarian'. I told him I had three files full of petitions with me. He nodded. I said the first file concerned cases of people of German origin who had applied to be reunited with their families; some of these petitions had already been granted. He nodded. File Two, I said, concerned cases of Soviet citizens in distress, the sort of people we called dissidents in the West. He nodded. File Three, I said, contained petitions from Jews who wanted to emigrate; their relations in Germany, Israel and the Soviet Union itself had written letters. When I had last ventured to mention such matters in Moscow I had been more or less cold-shouldered. In 1981 Brezhnev said, 'I know all about you, so don't try to persuade me you have followed in Nahum

Goldmann's footsteps and become President of the World Council of Jews.' Gorbachev's response was different: 'Who's your representative – someone who can discuss these matters tomorrow morning with a representative appointed by me?' It was done, and colleagues of mine helped to clear up many tricky cases of human rights even before the general situation had changed for the better.

It is hard today to understand what a turning-point it was when victims of despotism were set free; when it became possible to visit Andrei Sakharov in his Moscow apartment; when legal security, freedom of thought and belief gained ground; when there were even elections, inadequate as they might be; when people found that they could speak openly about the dimension of the terror and the accumulation of lies that went far beyond any normal power of comprehension; I myself had long underestimated it. Among the hopeful signs of normalization was something a respected writer told me in 1988. His grown-up daughter had asked him, 'Father, you must have known something about the crimes they're talking about so much now. Why didn't you ever mention them to me?' I do not like superficial comparisons, but did not such questions sound familiar?

In many places there were loose ends, ends that would not come together. However, revolutions do not take shape on the drawing-board but in the hearts and minds of contradictory human beings. People will tolerate mismanagement even when its absurdity is clear, and accept the suppression of national character even when anger is deeply felt. And then, suddenly, some small incident will be the last straw that breaks the camel's back, and enormous tensions will be discharged, tensions kept bottled up for who knows how long or why? When the Caucasus rebelled, and groups of people elsewhere began fighting each other, the General Secretary surprised me with his sober observation that he would rather have a serious problem on the table than swept under the carpet. There is no doubt it would be a good thing to allow national cultures within the Soviet Union greater scope. It was natural for the self-assured and orderly demonstrations in the Baltic states to arouse particular interest in Germany and Scandinavia. The Soviet Union is becoming more European, yet nothing can alter the fact that at the turn of the century its non-Russian nationalities will be dominant, at least numerically. Question follows hard on the heels of question, and if they are not answered Gorbachev's 'common European home' cannot be built.

In conversation with me, Gorbachev stressed the fact that *perestroika* also meant a qualitative leap forward in foreign policy. We have already seen something of this. So eminent a commentator as George Kennan, the expert on American–Russian relations, was ready to endorse this; he said that the morbid radicalism of Stalinist oppression was a thing of the past, and co-operation between states could be made considerably easier. I hope the Princeton professor was right.

Mao's Dark Shadow

Arrogant Europeans and Americans cannot be reminded too often that most of the Earth's population lives in Asia; they are expected to number 3.6 billion out of a world total of 6.1 billion by the turn of the century. Around the year 2000, moreover, 50 per cent of the world gross product will be created in the East Asian Pacific area. Although I was unlucky in the planning of my visits to Asia and had to cancel a number of them, my own observations have brought it home to me that change is not the same everywhere, and the face of Asia is changing at breathtaking speed.

I entertain no feelings of inferiority but, rather, am amused when American zealots threaten the shift of the USA's sympathies from the Atlantic to the Pacific. A transfer of American affections to the more able Asiatics? It is hard to take seriously. Some players in the game felt their Chinese card had failed them, but it would be foolish to overlook what is going on in the Middle and Far East. We should realize that according to all present indications China and India will each have a billion and a half inhabitants in the middle of the next century. Put another way, as many people will be living in each of those two countries as lived in the whole world at the beginning of the present century. India, like China, has succeeded in creating an industrial infrastructure in the last two decades and in increasing food production very considerably. Can the yield be doubled again in the course of a few decades? In 1988 one of the most learned men in the world, Jerome Wiesner, the inventor of radar and for many years director of the Massachusetts Institute of Technology, disarmed me with his resigned comment that in his head he had a solution for every other problem in the world, but not for population growth.

Seen on the global scale and not in Asia alone, the explosive growth of world population – it has tripled since my school-days – is particularly striking in the Southern Hemisphere, where many of the people live on or near the hunger line. I cannot say whether the experts on the subject are right, and eleven or twelve billion inhabitants would mean the end of the Earth. What we know does not suggest that we can judge for certain. Reproductive behaviour in different cultural groups does not lend itself to the simple approach.

It is not for me to remonstrate with the spiritual leaders of great religious communities, but one may ask what reference to the next world is worth if humanity is threatened in this one. I have often felt encouraged by kindly words from both Protestants and Catholics: for instance, when Pope John Paul II spoke to me and my colleagues in Rome of the essential links between development and disarmament 'and between the solutions of North–South issues and East–West problems'; his last predecessor but one, Paul VI, had called development 'another word for peace'. Condemnation of contraceptive measures is inimical to the world and the future, and does not sit easily with responsibility of this kind. Family planning is one of the essential factors for bringing order into humanity's struggle for survival.

There has always been less squeamishness in largely non-Christian Asia than in other continents. In China, and at times in India, the authorities have slowed population growth with measures that are sometimes draconian. Those who feel this is going too far are the last people who should approach the problem opportunistically or from the viewpoint of a fundamentalist ideology.

I have not seen much of Asia itself, and have gained an impression of its vitality and its poverty rather than experiencing them at first hand. During my travels on Berlin business I went to Pakistan, Burma and Sri Lanka, as well as Japan and India, which I visited again later. I went to Iran while the Shah was in power; this was held against me when I became Federal Chancellor, particularly over the issue of oil supplies. I first set foot in China in 1984. I became acquainted with other countries, such as Indonesia and the Philippines, Korea and Vietnam, through meeting leading representatives of those nations in Germany or at some third place.

Japan is an impressive example of what a drive to modernize can do if motive powers inside and outside the country complement each other. Although – or because? – the Second World War laid such a heavy burden on them, the Japanese embody the concept of an economic miracle almost more than the Germans. Who would have thought in 1949, except in wild dreams, that forty years later the world would be wending its way to Frankfurt and even more conspicuously to Tokyo, in search of means and guidance to keep the world's economic problems, particularly the debt crisis of the Third World, from going completely out of control?

And who would have guessed that within a few decades such high technological and organizational performance could be created out of the discipline, hard work and ability to learn which are part of the Japanese heritage? During my visits to Japan I saw the great changes which have brought the island state of the Far East to a leading position among trading nations. It was not until quite a late date that, for all the differences, I saw major parallels with German industrial development of the nineteenth century, involving a cheap labour force and profitable patents from the West. After the Second World War the Japanese made good use of another advantage: they spent little or nothing on military ends. They have resoundingly disproved the myth that military technique encourages economic growth. The Japanese invested energetically and effectively in civil technology.

Experts, of whom I am not one, argue as to why bureaucracy in Japanese life remained so dominant and so effective for so long, despite all the changes in the country, and why bribery is so widespread among those in political power there. Corruption occurs elsewhere too, both in the historically and socially different conditions of China and India and in America and Europe. And reformers in Russia and Africa have to do battle with bureaucracies even more than do reformers elsewhere, although those bureaucracies are not notable for their efficiency, so the comparison throws no light on the Japanese phenomenon. Could it be that Japanese democracy is still of rather a formal nature, and in combination with Japanese ability produces these strange fruits? Even during the half-century that will soon have passed since the end of the war, hardly any democratic structures or control mechanisms have been created.

In conversation with foreigners and in negotiations the Japanese appear extraordinarily self-assured. Whether in public or private, it used to be unusual for Japanese men to take an active part in discussions (and Japanese women were not present at all). They would listen, ask questions, make further inquiries, and say whether they were for or against something, but only if they were asked. I recall with particular pleasure my conversations with Foreign Minister Takeo Miki, because they

were so full of subtleties and so productive; he was also head
of government for a brief period, and a pleasant companion
outside his official functions. He asked about my experiences in
the Grand Coalition, and indicated the reasons for his interest.
His attempts to modernize Japan politically came to nothing.
In the context of the international Social Democratic
community, too, I found colleagues in that part of the world
whose remarkable intellectual powers are only just beginning
to make themselves felt in the reaction to some severe cases of
misconduct.

The Japanese are no longer the object of such great admiration and extensive study as before; that role has been assumed
by those Asiatic children of the economic miracle called by the
Americans 'the four dragons' and by the Germans 'the young
tigers': South Korea and Taiwan, Hong Kong and Singapore,
followed at a little distance by Malaysia and Thailand. They
are all imbued with the Chinese work ethic. They have all been
spurred on by the Japanese example and are looking to new
economic horizons. They show that nothing succeeds like
success, just as they teach us that progress and freedom do not
always move at the same pace. Despite all setbacks, however,
the development of Korea is particularly encouraging; the
dynamics of a market economy invite political democracy. We
need not look to South-East Asia to learn that in the long run
you cannot have one without the other.

The focal points of the world economy and world politics
are shifting. Should Europeans feel concern? I would say a firm
'No' to that. Why should the Asiatic and Pacific area not assume
a new importance and show the Old World that it has no claim
to a monopoly of success? Why should we object to seeing
Tokyo, Delhi, perhaps Beijing and certain other centres exert
stronger influence than before on the course of international
politics? I am rather sorry for those Americans who thought in
the eighties that they should conceal their fascination with Asia
behind a façade of disappointment in Europe; the Europeans,
they said and wrote, were 'arteriosclerotic' and must be forgotten.

The Japanese and representatives of the 'four dragons' tended to see Europe in a similar light at the beginning of the decade. However, the wide perspective of the European Community's home market taught them better, and the Americans along with them. Old Europe had suddenly been reinvigorated. Times and opinions can change very quickly.

It is not certain that the (Western) European Community will become a 'fourth world power', but it is possible. In Nixon's time – that is, when the Americans rediscovered China – there was talk of the geostrategic balance between the Big Three. Nixon's right-hand man provided an image of five fingers; to Kissinger's way of thinking, Western Europe and Japan should count as world powers. However, history marched on: to take a one-dimensional view of Europe was precipitate, and it was lacking in foresight to ignore India and Latin America, particularly Brazil. Excessive concentration on the geopolitical rivalry in which the nuclear powers became entangled in their competition for influence in the 'poorhouses of the Third World' was unrealistic – a classic example of a misguided policy of interest.

Both superpowers realized rather late in the day that the bipolar era was over, and new centres of gravity claimed their say in a multipolar world: India, for instance, which I first came to know through Jawaharlal Nehru, one of the great men of this century. We had made direct contact before the war when he visited Berlin, went briefly to Republican Spain, and visited Prague to show his solidarity with the victims of the Munich Agreement on their home ground. An intellectual from a high-ranking, prosperous Hindu family, Nehru had sympathies which took him well to the left until he realized that few such policies were suited to his native land. During the war I had been much taken with his view of world history, as told in the form of letters to his daughter, and recommended it to a Swedish publishing house. Nehru told his readers that the world was not to be seen as solely 'Eurocentric', and explained the weight carried by the Eastern religions which seem alien to Westerners.

When I was in Delhi in 1959 the Prime Minister gave a small dinner for me. Those present included his daughter Indira; she had become Chairman of the Congress Party that year, but did not take much part in the conversation unless her father asked her a question. Nehru showed a concerned interest in German affairs. He did so again when I met him a year later at his sister's; she was Indian Ambassador in London and visited me in Berlin. Would there be a solution for Berlin as a whole, Nehru wondered, and how did we envisage the future military status of Germany? We discussed European questions and other dangers to world peace. When I wrote to him about the building of the Berlin Wall, he said in reply that he was moved by the human aspect of our problems more than by legal positions. 'We must not cease to work for the easing of tensions.'

In the spring of 1984, twenty years after Nehru's death, I was a guest of his daughter, Prime Minister Indira Gandhi; this time our company at dinner included her son Rajiv and daughter-in-law Sonia, who were as reserved as Mrs Gandhi herself had been in her time. A few months later Rajiv, her elder son, was to take over the business of government after his mother's assassination at the gate of the garden in which we had spent some time discussing North–South and East–West problems in front of British television cameras. She was less imperious than I had expected, but more penetrating in discussion than I remembered her. She had visited Bonn when I was in office; I had also met her in Germany when I was Foreign Minister. At the end of 1977 – on my way back from a conference of the Socialist International in Tokyo – I visited Delhi and saw her in the unaccustomed role of a politician in opposition. Our ambassador had not invited her to a reception he gave for me, to avoid offending the Government in office. I put that right at once, thereby laying myself open to her vigorous complaints about the evils of the world in general and her political opponents at home in particular.

Some of those opponents thought they had been imprisoned at Mrs Gandhi's behest while she was head of government; as always, I had interceded for political prisoners. In a letter written in August 1976 to Tito, who figured among the leaders of the non-aligned countries, I had mentioned, more in surprise than in anger, how my friends Kreisky and Palme and I myself had incurred the wrath of Mrs Gandhi for this intervention.

At our meeting in June 1984 she was particularly concerned with the possibility of bringing some kind of movement into the rigid fronts of international politics. 'When will the Europeans be ready to co-operate with major forces in the non-aligned countries? Why don't we combine to put pressure on the superpowers to discuss the arms race and the world economy in the same context?' That was entirely in line with my own thinking.

I supported the endeavours of the Four Continents Initiative when the heads of government of Sweden, India and Greece met the Presidents of Mexico, Argentina and Tanzania in the spring of 1984. Like them, I thought peace too important to be entrusted solely to the White House and the Kremlin. At the time, and in my talks with Indira Gandhi, we were concerned with the topical question of a possible freeze on the deployment of nuclear arms and the encouragement of negotiations over reductions in stockpiling. We also agreed that more attention should be paid to the connection between the easing of tensions and the extension of co-operation.

In March 1983 Mrs Gandhi was appointed to chair the non-aligned countries' movement, which had grown ever larger in members, but rather thin in content. Like me, she wanted another summit meeting, to include discussion of those economic questions which were of burning interest to the developing countries, and she gave orders for thorough preparation of its agenda. Her authority died with her and was sorely missed amongst the non-aligned countries, which encountered a mixture of contempt and indifference in Western capitals – when they were not suspected of being the lackeys of Communism.

In Beijing, early in that summer of 1984, the General Secretary of the Chinese Communist Party, Hu Yaobang, had given me a few brief messages to be delivered to India: Beijing hoped relations would 'continue to improve', and it would be helpful if India abandoned 'sub-hegemonistic' attitudes towards its neighbours. Mrs Gandhi was sceptical: 'So what are *they* doing?' However, it was beginning to look as if the Chinese would succeed in three demands on which they made better relations with the Soviet Union dependent: fewer troops along their common border, the end of the Russian occupation of Afghanistan, and the end of the occupation of Kampuchea by the Vietnamese. None of these points did India any discernible harm.

Under Rajiv Gandhi India did not moderate its ambitions to be the guardian of order in the region. The country still has enormous problems at home, in spite of the great progress that has been made in supplying its population with goods and services: these problems include separatist movements, the plight of almost 250 million people living below subsistence level, and the consequences of far too long a period spent out of touch with Western technology.

Hu Yaobang, an energetic, humorous, reforming Communist, was deposed for too much 'liberality' in 1987; his death in the spring of 1989 set off the Beijing student demonstrations that were so ruthlessly crushed. The young people demanding less tyranny and more democracy wanted Hu's posthumous rehabilitation. He had been rather in advance of his party: in the early summer of 1986, when he was visiting Bonn, I had had some very animated conversations with him. Hu Qili, the Chinese Politburo theorist, had already visited the Federal Republic in November 1985. He had to pay for his open-mindedness when the real rulers of China stifled the pro-democracy movement in 1989. I met other Chinese leaders when they paid visits to improve inter-state relations.

At fourteen, Hu Yaobang had taken part in Mao's Long March, and had then known the vicissitudes of a Communist functionary's life. In Beijing, the General Secretary told me of his policy of more openness and economic reform. It was obvious that there had been some success, particularly in the provision of food supplies, although in big cities the housing shortage presented a horrifying picture. In other ways too the image of Communist China was no longer painted solely in shades of grey or blue, but was full of lively sound and colour. Intellectuals spoke of what they had had to endure under the regime of the 'Gang of Four'. Now and then, in hushed tones, there was mention of political prisoners, the demand for human rights, the struggle for democratic participation. Driving down a street, I was surprised to hear shots fired in a stadium – a particularly discreet companion told me 'in strict confidence' that it was 'only' some criminals being dealt with.

I have been unfairly accused of neglecting relations with China in favour of relations with the Soviet Union. Matters were not so simple. I never felt like following the example of those who thought they could achieve advantages for Europe and Germany by playing the 'Chinese card' or by praising Maoism as superior to Leninism. I also thoroughly disliked the excesses of the Cultural Revolution, and its reverberations echoed for a long time. I have never understood why China should be judged, by us and by America, more leniently on human rights than other nations.

In Bonn, even in the time of Adenauer and Mao, there were ideas in the air, as stirring as they were alarming, of exploiting opposition between the two Communist-ruled Great Powers for German ends. Smiling with satisfaction, the Old Man of the Rhine spoke of the deep sigh heaved by Khrushchev in Moscow in 1955 over *his* East; he added, meaningly: 'There are already 600 million (!) Chinese. They'll soon show the Russians that they must come to an understanding with the West.' In Bonn in December 1960, Adenauer said that in his view Kennedy, who was to take over the presidency next month, would have to deal with the China question very soon; America must decide whether to go along with China or Russia. He stuck by this 'either–or' even in the face of clearly expressed doubts. De Gaulle let it be known, in a very much less outspoken manner, that trouble between China and the USA need not do Europe any harm.

I thought it a mistake to suppose that we could derive any benefit from the Sino–Soviet conflict. At the first reading of the Eastern treaties in February 1971, I warned against pinning one's hopes on miracle weapons: 'China is not a miracle weapon either.' But I rejected the idea of laying down the law about inter-state relations and the protection of our normal interests. It was with this end in view – and because the export industries required it – that Ludwig Erhard had tried to formalize relations with China to some extent in 1964, thereby incurring American disapproval.

It was incumbent upon Federal German politicians to inform the USA as well as Japan and India when the time had come for us to think of establishing official relations with China. We also had what was in effect a duty to inform the Soviet Union and the Eastern European states, with which we were in the process of normalizing relations. On no account must we give any impression that we hoped to profit by tensions, but there was no need to wear blinkers.

At the conference of our ambassadors to Asia held in Tokyo in 1967, which I chaired, we said that the People's Republic of China could not remain a blank spot on our political map of the world; instead, it was in our interests 'for China to develop independently and be brought to co-operate in the family of nations'. But however important China would be for the future development of world politics, we said, it was certain 'that a settlement of the European and with it the German question cannot be decided without, or against the opposition of, the Soviet Union'. In 1969, at the Council of NATO, I advised against gambling on unchanging and persistent hostility between the Soviet Union and China.

The Soviets with whom I spoke in the sixties were horrified by the Cultural Revolution. In 1966 Abrasimov, Soviet Ambassador to the GDR, appealed to the common values of European culture. His colleague Zarapkin in Bonn sought to make us understand that the Russians would like to feel secure in Europe so that they could face the Far East. Tito, who soon afterwards fell prey to some wishful thinking about China, rather late in the day, spoke at the time of his fear that the Beijing leadership was including world war in its calculations. The hopes of Ben Gurion, the Israeli head of government, were much like Adenauer's. During the 'working funeral' for the first Federal Chancellor, he intimated to me that he was chiefly interested in what would become of the European Community – and of China.

Although we did not learn of it until later, Khrushchev was furious over Mao's 'Asiatic cunning, treachery, vindictiveness and deceit'; it was 'impossible to pin these Chinese down', he said. Brezhnev, at Oreanda in September 1971, said the same, but at greater length. It was very hard 'for a European' to understand the Chinese, said the Kremlin leader, adding, 'We both know the walls here are white; now if a Chinese walked in, he would swear they were black.' Chinese policy, he said, was 'extremely anti-Soviet, chauvinist and nationalist'; he even added 'bloodthirsty'. A tsar, he said, would have declared war in such a situation, but he, Brezhnev, wanted to improve relations. China would not be a military threat in the immediate future.

I was particularly anxious to hear the Soviet view because shortly before, in the summer of 1971, Nixon had announced that he was going to Beijing. Brezhnev said he had nothing against the relations of other states with the Chinese, but if Nixon went he would not have an easy time there. That summer the American President had told me he entirely understood that our priority was our relationship with the Russians: he would feel the same himself. And to ensure that there was no misunderstanding, he added that the great game for America was the one that involved the Soviets. I gave him to understand that I was familiar with the map of the world, and would not be lured into playing with marked cards by either left-wing or right-wing Maoists. When the question of normalizing relations arose, we would tell Moscow and Washington – and of course India and Japan too – in good time.

The matter was settled in October 1972 when Walter Scheel went to Beijing. When Brezhnev was in Bonn next spring, during a short walk with no one except an interpreter, a nervous curiosity still led him to inquire whether I intended to visit Mao. That was not on my programme just yet, and in the end I never did meet him. But I was aware of China's significance not just in general and in the long term, but in the present situation: the People's Republic had joined the United Nations at the end of 1971, and sat on the Security Council. It was also busy in East Berlin and elsewhere in the Warsaw Pact countries, with the obvious aim of obstructing the improvement of our relations with the Soviet Union.

During my visit in 1984, Hu Yaobang explained to me China's interest in world peace and in keeping an equal distance from Washington and Moscow, which had not been the case in Mao's time. Chinese interest in Europe and its attempt to achieve union was great, he said, and so was interest in European Social Democracy. There were indications that China's relationship with Moscow was about to be normalized. The return of the rich colony of Hong Kong to the People's Republic had just been negotiated with the British. Cultural, economic and touristic contacts with Taiwan, still ostracized by China, were on the way.

In the state guest-house I met Deng Xiaoping, a diminutive but energetic figure, although he could no longer articulate clearly. He was the man who determined the guidelines of policy; officially, he chaired the Advisory Commission of the Central Committee, and he was also chairman of the powerful Military Committee. I quote from our table talk, as we ate off porcelain of the Imperial period.

'I am instructed to give a dinner in your honour ... I am eighty years old. My head does not work so well any more. But Adenauer was an old man too when he became Chancellor ...

'Your visit to us is too short. You must come more often,

take a closer look at your engagements diary ... You are welcome here any time ... Only when you visit China do you really get to know it. I would like you to know China well ...

'I found my way to Communism in French factories. In 1926 I went from Paris to Frankfurt and then to Moscow by way of Berlin. I spent a week in Berlin. It was all very tidy, but I missed the cafés of Paris ...

'China is still relatively backward. Our problems are technology and skilled workers. We cannot solve them by ourselves. No one can develop in isolation. Hence our policy of openness to the world outside ...

'We have many old comrades; some of them have been working with us for decades. We set up the Advisory Commission as a transitional system. But the older functionaries are making way for younger people. At the same time, we put our wisdom at their disposal ... We have to pass on wisdom and experience to bring the coming generation security and stability.'

On such occasions it was obvious that much of present-day China could be understood only against the background of old systems of belief and thought. Early in 1988, at a congress in Madrid, there was some friendly questioning of an elderly Chinese delegate: could the next generation expect considerably greater prosperity? 'Oh yes,' he replied, 'in a hundred years we shall have made some progress.'

Before Deng asked me to dinner he brought the conversation round to a conversation between Adenauer and Churchill in which the Huns had been mentioned. He supposed they had meant the Chinese. I changed the subject, mentioning the great hopes the 'Old Man' had entertained of China's valuable role; a few years later the notion of Huns would have struck me as more relevant. In the short term, the students and workers demanding the murderous old man's resignation failed. The world had made a romantic picture of him, but he continued to spread fear and terror, translating the ideas he had always held into action and speaking of the educational function of executions. The world turned away in horror.

Olof Palme and the Cause of Security

Late on the evening of 28 February 1986 I was in Lübeck, where I was to speak next morning in the city election campaign. Inconceivable news came from Stockholm: Olof Palme had been shot in the street on his way home from the cinema with his wife. Years later people were still trying to puzzle out who did it. It was clear to many far beyond the borders of his country and the ranks of his political friends what we had lost. I felt as if a beloved younger brother had died.

Sweden had lost a leading politician of high international standing. A world thirsty for peace and justice was the poorer for one who had urged those things. In my first, rather awkwardly phrased comment, I said I mourned the loss of a close friend with whom I had been discussing ways of ending the arms race only a few days before by telephone. 'Together, we tried to do things which must now go on without him, but in the way he would have wished.'

Two weeks later, when we said goodbye beside his bier in the Stockholm Stadshus – many prominent people from all over the world, North and South, East and West, had come to the funeral – I said I would not call him simply a 'statesman': that would be too narrow a view, including neither his visionary force nor his extraordinary integrity. Had not the last two weeks shown how young people far beyond Sweden's borders realized what had made Palme so unusual and independent a political leader? I spoke in memory of the tall young man he still seemed to me, even at nearly sixty: 'He was always active, yet he never had difficulty in taking the long view, and he never neglected the cultural dimension. He could listen as well as talk, and he liked to laugh with us.'

When I was living in Stockholm Palme was still at school. He was of Swedish upper-class origin, his mother a member of the German Baltic aristocracy. Our friendship began in the mid-fifties, when Tage Erlander appointed him his personal secretary. Soon he was the youngest member of parliament and then of the Government. In 1969, when Erlander retired, Palme succeeded him at the head of the Government and of the Party. For six years, from 1976 to 1982, he had to be content with the role of Opposition leader, an unaccustomed one for a Swedish Social Democrat.

His sights were set to a great extent on full employment and a welfare state providing social security and a high standard of education. He felt bound to the special tradition of Scandinavian Social Democracy, and was proud when the Swedish model found European and international respect, even imitation. One of his fervent champions was Bruno Kreisky, Chancellor of Austria, who never denied the influence his Swedish exile had had on him. The fathers and mothers of the 'Volksheim', having weighed up all the pros and cons, accepted the bureaucratic burdens and determined that the blessings would more than compensate for them.

Abroad, Olof Palme attracted attention when he protested, loud and clear, against the Vietnam war – not just in the streets of Stockholm but on American television. He was already a Government minister. Richard Nixon recalled his Ambassador from Stockholm. Henry Kissinger, who spoke to me at a dinner in Washington about this clouding of inter-state relations, was rather surprised but not ungrateful when I explained how very much the Swede was a product of his student years in the USA: Palme's reaction was like that of the younger Americans. He spoke out on other subjects too, sharply attacking the Franco regime in Spain; he collected donations for its victims in the streets of the capital. He denounced the authorities who crushed the Prague Spring with all the passion in his heart. He made the troubles of South Africa his business on behalf of the international community of Social Democrats; he was one of the most vehement opponents of apartheid, and would accept no compromises. He visited Managua in 1984, the first and only Western head of government to do so. When we were among international friends in Slangerup, at the Danish metal-workers' school, his comments were: first, the representative of a country that was not especially large had to set particularly high standards in matters affecting the principles of international law, and second: 'No right-minded person can allow those in Nicaragua who oppose Somoza to go under.'

He pointed out earlier than most people that there would be further disasters in the Middle East if no solution were found to the Israeli–Palestinian question. He met the leader of the PLO in Algeria in 1974; the next year, at a conference of party leaders in Berlin, he was attacked by our Israeli friends Golda Meir and Yigal Allon for talking to terrorists, as they put it. Palme suddenly leaned forward from the window where he was following the discussion and raised his forefinger, interrupting firmly but amiably: 'And what were *you*, Yigal?' (He was referring to Allon's operations against the British protectorate before the State of Israel was founded.) At the beginning of the Iranian revolution we asked Palme, who had not yet returned to office as head of government, to take soundings in Teheran. At the end of 1980 the Secretary-General of the United Nations gave him the hopeless task of mediating in the first Gulf War. The time for that was nowhere near ripe yet, and so he concentrated, typically, on at least getting a number of children out of prison camps and sent home again.

In 1981 he was very anxious for the Iranian Foreign Minister, Sadigh Ghotbzadeh, to attend a meeting of the Socialist International in Oslo. We tried to follow Ghotbzadeh's line of thinking, which was moderate by Iranian standards. A few months later the Iranian let me know, by indirect ways, that he could not attend or speak again. He was executed soon afterwards.

In Kuwait in 1982 I saw Palme going back and forth over the nearby front line, ever-active, and in danger. This was on the occasion of a meeting of the North–South Commission, of which he was a particularly committed member. He wanted the representatives of the industrial nations to be readier with concessions, lest – as he told the US banker Peter Peterson – the motto of our report had to run: 'People of the world, unite to save Chase Manhattan Bank'. The Sweden he governed, like the other Scandinavian countries and The Netherlands, was conspicuous for its above-average generosity with development aid; large sections of the programme we drew up for immediate implementation bore our Swedish friend's handwriting.

When my Commission had completed its report Palme was not long in assembling his own. Its report, published in 1982, tackled the question of collective security in the nuclear age. The core of his group consisted, besides Palme himself, of the former American Secretary of State Cyrus Vance, the Soviet Institute director Giorgi Arbatov, and Egon Bahr, who brought the Commission our German experience of Eastern and security policy. On the Eastern side Jozef Cyrankiewicz, the former Prime Minister of Poland, took part; from my own Commission, there were the Japanese Ambassador Haruki Mori and the Commonwealth Secretary-General 'Sonny' Ramphal. As well as other representatives of the Third World, prominent European Social Democrats put their knowledge at the service of the undertaking: Gro Harlem Brundtland from Norway, Joop den Uyl from The Netherlands, and from England David Owen, who was to leave the British Labour Party after a bitter feud.

I had been kept well informed about the progress of the Commission's deliberations, and shared the conclusions they came to: collective security as an essential political task in the nuclear age, and partnership in security as a military concept to take over gradually from the strategy of nuclear deterrence; deterrence threatens to destroy what it is supposed to be defending, and thereby increasingly loses credibility. A new understanding of security also means taking account of the legitimate interests of the developing countries, and making resources hitherto tied up in armaments available for humanitarian and productive ends. But it quickly turned out that speaking and writing are easier than generating any kind of action, however modest.

The Palme Report contained the useful idea of a nuclear-free corridor, which was not taken up by those responsible for Western security, yet which helped to encourage new thinking in the sphere of defence. The American on the Commission had been strongly in favour, while the Soviet representative recorded his reservations. Some interesting suggestions were developed in technical discussion with representatives of the GDR – for a Central European zone with fewer armaments and no chemical weapons. Such discussions showed that representatives of 'the other side' had more ideas and were more open-minded than expected: they realized that the lives of people on both sides were at stake.

My own attitude to military matters has reflected the way problems have evolved between the thirties and the eighties. Growing up in an anti-militaristic tradition, I had quickly learned that the Nazi challenge could be met neither with radical maxims nor folded arms; none the less, it was still true that wars began in men's heads. After 1945 we Germans were not given the chance of dispensing with war materials entirely, as had initially been thought and hoped. I was among those who did not shrink from the consequences. It meant agreeing to the Western Alliance and the Bundeswehr, but it also meant agreeing to every reasonable form of arms control.

In Hanover in 1960, when I was nominated candidate for Chancellor, I had said that loyalty to the Alliance would be the guiding principle of our defence policy. Moreover, I added, we realized that armament and disarmament are two sides of the same coin: security is indivisible. I thought we should have to accustom ourselves to living with the balance of terror, and work out new political rules to fit the circumstances. The problem would be establishing the military status quo so as to allow freedom of movement, and surmounting it politically.

I said much the same in October 1969, in my first statement of Government policy as Federal Chancellor: 'Whichever of the two aspects of security policy we look at – whether our serious and determined attempt to limit and control arms simultaneously and in parity, or the provision of adequate defence for the Federal Republic of Germany – in both cases the Federal Government sees its security policy as a policy of equilibrium to ensure peace.' The Western Alliance, I said, was a defensive alliance, and our contribution was defensive too. With its allies, the Government would work consistently to decrease military confrontation in Europe. I was referring to the double reasons – readiness for defence and détente – which the Harmel Report had put to the Western Alliance at the end of 1967, and also to the projected Helsinki conference, of which we had great hopes while many others still felt unconstructively pessimistic about it.

The American monopoly of nuclear weapons lasted only a few years. Panting with eagerness, the Russians first pursued the Americans and then caught up with them in many areas. A situation of a new kind arose, and was not immediately understood in all quarters. People were inclined to sing the praises of the bomb. Had it not made an unusually long period of peace possible in our part of the world? Yet one must also ask whether the means of destruction piling up in ever-increasing quantities might not take on independent life of their own some day. And did not bringing nuclear arms down to a 'tactical' level mean the growing risk of miscalculation, with unimaginable consequences? American and Soviet scientists agreed in believing that by far the greater part of nuclear weapons on both sides could be eliminated without any danger to relative stability.

On the one hand, then, there were decades without war in Europe or between the nuclear World Powers. On the other, there were dangers that could hardly be comprehended: 'battlefield weapons' deployed in large numbers, mostly brought from those positions later; huge multiple-head rocket-launching systems, their numbers also hard to calculate; sea- and air-based weapons systems. My friends and I were already aware of the new risks, to which old rules no longer applied, when I expressed my thanks for the award of the Nobel Peace Prize in December 1971, in the great hall of Oslo University: 'Threatened as we are with the self-annihilation of mankind, coexistence has become a question of existence itself. Coexistence has become not one among several valid possibilities, but our only chance to survive.'

When the seventies were over, without catastrophe but also – despite *Ostpolitik*, Helsinki, and the setting of upper limits for intercontinental weapons of destruction – without any fundamental changes of principle in the East–West conflict, and with many 'small' wars being fought in the Third World, I argued more urgently: never before had the survival of humanity as a whole been in question. The world was in danger of arming itself to death. 'We are running faster and faster towards an abyss, or rather some are running and dragging all the rest along with them.'

I was very anxious, for détente threatened to evaporate as the seventies passed into the eighties. And yet the SALT treaty of May 1972, limiting strategic nuclear missiles, had been followed by various meetings which might have paved the way for peace. They included the agreement on consultations to help prevent an escalation of local conflicts made during Brezhnev's visit to the USA in June 1976. They also included the attempt to achieve 'mutual and balanced force reductions' at the MBFR negotiations in Vienna, conducted without guidelines predetermined by heads of government, although they never got further than a tedious and indeed boring diplomatic exercise with limited exchange of data. The arms race flourished. Soviet SS20 rockets were only a part of the entire picture, although a particularly alarming one for Western Europe. The Soviet Union felt disturbed by President Reagan's eulogy of the 'Star Wars' system, and the West itself was not fully convinced of its value.

Afghanistan and Poland brought a regression to the dark days of the Cold War, since critical views of the situation were not wanted.

I was ready to put up with criticism and sometimes suspicion for my unwillingness to take other people's mental short cuts. Instead, I tried to speak for moderation and willingness to negotiate, in many parts of the world – at the seat of the United Nations, at a hearing on Capitol Hill in Washington, at a conference of 'my' International in Finland in 1978 when representatives of the Soviet Union and America took part together for the first time, at a subsequent conference in Vienna in 1985 which also had Chinese and Indian delegates – the latter also representing the non-aligned countries. I supported the demand for a halt to nuclear tests, and other initiatives of the Four Continents group. The last document Palme signed was a peace proposal put forward by six heads of state and government. Such questions were discussed at the Socialist International by a disarmament committee chaired by the Finn Kalevi Sorsa. Like me, he had been Party Chairman, Foreign Minister and head of government before – unlike me – he became Parliamentary President. The well-informed and sober judgement of a Finn is no small consideration.

In September 1987 I was invited by the Swedish Institute for Peace Studies (SIPRI) to give the first of a series of lectures at the Riksdag in Stockholm in memory of Olof Palme. As chance would have it, a few days earlier the first real agreement on disarmament between the two nuclear World Powers had become a certainty: Ronald Reagan and Mikhail Gorbachev had agreed on the elimination of medium-range rockets. The significance of this step, I said as the first point in my lecture, could not be overestimated, even if only a small percentage of the nuclear potential for destruction was affected.

The Soviet Union had accumulated an enormous stockpile of conventional arms; its present acceptance of the principle of conventional stability on a lower level was something I described as great progress in the second part of my lecture. It opened up the prospect of successful negotiations in Vienna. However, it proved over-optimistic to expect simple subsequent negotiations on short-range missiles: nuclear weapons with a range of less than 500 kilometres.

Thirdly, I said that the concept of collective security, that great and reasonable proposition of the Palme Report, was being taken seriously in a manner that surmounted the blocs, even in conservative governmental circles. I mentioned Erich Honecker's recent visit to the Federal Republic. 'In 1970, when I made contact with the GDR, their authorities and I were always on common ground in saying that war should never start again from German soil. Now we are discussing what we can do together – and in our respective foreign policies – to secure peace in Europe and the world. Parties that were formerly at bitter odds now see, as a rule, that ideological struggle, or what goes by that title, can be civilized and must come second to the interests of peace.'

Fourthly, I indicated that the Geneva negotiations – in this case not between the nuclear World Powers, but in the broader-based committee acting on behalf of the United Nations since 1960 – had come close to a worldwide ban on chemical weapons. For reasons of only too obvious a nature, I emphasized that 'delaying complications' might set in, and for that very reason regional projects, such as the plan for a chemical weapons-free zone in Europe, must not be shelved. For the rest, those confidence-building measures concerning verification worked out and jointly recommended at the Stockholm Conference in 1986 might prove sensible and make military espionage unnecessary, in so far as spy satellites had not already done so.

Fifthly, logic suggested that a less tense relationship between the World Powers would help to defuse several of the so-called regional conflicts. 'I would certainly not advise us to pitch our expectations too high. But we should also recognize that a blasé and negative attitude has never got any project of importance off the ground.'

My experience, I said, had taught me that you make progress

faster when you do not ignore existing circumstances because you do not like them, but look at them and then try to improve them. Much can be changed, even in substance, under the political cloak of continuity. That had been tried and proved by ourselves in our time, with our *Ostpolitik*. Once the cold weather is over you no longer need your thick cloak. And the cold weather, I said, *was* over, even if the two alliances, NATO and the Warsaw Pact, remained essential factors of stability: essential for taking steps towards a firmly established peace in Europe, a peace which, so far as is humanly possible, could not be broken. There are very many ways of showing that account is increasingly being taken of this reality. Changing the map of Europe was not on the agenda, but that was not the case with the recognition of borders so that they ceased to be divisive and brought people together. The fulfilment of dreams from the past? No. But things that belong together can be brought together in this way.

Collective security for Europe through a structural incapacity to attack – history was presenting us with a great opportunity. Ideas that had seemed Utopian a few years ago had entered the sphere of reality: a distinct demilitarization of the East–West conflict, and substitution of peaceful competition and beneficial co-operation for military confrontation, principally but not solely in the spheres of the economy and the protection of the environment. A new chapter in the book of European history could be opened in this way.

There would still be differences, I said – if not of ideologies and systems, then of power. There would also be differences of taste, and of the ability of the occupants of rooms in the 'common European home' to furnish them. But conflicts arising from such factors were subordinate to the law of survival which included collective security. What a contribution Europe could make to the world! How greatly we would help ourselves, and what forces would be released for overcoming those great dangers that threaten humanity!

By the time Ronald Reagan handed over office to George

Bush in 1989, it was possible to check considerable achievements towards the slowing-down of the arms race off the list. Over and beyond controlled elimination of medium-range missiles, a 50 per cent reduction of 'strategic' nuclear weapons is being negotiated in Geneva. While attempts to achieve a world-wide ban on chemical weapons have come to a halt, the Vienna talks on conventional arms are making good progress. There is an agreement on the limitation and control of nuclear tests on the table again. A solution to savage conflicts in several parts of the world looks possible. The view that the great challenges of our time must be met on a world-wide scale is gaining ground.

Power and Mythology

I did not actively seek to become President of the international association of Social Democratic parties, membership of which extends far beyond Europe, but neither did I do anything to hinder my election to that office. I took it up in autumn 1976 with some pleasure and with the firm intention of overcoming the Eurocentrism of the organization traditionally known as the Socialist International. The mythology surrounding it has always been greater than its actual power. At my side I had not only those who had persuaded me to take the post, but others who were new to the organization. Léopold Senghor was accompanied by a colourful group of folk musicians from Senegal who came to thank the International for accepting their party. Carlos Andres Perez, President of Venezuela, came as a mark of his own interest and that of the Acción Democrática. Friends from the Middle East and South Africa let it be known that they hoped we would show increased commitment to their regions.

At our congress in Geneva, the seat of the International

Labour Organization, I described East–West and North–South relations and human rights as the main areas in which we should work. Concern for the environment as a supra-regional category was soon added. During these years my Finnish friend Kalevi Sorsa, an expert on Soviet affairs, led our deliberations in the field of arms control and disarmament. Michael Manley took on the economic sphere in 1983; when I had first met him twenty years earlier he was Opposition leader in Jamaica, and then became Prime Minister, an office he now holds again. The Swedes and the Austrians concentrated on questions of the environment and human rights. Certain regional committees seemed to have a special significance; this was frequently the case with the 'league' of parties within the European Community.

We never set out, in any committee, plenum or other group, to take majority decisions which would be binding on individual parties. All that a Social Democratic working community of independent national parties could and can do was to exchange notes and compare experiences, summarize opinions, and influence international and national decision-making. None of those involved has ever had a super-party in mind, certainly not a world executive. However, the value of the discussions away from the conference table which have become customary within the easy framework of the International cannot be overestimated or taken too seriously. They have helped to limit many conflicts; many new ideas have been proposed, much firm support promised and many new friendships formed. I am sure it is much the same in the international gatherings of conservative and liberal parties, which concede that the idea of an 'International' originated in the socialist organization and has a longer tradition than among them. The International may never have had sufficient influence in practical politics, but that is another matter.

The International of which I became President had been founded in Frankfurt in 1951. Initially, the parties of several countries where the Nazis had misused the name of Germany were doubtful about accepting Germans into the international community so soon. It was understandable that they should find it hard to distinguish between Social Democrats and other Germans. The old International – the Second, founded in Paris in 1889, as distinct from the First, set up by Karl Marx in 1864 – was revived when the Cold War was at its height. Consequently, several Social Democratic parties of Soviet-controlled Europe which had been suppressed or obliged to toe the line were not with us in Frankfurt.

As chance would have it, I had witnessed the revival of the Second International in May 1923, as a nine-year-old on an outing with a children's group of the Lübeck Labour Sports Club. The scene was the Hamburg trade union building in the Besenbinderhof; we children were allowed to put our noses round the door of its meeting-hall. I always imagined I had seen the Frenchman Léon Blum, the Dane Thorvald Stauning, the Swede Hjalmar Branting and the Belgian Émile Vandervelde, and was thus linked with the good old days of the European labour movement. Perhaps I had also set eyes on the German party theoreticians Kautsky and Bernstein, and the Austrian Friedrich Adler, whose opposition to war led him to shoot his country's prime minister, Sturgkh; he was pardoned at the end of the First World War, elected General Secretary in Hamburg, and held that post until 1940, when the Second International ceased to exist.

During my years of exile I had taken part in various international gatherings of a left-wing socialist nature in Paris and elsewhere, and during the war in Stockholm I had been part of the group which we rather grandly called the Little International. Although it worked almost under cover, word went round about it. One day a sympathizer on the staff of the Japanese Embassy in Berlin made his way to us and asked for asylum in a Stockholm hospital, but his country's secret service managed to lure him back to certain death. The intellectual influence of our discussion group in Stockholm continued far into the post-war period.

In the sixties – particularly after becoming chairman of my party – I attended several meetings of the International in London and Zürich, Brussels and Amsterdam, but I cannot honestly say I threw myself heart and soul into the movement. I was afraid that too much unrealistic speechifying would do the SPD no good. When I allowed myself to be elected a vice-president at a congress of the International in Stockholm in 1966, along with Guy Mollet, Harold Wilson and Tage Erlander, it was partly because I hoped to help channel its activities into a sensible course.

I recanted my views of the International in the years that followed, the years of German *Ostpolitik*: at its major meetings – at Eastbourne in 1968, Helsinki in 1971 and Vienna in 1972 – I encountered much understanding and even more support, not only of a rhetorical nature. The 1966 Congress also lives on in my memory: African delegations attended for the first time.

The Geneva congress at which I was elected had been preceded by a large Latin-American conference with European participants, held in Caracas in 1976. The end of 1977 saw a conference of party leaders in the Japanese capital, and the autumn of 1978 a congress in Vancouver, in western Canada. In the following years the International met in Tanzania and Botswana, Santo Domingo and Rio de Janeiro. In 1980 there was a particularly notable conference in Washington, organized by our American friends. Our disarmament committee also met in Washington, in Moscow and in Delhi. Before long the International had almost as many member parties in Latin America and the Caribbean as in Europe, although their stamina and inner cohesion still left much to be desired. More important was the fact that in more than one country we were able to contribute to the replacement of military dictatorships by democratically legitimated governments, although claims could not yet be made for their democratic stability – inevitably, in countries where democracy was neither economically nor socially assured. Where dictatorships prevailed, however, we could at least offer help and protection to persecuted democrats, as we did in Chile and Paraguay.

The Socialist International had a tradition of good contacts in North Africa; it was in the interests of Egypt and Tunisia in particular to extend these. We had difficulty in making contacts south of the Sahara, and had to direct our efforts at specific forms of co-operation appropriate to the regions concerned.

The Japanese Socialists, who chose their country's head of government after 1945, but were divided into at least two parties, had applied to join the International even before the First World War. Our other Asian ties were restricted to the Australian and New Zealand Labour Parties. Movements of a special nature had formed in India and Indonesia, the Philippines and Sri Lanka, Indo-China and Korea, Burma, Malaysia and Singapore, and finally in the new states of the Oceanic archipelagos. One of the great tasks facing the nineties lies in Asia.

Co-operation at party level has reinforced my belief that more weight must be given to the regional principle in the solution of international questions. The work of the United Nations was hampered by the Cold War. But the UN had always been a good place to exchange information, opinions and ideas, even against a background of international political tensions. And when the relationship between the world powers was eased, the UN gained a new profile. It would have been unthinkable for the Secretary-General to conduct operations to preserve peace with any prospect of success without getting the green light from Moscow and Washington.

The Socialist International and its representatives repeatedly tried to help make peace; in many areas its links went further than those of the UN – for instance in Cyprus and the Western Sahara, Eritrea and Kampuchea; it also received an appeal from Korea. People thought us more likely than anyone else to help in bridging great gulfs. But all of that pales into insignificance by comparison with those three areas of the world in which we invested our heart's blood and our prestige.

First, Central America. The countries between Mexico and the southern continent, and the nations of the Caribbean, kept us busy for years. It was no slight to other countries, and certainly not to the much-tried people of El Salvador, when we turned our special attention to Nicaragua after a conference in Lisbon in 1978, and had to face an unusual lack of understanding in North America. I made it quite clear that we did not by any means approve of everything done by the Sandinista commandos, but we firmly opposed the crushing, by repression, threats and violence, of the small country that had shaken off the yoke of Somoza's dictatorship. Why should Nicaragua not have a chance to determine its own future? To that end, we supported first the efforts of the so-called Contadora Group, and then the peace plan of the Social Democratic President of Costa Rica, Oscar Arias; I was present when he was awarded the Nobel Peace Prize in 1987.

I expressed my solidarity with the peoples of Central America on many occasions – for instance, on an emotional visit to Managua in the autumn of 1984. I spent hours with eight of the comandantes – the ninth was away – and assured myself of their determination to achieve national renewal and their almost Andalusian readiness to face death. Summing up the situation, I said: 'If those are all Marxist-Leninists, then I'm an ant-eater.' Attempts to exert a moderating influence on the Government of the USA were unsuccessful. While I was in the area, the Salvadorian Opposition also tried to have me attempt mediation. Talks were held, but the spirit of the times did not yet favour peace.

Fidel Castro wanted an extensive exchange of opinions, and sent a Cuban plane to bring me from Managua. The ageing revolutionary leader – his hair sparse now and his beard grizzled – was amiable and anxious to talk, and talk he did, for some seven hours. Now and then he asked if I would like coffee and I said that sounded a good idea, but nothing came of it. He talked and talked, drew breath and began again. He was proud of Cuba's record in education and health, and the development aid being given in many places by Cuban teachers and doctors. At the same time, he seemed to be aware that the times did not favour the export of his own revolutionary model. 'There will not be another Cuba.'

He obviously did not want to become over-involved in the chaos of Central America. Those countries must go their own way, he said. Even before Gorbachev, he realized that the Soviet Union's interests called for it to extract itself from expensive commitments in his part of the world rather than to incur more. I had already advised the Nicaraguan leaders not to forget what the map looked like; one of them told me a little later that *perestroika* did not bode well. The Cuban leader was reputed to like *glasnost* even less. In fact he was no longer under any illusions about the necessity of winding up his military commitment in Africa, although he justified it vigorously. Elsewhere too there was more going on than the general public could know. A high dignitary of the Church in Brazil had given me a message for Castro. The Americans had asked me to inquire into the fate of prisoners, and in my own baggage I had files on certain cases.

Castro's thinking was totally fixated on the USA. Without its repudiation, he would hardly have become what he was. Of the tens of thousands who attended the world baseball championship in the Cuban stadium, including Castro and me, the president of the international association, who came from America, received a more enthusiastic greeting than anyone else. Incidentally, it is pure invention for the sake of polemics that I ever drank to brotherhood with Castro.

The second crucial area was South Africa. I have visited many African states, one by one: first as Mayor of Berlin, and then as Foreign Minister and Federal Chancellor, and finally because of my international commitment. I met Haile Selassie in Addis Ababa and Jomo Kenyatta in Nairobi; I had met the latter at a conference in Paris at the end of the thirties, long before Kenya became an independent state. From Algeria to Nigeria, I saw the swift and usually radical ousting from power of leaders who had reached the top in their states during the struggle for decolonization. Among the exceptions were Julius Nyerere in Tanzania, Kenneth Kaunda in Zambia, and subsequently Robert Mugabe in Zimbabwe; I had particularly close contacts with all of them, and also with the presidents of Angola and Mozambique, because we supported the 'front-line states' in the struggle against apartheid in South Africa and for the independence of Namibia. Naturally we co-operated with the freedom movements of the African National Congress and SWAPO. The work of the International for southern Africa was co-ordinated by Olof Palme. He was succeeded by Joop den Uyl, and after den Uyl's death by Wim Kok of the Dutch Labour Party.

Effective measures were required to induce the Pretoria Government to abandon racial domination. I have long doubted whether economic sanctions were the right means. However, the urgent appeals of those who spoke for the majority of the South African population could not go unheeded; they were supported by 'white' South Africans, some from trade and industry. I visited Johannesburg and Cape Town in the spring of 1986 after a conference of the Socialist International in Gaborone, the capital of Botswana, where President Kaunda represented the front-line states.

I met white liberals and a large number of representatives of the black majority, including Winnie Mandela, many churchmen, and members of the fragmented but rapidly growing trade unions. The reforms that had been introduced seemed to me not inconsiderable, but those affected, and they were the people who mattered, thought they were too little and too late. Allan Boesak, the courageous Reformed Church minister, called apartheid an insult to human dignity, and said he could not negotiate over his human dignity. Before my visit, the South African Ambassador had suggested a conversation with President P. W. Botha. I did not reject the idea but I linked it to hopes of visiting Nelson Mandela in Pollmoor. By then, he had been behind bars for twenty-four years. I was to be given a decision in South Africa itself.

On 21 April 1986, at eleven in the morning, I met President Botha in Cape Town. My Bundestag colleague Günter Verheugen, who was with me, was amazed that I did not walk out after the extreme unpleasantness of the first ten minutes. But I was interested to see how much – in this case, how much Boer narrow-mindedness – could be crammed into an hour. Botha made such remarks as:

'What makes you think the blacks here are oppressed? You don't know the facts, and you've been talking to the wrong black representatives. What you say amounts to interference in South African affairs ...

'I believe you're a socialist. Well, look at socialism in the black African states. They export a lot of their products via South Africa, and they send us quite a few of their workers ...

'The idea of a white minority and a black majority does not correspond to the facts. Hostile foreign agitators call apartheid racism, and it's partly your fault we get unfair treatment. But you just remember this: we have survived 300 years of persecution, and we shall survive another 300 ...

'I have to refuse your request to meet the dangerous Communist terrorist Nelson Mandela. The man was legally found guilty at the time; he can't keep having foreign visitors now. Yes, I'm ready to release him and lift the ban on the ANC if he will renounce violence. As long as they refuse to do that I shall strike at the criminals again and again ...

'As for the rest of it, it is wrong to say I don't want to talk to the blacks. Our co-operation with the black homelands shows that. Why won't the West see it? After all, Luxembourg is regarded as a sovereign state ...

'There is trouble in Namibia only because the Soviet Union and East Germany want to extend their sphere of influence in Africa.'

It was an hour full of coldness, intransigence and self-righteousness. With the best will in the world, there was nothing to be done about it. I found evidence confirming Palme's belief that apartheid cannot really be reformed, but must be removed.

The third vital area was the Middle East. Hardly any other subject during my time with the International concerned its committees so often and gave them so much trouble as the tense relationship between Israel and its Arab neighbours. We felt strong sympathy because of the part Israeli Social Democracy traditionally played in our association, and out of a sense of co-responsibility for those European Jews who had escaped annihilation and were now devoting themselves to building up a national home. In the middle of the seventies the Austrian Federal Chancellor Bruno Kreisky headed three missions in an attempt to gather information on the spot which might help to determine ways of establishing stability and a lasting peace, not evading the issue of the future relationship between Israelis and Palestinians. The chairmanship of a Middle East committee was entrusted, at the suggestion of Mario Soares of Portugal, to the resourceful Hans-Jürgen Wischnewski, who also did sterling work in the search for peace in Central America.

Great tensions lay between vision and reality. I became acutely aware of that in the spring of 1978 when, at Kreisky's invitation, I was present at a long discussion between President Sadat and Shimon Peres, leader of the Israeli Labour Party, then in opposition. We envisaged a region where warlike forces would be put to productive ends, and desert lands turned into fertile gardens. A year later, in July 1979, Kreisky invited the PLO Chairman Yasser Arafat to Vienna and asked me to attend the meeting. We had the impression that even then he was ready to negotiate peace, a peace to include the secure existence of the State of Israel. We attracted a good deal of criticism for holding such a meeting at all, and not only from our friends in Tel Aviv and Jerusalem. But here again, experience was to show that, as a rule, it is a bad idea to put off unsolved problems for too long.

In autumn 1963 President Nasser of Egypt, about whom I usually had reservations, told me he would like to meet the officer, now a diplomat, whom he faced in the war in 1948. I passed the message on to Israel, but there was no response. Lack of Israeli reaction, with the questionable aim of gaining time, could be laid at the door of that amiable grandmotherly woman who had succeeded the prophet-like figure of Ben Gurion at the head of Israel. She also led the Labour Party, the main political power in the young state.

After all her people had suffered, Golda Meir, the 'iron grandmother', distrusted well-meant advice. Who could know her neighbours better than she did? Who could convince Mrs Meir, who had been Ambassador in Moscow, that the Soviet Union as well as the United States could play a part in achieving a Middle East settlement? Who could tell her that gaining time was not worth while? She had colleagues such as the Foreign Minister, Abba Eban, whose thinking was less simplistic but who had little say or who, like Nahum Goldmann, President of the World Council of Jews, were on the periphery of events. In the last years of his life he tried to enlist the aid of Pierre Mendès-France, the former French head of government, of Jewish origin, and myself in a dialogue between Israeli and Palestinian intellectuals. Nothing came of the attempt.

In May 1971, when the party leaders of the Socialist International met in Helsinki, Golda Meir asked me the rather baffling question, 'What has this got to do with the Six?' She meant the decision of the EEC, still limited to its six founding members, to enter into a European–Arab dialogue; Washington was officially against it too, for reasons different from those of the Israelis. The Israeli Prime Minister, half defiant, half resigned, commented: 'Israel has no friends left, but if necessary it will fight to the last man.' A year later, in Vienna, she was in a considerably milder mood. And in June 1973 she showed her appreciation of the fact that I was the first officiating Federal German Chancellor to visit her country. (Adenauer had been to Israel when he was no longer in office; my first visit to the country had been in the autumn of 1960 as President of the German City Assemblies.) She paid tribute to my attitude 'in the darkest hour of mankind', and said at a dinner that I gave in the King David Hotel: 'We are ready to compromise on anything and everything, with the sole exception of our existence and our right to live in this country and in this region of the world.'

I felt then as if Golda Meir and I were very close to each other, and emotionally we certainly were. But we were some way apart in our assessment of the situation and its dangers. In her office, a few months before the new military confrontation which was to become known as the Yom Kippur War, she said: 'The Palestinians' opportunities for action are getting less, and the refugee question is gradually losing importance.' She was not pleased when I pointed out – a recent conversation with Nixon still ringing in my ears – the uncertainty of the factors of time, money and oil. But it was easy to see that neither of the World Powers had any interest in getting drawn into a major conflict over the Middle East; the Suez crisis of 1956 had shown that. And there was no disregarding the fact that the Islamic Arab oil-producing countries had decided to use oil as a means of exerting pressure. Golda Meir, who also had reasons of her own for regarding our *Ostpolitik* with scepticism, finally said: 'Israel's problem is that in the end it always stands alone.'

After the Yom Kippur War she telephoned me asking for a discussion between socialist party leaders; it took place in London in mid-November and I asked Harold Wilson to preside over it. Golda was deeply discouraged; later, she claimed that one of her colleagues said oil had been found in the throats of the European Social Democrats. She spared me further reproaches, although the Middle East conflict had brought me into sharp conflict with the Americans. She knew that the West German government was helpful where it could be helpful without damaging its own interests. She will also have understood that, like Adenauer in 1956, I could not accept American attempts to make use of our territory as if it belonged to the United States.

At our Vienna meeting with Arafat I had met Issam Sartawi, an American-trained doctor and a brilliant intellectual, who had turned from a terrorist into a fanatical proponent of entente during his exile in Palestine. I met him a few times; French and Israeli friends of mine saw him more often. Some of his own people regarded him as a traitor. In 1983, he was shot in Albufeira in Portugal by one such blinkered extremist – in the lobby of the hotel where I was holding the final meeting of the International's congress. I had seen Sartawi only the evening before at a reception and joked with him about better days. I was deeply affected as I stood beside his body.

I fear that the aberrations of ideological and political fundamentalism will continue to give humanity a great deal of difficulty. Giving in to the acts of violence that they engender can only do long-term harm to the dignified coexistence of human beings. Survival and development demand more civilized forms of argument. Religious communities fail in their service to humanity when they condone murder and homicide. The International I represented was and is at one with its conservative and liberal counterparts in fighting for human rights and the total rejection of terrorism.

Building Plans

Open Doors

I have lost count of the times I have felt irritated by the inadequacies of the European Community, ranging from the awkward to the infuriating, but I know very well that I have never let myself be moved from the central idea of union. Now, as we move into the nineties, the Community is on the brink of a qualitative leap forward. The end of 1992 will usher in the single market for the twelve member states with their 320 million inhabitants, and monetary union, twenty years delayed, will begin to take shape. In spite of all the squabbling there will have to be correlation of the laws on taxation and social welfare. Will the European Union, going far beyond the co-ordination of foreign policy, crown the single market? Will it take precedence over the new membership negotiations planned for the years after 1992? Will a common framework be found for the organization of Western Europe's security? At the same time, will major elements combine into an all-European peaceful order that promises more success than earlier efforts? It is almost four decades since the attempt to found a European Defence Community failed.

The little book I wrote in exile during the winter of 1939–40, which fell victim, with much of more importance, to the occupation of Norway, bore the title *The War Aims of the Great Powers and the New Europe*. I did not have to find my way around Europe again after the war. But in what conditions would European policy be shaped in the post-war period? It turned out to have little in common with the ideas I had put together at my desk in exile. There was one exception: early realization that the future relationship between Germany and France would play a key part arose from neither clairvoyance nor wishful thinking.

One of my early fundamental views was that Europe, whatever area one understood the term to cover, could flourish only if Germany and France looked to the future in their dealings with each other. A fine tradition, rooted not least in German Social Democracy, had set me quite early along the path of reconciliation and friendship between the two countries; a call for a 'United States of Europe' featured on the agenda at a Heidelberg Party congress in 1925. To accuse the SPD of anti-Europeanism was always unjust. However, it must be admitted that in the early days of the Federal Republic justifiable efforts in the all-German interest did not always chime with pro-European endeavours.

At the beginning of the Second World War I did not regard either England (as we called the United Kingdom) or Russia (as we said when we meant the Soviet Union) as part of that Europe which Charles de Gaulle described as extending 'from the Atlantic to the Urals'. However, I had always counted the states west of the Soviet Union as part of it. Few guessed that they would come under Soviet domination at the end of the war. But then, no one could have predicted that in the mid-eighties a Soviet leader would proclaim as clearly as did Gorbachev that Russia was a part of the 'common European home'.

So far as the UK was concerned, I found myself in agreement with leading British politicians who saw their country's future role as a very special one. In his famous Zürich speech of September 1946, Winston Churchill argued vigorously for the union of the continent, but he did not see the United Kingdom as part of it. Instead, he thought that Britain, the British Commonwealth, the mighty state of America and, he hoped, the

Soviet Union too, would all be good friends to the new Europe. It was not widely foreseen in London and elsewhere that France would forge close economic bonds with its German neighbour the very year after the foundation of the Federal Republic, beginning with the coal and steel industries.

Understandably, in view of their past history, it was hard for the British to bid farewell to their all-powerful role in the world and accustom themselves to the idea of partnership within Europe. The idea of transferring national sovereignty to joint institutions was bound to seem even stranger to them than to others. The English Channel, in the British mind, marked more of a barrier than the Atlantic that had to be crossed to reach America. So open-minded a man as my friend Hugh Gaitskell, the Labour leader who died before his time, seriously greeted me even in 1962 as 'our friend from overseas'. The fact that the gulf could be bridged only slowly and with difficulty was a disadvantage to both sides. The British themselves paid a high price, delaying the modernization of their national economy for years.

Even in retrospect, however, it cannot be forgotten how firmly the French leadership intended to keep Britain at a distance; Paris wanted no challenge from London to its claim for leadership. And the General in the Élysée Palace was himself extremely suspicious of supra-national institutions. He foresaw systems and societies without any native land, failing to realize that at the time of his visit to Germany in 1962 the political leadership of Western Europe was there for the taking, and he could have had it. Was it a North German and Scandinavian feeling of reserve towards the French that made me a strong and early supporter of British participation in the process of Western European union? Certainly; but I also retained a lively sense of what 'the English' had done and suffered when the lights went out all over the Continent. My conviction, as I said at a reception given for me by Prime Minister Harold Wilson, was that we needed the creativity and wide experience of Great Britain, 'as an important part of that

European inheritance which still has much to give the world'.

De Gaulle frequently said, to me and to others, that it was ridiculous to deny the real existence of European nations; I had no objection to his idea of a 'Europe of fatherlands'. He thought it possible that in time a development towards a confederation might emerge – a federation of states, not a federal state. The original EEC should not be a defensive citadel: Britain, the Scandinavian states, Spain might well join. Couve de Murville, a Foreign Minister who was very conscious of tradition, let it be known in 1963 that the flat veto to British entry was not the result of his recommendation. He was conciliatory, but above all he was his President's man.

In my own time as Foreign Minister my non-French colleagues felt considerable impatience with Paris. The tall Dutchman Joseph Luns, later Secretary-General of NATO, was in favour of the Community and its extension, and so were his colleagues from Belgium and Luxembourg: their principles and their interests advised it. In Italy ministers changed more rapidly than elsewhere, but Italian goodwill was clear and constant, and the higher civil servants made sure that it was reflected on the record. I did not feel particularly happy to find the five of us meeting in semi-secret conclave now and again, but how else could we have agreed on any kind of sensible reaction to the gesture of an empty chair or a bombastic veto?

In the circumstances, the rump Community could not take great leaps forward. It continued running on the spot. The over-optimistic expectations of those who hoped for a quick, even an automatic transition from economic to political integration were bound to be disappointed in any case. When I represented the Federal Republic for the first time at the Council of Ministers in Brussels, I tried to move on from tariff and agricultural union to genuine economic union. This was in April 1967, a quarter of a century before the day, 1 January 1993, when the single market is to come into being. I urged that the authorities of the Coal and Steel Union, Euratom and the EEC be brought together to form the European Community. It got the blessing of a summit conference in Rome at the end of May 1967.

However, British entry still remained in the balance. Harold Wilson, Prime Minister since the end of 1964, and his eccentric Foreign Minister George Brown had been on a round trip to rally support, and came away under the misapprehension that a strong word from Germany was all that was needed to bring the General to his senses. He ignored further persuasions and my support for favourable study of applications to join from Ireland, Denmark and Norway, with a 'special memorandum' from the Swedish Government. These documents were handed over to the Brussels Commission without protest from the French. But before there could be any discussion of the Commission's report, de Gaulle had anticipated the outcome at a press conference: Paris would not agree.

The British were not especially adroit. When I met George Brown – as intelligent as he was mercurial – in the country, he told me, 'Willy, you must get us in, so we can take the lead.' This, to put it mildly, was a misunderstanding, since we wanted to observe the rules and not have one claim to leadership replaced by another. However, it was only another two years before Georges Pompidou and I came to agreement about the extension of the Community. This was by no means the end of difficulties with Britain. Further negotiations had to take place, first with the reasonable James Callaghan, then with the contentious Mrs Thatcher. It was impossible to keep to any timetable for extending the EC, and that was not solely the newcomers' fault. The miracle, if one likes to call it that, was that the Community survived all its crises. The 1974 crisis was particularly serious.

A less than accurate biographer claimed that I 'wrested' agreement to British membership of the European Community from President Pompidou at the end of 1969. There was no question of 'wresting' anything. The Frenchman had his own reasons for opening the door to the British. I spared him the trouble of naming these reasons at the summit conference in the Ridderzaal in The Hague at the beginning of December

1969: 'Anyone who fears that the economic weight of the Federal Republic of Germany could work against equilibrium within the Community should support its extension for that very reason, as well as others.'

Pompidou and I had clarified matters beforehand, in correspondence and with the help of able colleagues. On the evening of the first day of the conference, after the dinner to which the Queen of the Netherlands had invited us, the two of us got together to cross the 't's and dot the 'i's. The President wanted assurance that the extension would not impair the special Franco-German relationship of co-operation. I could give it with a clear conscience, since it corresponded to my own convictions. He wanted additional assurance that agricultural funding would be assured. I knew how important that aspect was for home policies in France, and that it had been a basic business principle between Adenauer and de Gaulle. I confirmed that money would continue to flow into the EC; I did not forget that our own farmers must have their livelihoods protected, but insisted that the regulations governing the agricultural market should be revised and the expenditure entailed by surpluses drastically reduced. But this reservation was unable even to act as a brake on the unfortunate developments of the following years.

In The Hague we agreed that we should not stop at tariff union. The organs of the Community – the Council of Ministers and the Commission – were requested to produce a graduated plan by the end of 1970 (!) for the extension of economic and currency union. In January 1971 (!) in Paris, at one of the regular Franco-German talks, Pompidou and I achieved basic understanding that the national banks should become a kind of European Central Bank – in about a decade ...

One man who was not discouraged by any setbacks, but kept working, more behind the scenes than on the platform, on ideas for furthering the European cause was Jean Monnet. A quintessential Frenchman – he came from a medium-sized cognac dynasty, but was very familiar with the Anglo-Saxon world – he had drafted the Schuman Plan, and became the first President of the Coal and Steel Union himself in 1952. He had been head of the planning authority under de Gaulle after the war, but the two men did not see eye to eye. The President very unjustly accused Monnet of lacking patriotism. I am glad to say that justice was done, at least later, to that fine man (he had taken part in co-ordinating the economic exertions of the Allies, and between the wars he had been Secretary-General of the League of Nations). Mitterrand ensured him a tomb in the Panthéon. I think, not without sadness, of occasions in Paris when I had to meet him under the seal of secrecy, so as not to give offence in the Élysée Palace.

Monnet was full of ideas. But he did not shrink from making much the same admonitory speech again and again; in this respect I sometimes compared him to Golda Meir. His ideas related to procedure as well as content: 'to re-arrange the scene' was one of his not infrequent metaphors drawn from the theatre. The same scenery, differently arranged, can indeed present a new picture. When he first visited me in Berlin we did not immediately think along the same lines. He thought it was too soon for British entry, and he knew little about the Scandinavians. On the other hand we quickly agreed that sooner or later the question of proper relations with the Eastern European states would arise. He recruited me for his 'Action Committee' – for a United States of Europe – which consisted of leading representatives of parties and unions; on the German side Herbert Wehner and the metal-workers' leader Otto Brenner played a particularly active part. Monnet and his committee offered many new ideas when the work for union threatened to flag or become confused.

One initiative aimed to give the Community a political leadership consisting of a committee of heads of government, and to curb the influence of the feuding ministerial bureaucracies. I did what I could to bring about a 'presidential meeting' in Copenhagen in December 1973; it subsequently acquired the name of the European Council. It does not diminish the role of the Brussels Commission, and it somewhat increases the importance of the European Parliament, at the least. However, the democratic anchorage and control of the work of the Community is still underdeveloped and largely unsatisfactory.

It would have been advisable, not just from the viewpoint of so well-informed an adviser as Jean Monnet, to tackle tasks in the early sixties which at last seemed to be coming to the fore at the end of the eighties: the introduction of economic and monetary union. The co-operation of Georges Pompidou and Edward Heath, who became head of the British Government in June 1970 and remained in office until 1974, should have provided the opportunity for a decisive breakthrough. But circumstances did not permit. I myself found how even a Chancellor can be kept in check by powerful departments – which does not, however, keep the ministers of those departments (and their capable state secretaries) from claiming credit later for achievements they prevented at an earlier date.

At the summit in The Hague I had made an important offer: the Federal German Government, which had not been backward in its support for solidarity in financial policy, was ready to co-operate fully in creating a European reserve fund. As soon as the necessary preconditions existed, we would help to set up such an instrument of a common policy and determine its procedures. We would then be ready to transfer a part of our own reserves to the European fund – 'to be administered jointly with the proportionate reserves deposited there by our partners'. It was no surprise to any of those partners that we intended to link this with a policy for the avoidance of inflationary risks.

At the Paris summit of October 1972 – as well as Heath, the Prime Ministers of Denmark and Ireland were attending for the first time – I had to back down over the monetary fund: the Federal Republic could not envisage a transfer of national reserves in the immediate future. The Finance Ministry and the Bundesbank had exerted a strong braking influence, obliging me to enter much less wholeheartedly that I thought we should into the development policy of the Community and the provisioning of the regional fund. Social welfare was also on the agenda in Paris, again at the German suggestion; others thought it should wait until much later. At the time I tabled a memorandum on European social union: it must be made clear to people, I said, what the Community meant and could mean in their work and their daily life. Social progress was not to be seen as a mere appendage of economic growth. 'If we develop a European perspective on social policy, many of the citizens of our states will find it easier to identify with the Community.'

However, the monetary question kept ousting all other subjects; it also dominated my correspondence with Pompidou. The French were more outspoken about the inconsistencies of American financial and monetary policy than we thought advisable or appropriate; I was not too bothered that the generally more flourishing state of German agriculture sometimes incurred their envy. In the spring of 1973 a British initiative had brought us very close to a point from which the breakthrough to monetary union might have succeeded. Heath visited Bonn, concerned, as we were ourselves, by a strong influx of dollars caused by speculation. Would we be able to secure long-term joint action? My answer was that we were ready for it ourselves, and would pay a high price for a European solution that must begin with a joint floating operation. Hours of discussion followed, with a few experts and between the experts themselves. It turned out that the ifs and buts of the experts weighed heavier in the balance than the political will of the British. I could not help getting the impression that a weight fell from the minds of our financiers, including the Bundesbank. However, they would have been ready to go a considerable way along a new path, and in matters of amount, interest and duration would have made possible a supporting action of hitherto unknown extent; reserves would have had to be found, and an understanding on the parity of the British pound reached. But the attempt failed. When Pompidou visited Bonn in June 1973 we could only agree that the crisis of dollar, pound and lira blocked the road to economic and monetary union for the time being.

Progress towards a common system – beginning with a 'currency snake' in which England and Italy did not participate and from which France too would depart now and then – remained a remarkably laborious business. Yet there was no mistaking its positive effects, particularly in greater stability of prices. My successor as Chancellor, Helmut Schmidt, did especially well in this area of European union, even after he was out of government office. I also agreed with him that if not all the member nations were expected to proceed with integration at the same rate in certain areas and over a certain time, it would not weaken the Community itself.

The spatial extension of the Community is on the agenda again now. When it was first extended I felt strongly committed to the project and had nothing to regret, with one exception: as Federal Chancellor I attended a meeting in Oslo before the referendum on Norwegian entry. On the evening of that meeting, sitting in the government guest-house, I was surprised to hear what a friend who had just come back from the more northern parts of the country had to say. There was a good deal of emotional reluctance to join. The temperance lobby had asked if they would be obliged to drink wine in the Common Market. Would the Pope want to undermine the Lutheran Church? Would the local girls be handed over to dark-haired southerners? After all, it was not so very long since the Norwegians had had the Gestapo in their country. What it amounted to was: would a small nation be able to retain its individuality or be swamped by a large supra-national association? I should add that the E C authorities were not particularly tactful in their negotiations with the Norwegians. Who was there in Brussels who knew about the traditions of the Norwegian fisheries, or farming conditions in the Arctic Circle? Except in Oslo, the majority of Norwegians voted against entry.

The Danish referendum came out in favour of joining, but a considerable part of the population continued to feel wary of the E C. Official Danish policy also showed some reservations about the activities and aims of the Community beyond the economic area. Last but not least, the British wanted to keep the co-ordination of foreign policy on inter-state and not Community level. None the less, work towards European political co-operation went well. The foreign ministries soon changed gear, and in the case of France and Germany regularly exchanged officials. Where the United Nations, the Helsinki agreements and crises anywhere in the world were concerned, the EC states conferred on a common stance. In 1973 it might have been possible to set up a permanent political secretariat if agreement could have been reached about its siting. The French insisted on Paris; most of the other states wanted Brussels.

The United States, which favoured European union in principle, found it difficult to accept joint European attitudes when they deviated from the Americans' own stance. In the time of Nixon and Kissinger it was said, inaccurately, that American interests were global and European interests were regional. We said, on the contrary, that we had no intention of renouncing our say in international politics. Bonn and Paris often differed in their reaction to Washington's expectations: we felt indebted to the Americans and knew how important the USA would be in the future structure of the East–West relationship. The French did not care to be reminded that they too had needed American aid. Even so level-headed a man as President Pompidou always jibbed if he felt the Americans wanted to be co-rulers of Europe or make claims as its guardians. He was particularly outspoken when he thought Europe was expected 'to finance the military, political and economic activities of the Americans out of its own deficit'; even my request for 'organic dialogue' with the United States was going too far for Paris. Edward Heath and I managed to prevent ourselves being played off against Paris, and we promptly received embittered letters from the White House – rather more reproachfully phrased to me than to my British colleague.

Subsequently, as the Community overcame one expansion

crisis after another, American attention turned to its own economic interests, concerned lest they should be restricted by Western European protectionism. This was a legitimate anxiety, although as usual in such cases a double standard was sometimes applied. When the planning of the single European market finally came up, the Americans became over-agitated about the dangers of a 'European citadel'. I tried to point out to friends on the American side of the Atlantic that world trade of as free a nature as possible was in our own interests, and I thought that was particularly obvious from the viewpoint of the export-orientated German economy. I also pointed out that many American firms had done very well in Community countries. In recent decades multinational companies have developed their own structures, which cannot be compared with the former economic links usual between nations. However, that side of the coin has only just begun to impress itself on the consciousness of active politicians.

In the eighties there was more and more speculation as to how far the EC might eventually extend; extension to the south had not only gone better than the sceptics expected, but turned out to be a genuine success story. Spain, and with a certain time-lag Portugal too, saw an impressive economic revival. Serious side-effects, particularly in social adaptation, were inevitable, and are not peculiar to membership of the EC. Greece gained clear advantages from membership but did not make adequate use of them. As I could see for myself on the spot after the fall of the military dictatorship, the country had primarily wanted membership to help secure the new democracy.

Turkey wanted its associate membership of the Community to become full membership. But the consequences for Turks of freedom of movement between countries were incalculable, and common sense advised postponing the decision. The island states of Malta and Cyprus became associate members of the Community, along with several littoral Mediterranean states including Israel. It seems logical to extend this co-operation with the Mediterranean region, and the matter should and will have a prominent place on the Community agenda.

Brussels has worked out a system making a certain stabilization of export earnings possible for the countries of the ACP group – the African, Caribbean and Pacific areas once dependent on the European colonial powers; they number over fifty states. Not all the expectations of these partners could be fulfilled, by a long way, but it was still possible to emphasize a policy of developmental co-operation going beyond that particular group of countries. There have also been regional initiatives towards the ASEAN states and the countries of Central America, in line with Western interests even when, or particularly when, Washington saw things otherwise.

The question remains: what about the other countries of EFTA, the European Free Trade Association? Austria applied for membership of the EC in the early summer of 1989, but on condition that its neutrality should not be affected. Sweden let it be known that it would like to have close economic links with the Common Market but did not want its freedom of alliance impaired in any way. The same goes for Finland. Iceland, which is part of NATO, is a special case. And Norway? It looks as if the previous 'No' is no longer valid, and that the Norwegians are now seeking a way to smooth their entry into the European Community. There are no obstacles that could arise from its status; Norway has been a member of NATO from the start.

During the eighties the EC made outline agreements of great potential with the Comecon group and its individual member states. But I do not feel able to answer the question of whether the EC will eventually become a structure covering the whole of Europe. Everything suggests that the closeness of relationships with the Community will vary, although despite differences there will be a trend towards a much higher degree of European common ground that would have been thought possible even in the early eighties.

Changing the Wallpaper

A change of consciousness, experienced particularly by the intellectually active social strata and extending to the higher ranks of the ruling parties, had begun in 'Eastern Europe' long before Gorbachev. Statements and initiatives from Moscow gave erratic impetus to the change taking place in the countries that lie between Germany and Russia, though not at the same time in all of them. The effects were felt even where people disliked the turbulence of *perestroika* or inquired, like the Politburo ideologist Hager in East Berlin, whether one had to change one's own wallpaper if one's big neighbour thought that was the thing to do. A very complex process was in train. The urge towards democratic decision-making, a more diverse society and the profit motive had found many outlets for self-expression even before ideas of renewal manifested themselves in the Soviet Union. There had been talk of more independence and new forms of equitable co-operation before the leaders in Moscow began drawing up new European building plans.

There was a good deal of rubble to be cleared away from the road towards a new clarification of ideas, and there still is. For instance, after it became permissible to say what the Hungarian rebellion of October 1956 was and was not – i.e., a popular rising and not a counter-revolution – the victims of particularly atrocious judicial murders had to be rehabilitated, at least on paper. But if Fascist monsters had *not* been at work in Budapest, leading the people astray, why should the mass demonstrations of June 1953 in East Berlin not be seen for what they really were? They began as protests by the workforce against the pressure of high norms and wretched living conditions. Then, as the demands of the protesters grew hourly, and the demonstrations affected a great many cities and industrial districts, they became a demand for self-determination in general and free elections in particular. Until the tanks rolled in.

The chapter of German and German–Soviet post-war history that deals with June 1953 awaits correction. However, the leadership of the Socialist Unity Party did not have to annul show trials, leading to work for the executioner, of dissidents from among their own ranks. Whatever else may be thought of him, Ulbricht did not go along with that particular expectation of the Soviet apparatus, nor follow the examples of the Balkans, Prague and Budapest. Now and then it even occurred to him, as a German Communist who had to follow every Soviet move, to cite the special situation of Germany. And he did not fail to point out that the leading cadres of the Communist Party in Germany, the KPD, had been decimated not only by Hitler's persecution but also by the Stalinist purges.

From the first – for historical reasons, and as a result of the broad interests of the dominant power and the divergent interests of the parties and state machinery involved – there were considerable differences between the countries on the borders of the Soviet Union. In many quarters the dominant role of the Soviet occupying and/or controlling power gave a false impression, and for years the somewhat pompous utterances of the Warsaw Pact countries were taken more seriously than they should have been, considering how they came into being. In Comecon, the Council for Common Economic Aid, the risk of overestimation was smaller.

It was not easy for me and my generation to equate the Warsaw Pact area with the concept of 'Eastern Europe'. At school we would have been more likely to apply the term to the Balkans. After the division of the continent, however, it soon became natural to call the entire region between the Baltic and the Adriatic Eastern Europe. Americans and others who saw things in a simple light did not find it difficult to regard Weimar and Dresden, Prague and Bratislava, and centres of European culture lying rather closer to Russia as all part of 'the East'. No wonder that Central Europe, believed to have vanished, has finally taken on new contours, although so far they are not as firmly drawn everywhere as they should be.

I spent a few days in Prague in the summer of 1947 and was surprised by the active, almost frenetic interest taken by the Czechs in their own post-war state. Six months later that bustling atmosphere was gone, and the solid uniformity imposed on the country by the *coup d'état* prevailed. It was not enough for the Communists to be the strongest party; they wanted no one else at all to have a say. The people did not even benefit from having let themselves be recruited into getting the Sudeten German part of the population expelled. In Poland, Hungary and the Balkans too, the sufferings of one part of the population interlocked with those of another: it was like running a film backwards. The Communists of those countries had suffered with their nations, distinguishing themselves by their readiness to make sacrifices; thereafter, they made themselves lords over life and death, persecuting people whose co-operation they had only recently been enlisting. Deranged witch-hunts began in their own ranks. But the defeats of nations, with all their intellectual and moral ravages, are not the whole story of their fate.

The nations found themselves again. Changes in the East of Europe went deep, yet they could not be perceived all at once, nor always clearly enough. The cultural and religious heritage, never entirely buried, resurfaced and was soon outstripping all other factors. The new-found national sense of self-worth was all the more impressive when it seemed to derive from the insecurity and helplessness of the Eastern superpower. The Soviet Union, it was generally felt, had bitten off considerably more than it could chew on its western borders. The attractions of Western life, although overestimated, came into it too. Furthermore, an awareness of links with the people of Western Europe had revived in the nations that lie between Germany and Russia even before the race to claim membership of the 'common European home' began.

In Berlin I felt, and at the time of *Ostpolitik* I hoped, that progress would be made in the Europeanization of Europe – particularly in the hearts and minds of many of the people in 'the East'. In the seventies it became a major theme, and not for me alone, to wonder how a part of that Europeanization could be realized in the foreseeable future. Whenever someone asked me to explain the other part of Europe, I spoke of the difference between a flat map and a relief map. In the years after 1945 you could have drawn a map in two colours, tracing in border changes here and there, and the political uniformity would not have justified any variety of colour. The changes visibly taking place in recent years could no longer be shown appropriately on a flat map in two colours; they called for a relief map with heights and depths to give an impression of living history.

Nineteen-eighty-five was the year that Gorbachev took office as General Secretary; later he became President as well. With him, people who had grown up some time after the October Revolution moved into positions of power. Although there was no direct connection with the change of leadership in the Kremlin, a change of personnel simply on grounds of age was occurring in most of the Eastern bloc states, although not in Poland. My impression was that the new man in Moscow would rather play for time than rush to make the acquaintance in a hurry of a whole series of new faces. I concluded that the old leaders would stay in power longer than they themselves had expected. Gorbachev had more at stake than the comparative age or youth of the faces surrounding him. He wanted to ease his military and financial situation in relation to the Warsaw Pact system and to certain expensive commitments in other parts of the world; political strategy and the overall accounting of the economy complemented one another.

In East Berlin – where I was welcomed with perfect courtesy in 1985 – it would not have been fitting to ask Erich Honecker about his successor. But of course it was no secret to him that there was talk, if in undertones, at the highest levels in the GDR about likely people to replace the Saarlander who became General Secretary of the SED; those names are never mentioned in discussion now. It was taken for granted that Honecker would stay on as Chairman of the Council of State, and not just for form's sake. But the question of the head of state was not the only one in the GDR. The leading cadres as a whole were superannuated; the formative experiences of all their members lay between the wars and in the struggle for survival before 1945. What do you do in that kind of 'predicament'? You make noises about a coming party conference which can be postponed or brought forward as required.

When Honecker paid his long-delayed visit to the Federal Republic in 1987 he was celebrating a small triumph over the Russians who had repeatedly prevented him from going to the Rhine. And he found confirmation of the belief he had expressed in the early eighties, that deteriorating relations between the World Powers need not necessarily affect the relationship between the two German states. His attitude to Gorbachev was one of cool friendliness, without any subservience. Honecker had already had dealings with other Kremlin leaders, and he had access to Moscow headquarters through channels of information not limited to the General Secretariat if he wished to use them. Well knowing that I had just seen the unpopular anti-alcohol campaign in progress in the Soviet capital, he asked, 'I suppose we shall carry on in the *German* way?' My rather light-hearted answer was not intended to produce vodka before lunch – 'breakfast' in the protocolary sense – although that was what happened; there was a double meaning involved, in that a West German product named after the Soviet General Secretary had been obtained.

In Budapest, Janos Kadar felt vindicated by the changes 'in Russia', but saw no need to prolong his personal commitment because of them. He had grown tired, and was content to have succeeded, under very difficult circumstances, in preventing a worse fate for his people after 1956. His wish to retire was not granted, and here the advice of 'Soviet friends' must surely have been at work. The circumstances in which he handed over his remaining functions in the spring of 1989, a few months before his death, seemed to me neither fitting nor dignified. I said so in terms that would be understood in the new Budapest.

Kadar was the Eastern bloc leader to whom I felt closest, outside routine matters. He and his supporters in a leadership not yet deformed by rigidity helped us with indications of policy direction when it was not easy to come by such things. However, they did not overlook their own, Hungarian advantage. Kadar let people travel and talk; at one period he was the one party leader in the bloc who could have offered himself for free election. He longed for Europe to come together again, and for the day when the divisions in the labour movement would be overcome. A picture of Mao in Moscow with leaders of the 'world movement' hung in his office, and he kept it there even when the Russians looked askance at it. I was more impressed by his remark during a long evening of conversation with me in the guest-house outside the city, in the spring of 1978: 'Must we really go on fighting the battles of 1914 or 1917 over and over again? Surely there are some very different questions socialists should ask themselves now and in the future?' It was difficult to deny that proposition. But despite all his resignation and worldly wisdom, he was far from thinking clearly about democratic socialism, unlike some of his colleagues and – less surprisingly – a number of the next generation.

At the beginning of the fifties Kadar, like Gomulka in Poland, had been imprisoned on suspicion of Titoism and tortured. He had never spoken to me about it, but he did hint at something that distressed him to the end: the fate meted out by the party in 1949 to its crown prince, Interior Minister Laszlo Rajk. Rajk was supposed to help 'the cause' by making a false confession, and was told he would then be allowed to go and live somewhere else under a false identity. Instead, he was hanged. There is room for doubt as to whether only a decade later Kadar – rather than the Soviets – broke the promise of safe conduct to Imre Nagy and his comrades who had sought refuge in the Yugoslav embassy. As a Hungarian and as a Communist – in that order – he admitted to thinking it advisable to come to an arrangement with the occupying power in 1956.

When I visited Gustav Husák in Prague in 1985, he did not

even try to hide his physical frailty; he seemed almost to be begging for someone to succeed him. When another man did at last take over the office of General Secretary it could not be seen as a sign of renewal. Prague, once a golden city, remained dull, grey and sour-smelling, as it had seemed for years.

The ruling party could neither summon up the strength to call the crimes committed under Stalinism by their true name, nor correct the pernicious misinterpretation of the Prague Spring, let alone reject the charge of 'counter-revolutionary' tendencies of which the reforming Communists, backed by the people, were accused. The victims of the Spring, particularly intellectuals, came together in the spirit of Charter 77 to put up tough if mainly silent resistance. The ruling apparatus could do nothing about either the trauma of 1968 or the ideas of the Charter.

Nor did Todor Zhivkov in Sofia – longer in office than any of the others; he came to power in 1955 – shrink from speaking of the successor he expected. There had been much forward movement in his country, he said (as was easily seen, not only in many indications of political openness but in considerable technological progress), but now new blood was needed. That did not prevent him from staying put and surviving, politically speaking, the successor who tried too soon.

I did not visit Bucharest in 1985. It was easy to tell, even from a distance, that the Romanian leader would be more likely to retreat into seclusion than open up to the world. Even in the early summer of 1978, when I went from the Bulgarian to the Romanian capital, I felt that I had passed from a reasonably pleasant climate to an almost intolerably Byzantine one. Yet I went in an unbiased state of mind, indeed rather inclined to feel well disposed because of Romanian independence in the past. However, if the term 'personality cult' (as also practised by those who were allowed to listen at the table and applaud) meant anything anywhere, it was in Ceausescu's Romania. Consequently, the head of state no longer even thought himself obliged to answer letters written to him about the ruthlessly anti-European treatment of minorities, or the ban on contact with former dignitaries such as foreign ministers. There was no denying that the aberrations of Bucharest showed little understanding of Europe, and it is not much comfort to know that 'government by neurosis' proves a blind alley even in Communist form. It is an alley paved with great suffering, and changing direction will be difficult.

Gorbachev did not hesitate to send out signals indicating that the Soviet Union would tolerate rather more than a change in its neighbours' wallpaper. He could not, of course, want secession from the Warsaw Pact to be seriously considered anywhere. But he would not threaten; what was called the Brezhnev Doctrine, which had attained notoriety in international affairs in 1968 when the Soviets marched into Czechoslovakia, was to be a thing of the past. Prominent Russians now praised the positive example set by Finland. In any case, the General Secretary in Moscow had no objection to his European neighbours making their relations with the West as productive as possible, and working for close co-operation with organizations previously seen as hostile to the (Communist) East; if prejudices, including prejudices against the Soviet Union, could be overcome in that way, all the better. From the new Russian viewpoint, similarly, it could do no harm for the signatories of the Warsaw Pact to table proposals on issues of European security that were more independent than before. On the contrary, it might help to break any ice that still had to be broken.

Honecker and his leadership group in East Berlin, not exactly in the first bloom of youth, were relatively successful economically – in their own area, under the conditions of their system, and certainly by comparison with 'the Russians', of whom it was said they should 'report back when they have reached our level'. Supplies of East German goods were important. Even more arrogant, in an unattractively 'Prussian' manner, were East German comments on the 'shambles'. However, when the Kremlin leadership changed direction shortly before Gorbachev's time and pursued a policy of isolating the Federal

Republic, and when jostling for position in Moscow blurred the picture of the situation both before and after Gorbachev, Honecker and his men dug their heels in and stayed put on the right side of détente. The sheer interest in survival of Germans both East and West weighed so heavily that the rulers of both states – in spite of everything else that divided them – declared their agreement that no kind of new Cold War should be an obstacle in the way of people on either side of the dividing line, and should certainly not lead to a military confrontation. Internal rigidity in dogmatic positions did not prevent the GDR from defining its own foreign interests and sometimes showing itself aware of problems where 'the Russians' would rather have had it otherwise.

Was it simply the characteristics of their own generation which prevented the East German leaders from looking critically at their own history and ideas, and led to such absurdities as the East Berlin–Bucharest axis, the only reason for which lay in the defiant admission that they wanted to show Gorbachev and his followers 'that we are still here'? No, the causes lie deeper, and touch on the very existence of a state without an identity of its own. Where national identity cannot produce internal unity, what is left? The dividing line between the brutal exercise of power and German self-assertiveness is too narrow for even a younger leadership to tread it safely for any length of time.

Hungary and Poland have been described as having 'advanced further' along the way to openness and democratization than other Eastern bloc countries that had made any headway. It is possible to justify such a special classification, but on the whole comparisons are out of place. Cultural variety had always been practised in Hungary and Poland, and the pressing demand for political pluralism came not only from outside and below, but from a considerable part of the leadership. There were typical differences: in Hungary a reforming Communist power was dominant, encouraging a multi-party system in defiance of all Leninist tenets. The possibility of standing down if that was what the voters wanted was taken into account. In Poland, there was a new development, one that was neither predetermined at the 'round table' between Government and opposition nor corresponded to the ideas of the representatives of 'Solidarność'.

'Solidarity' could be understood as an unofficial trade union fitting into no traditional framework. It could also be seen as a movement in which intellectuals and workers combined with the backing of the Church. Poland had become Poland again. It could not be assumed that the arm of that Church would be long and flexible enough to bless all would-be parts of the movement. However, unless one understands spontaneous movements and knows something about their anarcho-syndicalist and left-wing Communist interpreters (or precursors) and their corporate inclinations, one should not even think of trying to understand 'Solidarność'. Mrs Thatcher was extremely surprised to be acclaimed by simple 'trade unionists' on the Baltic coast of Poland. But again, that was Solidarność before it took on political responsibility as the opposition to the ruling regime, an opposition comprising very many diverse forces.

The heart of the matter, and it is of epoch-making significance, is that socialism without democracy is absurd and will not even work. That realization goes beyond the admission that no single party has a monopoly of truth and no single class a monopoly of progress. And it goes deeper than the acknowledgement that the outcome of the process we call history is open-ended.

It was not simply and perhaps not even primarily a question of the 'superstructure'. Experience had shown that structural changes – with more freedom for producers as well as consumers – were needed to adjust the rapidly deteriorating planned economies to modern requirements, if indeed adjustment was possible. The planning authorities had been quite unable to keep pace with technological change, and they largely blocked creativity and personal initiative. It was conclusively proved that social justice may be difficult to attain within the market economy, but is absolutely unattainable outside it.

There was no need to tell that to a man like Wojciech Jaruzelski: he knew. On a Sunday morning in December 1985 I was in Warsaw to commemorate the signing of our treaty fifteen years before, together with my Polish hosts. An unforgettable Chopin concert in the house where the composer was born was followed by a pleasant, lively dinner party in one of the old Radziwill castles; Jaruzelski's wife Barbara, a lecturer in German Studies at Warsaw University, speaks perfect German and is thoroughly at home with German literature of both the past and the present. The General, a patriot to his fingertips, was aware of the tragedy of feeling the wind go out of his sails:

'You have said, and we were glad to hear it, that Europe needs Poland. Please add something else to that: peace needs a stable Poland ...

'The Poles like to be admired, whether they are fighting or suffering at home or abroad ... but please understand: one day we would like to be an ordinary nation ...

'A state without democracy can only be strong now and then; to be strong in the long term it has to be democratic ...

'I will not stand in the way of a reconciliation.'

Jaruzelski was a more complex character than most of his adversaries guessed: not only a good, experienced army officer expert in all things military, not just cultured, and rooted in European tradition, but also not in the least servile to his mighty neighbour in the east. 'We did not have an easy time in Siberia either,' he remarked.

In 1981 I had asked Brezhnev what he thought of Jaruzelski and the situation in Poland. He first indicated the wretched party pontiff Suslov, who shook with discomfort at being sentenced to attend the forthcoming Polish party conference. He was clearly unable to exert any influence on it, and died soon afterwards. In the car, the day after I had posed my question, Brezhnev remarked of Jaruzelski: 'We know him, he was Defence Minister for some time. There's another man we know even better and who probably won't get a majority.' The 'other man' was Stefan Olszowski.

It was some time before the party's total loss of credit became

clear to the Soviet leadership. In December 1980 the military
leaders in Moscow were still pleading for intervention in Poland,
but they got no political backing – more particularly, they did
not get Brezhnev's. The way out was an emergency dictatorship
founded on the official text of the Polish constitution and called
'martial law'. Some of the members of the previous leadership
thought that they could get out of the morass they were in by
clinging to the General's coat-tails. As a result, Jaruzelski
became an object of hatred not only among his own countrymen
but in many circles abroad; it was hard to argue differently even
in the Socialist International, and unfair attacks were made on
the German Chancellor in Washington and in Paris. It was some
small comfort to think you could ask the more rigid ideologists
of Moscow, East Berlin or Prague if they had any idea how
Lenin would be turning in his sarcophagus if he knew what one
of the Communist states in Europe was like today: 'a general
at its head, and a Church with an influence extending far beyond
the party's'.

For a German Social Democrat – and this does not just apply
to the Poles – it was often difficult to have appropriate relations
with the men in power without being wrongly accused of thinking that the struggles of democratic opposition groups were
political folklore. I could not visit Andrei Sakharov in his
Moscow apartment until the spring of 1988, but in this case –
as in some others – I was able to put in a few words which
contributed to his return from exile. In 1985 I was unable to
combine an 'official' visit to Warsaw with a detour to Gdańsk,
where Lech Wałesa had invited me to talk to a number of his
colleagues. I had a long discussion with Jaruzelski about the
freedom to travel of Professor Bromislaw Geremek, who was
to become Parliamentary Party Chairman of Solidarność in
1989; the General paid a last brief visit to the guest-house before
I left to acquaint me with the abstruse objections made by his
security apparatus. Many years before I had pleaded the
cause of Adam Michnik in long discussions with the General
Secretary Edward Gierek; Michnik's restless, freedom-loving

spirit repeatedly brought him into conflict with the authorities (and the conflicts robbed him of his freedom). What can Gierek have thought when Michnik first became editor-in-chief of the opposition newspaper in Warsaw and then was invited to Moscow to expound his idiosyncratic theories there?

The Czech apparatchiks had the unfortunate distinction of supremacy in pettiness and chicanery. Among my good acquaintances, although I had never actually met him, was Jiři Hajek, Foreign Minister during the Dubček era, one of those left-wing Social Democrats who had joined the Communist Party after the war. He knew me better than I knew him, for he had been in Fuhlsbüttel concentration camp with one of my close Norwegian friends, the journalist and later state secretary Olav Brunvand. Hajek was one of the signatories of Charter 77. He suffered for it; among other things, his son was forbidden to study at university. Privately, Husák promised me to put that right. But yet again the state security forces were bent on showing they had more say in such matters than the President. Finally, and after much effort, young Hajek did get permission to go to Oslo and study there. I met his father for the first time when I visited Stockholm in June 1989, and Hajek was travelling back to Prague. Early in 1989 he was still unable to attend the dinner that Federal President von Weizsäcker gave for my seventy-fifth birthday.

Our relationship to old and new (and reviving) parties in the other part of Europe calls for much vigilance. It takes intelligence and courage to answer the questions that point the way forward. But nothing can be done unless the past is faced honestly: that is also true, indeed particularly true, of the East German SED. And who can tell what Eastern Europe, so-called, will look like by the turn of the century? How closely will its countries, or some of them, remain bound to the Soviet Union? How capable of development will their relations with the Europe of the Community prove to be in the short term? I do not know the answers, but it seems to me obvious that nothing will stay the same as it was in the shadow of Stalin.

Cornerstones

Mikhail Gorbachev has won considerable acclaim for his imaginative metaphor of Europe as a 'common home', even more in the West than in his own country. Yet the image was not so very new, and the emotionalism with which it was promoted often prevailed over conceptual clarity. When I first met Andrei Gromyko in New York a good twenty years ago, as Foreign Minister talking to Foreign Minister, he too pointed out that we lived 'under a common European roof'. Or did he say that we *were* to live there? Later, a famous Russian clown commented that he would have no difficulty in accommodating members of twenty nations in *his* house – a remark intended kindly rather than controversially, and certainly well-meant.

The image of the 'common home' suggests that its inhabitants must get on reasonably well together. Also, that they could do much for their own welfare by working together instead of making life hell for each other, like the generations before them – not in a common home, perhaps, but on common ground. For the rest, having the same roof overhead does not ensure unclouded friendliness. Still, before a home is built there are points that have to be cleared up. How far does Europe extend? Surely not all the way to Vladivostok? Where are the cornerstones being placed; where are the fences to go? And how will America remain linked to Europe?

Until long after the Second World War the two semi-European World Powers disputed power over Europe, while its caretakers, tenants and sub-tenants had difficulty in allocating floors, apartments and rooms between themselves and then furnishing them. How could the structure be called a 'European home' if it were not managed by the people who lived there and had grown up in it? The opportunities open to us in the early seventies were limited. They depended on Europe's participating in efforts for détente between the World Powers, and not being kept out. It would have been too much to ask us to set our sights on a 'common home' at the time. Some attempt at neighbourliness – of a 'civilized' nature – between contending parties and their adherents was required: no more, but no less.

The next step was to bring together elements of good-neighbourliness, so far as conditions allowed and when those involved did not become obstructive. However, it was clear to us that the Communist system would not last for ever, and that one day unnecessary fences and rickety barriers could be dismantled. I had indicated as much when I was nominated candidate for Chancellor in 1960, but to speak of it subsequently would have seemed over-optimistic.

And who could have known whether and when the subject of a 'common home' would arise, given the opposition not only between power blocs but between social systems? However, it was at least obvious that laying common tables in the open air would be some gain. The achievements of 'small steps', the treaties policy, and the all-European efforts at Helsinki still lagged behind the expectations of many of the people involved, and yet even these modest changes were welcome to Europeans. A particularly striking instance was the easing of travel between the two German states.

In any case, we in our part of Europe were right not to leave it entirely to the World Powers to decide under what auspices and by what stages the East–West conflict should be demilitarized, and alter its character in other ways too. This was our own business, and a case of gaining ground for practical co-operation and humanitarian relief. A realistic approach suggested, and still does, that the various parts of Europe cannot be either merged into a nebulous whole or fitted into some perfectionist building plan, but that by a process not yet clear in detail those parts – sections, states, communities – could come to stand in a new and probably productive relationship to each other.

The image of the common home included the hopeful notion

that there would be no breaches of its domestic peace, or if there were they would be corrected. The significance for ourselves of the change in the East aroused expectations which might be optimistic or pessimistic, but were generally exaggerated. There were those who announced instant bliss, and there were the professional messengers of doom who came on stage to warn of the dangers of successful reforms in what had been the Eastern bloc. This was nonsense in more ways than one. In any case probability suggested, as it still does, that the Soviet Union would still be a large and thus potentially dangerous military power even if it were continually shaken by unrest and if the pressure of its problems increased. You do not need to look very far back in history to see that internal unrest is not always reflected in a pacific attitude to the outside world.

For some time, the Soviet Union has been under the controlling influence of *one* party, even if that party should succeed in achieving some kind of tangible renewal and become Communist only in name. It will be a long time before the irritating bias that marked Russian thinking long before Lenin is overcome, if indeed it ever is. In other words: a Western style of democracy will not be quickly established in the Soviet Union, and everyone who wants to help build a European home should bear that in mind.

However, it would be foolish to ignore the historical caesura linked with the name of Gorbachev. I am sure that the reforms which have been introduced will not go unchallenged. I hope that what has been achieved will not be lost. For the rest, even if the division of Europe and the world – ideologically, economically and in power politics – should continue as it has been *without* major modifications, peaceful coexistence would still be an objective necessity. The world as it is now, on the threshold of a new century, leaves little room for the illusion that there can be absolute and definitive solutions. I have never seen the organization and extension of Europe as a rigid scheme, a simple matter of 'either–or', but as an intricately graduated pattern capable of change. I have never approved of making out that a part, however important, stands for the whole. At the very beginning of my chancellorship I made it clear that my government's foreign policy was primarily European. However, that did not mean just Western European – 'it will attempt,' I said, 'to orientate itself to Europe as a whole as well'.

After a year in the office of Chancellor, at the beginning of November 1970, I described my European political aims 'for this decade' to the Bundestag. Familiar themes came up: the extension of the European Community to include states willing to enter; the institution of economic and monetary union; Western European diplomatic co-operation with the eventual aim of political union; partnership with America as a further way of shouldering our responsibility in international politics. I added a fifth but no less important point: 'Last but not least, to pursue whatever opportunities arise for communication and co-operation with the states of Eastern Europe, and make use of them in the interest of all parties concerned.'

I sketched out that line of foreign policy in my Nobel Prize speech in December 1971. Thomas Mann had proposed it before me, even before the end of the war, urging 'Germany's return to Europe, its reconciliation with Europe, its free ... introduction into a European system of peace'. Through Europe, I said in Oslo, Germany would come home to itself and the constructive forces of its history, adding that this was the imperative task of reason, born of the experience of suffering and failure. Europe's future, I said, was not behind it. In addition to unity in the West, we had a chance of partnership for peace in Europe as a whole – 'if I did not know what practical and ideological obstacles still have to be overcome, I would even speak of a European peace federation'.

'Towards a greater Europe' was the watchword, I said in April 1972 at a congress in North Rhine-Westphalia. In the presence of Jean Monnet, I urged a socially responsible Europe, commenting that this was no new subject to us. 'A decade ago Monnet and his action committee were already suggesting the formation of a committee for co-operation between the Community and the Eastern European states. I devoted myself to that task when I was Mayor of Berlin. Political developments today, even when one is careful to steer clear of illusions, do seem to suggest that it will be possible once again to bring out our old ideas about the possibility of realizing it.'

Western European union on the one hand and the co-operation between Western and Eastern Europe on the other, I said, were not opposed but complementary. 'Western European union will not suffer if all-European co-operation makes progress; similarly, all-European security and co-operation will not suffer if Western European union makes progress. The extended Community does not constitute a bloc in opposition to the East, but – with the strengthening of social policy as one factor involved – can become a major building-block in a peaceful European order.'

If there has been unbroken continuity in any part of my political thinking and action, it is in this area. That has not prevented hostile and prejudiced critics from accusing me, quite unreasonably, of bias towards the East; even various scholarly modern historians have followed fashion in suggesting that my policy of détente lacked solid links with the West. Attempts to achieve détente and co-operation between Western and Eastern states did not run counter to Atlantic co-operation and Western European union. 'On the contrary, our *Ostpolitik*, or what goes by that name, began in the West and will always remain rooted in the West.'

Western European union was important in itself, but its purpose was not to impede developments beneficial to the continent as a whole. Co-operation in practical areas between states in the East and the West had its own value, and might even increase security. The landscape was changing for the better, partly because Washington and Moscow were reassessing their mutual interests, and partly because European partners on both sides of the Iron Curtain were re-evaluating the situation. Collective security was beginning to find expression in practical policies. For instance, there was concrete and not just general discussion of the level to which military potential could be reduced.

This development gained ground in the first half of the eighties, despite tendencies towards the fear of further or new confrontation. The Stockholm conference on confidence-building measures – as part of the Helsinki process – proved to be a decisive breakthrough, although most people did not immediately recognize it as such. In the autumn of 1986 a broad understanding on the subject of verification was reached in Stockholm. The combined system of land and air inspection was implemented at the beginning of 1987, and it was agreed that the movement of large bodies of troops must be made known some months in advance. In Vienna in 1989, negotiations on conventional arms stability – partly between the members of the two alliances, partly with the participation of all European states – reached a promising stage. If terms are agreed on the future upper levels for tanks and troops, artillery and aircraft, and then on 'tactical' nuclear arms as well, we shall see the basis of a new structure of European security. The parties concerned will assure themselves that the agreement is being kept by inspection on the spot and by keeping suitable records.

Such a system of arms limitation does not bring the alliances to an end. Indeed, any idea of discussing their dissolution prematurely is unrealistic. However, it is and will remain desirable for their nature to change if they are to safeguard the new European structure. The major influence exerted by the United States and the Soviet Union on Europe since the Second World War will be further reduced. Both World Powers will remain linked to the fate of the continent in many ways and yet will not prevent the Europeanization of Europe. An organization of European security overriding the blocs is hard to imagine without the inclusion of the 'semi-European' Great Powers. That was the case with the Helsinki conference of the mid-seventies, and it was the case again with the Vienna negotiations.

The leadership of the Soviet Union saw it the same way, and with increasing clarity; it would not previously have occurred to Moscow to describe the North American presence in Europe as a 'major factor in peaceful coexistence'.

None of this answers the question of the future organization of military security for Western Europe and the development – how soon? – of the European Community into a political union. The subject of appropriate Western European responsibility and co-responsibility has become no more urgent but no less important since President Kennedy recommended a two-pillar structure – North America here, Western Europe there – to NATO twenty-five years ago. Attempts to move in that direction did not get far, either within NATO with a 'Eurogroup', or outside it with the Western European Union which had once been created to put further brakes on any undesirable expansion by Germany. In particular, the question of the nuclear capability of France and Britain and its part in a European context remained unanswered. Germans were well advised not to put out their hands for something which – quite apart from any question of its significance – was not to be had anyway.

Perfectionists are always inclined to see Europe developing into either a European Community embracing the entire continent, or a new entity of all-European structures. History seldom presents simple alternatives. I think we shall see neither; instead, I would expect a wide spectrum showing different degrees of co-operation. It is certain that some day more Europeans will be living under the roof of the EC than can find space there today. It is probable that a few new members will join, but there will not be a definite extension eastward; there is no real comparison with the southward expansion which has proved a considerable success, despite many forebodings at the time. One reason I do not expect eastward extension is the existing membership of NATO.

Because of NATO membership, I shared the reservations of my like-minded Spanish friends after Spain's transition to democracy. The Yugoslavs feared coming under Soviet pressure if the strategic balance shifted in another part of the Medi-terranean area. There was also talk of Syria's entering the Warsaw Pact at the time. The situation changed, and Felipe Gonzales achieved Spanish membership not only of the EC but also of the Atlantic Alliance – without full integration, and under conditions which were advantageous to his country in other ways as well.

For the rest, it seems likely that we shall see broad-based co-operation, of various degrees of intensity, between the EC and the Eastern states, including the Soviet Union; helpful criticism along the way will be useful. Along that way, too, they will become responsible partners in important international organ-izations.

I do not think it impossible that some supra-bloc institution for Europe as a whole will come into existence. If the EC makes its environmental policy a proposition in which the other side can participate, that will be a sensible and highly welcome move. And if neighbouring countries co-operate to take those protective measures which must necessarily cross borders, thinking in terms of blocs will disappear almost of itself. An effective environmental authority, equipped with means and powers applying to the whole of Europe, cannot come a day too soon; an awareness of the explosive nature of the problem of the environment may help to hasten it.

Over and beyond countering new threats to society, it would be useful for East and West to work together to surmount the international North–South divide. Endeavours going further than traditional development aid would be good for Europe's reputation – not only in other parts of the world, but among its own rising generation, which responds to various forms of actual European co-operation, public or otherwise, far more than to official texts and statements.

The Final Act of Helsinki and the recommendations of sub-sequent conferences contained many suggestions providing material not just for joint papers but also, perhaps, for agreements and thus a binding European law, or common

European action. At the Council of Europe in Strasbourg – with its twenty-three members including Finland, which became a full instead of an associate member in 1989 – well over a hundred conventions have been passed, mainly concerned with legal, technical and cultural matters. The setting-up of the Commission and Court of Human Rights has been the major achievement.

I have always felt it most significant, in principle, that the work of the Commission of Human Rights could be applied to both the Greek colonels' regime and Turkish military rule: Europe cannot be seen in isolation from human rights, and anyone who wants to belong to Europe must maintain them. Once Eastern ideas came closer to Western ideas, it could surprise no one, whatever may eventually come of it, to find several Eastern European states attempting to co-operate with the Council of Europe. The Council itself cannot be divorced from the principle of human rights in which it is rooted, and its citizens' claim to them. Measured against future possibilities, such an assessment of Strasbourg may not seem much; measured by what lies in the past, history seems to have made a great leap forward.

Cracks

The Nazi and post-Nazi expulsions left Europe the poorer. A democratic law on minority groups could have provided a secure basis upon which many different national and cultural forces might have flourished, to their own and the general good. Where the more or less centralistic nation-state gives way to common European structures, the regions will acquire more weight of their own. Important changes in that direction have at least begun, particularly in Spain but also in France.

The Soviet Union obviously feels no inclination to give its regions more responsibility. Along with the economic question, the regional question stands high on the agenda of changes pending. It will be hard to go on fobbing off the non-Russian peoples of the Soviet Union with a show of federalism – that may prove the trickiest factor of all in the uncertainty of the years ahead.

In the Balkans, particularly Romania, national minorities are constantly being oppressed. After Tito's death, the federal constitution of Yugoslavia looked like facing a new challenge. It was not and is not in any sensible European interest for the Yugoslav Republic to run a serious risk of falling apart. The friends of that country, among whom I count myself, could only advise that the necessary economic and democratic reforms should not be postponed; intensive participation in advanced European co-operation could do much to ease matters.

As a leading member of the non-aligned movement, Yugoslavia may sometimes have overtaxed itself; on the whole, it has exerted constructive influences in and beyond Europe. The same applies in differing but impressive degrees to all the democracies outside the alliances: Switzerland and Austria, Sweden and Finland have swept away the old clichés about historically conditioned neutrality by their conduct in European and international affairs: neutrality is no longer regarded as an amoral failure to take a stance.

Whenever flaws or cracks appeared in the European structure, however, there was always talk of the Germans. What might come of the relationship between their two states? Would they, as long appeared likely, merge so completely into their respective opposing blocs that the question of a closer common future would disappear? Or could a common roof, whether of the same state or not, be a possibility after all, brought into existence by a changing East–West relationship? Would the Germans actually want it, despite all the difficulties and – from the Western viewpoint – all the inconveniences it would mean? And would the neighbours continue to be friendly if they were asked for more than general declarations of goodwill? If they were asked, perhaps, to consent to the emergence of a Central European state of a dominant nature because of the sheer number of its people, its economic power and its other potentials? Or would old fears be overcome by new trust? A trust springing from new European structures?

Many of my countrymen – and many of those who speak for them – are only too ready to evade such questions. They prefer to imagine that first, there is a kind of natural right to *one* state per people, and second, that the Western powers promised the Federal Republic to help the Germans to regain state unity, the unity that Bismarck achieved in 1871 and that broke up in the aftermath of the Second World War.

Those who should have known better asked whether the Americans, the Russians and the British had not indicated at the Potsdam Conference in the summer of 1945 – and the three of them together with the French in the Allied Control Council – that they intended to restrict the German Reich territorially but not fragment it in the long term. Germany, it was said, should be able to return 'to the comity of civilized nations', and meanwhile should be treated as an economic unit. And was there not talk of an interim solution in the third year after the end of the war, when the victorious coalition had fallen apart and political reorganization of the Western zones was in progress? Could it not be deduced, from the introduction to the Basic Law of the Federal Republic of Germany, that over the following years all that had to be done was to reassemble the parts so drastically divided by the collapse of the victorious wartime coalition?

Matters did not have to stay as they were, but many people, including those with great political responsibility, found it hard not to lose sight of a fundamental factor in European history: Germany's neighbours, of which it has a considerable number, had always helped whether directly or indirectly to determine how it was constituted as a state. Indeed, the Germans will not decide alone on their national political future, however it may be formed, in any forthcoming rounds. Nor will the victorious powers of the Second World War be the only forces involved.

The reverse of the coin is to ask whether the perversion of German nationalism, ever-present in the minds of neighbouring nations and large parts of the world, must always exclude the possibility of the concentration and perhaps the expression of national revolutionary energies not directed at destruction, without the express intervention of any authority? We may assume that the scene of such events would be that part of divided Germany in which people are less well off than in the other. Why, by what right and on the grounds of what experience do we think it impossible that not hundreds but hundreds of thousands should stand up some day in Leipzig and Dresden, in Magdeburg and Schwerin – and in East Berlin – and demand their civil rights? Including the right to emigrate from one part of Germany to the other? That would be something of an embarrassment not only to the Russians but also to the Allies, because of the question of rights in Germany as a whole. They might not even have given enough thought to that type of self-satisfied West German who would do anything rather than share what he has with those who drew the short straw at the end of the war.

As for the victorious powers, no members of the Soviet leadership have ever tried to win my goodwill with offers or even hints suggesting German unity. They have contented themselves with generalities about change being an essential historical factor, distancing themselves very clearly from the idea of retreating, sooner or later, from their advance post of direct influence in Europe. Gorbachev and his people remained non-committal when questions were being asked in Bonn about their future policy on Germany. In Paris there were knowing smiles, and the heads of state reminded each other of the notorious Four-Power responsibilities. Among the immediately significant changes, however, is the fact that the new leaders of Eastern Europe – including Poland! – no longer necessarily think that the frozen status quo in Germany is the only way their own interests will be served.

As for the United States, when Washington gave its blessing to our treaties policy it did not conceal the fact, at home, that it did not expect so-called reunification to come closer in this or any similar way. On the other side of the Atlantic, they were especially inclined to think the division of the continent an epoch-making event and expect little to come of the winds of change invoked by Kennedy. Why make things more complicated than they were already? Richard Nixon used to flatter us by saying Germany was the key to Europe. In the summer of 1971 he told me that Europe would need time, but that the Germanies would play a larger international part for the rest of the century. When I lectured at several American universities at the end of the eighties, I could be sure, from California to New England, that I would be asked about reunification and its likely date. (And the next question was: could the American soldiers come home at last after that?)

Harold Wilson and Edward Heath both expressed the concerns of British policy with great discretion. Much like their colleagues in Paris, the administrators of the diplomatic inheritance in London were moved partly by a guilty conscience and partly by a vague hope. They had been unable to help the Poles as little in 1939 as the Czechs in the previous year. From their point of view, it would not necessarily be the worst of all possible prospects to see the smaller part of Germany merge into Eastern Europe, however Eastern Europe developed.

In France, from Charles de Gaulle to François Mitterrand, the general rule was to think of the danger that an all-German state might represent, but to avoid as far as possible the embarrassment of having to discuss it. As intelligent a man as Jean Monnet seriously thought Western European integration might offer the people of the Federal Republic an acceptable substitute for the national unity they could not regain. Meanwhile, the general public did not absolve the Federal Republic of all suspicion of setting the bar so high for the EC in general and monetary union in particular in order to have a 'free hand in the East'.

Georges Pompidou, that cautiously calculating son of the Auvergne, said in the summer of 1973 that even unarmed neutrality in Central Europe – 'and all that that could lead to' – was bound to make France very uneasy. Two years before, however, he had said: 'The day will come when the East decides to take the path of liberalization.' Therefore, he said – like de Gaulle before him – the West must not represent itself as a bloc that could never change. In his remarks in Bonn in June 1973, which were rather in the nature of a political testament, President Pompidou said that France would be delighted if the GDR were to shake off Communism and reunification came closer, but it was extremely improbable. So what *was* to be expected? My cautiously drawn picture of national coherence within the existing division of Germany carried no conviction in Paris. It was only two years since the President had briefly let himself be persuaded that I had agreed with Brezhnev in the Crimea that the Federal Republic would leave the Western Alliance. The French themselves soon realized this was pure nonsense, but the mere fact that Germany was making headlines in the international press appeared suspect to the politicians of Paris. The Western Allies had always observed our interest in *Ostpolitik* with a mixture of understanding and scepticism; in Paris, however, criticism always outweighed sympathy.

Early in the summer of 1987, when I had retired from the chairmanship of my party, François Mitterrand invited me to dinner and surprised me by asking whether reunification did not come top of the list of German interests. I corrected his view of the present state of affairs, rather as if I were administering a tranquillizer. Did I really mean, he said, that ecological concerns and not the national question were easily our prime concern? That was typical of German *romanticisme*. It can be difficult for neighbours, and in this case friends too, to explain themselves to each other. Even the peace movement was fundamentally misunderstood by our French partners – as unrealistic *pacifisme*, and mealy-mouthed at that. As for explaining the relationship between the hostile – yet well-disciplined – German brother states, it was more or less impossible.

Mitterrand was greatly surprised when, early in 1981 and at the beginning of that presidential campaign which took him to the Élysée in May of that year, we met in an 'East German' hotel and a complacent First Secretary suggested to him that all was well with socialism in the GDR. The very French Socialist leader was even more surprised when he saw the special attention the GDR authorities paid me. While he and one of my colleagues visited the place in Thuringia from which he had escaped as a prisoner of war in 1940, I went by car from Berlin to our meeting-place at the Hermsdorf crossroads – on a completely cleared autobahn: a special kind of quarantine. When we crossed the border into Franconia, the Frenchman was again slightly surprised to see how civilly I was treated and how punctiliously we were saluted. He may well have been asking himself how you could ever understand the Germans.

At one of our first meetings early in the seventies, Mitterrand had spoken in lyrical terms of his two escapes as a prisoner of war. We agreed that some day we would drive along the road he had taken on foot with his companion, a priest, before they were recaptured in Swabia. Seven years earlier he had just failed to get elected with 49.3 per cent of the vote; there was no mistaking the bitterness (and some desire for revenge) in his voice when he spoke of it. He was convinced that German eulogies of his opponent Giscard d'Estaing had robbed him of success. In 1975, a year after this defeat, Prime Minister Jacques Chirac tried to explain to me, at a dinner given by Helmut Schmidt for the French in Hamburg, that Mitterrand's gullibility would guarantee the victory of Communism in France. In Social Democratic circles too we were concerned and incredulous when, at a conference of party leaders at Elsinore, Mitterrand assured us that the party he led would defeat the Communist Party and not the other way round; he was not short of self-confidence. Subsequently, Harold Wilson remarked to the

German Chancellor that Mitterrand had not only said it, he actually believed it.

The other partners in the European Community kept any sympathy for the increasingly close bond between Bonn and Paris well within bounds. The British thereby deprived themselves for a number of years of the chance of playing a more prominent part in the Community; however, they acquired a reputation for extreme correctness in German affairs. The Benelux countries would rather have seen a good working Franco-German relationship than its opposite. The Spanish and Portuguese were anxious not to appear too dependent on France. Among the most faithful friends to the Germans, and not always properly appreciated in Bonn, were the frequently changing but on the whole remarkably successful representatives of Italian policy: de Gasperi and Pietro Nenni, Aldo Moro, Andreotti and Craxi – and Enrico Berlinguer. It was the Social Democrat Giuseppe Saragat who visited Auschwitz when he was President of Italy and said, quietly, 'The Nazis did that, not the German people.'

The Germans had more friends than they realized, or were willing to realize, or than it sometimes appeared. But there was no approval anywhere for the allegedly legally valid view that the Reich, and moreover the Reich within its 1937 borders, had never really ceased to exist. Expressions of goodwill for 'reunification' in the abstract were easily obtained, but the (new) allies of the Federal Republic went no further than lip-service. Considering the past, anything more would have been surprising.

More clearly than the Germans themselves, their neighbours recognized that consideration of the German future, unavoidable as it may be in the context of European co-operation, is neither expedient nor timely, and the question must go unanswered for the time being. The bloodless 're' in 'reunification' is and will be even less persuasive than it has been in the past. Nor do the configuration of international politics and the realities of the Continent encourage simple thinking. And who would believe that some day the GDR will be united with the Federal Republic, and that will be all?

History is certainly open-ended and holds good and less good things in store, but it does not invite us to shed our sense of realism.

Today I find increasing approval of a policy that might make the borders less sharply divisive, preserve national substance, and smooth the way for a peaceful order in Europe. I have assumed the division of Germany as a fact, and I regard it as a success that improvised forms of co-operation between Bonn and East Berlin prove enduring and go far. Was it for that reason that I did not touch upon the right to self-determination? No, certainly not. The right to self-determination is rooted in the United Nations Charter, and on principle it is not divisible either between nations or within a nation. And what would the Western community be if it did not embody that very right? Whatever our understanding of our neighbours' fears, we must be allowed to recall that fact too.

The Basic Treaty between the two German states – apart from the well-known difference of opinion on the national question – has proved its worth. The agreement on transport communications has made everyday life much easier. Trade within Germany and practical co-operation in a number of areas have been more useful to one side than the other. The Federal Republic is ready to pay something for the settlement of a number of affairs; it can afford to do so, and is willing – perhaps partly to soothe a guilty conscience for being so much better off?

The once hotly debated policy of taking small steps has become an attitude that overrides political parties. When, towards the end of his life, Franz Josef Strauss used his influence to obtain a GDR special credit, he was criticized not by those who had been his opponents for so long; the people who distanced themselves from him were those who thought they owed it to their particularly right-wing stance.

It was easy to see the advantage of internal German settlements for the GDR as a whole and not just its rulers. The increased flow of visitors allowed by the Government – initially very restricted, later permitted even from East to West – was more than we could have hoped for at the start. But once pressure was slightly reduced at the top, people at the bottom wanted and still want more. Much more. The wish of a considerable number of GDR citizens to emigrate to the Federal Republic (and be personally 'reunified', or reunified as a family) is insatiable, and cannot even be brushed aside. Where two have emigrated, ten more immediately apply for emigration permits.

The GDR leadership thinks highly of its state economic policy and its success by comparison with others in the Eastern bloc. But it still exemplifies the disadvantages of bureaucratic central planning. And the Communists who call themselves members of a Socialist Unity Party have no sensitivity towards critical feeling among the citizens who have no say in government and do not feel involved in the state process. Some sections of the Protestant Churches have been able to show a fraction of the readiness for dialogue which the state and the party are neither willing nor capable of showing, but that is all.

I have more than once observed the neurotic fear of its citizens' reactions felt by the GDR's security services. Many years after that visit of mine to Erfurt, they still would not risk orderly meetings and demonstrations. In 1985, when I managed to make a detour to Weimar, with much difficulty and some persistence, the many people who came to welcome me became rather unruly and were put to flight in a matter of moments. Three years later a lecture I was to have given on the subject of the North–South divide on Church premises in East Berlin was cancelled, and so was a television programme that I was going to make in Rostock, a place familiar to me from childhood.

The Socialist Unity Party endeavoured, not wholly without success and certainly not with the approval of its Polish and Czech neighbours, to revive certain German traditions of the Prussian variety. Entirely in line with this attitude, the group around Honecker feels intellectually and emotionally close to the idea of 'all-German' resistance to Hitler. In 1985, during a drive through East Berlin, the Chairman of the Council of State asked me: 'And where were *you* when I was agitating here just fifty years ago?'

The GDR has not been able to create itself a national identity out of this; the official description of a 'socialist state of the German nation' is still as empty as ever. The West is economically successful, highly attractive, and there is no language barrier. GDR citizens have more in common with the Federal Republic than our electronic media offer them.

It was not self-evident that the GDR rulers would think it to their advantage to reduce arms stockpiling in Central Europe. In essence, Social Democratic suggestions from the Federal Republic sustained an unofficial but important dialogue on security between the two Germanies, on the fringe of the Vienna negotiations. Despite the continued existence of the differences in their systems, this has been a clear and objective piece of co-operation going beyond the economy and culture.

Less fruitful was the attempt of Western Social Democrats and Eastern Communists to conduct their argument on irreconcilable positions in a more civilized way than in the past. The real nub of the matter, the subordination even of ideological confrontation to the necessity of peace, was quickly identified, and accepted by those who do not think dogmatically. There was also the practical consideration that the Germans did not have to be involved in every kind of substitute conflict. But history has decided the argument between Social Democracy and Communism – and for a long time it was more than just an argument! It is not worth pursuing it now, although the incorrigible arrogance of ideologists should still be opposed.

Not much is said either cogently or publicly in the Federal Republic about the tension between European union and German unity. That is not just because people are baffled by it, but because of a fear of changed perspectives and circumstances.

The simple formulae of the immediate post-war decades are no longer valid, and no new ones are in sight.

In the process of European change, the Germanies face the old question, but put in a new way: is unity possible only under the state roof, or can the divided states, should they continue to exist, come closer in some other way? Especially if the difference between the systems is reduced to such a point that it hardly matters any more? And if both parts of Germany belong equally to Europe?

Who could determine, from the outset, the form in which the national community might find expression if the power interests of others and the opposing systems no longer stood in the way?

And what about Berlin, and the Wall? The city will live, and the Wall will come down. But the idea of a solution for Berlin alone, not bound up with far-reaching changes in Europe and between the two Germanies, has always been an illusion, and has become no more likely over the years.

Soon Berlin will have been in its peculiar position for as long a time as it was the capital of the Kaiser's Reich, and longer than it was the capital of the Weimar Republic and the Third Reich. Against the expectations of pessimists, and indeed other people too, it has neither fallen victim to pressure from outside nor been consumed by its internal shortcomings. If, after the blockade or after 17 June 1953, Reuter and I had been told it would be so, we would have shaken our heads incredulously. We saw no prospect of the defensive operation's lasting more than a few years.

Meanwhile, the two parts of the old capital are not so far from each other as they were two or three decades ago. West Berlin is rooted in the West, and sensibly seeks tasks that make sense for both (or all) parts of Europe. Building plans are important in Berlin too, but life does not predominantly run according to plan, in Berlin or anywhere else.

One thing is certain, however: the building-blocks of the post-war order will not lie for ever where they fell during the confusion of those years. And they will not be put together again in precisely their former structure. I do not know what part peace treaties may still play, and if they will establish a new normality or fix the status quo. Germany will have particular difficulty in mending the cracks that run through Europe, and yet must try. Why should what is good for Europe be bad for Germany?

For what is true of Europe as a whole is particularly true of its centre.

Room to Breathe

This century of ups and downs is not yet over: a century that had so much potential and leaves behind very mixed feelings. Anyone born in 1913, as I was, cannot complain of any lack of grim experiences and bitter disappointment. But have there not been encouraging signs? Humanity has been given the ability to free itself from want and misery. Humanity has also been given the ability to reject oppression and despotism. However, I do not overestimate the capacity of nations to correct the mistakes of those who should have been in duty bound to rule with understanding.

A German European of my generation and way of thinking must be glad that our part of the world still has a future ahead of it and has entered upon the fine venture of a league of free nations. We must feel relief that the Germans survived their fall into the abyss and did not suffer lasting harm. In the larger part of their country, they seized and used the welcome chance of proving themselves once again in productive co-operation.

Do we learn from history? In so far as a nation does learn from history, it is not a painless process. But there is so much ground to be gained: ground on which it can overcome misfortune and find its way back to dignity. However, it is still important to preserve our memories and not to forget. To deny individual guilt and suppress collective responsibility would surely lay heavier burdens on the coming generations than they should reasonably have to bear.

When I started school the end of the First World War was little more than a year in the past. The dual hope that the Europeans would take that catastrophe to heart, and the Germans would give democracy more room, turned out to be deceptive. At twenty, when I had left the country, I had behind me an experience that I could never forget: the seizure of power by those who set up the murderous Nazi regime, and the failure of those who stood by and watched the Weimar Republic founder. Where there is no civil courage, freedom will not get far. And where freedom is given no timely defence, it can be won back only at the cost of great and terrible sacrifice. This is the lesson of the century.

I was lucky enough to discover Europe in my early youth. But I saw little that could put up a strong defence against the powers of darkness, and little solid progress towards freedom. The crimes of Stalinism, long underestimated, contributed to this sobering assessment. The war willed by Hitler could not be won: that was a different matter. The Scandinavian countries of Europe where I found refuge showed me a culture and a democracy rooted in the people and not just for outward show. The sense of gratitude I owe Scandinavia has left a deep mark on me.

When the Second World War ended I was over thirty. I went home to the ruins of Germany, became a member of the Bundestag and had to prove myself in Berlin. I underestimated the depth and duration of the division in the continent and within my own country, but not the future strength of European democracy, nor the power of the United States. In the Federal Republic, despite much looking backwards, the major political parties came to an understanding on a national order which sprang from the democratic traditions of the West. The consensus on the Constitution held together, and that meant much.

At fifty, I was setting out on my endeavour to counter the inhumane division with a policy of small steps. Concrete German contributions were required to help in reducing those tensions that endanger peace. We even thought that, with the help of like-minded people in Europe and America, we could transform the dreadful conflict called the Cold War. One of my less-regarded remarks twenty-five years ago was that it was time to look at Europe as a whole.

It was Albert Einstein who said the atom bomb had changed everything except human thinking. My thinking did not go unaffected by the situation faced by Berlin, but it led me to conclude that in the nuclear age the future could be safeguarded only by the securing of a common peace.

By the time the working-class boy from the seaport of Lübeck had reached sixty-five, he had been Chairman of the Social Democratic Party for some time, had been a member and then head of the Federal German Government, and had recently taken on the presidency of the international association of Social Democratic parties. I remained active in European affairs beyond the West, and would not decline to involve myself more than before in relations between the rich and the poor nations.

It would take another book simply to list the great changes to which Germany and the world have been exposed since my youth. Someone from a very humble background can only be filled with pride to think that formal education is no longer the privilege of a narrow social class, and that the material circumstances of broad strata of society are now quite good. Most of today's states did not exist a generation ago, and there has been a fundamental shift in the balance of the community of states as a whole. Many of the technical achievements which we take for granted today began in recent decades. The scientific and technological revolution is still in progress. But wisdom and morality lag behind that progress.

In my old age, I am glad of the measurable gain for human rights and civil liberties. First in the centre of Europe. Then in the South, written off by the faint-hearted only a decade and a half ago. And now in the East, which many strategists of the 'status quo' persuasion were too hasty in allocating to the Soviet Union. In other parts of the world too – not least in Latin America, large parts of Asia and here and there in Africa – the idea of democracy is alive.

None of this goes unchallenged, and the naïve optimism of my youth will not be seen anywhere again. Who would wish to extinguish our knowledge of humanity, what it can do, and to what ends it will let itself be misused? Yet much of what I first hoped for and then sought to work for is beginning to take promising shape.

Setting priorities is a useful political activity. When I resigned from the Party chairmanship in the early summer of 1987, I asked myself what mattered more to me than anything else, besides peace, and replied: freedom. I spelled it out further: freedom of conscience and opinion. Freedom from want and fear. Democracy cannot exist without bread and with a secret police. Or without pluralism and with a claim to monopoly. I would add that wishing to ordain happiness by decree means stifling freedom.

Through no merit of my own, I was born into the tradition of the labour movement and the intellectual world of European Social Democracy. I have seen their weaknesses, particularly in Germany, as well as their greatness. Readiness to suffer overcame the determination to struggle. Totalitarian Communism has shown itself to be the wrong road, claiming many victims, a road paved with economic and social failure.

Civil liberties and social justice always have to be weighed against each other. A social state is free only if it avoids the danger of proliferating bureaucracy, does not allow itself to be constricted by planning, and emphasizes its commitment to individual responsibility. Having room to breathe is what matters.

Germany cannot dispense with a strong tradition of Social Democracy. Its ethical impulse is not worn out. The European Left will either be Social Democratic or feel the lack of its formative influence. Actual party names are of minor importance;

if various ideological currents flow together they may provide additional force.

Politicians who rely on dogma or expect to be raised on to a pedestal of infallibility do not deserve trust. Arrogance and stubborn persistence in error cannot be reconciled with honest dealing towards one's neighbours and fellow citizens. And suspicion is in order when people cite unproven necessities or proclaim national interests or geo-strategic constants as an excuse for taking no action and asking no critical questions. Even in a democratic atmosphere, stupidity lies in wait and ill will can be mobilized.

Nothing can be achieved without patience. But it is reasonable to be angry when evident knowledge is not translated into appropriate policy at all, or only very slowly, so that resources are wasted. That is true, not least, of issues transcending borders or affecting humanity as a whole. For some time, it has been a notorious fact that our earth cannot long support the foreseeable growth of its population, the exhaustion of its natural resources, and the damage being done to the environment. For some time we have been living at the expense of coming generations. We need determined and courageous political leadership to tackle those tasks that clearly lead beyond the immediate present. There is no inevitable, direct road to rational action and humane progress. To come close to it is the opportunity inherent in democracy.

Even if there is no nuclear war, the danger of humanity's destroying itself is not averted. Individuals can have only a limited influence on the threats to our existence. But we have found in the Federal Republic that our country carries some weight, and Europe most certainly does. And one of the conclusions I have come to during my life is that the situation is never hopeless.

To have helped in causing the German name to be linked with the concept of peace and the prospect of European freedom is the true satisfaction of my life.

POSTSCRIPT
End of November 1989

Nothing will be the Same Again

On one of the last pages of the manuscript of my *Memoirs*, writing in the summer of 1989, I conjectured that some day 'not hundreds but hundreds of thousands' would stand up in Leipzig and other cities of the GDR and demand their civil rights. Even I did not foresee in detail the subsequent course of events as it unfolded week by week, ushering in the radical but peaceful revolution of the autumn of 1989. And although the emphasis must be on the lead taken by the people of Saxony, the role of more northerly parts of the GDR should not be forgotten.

Berlin – where else? – was the place where German feeling united, and the fascinated attention of the world concentrated on the city. On the night of 9 November holes were knocked in much of the length of the Wall: the dramatic changes along the border between East and West Germany followed. A month earlier, speaking in East Berlin, Mikhail Gorbachev had said that life would penalize those who could not keep pace with developments. Soon afterwards – in the 'capital of the GDR' – we saw the first but already remarkable signs of change at the head of the state, and in the leadership of the party that had held power for over forty years. Now its time was running out.

On 10 November 1989 I spoke – with Mayor Momper, Federal Chancellor Kohl and Foreign Minister Genscher – at a mass meeting outside the Schöneberg Rathaus. I remembered the August of 1961, when I had to express the bitter disappointment of my fellow citizens on the same spot. Matters were not as simple as in the old days. We did not have to resist threats from outside, or urge ourselves to defy the dividing Wall, refusing to let it deter us from our resolve or from the work of reconstruction. Deeply moved, a witness to countless reunions, I saw that the city was full of spontaneous cheerfulness, with not a trace of aggression. The unity urged for so long and with so many words was imposing itself 'from below', and it meant more than the reunion of divided families. I was overcome by a sense of great relief, mingled with hope that we would master the tasks that still lay ahead. My mind went back to that August of 1961. What a road we had travelled since then! We had not been content to call for the Wall to go; we had said to ourselves and others that Berlin must survive in spite of it, and for all the many deep divisions between us our nation must be held together – in the context of its European duties, among other things.

And now we were back outside the Schöneberg Rathaus, in the square named after John F. Kennedy in 1963. This time thousands of people from the 'other side' were there too. Addressing them, I was not ashamed of my tears. And I was moved by the many letters and calls I received afterwards expressing gratitude.

It had been important to alleviate the harsh consequences of separation by taking small steps while it was impossible to take larger ones. Few would dispute that now. And only now do we see the full importance of those tiny milestones. What would become of a nation if its families could not be united?

The Germans, I said on that November afternoon in Berlin were coming together in a way no one had guessed at, and no one now should claim precise knowledge of how the people from both sides of the Wall would get on in their new relationship. What mattered was the fact that they *could* come together in freedom. 'And it is certain,' I said, 'that nothing in the other part of Germany will be the same again. The winds of change that have been blowing over Europe for some time now could not pass Germany by. I have always been convinced that division by concrete, barbed wire and armed patrols ran counter to the current of history.' I felt great inner satisfaction in recalling the words I had set down on paper in the summer: 'Berlin will live, and the Wall will come down.'

I asked my fellow citizens and countrymen to understand and adapt to the process of change: 'I know that our neighbours in Eastern Europe understand our motives, and that they are a part of the new ways of thinking and acting which are challenging the people of Central and Eastern Europe themselves. We can assure our neighbours and the great World Powers that we do not aspire to any solution of our problems which is incompatible with our duties to peace and to Europe.' We were guided, I said, by the conviction that the European Community must continue to develop, and the fragmentation of our continent be gradually but definitively overcome.

My main subject – and not just in the spirit of a general conjecture – was that close links are developing between the various parts of Europe. This new statement of unity between Germans, arising to a great degree from the new self-confidence in the eastern part of the country, became a subheading for a chapter as pleasing as it was significant. The 'winds of change' implied not just a change of climate in the countries lying between Germany and Russia, but new factors and new attitudes at work within the great Eastern Power itself. However, there was no need for me to apologize for being fascinated by the changes in once-divided Germany – changes which went beyond anything that could reasonably have been expected.

The fundamental change in the situation had been brought about by the way the Germans of the GDR took their fate into their own hands. 'The people themselves' raised their voices, at long last shaking off the pall of dependency and deprivation. Not least among their demands was the right to freedom of information, freedom of movement, freedom of assembly, and appropriate financial rewards. It was clear that the popular movement would lead to free elections. Free elections worthy of that name. And while I could understand those who had decided to emigrate, I thought that working for renewal in the GDR itself was worth while and deserved encouragement.

My final remarks in Kennedy-Platz on 10 November 1989 ran: 'Nothing will be the same again. That applies to us in the West as well: we shall not be judged by yesterday's slogans, fine or otherwise, but by what we are ready to do, to achieve, today and tomorrow, and by what we are in a mental and material position to do. In the mental sense, I hope the cupboard will not prove to be bare. In the material sense, I hope aid will be forthcoming. And I hope engagement diaries will allow room for what is needed now. Our willingness to show solidarity, to compromise and to make a new start rather than wag an admonitory finger will be put to the test. We must move closer together again, keep our heads clear, and so far as we are able we must act in line with both German interests and our duty towards Europe.'

Berlin became a city of many meetings, attracting the attention of the world's media. But only Leipzig, once the market-place of Europe and the capital of the German book trade, a city with an old tradition of public spirit and the cradle of Social Democracy in Germany, could have been the scene of those extraordinary, powerful demonstrations that took place month after month. It was in Leipzig, too, that astute Russians and prudent Germans averted the danger of bloody confrontation. General Secretary Honecker had already signed the operations order for the armed forces; live ammunition had been handed out. At the last moment a 'Council of Six' intervened, and managed to prevent 9 October becoming known as Bloody Monday. Furthermore, the Soviet Union was disinclined to use its army to keep the Communists of the Socialist Unity Party in power, even when – as was later revealed – the tanks had already arrived in Dresden. I could be sure I was speaking for the vast majority of my countrymen between the Elbe and the

Oder, the Baltic and the Erzgebirge, when I said at the Berlin meeting and elsewhere: 'No one wants any problems with the Soviet troops who are still on German soil.'

Let there be no misunderstanding on this point: in mid-October 1989, when I was in Moscow for lectures and talks, I had received a clear impression that the Soviet leadership did not intend to dismantle its military (or 'strategic') presence in the GDR unilaterally. Nor did it want to see the flow of industrial goods from the GDR cut off. Discussion of the German question was ambiguous; no clear attitude could be discerned. There was an evident desire to see the post-war frontier between Germany and Poland firmly fixed. What else? No one was ready even to think of the GDR leaving the Warsaw Pact. But everyone, even in the higher echelons of the Moscow leadership, expected to see the two German states enter into a closer relationship with each other. It was said, not without malice, that the views conveyed to the Soviet side by the major Western powers, independently of each other and with different degrees of emphasis, contained rather more reservations.

Important as our own affairs may be to us, we should not forget that Gorbachev and his colleagues see firstly the enormous internal problems of the Soviet Union, and secondly continued improvement of relations with the USA, as taking priority over the German question. Even less than before did I doubt that the Kremlin leader was serious in his proposals. But the obstacles in their way and the forces working against them seemed to me, if anything, to have increased. We might hope for peaceful change, but we could not be sure that it would get its chance if shortages led to the brink of chaos.

As for the other part of Germany, the GDR, besides the suppressed discontent in the country there were many factors, both external and internal, turning what began as uncoordinated and timid protests into a powerful mass movement, which received momentum from neighbouring countries and passed it back to them.

The extensive changes in Poland and Hungary had aroused

lively interest, while SED carping at the Soviet efforts towards reform became an irritation. Unfortunately anti-Polish feeling, supposedly a thing of the past, flared up again too, with over-zealous Communist Party members stirring the embers. The influence of German developments was felt, in turn, in Czecho-slovakia – a small reparation for what the troops of the Warsaw Pact, with the shameful participation of the GDR, had done to that freedom-loving and traditionally minded nation in 1968. The opposition – including those who still cherished the hopes of the Prague Spring – made good headway that November of 1989.

The rapidly swelling wave of refugees that had begun leaving the GDR by way of Hungary and Austria late that summer – most of them young, well-qualified East German citizens who were not materially destitute – had had a profound effect on family and economic life. The fragility of the old order was further revealed by the way in which the Hungarian Govern-ment ignored protests from East Berlin. The authorities in Prague and Warsaw allowed those who took refuge in the embassies there to travel on *en masse* to the Federal Republic. The East Berlin leadership looked foolish as well as isolated.

There had been falsification on a massive scale in the GDR local government elections in the spring of 1989, something that stuck in people's minds. Falsification itself was nothing new, but against the background of general discontent it was the proverbial last straw that breaks the camel's back, making life difficult for Honecker's successor Egon Krenz. There was no overcoming the handicap of the facts, and the various separate opposition groups found common ground here.

Then the police attacks on demonstrators – again, mainly young people – in Berlin, Dresden and other East German cities in early October aroused cold fury. These attacks involved the rough treatment of the demonstrators during arrest and while they were in the custody of the security police, the humiliation of young women, and the rest of the stock-in-trade of badly rattled mercenaries. It was no comfort that this was not solely a German outrage, for there had been police brutality in Prague too up to the last few days before the turning-point came, and in Warsaw it proved almost impossible to call to account those responsible for the violence.

In the GDR the shouts of 'Wir sind das Volk' – 'We are the people' – rose above everything else, exposing the arrogance of the single party to ridicule. The people had championed their own cause, with great self-discipline but in a way that could not be ignored. They were insisting on their right to be taken seriously as citizens and not spoon-fed any longer. The state – shrinking from the temptation to use force, and with the Soviet side urging moderation on it – reconciled itself to major concessions: the change to genuine freedom of information took place almost overnight. Gifted journalists set to work forcefully and without inhibitions, proving that the news can be made interesting even under a transitional regime. Most of the public, not to mention the majority of civil servants and party functionaries, were already well used to television programmes from the West.

Requests for easier travel between East and West Germany were granted so far as was possible for the time being. There may even have been a willingness to see a certain amount of chaos, so as to provoke demands for 'more order'.

The Socialist Unity Party changed rapidly, underwent much differentiation and showed tendencies to split. The number of its members who ceased to pay their dues increased. Activists from the hard core of the party organized a special conference. Even before it took place it became clear that the party's claim to authority was going to be removed from the Constitution. Among the less attractive ways in which the revolution manifested itself was the hunt for scapegoats, intended to divert attention from the great numbers of those responsible for the wretched state of the GDR. However, many leading figures in the so-called coalition parties also wanted it forgotten that they had not previously opposed the authority of the SED, but had usually gone along with what its leaders said.

As early as the summer of 1989, new political forces had begun to team up in a remarkable, almost sensational manner. They developed largely out of civil rights groups, peace groups and environmental groups, which had led only a semi-legal existence before. The protective and moderating part played by leading figures and institutions of the Evangelical Church in the formation of the GDR's 'New Forces' can scarcely be overestimated, nor the commitment of its pastors over and above the call of duty. Initially, the Church had said it 'only' wanted to appeal to the conscience of the state leadership.

It was no coincidence that a Social Democratic Party – a GDR Social Democratic Party – was re-founded in a parsonage near Berlin early in October 1989. The preparations had begun in August. In those weeks of late summer other, overlapping initiatives also took clearer shape: the New Forum, Democratic Awakening and Democracy Now groups. Some of those involved had long been known to me. With the SPD Chairman Hans-Jochen Vogel, I visited friends of the East German SDP on the evening of 10 November, when we had celebrated the fall of the Wall.

Nothing would be the same again. But the end of the road was not in sight yet, and setbacks could not be ruled out. The situation remained particularly unstable in the GDR. Clearly, this state of affairs could be rectified only if people were sure that the movement towards genuine civic co-determination would continue to make headway, that tangible material improvement could be expected in the foreseeable future, and that the country's relationship with the Federal Republic would be set on a new footing. At the same time, it had to be realized that not too many months must go by before the democratic movement was ratified by the holding of free elections.

Serious reservations about speedy elections were expressed by the opposition: how could they be fair without organizational preparation, access to the media, and party finances, however minimal? And if the nomination of candidates were not to depend too much on chance, surely that was not something to be done in a hurry, either? Serious doubters even wondered whether an assembly to draw up a constitution should not come first, and whether it might not be better to shed the burden of the past and regulate the transitional period at a 'round table' conference. There is no denying that such suggestions carried weight. But I advised against too much delay. Revolutions do not commonly wait until the agenda has been thoroughly discussed and 'proceedings' bureaucratically transacted. There is a case for thinking that the second phase of a revolution has sometimes become violent because there was too much hesitation and too little improvisation during its first phase.

The disinclination of the confident New Forces to be told what they ought to do was obvious. And the general public of the GDR was unwilling to see what it had achieved in unfavourable circumstances denied proper respect. Nor did the East Germans particularly like to hear the object of their efforts discussed as if it were a bankrupt's estate. While well aware that they needed radical and thus painful economic reforms at home, they regarded union with the more prosperous, western part of their country as more than just a take-over. The connection with developments affecting Europe as a whole also dawned upon people who guessed more than they knew of such things.

It was not difficult to get that impression, and to feel that yet again the overriding issue was the forging of close links between the various parts of our continent. For all the obvious difficulties, it proved objectively useful that the two German states had already been working together in and for Europe even before the revolutionary upheavals took place.

Bonn and East Berlin did not oppose one another at the Vienna talks on troop reductions and conventional arms control; on the contrary, they worked harmoniously together even under the old SED leadership. Outside the framework of government routine, Egon Bahr had done much to create the climate where that was possible. In such a context it showed unnecessary prejudice to fulminate against Party contacts with the GDR. It depended on what they were for. Similarly, as I knew from personal experience, aid for individuals and families with problems could generally be provided only in ways that are unusual because unnecessary in the West.

Both parts of Germany had supported the findings not only of the Final Act of Helsinki in 1975, but of subsequent conferences. I was sure that the ideological relaxation and change to democracy in the GDR would give new force to their cooperation in the European context. Both states, for instance, are members of the United Nations Economic Commission for Europe (ECE), based in Geneva, and may be able to reinvigorate that body, which has been inactive for some years. Moreover, the GDR, like other states of the former Eastern bloc, is at liberty to interest itself in joining the Council of Europe in Strasbourg (not to be confused with the EC's European Parliament). More important, however, is the issue of how the territory of the GDR could be linked more closely with the European Community. The EC Commission in Brussels, like the Government of the GDR (and the Government of the Federal Republic) showed interest in the question.

Action relating to Germany alone would inevitably be inadequate. But if the parts of Europe are coming closer to each other, who could give any good reasons for keeping out Germany or the two parts of Germany? Rather, the question is one of how to meet what security interests.

Such considerations were behind the outline of a graduated all-German plan laid before the Bundestag by Federal Chancellor Kohl on 28 November 1989; in essence, the Social Democrats as well as the Government coalition approved it. I was in Berlin again that day, acquainting Senator Edward Kennedy with the new state of affairs. I was able to tell him that the vision of his brother the President was about to be realized:

'Solidarity between the Germans, between those living on German territory, has increased, going hand in hand with an awareness that we bear joint responsibility for our part of the world. But first and foremost, with due respect for our various responsibilities, people's immediate needs must be met. Not just here and in anticipation of a new German federation in the near future, but in our relations with neighbouring countries which are also in the process of democratic, social and economic regeneration.'

Some Western governments might find it difficult to reconcile old opinions with more recent developments. But any idea that anyone could still make the arrangements for Germany was bound to be misleading: that was not and would not be the case.

Nor was calling on the victorious powers of nearly fifty years ago for advice before making up our own minds a convincing course of action. We must shake off any inclination to ask the opinion of the great ones of the world (or even ask them to tell us what to think) before expressing our own ideas in written or spoken form: such notions, like thinking in either/or categories, were irrelevant now.

Making the existence of two German states a point of dogma had never carried conviction; nor did the idea that an enlarged nation-state was the sole possible outcome to be deduced from the Federal German Basic Law. To achieve unity through self-determination was the task handed on to us by the fathers of the Constitution. There is more than one way to go about carrying it out, but to neglect it would be seen as failure on the part of those responsible in a national *and* a European context.

The end of Communism – with its totalitarian party leadership and its centrally planned economy – now seems irreversible. The process of democratic reform will not go unopposed. I see a renaissance of free Social Democracy in Central and Eastern Europe, in parts of the Soviet Union and in certain influential circles there. But that can be only one among other motive forces, and to my mind the united Europe of the future should and will be of more than one political colour.

The benefits of the end of Stalinist and post-Stalinist rule extend far beyond Europe. One anxiety in other parts of the world is that the industrial states may set their sights even lower where development policy is concerned, if their financial power is needed in Eastern Europe. This is not an idle fear, and it must and can be countered. Now of all times it would be right to put some of the funds freed by arms reduction towards fighting world-wide famine and poverty. That means co-ordinating national interests, European duties and global responsibilities to the best of our ability.

I am not forgetting the many uncertainties and risks still paving the way ahead of us. But to see ideas that were once held in the face of much persistent inertia and doubt come within reach of being realized is a source of great satisfaction.

Biographical Data

1913   Born Herbert Ernst Karl Frahm in Lübeck. Active in positions in the Socialist Youth Movement from a very early age.

1930   Member of the SPD; goes over to the SAP (Socialist Workers' Party) the next year.

1932   Takes *Abitur* at the Lübeck Johanneum.

1933   Flees to Norway by way of Denmark. Active as a journalist; studies history. Lectures to various organizations of the Norwegian labour movement, particularly on the Nazi regime and support for the German Resistance. Many visits to centres of Germans in exile.

1936   Takes part in Heinrich Mann's efforts to set up a German Popular Front against Hitler. Undercover work in Berlin under a false name in the second half of this year.

1937   Spends several months in Catalonia, reporting on the Spanish Civil War and working for humanitarian aid.

1938   Secretary of the Norwegian People's Aid organization. Stripped of German citizenship by the Nazi government.

1940   Briefly imprisoned by the Germans during the occupation of Norway, but not recognized. Flees to Sweden. Journalistic work there. Norwegian citizenship confirmed by the Government in exile in London.

1942   Honorary secretary of an international working-party which draws up the 'peacetime aims of democratic socialists'.

1944   Links with the attempt to overthrow Hitler (the 20 July Plot). Member of the local group of German Social Democrats in Sweden, integration of the various groups into the reviving SPD.

1945   Return to Oslo at the end of the war. Correspondent in Germany for Scandinavian journals.

1947   Press attaché at the Norwegian military mission to the Control Council in Berlin.

1948   Special representative of the SPD executive committee in Berlin and to the Allied Control authorities. German citizenship restored by the *Land* government of Schleswig-Holstein.

1949   Sits as deputy for Berlin in the First German Bundestag; also in the Second Bundestag from 1953.

1950   Member of Berlin City Assembly; re-elected 1954 and 1958.

1954   Deputy Chairman of the Berlin branch of the SPD (previously local borough chairman), Chairman of the Berlin SPD from 1958.

1955   President of the Berlin City Assembly.

1957   Governing Mayor of Berlin (until entry into the Federal Government in December 1966). Does not stand for the Third Bundestag because of membership of the Bundesrat. President of the German Congress of City Authorities (until 1963).

1958   Member of the SPD executive committee; becomes Deputy Chairman in 1962.

1960   Nominated the Social Democratic candidate for Chancellor in the Bundestag election of 1961 (and again in 1965).

1964   Elected Chairman of the German Social Democratic Party at Bad Godesberg after the death of Erich Ollenhauer. Re-elected at Karlsruhe in 1964, Dortmund in 1966, Nuremberg in 1968, Saarbrücken in 1970, Hanover in 1973, Mannheim in 1975, Hamburg in 1977, Berlin in 1979, Munich in 1982, Essen in 1984, Nuremberg in 1986.

1966   Federal German Foreign Minister and Deputy Chancellor in the Grand Coalition Government.

1969   Federal Chancellor after the elections for the Sixth German Bundestag, with a coalition SPD and FDP government.

1970   Meetings with Chairman of Council of Ministers of the GDR in Erfurt and Kassel. Signs the Moscow and Warsaw treaties (and the Prague Treaty at the end of 1973).

1971   Awarded the Nobel Peace Prize in Oslo. Given the freedom of Berlin (and of Lübeck in 1972).

1972   Vote of no confidence fails in the Bundestag. Early new elections bring clear mandate for the Brandt–Scheel Government. SPD the strongest parliamentary party in the Bundestag, with 45.8 per cent of the vote.

1973   First Federal Chancellor to address the General Assembly of the United Nations.

1974   Resigns as Chancellor over the GDR spy affair.

1976   Re-elected to the German Bundestag (on the list of candidates for North Rhine-Westphalia), also re-elected in 1980, 1983, and 1987. Elected President of the Socialist International in Geneva (Vice-President since 1966). Re-elected in Vancouver in 1978, Madrid in 1980, Albufeira in 1983, Lima in 1986, Stockholm in 1989.

1977   Agrees to chair the Independent Commission on International Development Issues. Early in 1980 presents report *North–South: A Programme for Survival*. Additional report, *Common Crisis*, early 1983.

1979   Elected to European Parliament; resigns seat in 1982.

1987   Retires as Party Chairman; appointed Honorary Chairman of the SPD.

Many honorary doctorates and distinctions, including the Third World Prize (New York 1985) and the Albert Einstein Prize (Washington 1987).

Index

READ MORE IN PENGUIN

In every corner of the world, on every subject under the sun, Penguin represents quality and variety – the very best in publishing today.

For complete information about books available from Penguin – including Puffins, Penguin Classics and Arkana – and how to order them, write to us at the appropriate address below. Please note that for copyright reasons the selection of books varies from country to country.

In the United Kingdom: Please write to *Dept. JC, Penguin Books Ltd, FREEPOST, West Drayton, Middlesex UB7 OBR*

If you have any difficulty in obtaining a title, please send your order with the correct money, plus ten per cent for postage and packaging, to *PO Box No. 11, West Drayton, Middlesex UB7 OBR*

In the United States: Please write to *Penguin USA Inc., 375 Hudson Street, New York, NY 10014*

In Canada: Please write to *Penguin Books Canada Ltd, 10 Alcorn Avenue, Suite 300, Toronto, Ontario M4V 3B2*

In Australia: Please write to *Penguin Books Australia Ltd, 487 Maroondah Highway, Ringwood, Victoria 3134*

In New Zealand: Please write to *Penguin Books (NZ) Ltd,182–190 Wairau Road, Private Bag, Takapuna, Auckland 9*

In India: Please write to *Penguin Books India Pvt Ltd, 706 Eros Apartments, 56 Nehru Place, New Delhi 110 019*

In the Netherlands: Please write to *Penguin Books Netherlands B.V., Keizersgracht 231 NL–1016 DV Amsterdam*

In Germany: Please write to *Penguin Books Deutschland GmbH, Friedrichstrasse 10–12, W–6000 Frankfurt/Main 1*

In Spain: Please write to *Penguin Books S. A., C. San Bernardo 117–6° E–28015 Madrid*

In Italy: Please write to *Penguin Italia s.r.l., Via Felice Casati 20, I–20124 Milano*

In France: Please write to *Penguin France S. A., 17 rue Lejeune, F–31000 Toulouse*

In Japan: Please write to *Penguin Books Japan, Ishikiribashi Building, 2–5–4, Suido, Tokyo 112*

In Greece: Please write to *Penguin Hellas Ltd, Dimocritou 3, GR–106 71 Athens*

In South Africa: Please write to *Longman Penguin Southern Africa (Pty) Ltd, Private Bag X08, Bertsham 2013*

READ MORE IN PENGUIN

BIOGRAPHY AND AUTOBIOGRAPHY

Freedom from Fear Aung San Suu Kyi

This collection of writings gives a voice to Aung San Suu Kyi, human rights activist and leader of Burma's National League for Democracy, who was detained in 1989 by SLORC, the ruling military junta, and today remains under house arrest. In 1991 her courage and ideals were internationally recognized when she was awarded the Nobel Peace Prize.

Friends in High Places Jeremy Paxman

'The Establishment is alive and well ... in pursuit of this elusive, seminal circle of souls around which British institutions revolve, Jeremy Paxman ... has written a thoughtful examination, both poignant and amusing' – Jessica Catto in the *Independent*

Last of the Hot Metal Men Derek Jameson

Following on from his hugely successful *Touched by Angels*, Derek Jameson presents the second volume of his astonishing memoirs. Here is the inside story of the ten years when he was editor of three national newspapers, ended up unemployed and then bounced back as a media megastar. 'The great personality of today' – David Frost

When Shrimps Learn to Whistle Denis Healey

The Time of My Life was widely acclaimed as a masterpiece. Taking up the most powerful political themes that emerge from it Denis Healey now gives us this stimulating companion volume. 'Forty-three years of ruminations ... by the greatest foreign secretary we never had' – Ben Pimlott in the *New Statesman & Society*

Stone Alone Bill Wyman with Ray Coleman

Ruthless, cynical, electrifying and exuberant – the Stones played a revolutionary soundtrack for the sixties. Offstage, bass guitarist Bill Wyman has always been 'the silent Stone'. But here he reveals the intimate and gripping story of the 'bad boys' of British rock and the era they helped to shape.